TRINITY AND ALL SAINTS

CHILD LEGISLATION 1969

CHILD LEGISLATION 1969

Including the

REPRESENTATION OF THE PEOPLE ACT 1969, s. 1
FAMILY LAW REFORM ACT 1969
CHILDREN AND YOUNG PERSONS ACT 1969
TATTOOING OF MINORS ACT 1969

By

D. A. HOLDEN, B.A., LL.B., Dip. Ed.

and

BUTTERWORTHS LEGAL EDITORIAL STAFF

LONDON
BUTTERWORTHS
1970

This book is also available as part of Butterworths Annotated Legislation Service

ENGLAND: BUTTERWORTH & CO. (PUBLISHERS) LTD.
                 LONDON: 88 KINGSWAY, WC2B 6AB
AUSTRALIA: BUTTERWORTH & CO. (AUSTRALIA) LTD.
                 SYDNEY: 20 LOFTUS STREET
                 MELBOURNE: 343 LITTLE COLLINS STREET
                 BRISBANE: 240 QUEEN STREET
CANADA: BUTTERWORTH & CO. (CANADA) LTD.
                 TORONTO: 14 CURITY AVENUE, 374
NEW ZEALAND: BUTTERWORTH & CO. (NEW ZEALAND) LTD.
                 WELLINGTON: 49/51 BALLANCE STREET
                 AUCKLAND: 35 HIGH STREET
SOUTH AFRICA: BUTTERWORTH & CO. (SOUTH AFRICA) (PTY.) LTD.
                 DURBAN: 33/35 BEACH GROVE

ISBN 0 406 23351 9

MADE AND PRINTED IN GREAT BRITAIN BY
WILLIAM CLOWES AND SONS, LIMITED
LONDON AND BECCLES

FOREWORD

Whatever his political complexion, no responsible citizen would dispute the quantity of social legislation engendered by the Parliament which by the time this book appears in print, will be in dissolution.

1969 was a prolific year in which there was some concentration on the interests of children and young people, and I welcome the collection of the enactments relating to children into a very readable volume, which will surely find its way on to the desks of many members of the legal and social work professions.

Never in our history have events moved so quickly and in the field of social work the pace is faster than anywhere. There are times when practitioners feel themselves to be impelled by forces quite beyond their control towards an unseen goal whose form is unpredictable.

Young people are the focus of much of our attention. We are, on the whole, ambivalent about them. We look upon them with a mixture of pride, envy, patronage and apprehension, seeing in them a reflection of that part of ourselves which was unfulfilled, that part which we most like to project and that part of which we have always been somewhat afraid, and have, therefore, repressed. They, on the other hand, are much less prone to repress and very prone to express their feelings and attitudes, sometimes in ways not palatable to the rest of society.

The legislation concerning young people which was promulgated in 1969, and which is the subject of this book, provides one opportunity for the sociologists and the historians to examine how in Britain we are attempting to deal with the continuous demand, both articulate and implied, of young people to be permitted to occupy a responsible and accepted place in society. From their findings they should, with confidence, deduce that the concept of children as no more than undersized adults, first assailed with vigour in the latter half of the nineteenth century, has now been finally demolished.

It is too soon to know what effect the lowering of the minimum age of enfranchisement will have upon our legislature. What becomes ever more vividly important is the need to educate our young people to exercise their rights as citizens in a way which will assist the development of our democratic way of life. More of our resources must be devoted to ensuring that our youth understands its civic responsibilities and is properly prepared to undertake them.

It has taken us a long time to come to terms with our subjective feelings about illegitimacy and to allow ourselves to concede that the circumstances of birth are no more than an accident. Some sections of the Family Law Reform Act will come as a relief to those consciences which for long have been troubled by the past punitiveness of the law towards those born out of wedlock. Not before time, the stigmas in this area are receding.

Now, moreover, in the eyes of the law, boys become men, and girls become women at the age of eighteen. Thereafter, they may freely marry, make their wills, and dispose of property and in the future will not have to endure the term "infant". Child care officers and others will not have failed to notice that wards of court may now be placed in the care of local authorities.

The most far-reaching of the measures included in this volume is the Children and Young Persons Act. It should be regarded, not as an entity in itself, but as the culmination of a protracted train of legislative thought which found its earliest expression in the establishment of juvenile courts, with the implied acknowledgment that children and young people are a special sector of the population, with special problems and entitled to special attention and treatment. The philosophy of the Act is well described in the Introduction.

The Act confers more responsibility upon the children's service of local authorities. This service, formed as recently as 1948, has in the twenty-two years of its existence been called upon to assimilate and digest such formidable enactments as the Children Act of 1948, the Adoption and Children Acts of 1958, and the Children and Young Persons Act of 1963, as well as a number of minor but, nevertheless, important measures. It would appear to have been the intention of Parliament ultimately to give to this local authority department the entire task of helping, caring for and treating those sectors of the juvenile population which are in some measure deprived, disturbed or delinquent.

The history of the children's department administered by local authorities and presided over by the Home Office has been a memorable one. It has accepted the successive demands made upon its limited but feverishly expanding resources with enthusiasm, devotion and imagination and has applied itself diligently and with developing skill. It is right that the responsibility for this task should be concentrated upon one service and not be fragmented; there is little doubt that child care officers will meet the challenge with the same resolution as they have always shown.

I return to my initial theme. As a part of the whirlpool of change, children's departments and their children's officers are to lose their separate identity and will become integrated into a new social services department which will be geared to meet the needs, not only of children and their parents, but of the elderly, the handicapped and the mentally sick. This will result from the Government's implementation of the recommendations of the Seebohm report, and few social workers practising in these fields would doubt the wisdom of it. There are, however, those who might have wished for a period of time to have elapsed in which the reforms envisaged by the Children and Young Persons Act 1969 could have been firmly set in motion before the service found itself engulfed in an administrative upheaval of this magnitude.

Great vigilance will need to be exercised in the short term to safeguard the foundation of an Act of Parliament which, if implemented sensibly and courageously, is likely to have significant implications for the treatment and rehabilitation, not only of children and young people in the age groups whose immediate interests it seeks to serve but ultimately of the older adolescent and adult delinquent population.

E. P. Brown
Children's Officer
(Hon. Sec. Association of

May 1970   Children's Officers)

CONTENTS

REFERENCES AND ABBREVIATIONS

ANNOTATED LEGISLATION SERVICE

References to previous Statutes Supplements are given thus:—
5 Statutes Supp.

HALSBURY'S STATUTES OF ENGLAND

References to the Public General Statutes (other than to Acts or sections printed in this service) contained in the second or third editions of Halsbury's Statutes of England are followed by a reference to the volume and page in those editions where the Act or section will be found, thus:—
Wills Act 1837, s. 6 (26 Halsbury's Statutes (2nd Edn.) 1331)

or

Royal and Parliamentary Titles Act 1927, s. 2 (6 Halsbury's Statutes (3rd Edn.) 520)

PARLIAMENTARY OFFICIAL REPORTS (HANSARD)

House of Lords and House of Commons Official Reports are referred to by reference to the volume followed by the number of the column. References are to column numbers of the daily issues; the weekly issue normally agrees with the daily issue but the bound volumes do not necessarily so agree. Thus:—
121 H. of L. Official Report 1200.
376 H. of C. Official Report 1600.

House of Commons Standing Committee Official Reports are referred to by reference to Standing Committee A, B, or C, etc., followed by the date and the number of the column, thus:—
H. of C. Official Report, S.C.B., 17th April 1969, col. 12.

TABLE OF CASES

In the following Table references are given where applicable to the English and Empire Digest where a digest of the case will be found.

PAGE

INTRODUCTION

If the United Kingdom followed the practice of some oriental countries, the year 1969 might well have been called "the year of the children". For the volume of legislation passed during that year and directed towards the interests of young people was very considerable and penetrated into almost every field of law: the Representation of the People Act, by conferring the power to vote upon persons aged 18, affected the Constitution; a similar provision in the Family Law Reform Act made inroads into many realms, including contract, real property, marriage, executorship, administration and testamentary capacity; the Children and Young Persons Act, by far the longest and most complex of these enactments, took great steps forward in its provisions for dealing with children in need of care and protection—the greatest step forward, some people said, since 1933. Finally the Tattooing of Minors Act, the shortest and most simple of the series, provided for the protection of young people against adorning themselves in a way they might later come to regret.

THE REPRESENTATION OF THE PEOPLE ACT 1969

The Representation of the People Act 1969, gives effect to the proposals contained in the White Paper "Conclusions on Review of the Law relating to Parliamentary Elections" (Cmnd. 3717). It amends not only the law relating to the return of Members to Westminster, but also cancels many of the special qualifications which prevailed in local government and its elections. By so doing, the two forms of suffrage are brought into line.

The most important provision, and the one that is dealt with in the following pages, is contained in s. 1, which provides that the age at which a person shall be able to cast a vote is 18 (and not 21 as formerly).

During preliminary discussions, while it was generally agreed that the age of majority could rationally be reduced to 18 for most of the common purposes of life, considerable doubts were expressed as to the wisdom of extending the franchise to that age-group. Even the Committee of Inquiry on the Age of Majority whose Report (the "Latey Report"; Cmnd. 3342: 1967) had most attractively advocated the cause of young people was noticeably less enthusiastic on this subject and confined itself to saying:

> "It does not seem to us that changes in the civic field are at all likely to follow changes in the private field even if we wished that they should. It

is a very different thing to cope adequately with one's own personal and private affairs and to measure up to public and civic responsibilities."

The Speaker's Conference on Electoral Law published its recommendations during February 1968 (Cmnd. 3550) and suggested that the minimum age for voting should be 20 years. However the Government decided that 18 was to be the new voting age and its reasons are well expressed in the words of its spokesman in the Lords. Introducing the measure for its second reading, he said:

"As for the voting age itself, which, under the present law is 21, I think we are all agreed that some reduction is justified. The Speaker's Conference recommended the age of 20, and as the Government sees it, the choice lies between that and the age of 18, which was the age of majority recommended by the Committee on the Age of Majority for purposes other than civic law and which the Government [has implemented] in the Family Reform [Act]. This is very much a matter of judgement and opinion, but the Government came down in favour of 18. The decision was based partly on the argument of consistency but there were other factors of far greater weight. There is no disputing that there is a real change in the social climate from what it was, say 20 years ago. Physical maturity now comes earlier than it did, but—more important—social and moral maturity is assumed and conceded at an earlier age. Improved education, and the impact of mass media, particularly television, means that everyone is better informed than ever before on public and social issues. Information arouses interest, and interest arouses a desire to have a voice in the way things are run. There is evidence that the present arrangements for young voters—popularly called the 'Y' voters—lead to frustration and there is still more evidence in the shape of demonstrations and the so-called 'student unrest', which the Government regard as symptoms, which, while they are not always desirable in the form they take are nevertheless indicative of a healthy state of affairs. Our young people are no longer children and they resent being treated as such. Our view is that, if we entrust them with responsibility, they will act responsibly. With all respect to the Speaker's Conference and to those who share its view, we think that to fix the voting age at any point between 18 and 21 would be a half measure which would be neither understood nor appreciated, and which, for that matter, would not be allowed to stand for long." (298 H. of L. Official Report 1033.)

Section 1 (2) gives effect to the recommendation of the Speaker's Conference that when persons reach the voting age during the period of validity of any register, the date of the birthday should be shown against the name of the elector, and that he or she should be qualified to vote in any election held on or after that date. This gets rid of the cumbersome and confusing arrangements about "Y" voters which were always being criticised. The subsection also provides that if a person who is on the register will be of voting age by the date of the poll he may be treated, in effect, as an elector before that date for such purposes as, say, applying for absent voting facilities or being appointed as a proxy.

The form of the Act should be noted. It is not as easy to follow as one might wish, but this arises from the fact that the present electoral law, made generally in 1949 has worked exceedingly well. Accordingly the present Act is built into the earlier enactment, and the greater part of its sections simply amend relevant provisions. In quite a few cases sections of the 1969 Act are actually to be incorporated into the 1949 text as additions or replacements. (See s. 26 (5), *post*.)

THE FAMILY LAW REFORM ACT 1969

The Family Law Reform Act was frequently described as being "three Acts in one". Its purpose is to make three major changes in family law and each of its main parts stems from the Report of a separate Committee—or, as another speaker put it, "it is an amalgam of the Latey, the Russell and the Law Commission Reports".

The Latey Report—officially known as the "Report of the Committee on the Age of Majority" (Cmnd. 3342: 1967)—was responsible for the recommendations implemented in Part I of the Act, the most important of which is that for the purposes of the civil law, the age of majority, which has stood at 21 for nearly 800 years has been reduced to 18.

The Russell Report—officially known as the "Report of the Committee on the Law of Succession in Relation to Illegitimate Persons" (Cmnd. 3051: 1966) was responsible for the recommendations (with one important exception) now appearing in Part II of the Act. This gives illegitimate children the same rights of succession on the intestacy of their parents as if they had been their legitimate offspring and improves their status generally.

The Law Commission's "Report on Blood Tests and Proof of Paternity in Civil Proceedings" (Law Com. No. 16: 1968) relates to the use of blood tests in civil proceedings in which paternity is in issue and provides the substance of Part III.

Part IV contains only two provisions: that the presumption of legitimacy may be rebutted on a balance of probabilities rather than by proof beyond reasonable doubt; and, in order to facilitate the entry of a father's name on the birth certificate of his illegitimate child, a new procedure has been prescribed. Both the foregoing provisions emanate from the Russell and Law Commission Reports, but, for various reasons, it was not found desirable to include them in their related Parts.

PART I: REDUCTION OF AGE OF MAJORITY AND RELATED PROVISIONS (ss. 1–13)

The provisions of this Part of the Act, which lower the age of full legal capacity from 21 to 18, arise from the recommendations made in the Report of the Committee on the Age of Majority (Cmnd. 3342: 1967).

The Committee dealt exhaustively with topics relevant to the age of majority and conducted its enquiry with a thoroughness and skill which was described as "impressive" and "a very considerable public service". Having examined the historical case for the age of 21 (see Appendix I, *post*), the Committee decided, by a majority of 9 to 2, that the age be reduced to 18 in the field which they had examined. It is important to note that the minority dissent was in substance confined to the field of marriage, wardship, and, to a limited extent, contract. There was complete unanimity in the other 44 recommendations out of the 52 which were made.

Apart from the reduction of the age of majority and its effects upon marriage, wills, inheritance, maintenance (which are dealt with specifically), and its incidental effects upon certain enactments—in particular those relating to trusts, administration of estates, property, settlements and perpetuities and accumulations, this Part of the Act makes considerable inroads into other legal matters. A major effect of Part I is to enable those who have attained the age of 18 to enter into contracts in their own right. In litigation, any person over the age of 18 is free to take part in proceedings in any court in England and Wales without the intervention of a next friend or guardian *ad litem*. Several medical matters have also been cleared up: any person, having attained the age of 16 is at liberty to consent to any medical, surgical or dental treatment, and any person having attained 18 may be a blood donor. A young person, having reached the new age of majority may apply for a passport and acquire an independent domicile.

Two smaller items are also dealt with in this Part: the time at which a person attains a particular age expressed in years is now the commencement of the relevant anniversary of his date of birth, and the terms of s. 12 indicate that the designation of any person under the age of 18 as "minor" is more acceptable than "infant".

It was specifically stated during the passage of the Act through Parliament that it had no effect upon the criminal law, wages or education.

Reduction of age of majority from twenty-one to eighteen (s. 1)

Section 1 provides, in general terms, that full age shall henceforward be attained at 18; that all those already over 18 but under 21 shall automatically attain full age on the date when the section came into effect (*i.e.*, 1st January 1970); and that in all statutory provisions, whether passed or made before or after that date, words importing the old status, such as "infant" or "minor" should be construed accordingly. Private dispositions of property—wills, deeds, trusts, etc.—unless specifically amended so as to conform with the new law, remain undisturbed.

There are three Schedules appended to this Section. Schedule 1 gives life to the new law by directing that in a range of statutes running from the days of Charles II references to the age of 18 are to be substituted for references to the age of 21. While one hopes that the Parliamentary draftsmen have succeeded in locating all the relevant enactments to which the new rule applies, there is always the possibility that an odd one may have been overlooked. As far as local enactments are concerned, the provisions of s. 1 (5) may be invoked; but the position with regard to Public and General Acts remains uncertain. It may be noted that from time to time during the passing of the Act, it was found necessary to introduce amendments so as to insert into the Schedule further enactments which had subsequently come to light.

Schedule 2 contains three exceptions to the general change which is brought about by s. 1. The first is the Regency Acts 1937 to 1953. It has long been the case that the age of 18 is that at which the Sovereign becomes capable of exercising His or Her functions as such and that the Heir Presumptive or the Heir Apparent can act as Regent or Counsellor of State. Other members of the Royal Family cannot act as Regent or as Counsellor of State until they are 21 and it is not proposed to alter this. The second exception refers to the voting age, which was dealt with in the Representation of the People Act 1969. The exclusion of s. 7 of the Parliamentary Elections Act 1695 means that a person will still have to be 21 before he can become a member of Parliament—so, as the Attorney-General said, "there will be no teenagers in the House yet". The last exception referred to taxation, which would not have been appropriate for inclusion in a measure of this nature and was, in fact, dealt with in the Finance Act 1969.

Schedule 3 makes allowance for the fact that the sudden lowering of the age of majority might put some parties at a disadvantage or upset existing arrangements. For example, under the Limitation Act 1939, the right to bring an action usually expires after six years from the date a claim first arose. Any person under full age, however, was permitted to date his rights in this respect as from attaining the age of 21, the right thus expiring upon his attaining the age of 27. The new age of majority reduces the corresponding age to 24. This might operate to the disadvantage of a party who, for various reasons, had not been able to commence proceedings until, say, his 25th or 26th birthday. As it is the provisions of para. 8 of Schedule 3 are designed to keep open such and similar rights, until, with the natural effluxion of time, they have all expired.

Provisions relating to marriage (s. 2)

Section 2 provides that 18, instead of 21 is now the age at which a person can marry without parental consent. It also empowers a superintendent registrar, in cases where consent is still necessary to require written evidence of that consent if he thinks fit.

It is not too much to say that this section and its proposals were the most controversial of the entire Act. Of the 52 recommendations put forward by the Committee, this was one of the few upon which there was a dissenting memorandum and its passage, through both Houses of Parliament was far from easy. The arguments advanced in favour of lowering the age for what was currently termed "free marriage" were so evenly balanced against those which supported the status quo, that the ultimate choice was simply an expression of opinion on the part of the Government. It followed the line that since a person was to attain full legal capacity at 18 (and this, the Government had decided, was to include the right to vote; see the Representation of the People Act 1969, s. 1, *post*), to have made an isolated exception in the case of marriage would have served only to complicate and irrationalise the law to such an extent that there would most certainly have been demands for its alteration.

Provisions relating to wills and intestacy (s. 3)

Section 3 reduces from 21 to 18 the age at which a person can make a valid will. It also provides that a "soldier's will" can be revoked notwithstanding that its maker is still under 18 whether or not he is still on active service.

Referring to this aspect of its enquiry, the Committee said that it had yielded little controversial evidence; and during the passage of the Act through Parliament, the section was never discussed.

Maintenance for children under Guardianship of Infants Acts to continue to the age of twenty-one (s. 4)

Section 4 enables maintenance orders under the Guardianship of Infants Acts 1886 and 1925 to remain in force until the child for whose benefit they are made reaches the age of 21. Where a person is over 18 but under 21 and has at any time while still a minor been the subject of an order under these Acts, the courts are empowered to make a fresh maintenance order against either or both of his parents, as long as they continue to live apart.

This section was referred to in the House of Lords during the second reading debates as "a holding operation". The Government explained the position thus:

> "The Law Commission are at present considering the whole law of financial relief in matrimonial proceedings and the Government do not consider it wise to change the law on this subject any more than is necessary before the Law Commission have finished their task. The Latey Committee recommended that a court should have power to make maintenance without any age limits; in general the present law is that this jurisdiction ends at 21 and the [Act] preserves that position for the time being." (297 H. of L. Official Report 1137.)

Modification of other enactments relating to maintenance of children as to preserve benefits up to the age of twenty-one (s. 5)

The principle of s. 5 is identical with the foregoing and is intended only to modify certain existing enactments relating to maintenance and financial benefits for those over 18 but under 21 so as to preserve their existing position. The right of a deceased person's son to make an application under the Inheritance (Family Provision) Act 1938, ordering provision to be made for him out of his parent's estate where he has not otherwise been reasonably provided for, is continued until the son is 21; so is the right of an illegitimate child of 18 or over who is receiving full-time education to receive maintenance from his father. The right of a mother to apply to the court for maintenance where the father has been guilty of wilful neglect is also preserved until the child in question is 21.

Maintenance for wards of court (s. 6)

The intention of s. 6 is simply to give the Chancery courts the power to award maintenance in wardship proceedings. The section is directed solely to administrative convenience and is intended to make no alteration in the law as to maintenance or wardship whatsoever. Because it was doubtful whether in wardship proceedings the Court of Chancery had the same powers as has the Divorce Division to make maintenance orders in favour of children where parents are in dispute about it, a tiresome procedural device was resorted to whereby a wardship application was coupled with another under the Guardianship of Infants Acts. This certainly achieved its object, but it savoured of deviousness, and involved unnecessary expense and work and it was the Chancery judges themselves who recommended to the Committee on the Age of Majority that they should enjoy this new power.

Committal of wards of court to care of local authority and supervision of wards of court (s. 7)

Section 7 enables wards of court to be placed in the care of local authorities whenever it seems desirable. The Divorce Court has, since 1965, had the power to commit a child to the care of a local authority and found it valuable. The Judges of the Chancery Division suggested to the Committee on the Age of Majority (Cmnd. 3342: 1967) that they too would find it useful. The provision is, in terms, very similar to the corresponding sections of the Matrimonial Causes Act 1965.

Consent by persons over sixteen to surgical, medical and dental treatment (s. 8)

Section 8 enables anyone over the age of 16 to give a valid consent to medical treatment for himself. The question of consent to medical treatment did not lie strictly within the terms of reference of the Latey Committee but since so many witnesses declared that there was a good deal of confusion about the correctness of certain procedures and the legality thereof, the Committee thought it desirable to investigate and clarify the matter. It was agreed that in emergencies, doctors would be perfectly justified in setting aside the rules as to consent if by so doing they were to save any party from permanent disability and unnecessary pain and suffering. When, however, there was no emergency and the patient was not of full age, the situation was fraught with ambiguity: while there was the general rule of law that such a person was subject to the control of his parent or guardian and had little or no consensual capacity, it was not certain how far this extended to medical treatment. Apart from there being no judicial authority either way, there was the direction in the National Health Service Regulations that a person could choose his own practitioner at 16 and so was presumably free to accept the treatment advised. It was said to be absurd to permit a girl to marry at 18 and have a baby and still require the consent of older parties—husband or parents—should she need an anaesthetic. It was equally as illogical to suggest that a young mother, under age, should be unable to consent to the treatment of her own child.

The provisions of this section were not expected to bring about any radical alteration in current practice: most of the great teaching hospitals already regarded the consent of a sixteen-year-old, countersigned by an administrative officer, as adequate authority to proceed, but there was no consistency elsewhere. However, the section clarified the matter and medical practitioners and hospital authorities henceforward would know exactly where they stood.

Persons under 18 cannot however consent to blood donation. In practice the matter is not likely to become pressing. The medical objections to lowering the age to 16 are that growth is still proceeding at quite a high rate, that blood volume will not have reached its adult extent in many members of this age group, and that it seems unwise deliberately to produce anaemia, even of short duration, under such circumstances. This experience and reasoning is wholly sound and supports the conclusion that the age of 18 should be the earliest at which persons are free to be blood donors.

Time at which a person attains a particular age (s. 9)

Section 9 contains a general provision that a person shall attain any given age at the first moment of the relevant birthday, and not, as hitherto, in most cases, at the first moment of the preceding day.

The reform of the law relating to the time at which a person attained a given age had long been advocated. The rule at common law was that a person was deemed to have attained a given age at the first moment of the day preceding the relevant anniversary of his birth. The case which has been most frequently quoted to support this curious view is *Re Shurey: Savory* v. *Shurey*, [1918] 1 Ch. 263.

On the other hand, statutory provisions frequently specify that a person shall be taken to have attained a particular age at the commencement of the appropriate anniversary of the date of his birth—*e.g.*, the National Service Act 1948, s. 34 (3) (56 Statutes Supp.) ; the Mental Health Act 1959, s. 147 (5) (119 Statutes Supp.) ; the National Insurance Act 1965, s. 114 (4) (*c*) (45 Halsbury's Statutes, 2nd Edn., p. 1057).

The inconvenience to which the former rule could give rise is well-expressed by the Institute of Hospital Administrators:

> "It is quite unnecessarily confusing that for different purposes *e.g.* for consent to operations, for the making of a will and for the making of a contract for an amenity bed a patient should attain the relevant age on one day, but for other purposes, as, for example, s. 147 (5) of the Mental Health Act 1959, he should attain it on the next."

Modification of enactments relating to the Duke of Cornwall and other children of Her Majesty (s. 10)

Section 10 was inserted during the Committee stage in the Commons and passed through that Chamber without discussion. It was introduced into the Lords and explained as follows:

> "It has been agreed as a matter of principle that if it is right to fix the age of majority at 18 years for the generality of Her Majesty's subjects, it is right to do so for Her Majesty's children; and so it is only logical to extend the application of the present Act to those statutes which particularly affect them—as for example those which refer to the revenues derived from the Duchy of Cornwall." (304 H. of L. Official Report 986.)

Repeal of certain enactments relating to minors (s. 11)

The Infants Settlements Act 1855 applied to male infants of 20 and female infants of 17 and enabled them to make binding settlements of property, with the sanction of the court, in contemplation of marriage. With the reduction of the age of majority to 18, the section became largely superfluous, and the Committee recommended that it should be repealed.

Under the repealed provisions of Employers and Workmen Act 1875, s. 6, an apprentice could be sent to prison for up to fourteen days if, in relation to a dispute between a master and an apprentice, he failed to carry out an order, made by a magistrates' court, to perform his duties. The Committee considered this provision to be "anomalous" and "thoroughly out of place in modern law" and recommended that it should go as soon as possible.

Under the Sexual Offences Act 1956, s. 18 (36 Halsbury's Statutes (2nd Edn.) 226), which re-enacted s. 56 of the Offences Against the Person Act 1861 (5 Halsbury's Statutes (2nd Edn.) 808), it was an offence for a person to take a girl under the age of 21 out of the possession of her parents or guardian against their will, if she had property or expectations therefrom, and was taken or detained by fraud with the intent that she should marry her captor or have unlawful intercourse with him. The repeal of this provision is in the interests of consistency, otherwise, if it were allowed to stand, the section could provide the means whereby an irate parent could penalise a young man who ran away with an eighteen-year-old daughter with "great expectations".

Persons under full age may be described as minors instead of infants (s. 12)

In English law "infant" was the technical term applied to all persons not of full age. In non-technical usage, however, the word is usually reserved for persons of tender years. Webster's dictionary, for example, defines an infant as "a child in its first period of life; a babe; sometimes a child several years of age". The applicability of the term to a young man of 18, carrying certain responsibilities was decidedly questionable. The topic lent itself to many amusing illustrations, usually featuring "a 14-stone rugby player, aged twenty, married, with three children and a car". Reformers in this field also pointed out that the word had emotive qualities, the force of which ought not to be ignored.

Powers of Parliament of Northern Ireland (s. 13)

Section 13 gives power to the Parliament of Northern Ireland to enact legislation similar to Part I of the Family Law Reform Act. The present Act cannot be made directly applicable to Northern Ireland because the law relating to minors in that country, although substantially similar to that in England differs in points of detail. Since it would be very inconvenient to have two conflicting systems of law between the two countries this section has been enacted. It is not perfectly clear what is contained in the Government of Ireland Act 1920 (17 Halsbury's Statutes (2nd Edn.) 56) that would preclude the Parliament of Northern Ireland from enacting legislation to bring the law of their country into line with the new law in this Act, and the provision is no doubt enacted for the avoidance of doubt.

PART II: PROPERTY RIGHTS OF ILLEGITIMATE CHILDREN (ss. 14–19)

The provisions of this Part of the Act flow generally from recommendations made by the Committee on the Law of Succession in Relation to Illegitimate Persons (Cmnd. 3051: 1966). The Committee made two proposals, both of which were implemented in ss. 14 and 18 of the Act and both of which were welcomed on account of their humane intent. The reform contained in s. 15, however, is diametrically opposed to what the Committee suggested in their Report.

Right of illegitimate child to succeed on intestacy of parents, and of parents to succeed on intestacy of illegitimate child (s. 14)

Section 14 provides that an illegitimate child and his parents shall have the same right to share in each other's estates on an intestacy occurring after the section comes into force as if it were legitimate. The benefit accrues only to illegitimate children and their parents and not to remoter descendants or ascendants. The existing rights of adopted and legitimated children are pre-served.

The humanity underlining this new provision was never in dispute: the Bishop of Leicester spoke for everybody, when he said: "We all start from the same assumption, that whoever is at fault, it is not the illegitimate person and we must draft the law in such a way that every possible disability of the illegiti-mate person is removed, so far as it can be done." (297 H. of L. Official Report 1150.)

It is true that the section was heavily debated but it was on a point of administration rather than on one of principle. The objection, which was cer-tainly valid, was that "a claim to share in an intestate's estate will only arise in the average case some 50 years after the birth of the claimant", and, as one commentator suggested, "after the death of one of the principal parties". It was strenuously urged, therefore, that participation in the estate should, in the case of illegitimate parties, be confined to those who had been recognised or acknowledged by their natural fathers. The suggestion certainly had respect-able antecedents, but even so, it did not find favour since it would have given the father an absolute right to disinherit an illegitimate child which he does not have with regard to those who are legitimate. This would be visiting the sins of the father upon the head of the innocent with a vengeance and would also give the father a most undesirable hold over the mother of his illegitimate offspring. That this has been recognised in other countries may be tested with reference to s. 38A of the Decedentes Estates Law, New York, 1965, which, as from 1st March 1966, enacted that, given certain conditions, an illegitimate child is en-titled to succeed to its father's property and that this rule may not be set aside by agreement, compromise or approval.

On practical grounds, the Government rejected what became called the "familial relationship test" along the following lines:

A suitable test of familial relationship is not easy to formulate. Mere formal recognition is not satisfactory because it may be consistent with a determination not to treat the child as a member of the family in certain cases. For example, recognition may be embraced in a written agreement entered into for the pur-pose of excluding affiliation proceedings, with all the embarrassment that might cause. "Living with father" is, again, a difficult test. Any test based on the formula, "living with the father of his acknowledged child for a period, however short, as his acknowledged child," or living with him "for some material period" is obviously capable of unrealistic construction—especially if the period is to be calculated in days. The Government somewhat wryly pointed out that those who pressed for this arrangement had not specified any length of time.

The objection to the proposal was also sounded in principle. There is a widely held view that property in some sense belongs to the whole family and not solely to its legal owner—therefore, since the Family Provision Act 1937, the court has power to override a dead person's wishes in favour of dependants. If it is now to be held that illegitimate children are to be regarded as much a part of the family as legitimate issue, it follows that it is only reasonable that simple blood relationship be the test and not an ill-defined one based on whether a father had chosen to acknowledge the children for whose existence he had been responsible.

The Government drew confidence in the practicality of its proposals, on the grounds that: the courts are used to dealing with claims against the estates of deceased parties, and, in the absence of written evidence or proof of a clearly established, settled irregular union, there would be few cases in which an alleged bastard would succeed in a claim against his father's estate. Any court would view with considerable suspicion and examine with great astuteness, the claims of a 50-year old bastard who suddenly emerged out of the blue to put in a claim against the intestate estate of his alleged father. The courts are remarkably gifted in smelling out fraud and there is no reason to believe that they would fail to continue to do so.

And, if no other argument were to prevail, the Attorney-General certainly found this powerful:

> "The same change in the law of Scotland was considered by Parliament in the last session and was enacted by s. 1 of the Law Reform (Miscellaneous Provisions) (Scotland) Act 1968. No doubt it was debated with great skill and care in the Scottish Grand Committee, and on Report and Third Reading and it was passed in the other place. So that this matter, so far as it affects the law of Scotland, has already been adjudicated upon by Parliament. While I agree that there is no absolute need for the law of both countries to be kept in step in a subject like this—there are many respects in which the laws of our respective countries are not in step—there is nevertheless a clear advantage in avoiding the creation of differences which can lead to anomalous results. In my submission, what Parliament decided for Scotland in this matter is right in principle and practice for England and Wales and, therefore, s. 14 should stay as it is."
> (H. & C. Official Report, S. C. B. 24th April, 1969, col. 93.)

Presumption that in disposition of property references to children and other relatives include references to, and to persons related through, illegitimate children (s. 15)

Section 15 reverses the existing rule of construction and provides (with certain specified exceptions) that in any deed, will or other disposition of property, whether written or oral, made after 1st January 1970, a reference to the children of any person shall, unless a contrary intention appears, be taken to include a reference to his illegitimate children and an expression denoting a blood relationship to include such a relationship traced through an illegitimate child. (It should be noted that the terms of this section have been expressly extended to insurance policies—for which see s. 19, *post.*)

The section is, of course, a vindication of Lord Denning's celebrated dictum on the law as he thought it ought to be in *Sydall* v. *Castings*, [1966] 3 All E.R. 770.

During the passage of the Act through Parliament, the following extract was several times quoted:

> "'Relations', it is said, includes only legitimate relations; and 'descendant' means only a legitimate descendant. If this contention be correct, it means that because Yvette (the relevant child: a little 4-year old girl) is illegitimate, she is to be excluded from any benefit. She is on this view no 'relation' of her father: nor is she 'descended' from him. In the eye of the law she is the daughter of nobody. She is related to nobody. She is an outcast and is to be shut out from any part of her father's insurance benefit.
>
> I have no doubt that such an argument would have been acceptable in the nineteenth century. The judges in those days used to think that, if they allowed illegitimate children to take a benefit, they were encouraging immorality. They laid down narrow pedantic rules such as that stated by Lord Chelmsford in *Hill* v. *Crook* ([1874–80] All E.R. Rep. 62 at p. 389): 'No gift, however express, to unborn illegitimate persons is allowed by law . . .' In laying down such rules, they acted in accordance with the then contemporary morality. Even the Victorian fathers thought that they were doing right when they turned their erring daughters out of the house. They visited the sins of the fathers on the children—with a vengeance. I think that we should throw over those harsh rules of the past. They are not rules of law. They are only guides to the construction of documents. They are quite out of date. We no longer penalise the illegitimate child. We should replace those old rules by a more rational approach. If they are wide enough to include an illegitimate child, we should so interpret them. Just as Mackinnon, J., did in *Morris* v. *Britannic Assurance Co., Ltd.*, ([1931] 2 K.B. 125), when he held that in a statute concerning industrial assurance benefits, the word 'child' included an illegitimate child. So here the words 'relations' and 'descendants' in a group assurance scheme are wide enough to include illegitimate children and we should so interpret them."

The two other judges who sat with Lord Denning on that case were not, however, prepared to upset a rule of law as it was then generally understood— and, indeed, could hardly do otherwise. It had subsisted for several centuries and there was a considerable body of informed opinion against reversing it. The most authoritative expression along those lines was set out in the Report of the Committee on the Law of Succession in Relation to Illegitimate Persons (Cmnd. 3051: 1966):

> "Any change in the present *prima facie* rule of construction would in our view lead to more problems than it would solve. A father would be faced with the alternative of either benefitting against his wishes bastards who might be born to his daughter, or, of extending to her by the terms of his will the gratuitous insult of expressly excluding the possible outcome of her possible immorality. We feel considerable sympathy for the suggestion that in the case of at least a mother's will a reference to her children should include her bastard as well as her legitimate children, as being more

likely than otherwise to accord with her intentions. But it would be un-acceptable to impose on a mother who did *not* want to include the former the need to reveal in her will that which might not be generally known, either by express exclusion of individuals, or of bastards as such, or by some device which might well reveal the position to those with knowledge of the family. Further it would we feel lead to confusion to have differing principles of construction of such phrases applied to different documents. Accordingly we do not recommend any change under this head. It is right to recall that there are many occasions in which the circumstances are held to justify the construction of such phrases in a particular docu-ment as extending to the illegitimate link: the rule of construction is *prima facie* and by no means absolute." (Cmnd. 3051: 1966, p. 13.)

As the Attorney-General said, when introducing this section on the second reading:

"There are arguments both ways and the matter is nicely balanced. However, the Scottish Law Commission took the opposite view to the Committee and this has now been incorporated in the Scottish Act [*i.e.* the Law Reform (Miscellaneous Provisions) (Scotland) Act 1968.] My Right Hon. Friends and I have considered this carefully and are of the opinion that it would be best to follow the Scots and that is why [s. 15] appears in this form." (778 H. of C. Official Report 45.)

Even so, the proposals were by no means greeted with overwhelming en-thusiasm and the section was strongly attacked during Committee, and on report—in fact, in the House of Commons, it led to the only division. Most of the confidence that the Government displayed was drawn from the "high auth-ority of the Scottish Law Commission". Furthermore, "the justification for having a settled rule of construction applicable to the expressions affected by this section is that it makes for certainty and enables testators, settlors and their advisers to ensure that the words used give effect to the intentions of those using them. From this point of view, a rule that these expressions *prima facie* include illegitimate relationships is neither better nor worse than its converse. But such a rule ought also to tend to a construction which is likely, more often than not, to bring about a result consonant with the intention of a testator who is unaware of the rule and has not sought advice from those who are familiar with it."

During the passing of the Act sincere doubts were raised as to whether the humane principles implicit in this section conflicted with the well-established policy that arrangements tending to immorality ought not to be encouraged. In particular, great stress was laid on the fact that many dispositions as con-templated by this section, were going to be in favour of "unborn bastards". The topic was still more ambiguous in that it was not really certain whether such a rule of law subsisted in any case. For the removal of doubts the Govern-ment inserted sub-s. (7) which abrogates any such rule, explaining the matter thus:

"[Many judges] have questioned the extent of the survival of the rule— if any such rule did in fact exist. In the nature of things, many of those capable of benefitting on the basis of this section will be unborn at the time the disposition is made and it would be absurd if Parliament were to provide, on the one hand, that such a disposition should be construed as intended to benefit those persons, but, on the other hand, that public policy required this intention to be frustrated." (786 H. of C. Official Report 1424.)

It is salutory to reflect upon the words spoken by Lord Selborne nearly a century ago in *Dorin* v. *Dorin*, [1874–1880] All E.R. Rep. 71 at p. 74:

> "I am by no means sure that the law would not be in a better state than it is at present if the word 'children' in a will were regarded as large enough, when used concerning the children of the testator by a particular woman, to include within its proper and *prima facie* construction any children living at the date of the will, who might be recognised by the testator as being his own by that woman, as well as those who might afterwards be procreated between them in lawful marriage."

Almost at the very end of the measure's parliamentary life, the following words of caution were spoken:

> "What emerges most clearly from what was said, both in the debate on [sub-s. (7) and] on Part II in general, is that it will be absolutely essential in future (because none of this is retrospective) that those who draft documents into which this type of interpretation might at some stage come should be fully aware of what is in [this Act]. They should also make quite certain that their drafting takes account of the changes in the law which have been brought about by this [Act]. It will no longer be apposite or sufficient to deal with the intentions of testators and settlors, and other people, in accordance with rules which have for so long governed these matters—and indeed [that concerning 'future bastards'] was an obscure one. They will now have to be specific, if they do not wish illegitimate children to be included. So long as the legal profession—and anybody else who has to draft deeds of this sort—realises that this is now the situation, then [it may be taken] that the intention of the person for whom the deed is being drafted will be adequately safeguarded." (304 H. of L. Official Report 989.)

For one view as to the undesirability of excluding the presumption, see the note to this section in the Second Cumulative Supplement to *Williams on Wills* (3rd Edn.), at p. B 44.

Meaning of "child" and "issue" in s. 33 of Wills Act 1837 (s. 16)

Section 16 is consequential upon the provisions of the foregoing Part of the Act.

Protection of trustees and personal representatives (s. 17)

Section 17 confers protection upon trustees who deal with property without having first ascertained that there is no person who might have a claim to it under ss. 14–16 of the Act. Such a person would still be able to follow the property into the hands of anyone receiving it unless such a one was a purchaser.

Illegitimate children to count as dependants under Inheritance (Family Provision) Act 1938 *(s.* 18)

Section 18 gives illegitimate children, in relation to the estates of parents dying after the 1st January 1969, the same rights under that Act as if they had been legitimate.

Policies of assurance and property in industrial and provident societies (s. 19)

Section 19 was introduced during Committee and corresponds with those foregoing in that it extends the general provisions of this Part of the Act to certain enactments concerned with the distribution of estates among the children of specified policy-holders. The enactments referred to are the Married Women's Property Act 1882 (11 Halsbury's Statutes, 2nd Edn., p. 799) and the Industrial and Provident Societies Act 1965 (45 Halsbury's Statutes, 2nd Edn., p. 755). The section attracted little comment but the Government added sub-s. (2) to settle certain misgivings.

PART III: PROVISIONS FOR USE OF BLOOD TESTS IN DETERMINING PATERNITY (SS. 20–25)

The provisions of this Part of the Act, which empower the Courts to order blood tests in cases of disputed paternity arise from the Law Commission's Report on Blood Tests and the Proof of Paternity in Civil Proceedings (Law Com. No. 16: 1968).

The justification for the legislature providing for this new power is to be found in the *cri-de-cœur* uttered by Ormerod, J. in *Re L.*, [1967] 2 All E.R. at p. 1126: "If ever a case illustrates the extreme necessity for some statutory power in the court to enable this sort of problem to be resolved, it is this case."

Until the passing of this Act, the limited power to order a blood test was vested only in the High Court. Otherwise in the case of magistrates' courts, there was no corresponding power at all: and such a test could only be carried out with the consent of all the parties. Furthermore, any refusal could not be taken into account on arriving at a decision. In the case of undefended proceedings before a county court under the Matrimonial Causes Act 1967, where it might be thought desirable in the interests of a child to have a blood test, the matter had to be referred to the High Court as one demanding ancillary relief.

All this is now obviated by the provisions of s. 20.

The Law Commission derived confidence in its recommendations from the high degree of certainty which medical evidence can provide. Its comments were expressed thus:

> "We are satisfied that as medical knowledge stands at present blood tests may provide conclusive evidence in a negative sense; that is, they can prove that a given man could not, according to the biological laws of heredity, be the father of a particular child. They cannot prove conclusively that he is the child's father but they can show, with varying degrees of probability that he could be. Where blood tests indicate that the man concerned could not be the child's father we shall term this an 'exclusion result'; where the tests indicate that he could be the father we shall term

this a 'non-exclusion result'. Where a man is wrongly accused of paternity there is now at least a 70 per cent. chance that an exclusion result will be obtained from blood tests. The chances of obtaining an exclusion result will no doubt be increased as further blood groups are discovered and more refined techniques developed. Even now, where uncommon blood factors are present or where, for example, it is known that the father must be one of only two men both of whose blood groups are known, the chances of excluding a wrongly accused man can be very much greater than 70 per cent. Where blood tests provide a non-exclusion result they indicate a possibility that the man concerned is the child's father. The strength of this indication will depend primarily upon the incidence of the relevant blood factors in the population. Where common blood factors are present there may be a statistical possibility that any one of, say, 50 per cent. of the adult male population could be the child's father, but in an extreme case where uncommon blood factors are present the incidence of possible fathers could be as low as one in fifty million. The circumstances of an individual case may also increase the evidential value of a non-exclusion result. The presence of certain factors in a child's blood, for example, may be almost conclusive proof that a parent is of a particular ethnic group. There may be cases, for example the Scottish case of *Sinclair* v. *Rankin,* where it is clear that the father of a child must be one of only two men. In such a case a non-exclusion result in respect of blood tests on the first man and an exclusion result in respect of the second man might be acceptable as proof that the first man is the child's father." (Law Com. No. 16: 1968 at pp. 2, 3.)

Power of court to require use of blood tests (s. 20)

Section 20 gives a court power to order a blood test in any civil proceedings in which paternity is disputed and provides that the report of the blood test shall be receivable as evidence in such proceedings.

The reason for this new power arises from the fact that under the old law a court had very limited authority to order adults to submit to a blood test—see *W.* v. *W.* (*No.* 4), [1963] 2 All E.R. 841, in which the topic is fully discussed. This did not mean that it could not accept and act upon evidence submitted by parties who had volunteered among themselves to undergo blood-testing: it most certainly could, even if the result were to bastardise a child in whose favour the presumption of legitimacy would have prevailed (as to which see s. 26, *post*). Referring to voluntary blood tests, the Law Commission said:

"If, in any proceedings, under the law as it stands now, the parties agree to submit themselves and the child to a blood test before there is any question of the appointment of a guardian *ad litem* the results of these blood tests are admissible in evidence. We think that no obstacle should be put in the way of the continuance in future of a practice which will tend to reduce the questions in dispute in litigation and cut out a number of contentious proceedings. It would be desirable for such voluntary testing to be carried out in the way which we recommend later in this Report. There will clearly be cases where the procedure cannot be complied with, for example, where one of the parties is abroad and the tests on his blood are done in the country where he is living, but in general we consider that it is important that the recommended testing procedure should apply wherever this is possible." (Law Com. No. 16: 1968, at p. 14.)

The former powers of the court to direct the blood testing of a child remain undisturbed: they are succinctly set forth in *B. R. B.* v. *J. B.*, [1968] 2 All E.R. 1023, at p. 1025, C.A. *per* Lord Denning, M.R.:

"... a judge of the High Court has power to order a blood test when-ever it is in the best interests of the child. The judges can be trusted to exercise this discretion wisely. I would set no limit, condition or bounds to the way in which the judges exercise their discretion. The object of the court always is to find out the truth. When scientific advances give us fresh means of ascertaining it, we should not hesitate to use those means whenever the occasion requires."

At the time of delivery, however, this judgment was received with some reservation by other judges, and, being a Court of Appeal decision, there always remained that element of doubt which a decision of the House of Lords alone could have resolved. The terms of the present Act put the matter beyond dispute.

It should be noted that since the power is discretionary, it may be taken that the spirit of the foregoing judgment will prevail, and that courts will not feel themselves called upon to exercise it where no useful purpose would be served. As the same learned judge remarked in *M. (D.)* v. *M. (S.)* and *G. (M. D. A.)*, *intervening*, [1969] 2 All E.R. 243, at p. 244:

"If it were possible, by means of the blood test, to show that the husband was the father, it might be to the child's benefit. But it cannot show that. This is not a case where one of two known men is the father. The only known man is the husband. There is a 70 per cent. chance that it may show that the husband was *not* the father. But, if that is shown, what good is it to the boy? It would only show that he is illegitimate, and that the wife was telling lies when she said that the husband was the father. That does the boy no good. On the other hand, if the blood test should show that the husband *could* be the father, that will not do the boy any good either. Hundreds of other men also *could be* the father. This husband will not recognise the child as his. He has always denied paternity and will doubtless continue to do so.... I cannot help thinking that the sole reason why the husband wants the blood test is to prove that the wife was guilty of adultery over ten years ago. Now in most cases it is best to know the truth.... But I do not think the infant should be made a pawn in a contest between husband and wife—not, at any rate, in the case of an infant of ten who can understand what is happening.... In all the circumstances, I think these adults should fight out their own battle without bringing the infant into it. The divorce proceedings should go for trial, as they are....."

Consents, etc. required for taking blood samples (s. 21)

Section 21 provides that a blood sample shall not be taken from any person without his consent, and that any person over sixteen may validly consent for this purpose. Provisions are also included for consents on behalf of persons under 16 and persons who are mentally incapable of acting for themselves.

The terms of this section uphold the well-established principle that no person should be compelled to submit to a medical examination unless his consent is freely given or that power in that behalf is expressly conferred by statute.

In spite of its inherent sanction, contained in s. 23, the new power attracted very little comment, even during the Committee stages. The most that was said arose in the second reading debate—

> "It affects the rights of the individual. The Attorney-General said that there is really no sanction, but, of course, the inference that can be drawn by the refusal is really the sanction. There are people with conscientious objections to that sort of thing . . . . The court must—I hope that it will—take into account that there are many people who have such objections. (778 H. of C. Official Report 55.)

Power to provide for manner of giving effect to direction for use of blood tests (s. 22)

Section 22 prescribes with some particularity for matters upon which the Home Secretary may make regulations as to how blood tests are to be conducted. It should be noted that these regulations are directed only to tests carried out under statutory powers and would not necessarily be applied to tests undertaken voluntarily.

Failure to comply with direction for taking blood tests (s. 23)

Section 23 provides that the court may draw any inference it thinks right from a person's refusal to participate in a blood test which it has ordered under s. 20. As an additional sanction, if such a person is claiming relief in reliance on the presumption of legitimacy (which frequently arises in cases within the contemplation of this section), the court may dismiss such a claim on the ground that persons ought not to be permitted to secure a tactical advantage from their disobedience. The subject of sanctions occupied a great deal of the attention of the Law Commission and they discussed it at length in their Report.

The solution embodied in the Act is certainly the best that can be devised: namely, that the court should be given the power to make a direction (not an order) for blood testing and if this is not complied with, the court should be empowered to consider the failure as evidence from which it can draw whatever inferences it thinks warranted.

The Commission was not slow to recognise that a refusal to allow a test could be turned into a tactical advantage. It described the situation in which a wife had been committing adultery and at the same time participating in sexual relations with her husband. The subsequent birth of a child could be attributed either to the husband or to the adulterer—and the wife herself might not know who. While she is prepared to suffer the consequences of a refusal to be blood tested in subsequent divorce proceedings—*i.e.*, that her refusal can be construed as an admission of misconduct—nevertheless it is impossible to come to any conclusion as to who is the child's father. In this matter the court can draw no inference and must, unless there is potent evidence indicating otherwise, apply the presumption of legitimacy. This is exactly what the wife desires, since she can then claim maintenance from the unproven "father". To prevent this the Commission recommended, and this has been incorporated into the section, that where paternity is disputed and a party has refused to comply with a direction of the court for blood tests to be made, then, on an application by that party for custody of, or maintenance for the child, the burden will be on the party applying (until the direction for blood tests is complied with) to prove the paternity of the child.

Penalty for personating another, etc., for purpose of providing blood sample (s. 24)

Section 24 makes impersonation in connection with a blood test a criminal offence punishable on indictment with up to two years imprisonment and on summary conviction with a fine of up to £400.

The position in common law as to this offence is somewhat ambiguous, being obscured by the fact that this form of cheating has usually to be shown as being carried out to secure some material advantage. It is certainly well established that conspiracies or frauds designed to pervert the course of justice are actionable, but the provisions of this Act leave no room for doubt or dispute.

PART IV: MISCELLANEOUS AND GENERAL (ss. 26–28)

The provisions in this Part of the Act, are mainly limited to miscellaneous connected matters arising out of the question of paternity. The first is derived from a recommendation of the Law Commission that the old "presumption of legitimacy" rule be no longer subject to such stringent standards of proof as formerly. The second, arising during the passage of the Act through Parliament, is that the paternity of an illegitimate child may be more easily registered.

Rebuttal of presumption as to legitimacy and illegitimacy (s. 26)

Section 26 provides that the presumption of legitimacy may be displaced on a balance of probabilities instead of proof beyond reasonable doubt.

The subject was closely studied by the Law Commission whose Report made the following points:

Bastardy is no longer the source of reproach and ridicule that it once was, and the lot of the illegitimate child, particularly since the Legitimacy Act 1959 and Part II of the present enactment, is less unfortunate. Even so, despite the changes in public and legal attitudes towards illegitimacy, the courts are still very unwilling to make a decree which has the effect of bastardising a child. Some recent decisions have reflected this reluctance, but it has been taken to such an extent as to inflict a hardship upon husbands, who can only feel a contempt for law which requires them to maintain children who are more than likely to be those of another man.

It is probably more important today for the courts to arrive at a correct decision rather than exhibit an apparent lack of worldly wisdom and declare a child to be legitimate at all costs. It is in a child's best interests to know, if possible, the true position as to its paternity.   Where a husband has denied being the father of his wife's child, but has been unable because of the strength of the presumption of legitimacy to prove that he is not, the emotional and financial effect on the child is not likely to be beneficial if the husband is never-theless still firmly convinced that he is not its father.   It can be strongly argued that on balance it would be better for the child if it was firmly established who his father was rather than to leave this in doubt, even if leaving it in doubt secured for him the legal status of legitimacy.   Also, it is to be remembered that the fact that a child is illegitimate at birth no longer means that he will remain illegiti-mate for all time.   Since the Legitimacy Act 1959, the subsequent marriage of the natural parents legitimates a child even though one or both of them were married to another at the time of its birth.   In a great many cases the wife, after divorce proceedings, marries the co-respondent, thereby legitimating any child she has had by him.   This is likely to be far more beneficial to the child than to leave it in a position in which, while it is in law a child of the previous (dissolved) marriage, none of those concerned really believes that it is in fact such.   (Law Com. No. 16: 1968, at pp. 6, 7.)

Entry of father's name on registration of birth of illegitimate child (s. 27)

The Russell Committee concluded that in cases where paternity is established or not disputed, the position of an illegitimate child in relation to the father's es-tate, and of the father in relation to the illegitimate child's estate, should be the same as in the case of the mother. But though the Committee talked of paternity being established, it did not make any recommendation as to how it might be established.   The only thing said was contained in paragraph 43 of its Report: "We think that the facilities for recognition in connection with birth registration might well be reviewed and extended as they have been in Scotland under ss. 18 and 20 of the Registration of Births, Deaths and Marriages (Scotland) Act 1965".

Section 27 meets this suggestion and authorises the name of the father of an illegitimate child to be entered on the register of births without the need for his attending personally to sign the register on the occasion of first registration and on the re-registration of a birth that has already been registered.

Short title, interpretation, commencement and extent (s. 28)

There were some criticisms made as to the choice of a title and the Lord Chancellor made the following observations:

> "Of course this is not really one [Act]; it is three [Acts] to implement these three Reports: [the Latey Report, the Russell Report and the Report of the Law Commission as to Blood Testing.]   This [might] not be the right way to draft legislation but those who manage our Parliamentary time say that three measures always take up more time than one and therefore, if you want to get your thing done, you have to put three in one. Then I was faced with the question 'What is the measure to be called?'   I appreciate that 'Family Law Reform' sounds like [an enactment] about which anybody who had any proposal to make about family law could put

down an amendment and push it in, but of course that would be quite outside the scope of the measure. The difficulty was that the alternative was the 'Law Reform (Miscellaneous Provisions) [Act]'. For the main customers of Statutes, who are the lawyers, this might mean anything. You cannot tell by the name what it is. Technically the correct name of this [enactment] is 'Law Reform (Miscellaneous Provisions) (Age of Majority, Rights of Succession of Illegitimate Children, and Proof of Paternity) [Act 1969]'. This would have been perfectly terrible and, after many consultations with many people, we ended by choosing this title as being, on the whole, less objectionable than any alternative." (297 H. of L. Official Report 1194.)

The Act received the Royal Assent on 25th July 1969 and Parts I, II and IV were brought into operation on 1st January 1970 (see S.I. 1969 No. 1140).

THE CHILDREN AND YOUNG PERSONS ACT 1969

This Act, in spite of its 73 sections and 7 Schedules, is not as formidable as it appears. In the first place it reproduces a great deal of what is already on the statute book: for example, the greater part of the law relating to hostels, children's homes, remand homes, reception centres, approved schools, and the voluntary establishments has been repealed, and the new law with regard to residential accommodation for children in care, which now falls under the simple designation of the "community home system" combines and consolidates in a single Act what once was distributed through several. In the second place, it was indicated by both the Home Secretary and the Minister of State, that the essentials of the Act are contained in only five sections (ss. 1, 4, 5, 12 and 35).

Probably no better exposition of the philosophy of the Act is to be found elsewhere than in the White Paper, "Children in Trouble" (Cmnd. 3601: 1968):

"Juvenile delinquency has no single cause, manifestation or cure. Its origins are many, and the range of behaviour which it covers is equally wide. At some points it merges almost imperceptibly with behaviour which does not contravene the law. A child's behaviour is influenced by genetic, emotional and intellectual factors, his maturity, and his family, school, neighbourhood and wider social setting. It is probably a minority of children who grow up without ever misbehaving in ways which may be contrary to the law. Frequently such behaviour is no more than an incident in the pattern of a child's normal development. But sometimes it is a response to unsatisfactory family or social circumstances, a result of boredom in and out of school, an indication of maladjustment or immaturity, or a symptom of a deviant, damaged or abnormal personality. Early recognition and full assessment are particularly important in these more serious cases. Variety and flexibility in the measures that can be taken are equally important, if society is to deal effectively and appropriately with these manifold aspects of delinquency. These measures include supervision and support of the child in the family: the further development of the services working in the community: and a variety of facilities for short-term and long-term care, treatment and control, including some which are highly specialised.

The social consequences of juvenile delinquency range from minor nuisance to considerable damage and suffering for the community. An important object of the criminal law is to protect society against such consequences: but the community also recognises the importance of caring for those who are too young to protect themselves. Over recent years these two quite distinct grounds for action by society in relation to young people have been moving steadily closer together. It has become increasingly clear that social control of harmful behaviour by the young, and social measures to help and protect the young, are not distinct and separate processes. The aims of protecting society from juvenile delinquency, and of helping children in trouble to grow up into mature and law-abiding persons, are complementary and not contradictory."

As will be seen, this philosophy of "variety" and "flexibility" is put into effect in the Act by placing the choice of treatment or care in the hands of supervisors and the local authorities and not on the courts.

The Act is divided into three parts: the first Part deals with how children and young persons are to be dealt with when appearing before the courts; the second establishes the administrative machinery for setting-up a comprehensive system of residential establishments for children who need them; and the third Part contains various miscellaneous provisions.

PART I: CARE AND OTHER TREATMENT OF JUVENILES THROUGH COURT PROCEEDINGS (SS. 134)

Care of children and young persons through juvenile courts (ss. 1–3)

Section 1 sets out all the circumstances under which a child or a young person may be brought before a juvenile court: a "child" is a person up to the age of 14; a "young person" is one up to 17. Committing an offence is only one of several factors which should entail the presence of a youngster in court. This arises from the philosophy of the Act which regards the child who does wrong as being in need of the same care and control as the child who is ill-treated or neglected. However, the Under-Secretary for the Home Department on concluding the Second Reading, said:

"Nothing in the [Act] has been spawned by sentimental notions of curing all problems by kindness alone. The compelling motive is not softness or permissiveness, but rather a realistic appreciation of the range and the variety of assets which modern society has available and which can be further developed to deal more effectively with the problem of juvenile delinquency." (779 H. of C. Official Report 1292.)

The circumstances which would justify a person bringing a child or young person to court are (1) that he is neglected; or (2) that he is living in a bad home from whence his removal is desirable before anything happens to him; or (3) that he is being exposed to moral danger; or (4) that he is beyond control; or

(5) that he is not attending school; or (6) that he has committed an offence (except homicide, for which special arrangements are necessary), and that unless the court does something about it, nobody else will.

Since a child can hardly speak for himself and parents, if they are unkind to him, are not likely to come forward, and, in any case should be protected against officious interference, the only parties who are permitted to bring proceedings are the police, the local authorities or the officers of the N.S.P.C.C.

The steps that a court can take are several. Obviously if the child is seriously disturbed in its mind, then it is best for an order to be made, putting him into the hands of those most qualified to help him. Where the parents are willing to face up to their responsibilities and co-operate with the authorities, they can enter into a recognizance to keep their child from trouble. If it is best for the child to be taken away from them, then an order committing him into the care of the local authority can be made; otherwise it might suffice simply to make an order putting the party under the supervision of the local authority—to keep an eye, as it were, upon him and to "advise, assist and befriend" him.

Only one order at a time can be made—unless it refers to mental cases, when two concurrent orders are possible. Nor can an order be made against a person aged 16 and who is, or has been, married.

The first thing a local authority must do upon receiving information about a child or young person, is to initiate an enquiry—unless it thinks that this will serve no useful purpose (s. 2 (1)). If these enquiries indicate that it would be desirable to begin care proceedings on behalf of a youngster, it should do so on its own account unless some other party has intimated its intention of doing this—usually the police or an officer of the N.S.P.C.C. (s. 2 (2)). Since it is only reasonable that a local authority should have advance notice that a youngster may be committed to its care, it is entitled to notification from these other people that they do in fact intend to bring these proceedings (s. 2 (3); cf. also s. 5 (8)). If the care proceedings are going to be based on the fact that a youngster is not attending school, etc., then only the local educational authority may bring them (s. 2 (8)).

If a child is under the age of five it is not always necessary—nor is it sometimes desirable—for him to attend the court where proceedings are being conducted on his behalf, but of course his parents ought to be present or at least have been given an opportunity to be heard (s. 2 (9)). Otherwise the attendance of any youngster can be secured in the usual way, either by summons or by warrant—a proceeding which also applies to witnesses (s. 2 (4), (6)). Young people who are arrested and in custody following the issue of a warrant to bring them to court must make an appearance within 72 hours so that the appropriate steps may be taken (s. 2 (5)).

A court is not obliged to make a definitive order upon the youngster's first appearance: it can, if it is not in a position to decide there and then what would be the best course to take, arrange for an interim order (s. 2 (10)).

As is usually the case there are conferred rights to appeal to quarter sessions against the orders made—unless it is a recognizance; but since this would be entered into voluntarily, no appeal would be relevant (s. 2 (12)). There are also provisions made to ensure that as far as possible a person on whose behalf care proceedings are brought is dealt with by his own people and in his own area;

consequently arrangements are made to remit proceedings from the area where-in the lapses take place to the area wherein the youngster lives—or at least to send notice to his own local authority that proceedings are taking place, and giving it 21 days in which to decide what to do (s. 2 (11)).

Once a youngster is before the court with regard to having committed an offence, all the safeguards built into the criminal law are brought into play (s. 3). In the first place his presence there will only be possible if the proceedings are initiated either by the local authority or the police—and they will have con-ducted preliminary enquiries beforehand as to the merits, if any, of acting thus. Although only the police or the local authority may proceed against the offend-er, other authorised persons are not precluded from adducing evidence. All the established rules as to the burden of proof, the standard of proof and matters with regard to the form and nature of evidence, previous offences, and the "autrefois" principles, etc., are to be observed.

The courts may, whether an order is made or not, call upon the parents to pay compensation up to £100 for whatever damage their child has caused. If the offender is over 14 he may, but only if he consents, be required to enter into a recognizance for a sum not exceeding £25 and to promise to behave himself for a year (s. 3 (6)).

While it is open to the court before which the offender appears to determine the proceedings—since it would be unfair to expect witnesses to travel to other places, it may remit the offender to his own home town for the local court to make the appropriate order—again on the principle that it is better for him if his own people attend to his care and control (s. 2 (5)). If however he wishes to appeal, this must be made back in the area where the original findings took place (s. 3 (9)).

Consequential changes in criminal proceedings (ss. 4–10)

Criminal proceedings against children will ultimately cease, except where the offence is homicide (s. 4). As to the full implementation of s. 4, the Under-Secretary said:

> "It is the Government's intention that this section should be brought
> into operation up to the twelfth birthday in the first place and that this
> age level will not be raised higher until we have been able to satisfy our-
> selves of two conditions: first, that the resources which are necessary are
> available and secondly that our experience is such as to justify raising the
> age level to 13 and ultimately to 14."

In the case of young persons, criminal proceedings are severely restricted (s. 5). In the first place, when an offence alleged to have been committed by a young person comes to the notice of the police, they have an obligation to ask for any observations from the local authority (s. 5 (3)). If the authority thinks it desirable, they will then undertake the task of:

> "assembling and considering the available information about the child
> and his background (*e.g.*, from his teachers), consulting any others known

to be involved already with the child or his family (*e.g.*, the probation service), and a home visit if this seems required before the children's department can decide whether voluntary action with the family would be worth attempting.

    (*a*) If, after this consultation, it is agreed that voluntary action without the support of a court order should be tried or continued, or that a formal caution would be appropriate, or that no action is necessary, the case will be dealt with accordingly and there will be no application for process.

    (*b*) If the police and the children's department agree that it is a case for prosecution or for care, protection or control proceedings, process will be applied for accordingly." (Cmnd. 3601: 1968.)

Only a limited class of people are to be permitted to bring proceedings, so the private prosecutor is eliminated (s. 5 (17)). Such persons as are authorised to act are designated "qualified informants" and are carefully defined in the Act. They are mainly drawn from the ranks of the police and the staff of public and local authorities. Proceedings attracting the attention of the Director of Public Prosecutions and the Attorney-General are specially exempt from the process.

In order to assist the police, etc. to direct their minds as to whether a process should begin or not, the Home Office will issue regulations under s. 5 (4) specifying the circumstances in which it will be possible for criminal proceedings to be brought for an alleged offence (s. 5 (2)).

The formalities begin with the "qualified informant" presenting the justices with a statement in writing setting forth the age of the offender and certifying that the local authority has been informed and have made no representations. If this is not forthcoming, the justices must quash the information, but this is no bar to subsequent proceedings nor does a want of form invalidate those undertaken inadvertently (s. 5 (6)).

Since it is now generally agreed that a full-scale mounting of a trial, with judge and jury, is quite inappropriate for dealings with young persons, they are normally to be proceeded against summarily. Homicide and a few very grave crimes, such as wounding with intent to do grievous bodily harm and (but only if the courts think it would be in the interests of justice), cases where a young person is charged jointly with an offender over the age of 17, still attract a trial on indictment (s. 6 (1))—but of course, this is only with regard to a *young person*; no criminal proceedings (except in the case of homicide) are to be possible against a *child*. On a finding of guilt under the new procedure, the court will have power to fine up to £50 (s. 6 (3)).

With the elimination of criminal proceedings against children and their restriction against young persons, as well as the assimilation of many "sanctions", many of the old forms of punishment disappear: borstal training may be directed only after the age of 17 (s. 7 (1)), and a probation order, since it can only follow upon, a conviction, will be replaced by the new "supervision order" (s. 7 (2), (7)). The approved school order which depends for its existence on an approved school must of necessity expire when those schools become part of the community home system to which the "care order" will apply instead (s. 7 (5)). That will also take the place of the "fit person order" (s. 7 (6)). The same community home system will provide the necessary places to which those found guilty of serious offences, such as homicide or manslaughter, may be sent—again under a care order. Children who are charged with homicide may be sent to a community home or be put under supervision or may have their parents enter into recognizance to take care and control of them (s. 7 (7)).

A few points of procedure need to be mentioned: the police may take a young person's finger prints only if authorised to do so by a court order (s. 8). A general duty is laid upon local authorities, whether in respect of proceedings under s. 1 of this Act or because they are so requested by the court, to compile and present a report as to the home background, health, school record and character of persons in respect of whom proceedings are brought (s. 9). A young person who is 17 when proceedings begin and attains the age of 18 during any interval which might arise is deemed still to be a young person. The publication of particulars of the proceedings involving young persons is still further limited (s. 10).

Supervision (ss. 11–19)

Existing forms of treatment available to the juvenile courts distinguish sharply between those which involve complete removal from home and those which do not. The juvenile courts have very difficult decisions to make in judging whether circumstances require the drastic step of taking a child away from his parents and his home. The view has often been expressed that some form or forms of "intermediate treatment" should be available to the courts allowing the child to remain in his own home but bringing him also into contact with a different environment.

The present Act now establishes a framework for the development of a variety of forms of intermediate treatment for children and young persons placed under supervision by the juvenile courts. One object is to make available for this purpose the use of facilities not provided expressly for those who have been before the courts. The new methods will be linked to supervision, but a straightforward "supervision order" will remain possible.

At present children and young persons who have committed an offence may be placed on probation and are supervised by probation officers. Those found in need of care, protection or control may be placed under the supervision of a probation officer, the local authority or any other person. Under the new arrangements the supervision of a child under 14 found to be in the need of care, protection or control will normally be undertaken by the local authority. For young persons aged 14 and under 17, supervision following both criminal proceedings and care, protection or control proceedings will be carried out either by the local authority or by a probation officer (but not as at present, by any other person) as decided by the court. This means that the association of the probation service with young persons will be preserved. Supervision will be for a specified period of not more than three years.

The supervision order which the court may make under the new Act is in many respects similar to the present probation order—in fact, if the probation officer already knows the family involved, it is more than likely that the local authority will request him to undertake the task of supervision.

The duty of the supervisor (as of the present probation officer) is to "advise, assist and befriend" the supervised person and also, if such a requirement is included in the supervision order, to give him directions as to how best to adjust his way of living so as to prevent the lapses recurring which caused him to fall under the order in the first place (s. 12 (2)). These directions are entirely at the discretion of the supervisor, but it is anticipated that they will offer tremendous possibilities since it is to be the duty of regional planning committees to build up facilities to assist in this remedial process.

There are many things that a supervised person can be asked to do: live with a certain person or at a certain place; attend regularly at a place specified and so forth. While the order itself may subsist for three years, the activities which a supervised person may be called upon to perform may not extend beyond thirty days in any one year, and if he is required to live in a certain place or with a certain person, the period may not exceed three months in all.

Naturally if a supervised person makes good progress the order may be discharged before time, and equally so, if he proves recalcitrant sterner alternatives may be substituted (ss. 15–17).

Committal to care of local authorities (ss. 20–24)

Sections 20–24 largely replace the corresponding sections in the Children and Young Persons Act 1933 (*i.e.*, ss. 62, 75 and 76). There may be cases in which it is not certain what ought to be done about a person and it may be equally as certain that his whereabouts should be known. Consequently it is possible to make an "interim order" committing him to the care of the local authority for any period up to 28 days. When the court has decided that the person needs finally to be committed into care, it may make a "care order" which may subsist until he is 18. To this there is one important exception. If the person is aged 16, the order may go on until he is 19. Persons who are detained because of some serious factor which might render them a public danger may also be kept in care until they are 19, but only if the local authority makes application: equally so, an order originally made under those conditions can be discharged before time. Generally speaking, the nature of the offence is irrelevant, and children guilty even of homicide will go into such a community home selected as is thought suitable for them: behaviour is however extremely relevant and if a person proves to be unruly he may be despatched to a remand centre or even prison (s. 23). Persons once in community homes are to be brought up in the religion to which it is presumed they belong, and if over five and not used to leaving the home regularly and making contacts outside, are to be provided with "visitors"—unless their parents fulfil this role.

Transfer (ss. 25, 26)

Sections 25 and 26 provide for transfer between the various parts of the British Isles. of persons to whom the new legislation applies. For details, see the notes to the text of the Act, *post.*

Consequential modifications of ss. 11 and 12 of Children Act 1948 (s. 27)

Section 27 makes consequential modifications to the duties of local authorities under Part II of the Children Act 1948. It incorporates references to the present Act, and, out of deference to public apprehensions, directs that where the public interests and those of a child in care conflict, those of the public should prevail. They are to be assisted in this by directions from the Home Secretary and must review every child's case at intervals of not more than six months.

Detention (ss. 28–30)

If any person sees that a youngster is being ill-treated or is neglected or not attending school or is exposed to moral danger, he may make application to remove the child (or young person even) to a place of safety—*i.e.*, to a community home, hospital, police station, etc. Naturally a time limit must be imposed and after eight days if not sooner the child or young person is to be brought to open court. Where however a child or young person is found committing an offence he must be brought to a police station and, if it is thought necessary, committed to the local authority for no longer than 72 hours. In all cases there must be good reason for the detention and interested parties must be given information as to their rights to apply for release. Certain community homes, if so designated by the Home Secretary, may be used for the reception of young offenders who are convicted of grave crimes, and young offenders who prove so unruly that their remaining in a community home would be most undesirable may be removed to borstal, notwithstanding they may only be 15.

The existing law with regard to absentees has been re-enacted to correspond with this Act.

Legal Aid (ss. 33)

The facilities of the legal aid system are extended to proceedings under this Act. Since young persons under 16 are hardly likely to be able to make any contribution, their parents can be called upon to make some contribution. The technicalities of applying this Act to the Criminal Justice Act 1948 are contained in Schedule 1.

Transitional modifications of Part I for persons of specified ages (s. 34)

Section 34 gives the Home Secretary power to specify ages up to or above which a number of the provisions of the Act will operate; see the note to s. 4 on p. 24, *ante*.

PART II: ACCOMMODATION ETC. FOR CHILDREN IN CARE, AND FOSTER CHILDREN (SS. 35–59)

"We on this side of the Committee generally give Part II a warmer welcome than that which we gave Part I. I for one can see that the blurring of the line between the deprived and the depraved child in the matter of accommodation may well have a beneficial effect on a number of children who are, as it were, accidentally depraved." These were the opening remarks of the Committee when the provisions as to accommodation, etc., for children in the care of local authorities and similar organisations came up for scrutiny.

The welcome extended to Part II is not surprising. For a long time it has been the opinion of those concerned with the social services which are directed towards the needs of children and young persons that many changes and improvements are highly desirable. This attitude was strengthened by the ever-increasing expressions of concern at the increase in juvenile delinquency in recent years.

Among many items singled out for criticism has been that the system of residential treatment and other services for the care and supervision of young people who have become involved with the law, is divided among too many parties and that categories are too inflexible. At present the care and treatment of children who have become involved with the courts is distributed between:

   (i) *the probation and aftercare service,* which is responsible for the supervision of all children and young people placed on probation, most social enquiries for juvenile courts, some supervision orders under the Children and Young Persons Acts 1933–1962, the aftercare of about half the children and young people on licence from approved schools, some work in respect of adoptions, and matrimonial work which often involves children;

   (ii) *the children's service,* which is responsible for some social enquiries for juvenile courts, some supervision orders under the Children and Young Persons Acts 1933–1963, and the aftercare of the other half of the children and young people on licence from approved schools, the discharging of fit person orders and a considerable amount of work connected with adoptions. Children's departments are also responsible at present directly for running 30 out of the 122 approved schools and 56 out of the 58 remand homes;

   (iii) *voluntary bodies,* including denominational bodies, some operating on a national scale and some locally, who administer 92 approved schools and 2 remand homes, all of them largely financed from public funds;

   (iv) *the education service and the national health services* (both local authority and hospital service) which, besides their general concern for the welfare of young people, provide educational and child guidance services for remand homes and approved schools, medical and educational reports for the courts, and places in special schools and hospitals for young offenders and "non-offenders" who are the subject of fit person orders and are thought to require these kinds of care and treatment.

Apart from the evils incident upon fragmentation, there is another which, during the passing of the Act, was repeatedly singled out for criticism: that the separation of establishments into rigid, legally-defined categories, leads to an inflexibility having most undesirable results. For example, once a court has made an "approved school order" the local authority has no alternative but to arrange for the child to be sent to such an establishment, however much they might regret it and in the knowledge that it will have an effect upon the child which will be anything but beneficial.

The purpose of this Part of the Act is to remedy this deficiency, and almost, some have suggested, to work, as it were, a miniature "Redcliffe-Maud" within the children's services. The new system emphasises that "a child committed to the care of a local authority for remedial treatment should be placed in the most suitable establishment that has a place available"—a choice which is best left to the local authority: there, the officials and child workers have much better opportunities of assessing the needs of a child than have courts, which may need to act upon a single appearance. The new process, will, in the case of the individual child be initiated by the court simply committing him to the care of the local authority which will then be free to allocate to him a place in whatever establishment it thinks appropriate to his needs.

Community Homes (ss. 35–48)

All the "homes" and hostels, remand homes, reception centres and the approved schools are swept away, and in their place emerges one single legally defined category: the "community home". This means that establishments will no longer be confined to carrying out purposes limited by definition, as formerly, but will be free to experiment.

The new system also continues a process which has been carried out for many years with conspicuous success, with regard for example, to the hospitals and the police forces: *i.e.* that the grouping of local authorities is one of the best ways of ensuring that staff, premises, equipment and resources are deployed to much better advantage than they are at present. At the moment, no authority is really large enough, nor will the administrative units proposed by the Redcliffe-Maud Commission be suitable, for the provision of a range of community homes sufficiently comprehensive as to embrace every type contemplated or required. The Act therefore provides that local authorities are to be grouped into "regional planning areas". The boundaries will be drawn after the Secretary of State has consulted with all the authorities concerned and one of the objects will be, with regard to the drawing of the new "frontiers", that there is a sensible relationship between these areas and those of other services, such as the regional hospital boards, the police, special education and the probation service.

The first task of the regional planning area authorities will be to form a "children's regional planning committee" in accordance with Schedule 2 (see s. 35 (3), (4)). The majority of members must be drawn from persons representing local authority interests, but other associations, such as those involved with health and the educational services may also be represented. All through this Part of the Act, great stress is laid upon the value of consultation and the need for a unified approach and a flexibility in administration. The resources of central government departments concerned with child care, education and health will be made available so as to assist these committees in their work, particularly by identifying needs for which provision must be made on a national basis.

The initial task of the children's planning committees will be to prepare and submit for the Secretary of State's approval, comprehensive plans for a system of "community homes" in their region (ss. 36, 37).

This, it is anticipated, will be best achieved by the Committees first aggregating all the resources which the process of amalgamation has yielded and then setting them alongside the requirements of all the young people in their care.

From the data thus provided it should be possible to evolve schemes whereby every facility may be most advantageously utilised.

All this was put to Parliament in the following way, during the second reading, by the Home Secretary:

"Groups of local authorities will establish regional committees which will plan an integrated system of community homes. It will be the aim to accommodate as many children in local homes as possible and also to provide much the same facilities as a family home and to use the local schools and other services. Most Hon. Members know the housing estates and the houses where these families live. They are frequently unknown except to the immediate neighbours and that is as it should be. The fact that we have been able to use these homes in this way is part of the process of ensuring that the children can develop in a way which will enable them to grow up into the kind of citizens that we hope to see.

But for some children more specialised homes will be needed. Some such homes will require secure accommodation. They must be provided and the regional plans will enable authorities to co-operate in making the best use of the available resources to develop the wide range of specialised facilities which will be needed. I need not particularise: Hon. Members will know some of my difficulties in trying to place children in suitable homes at present because of the fractionalising of control. I believe that this will help to remove that.

The excellent facilities provided in establishments provided now run by voluntary organisations as approved schools or voluntary homes will, I hope, through partnership with the local authorities become available to them. Part II of this measure enables this to be done while preserving for the voluntary organisations a part in the management of these establishments."

As well as building-up a co-ordinated plan for residential facilities, the regional planning committees will also be required to prepare schemes of "intermediate treatment" which the court may prescribe for youngsters under the terms of the new supervision orders (see p. 26, *ante*, as to "intermediate treatment" and as to the provisions of ss. 11 to 19, relating to the new orders). Wide scope is now given to local authorities, the probation service, juvenile court magistrates, the police and voluntary agencies working with children, to make use of all the resources they have available in their locality and elsewhere, for children placed under supervision. The provisions open the way for many constructive possibilities for giving new experiences, a taste of adventure, particularly to children from deprived backgrounds, without the need for long-term removal from their homes and their own environment.

"The great function is to bring young people in trouble with others taking part in the normal constructive activities of young people of their own age—social, educational, recreational, helping others, etc. These activities may take place in the evenings or at the week-end and the children may go away under supervision perhaps for longer periods. They may involve going away, for instance, for adventure training or to a harvest camp. In some cases a supervision order might involve spending as much as three months away from home." (779 H. of C. Official Report 1130— *per* the Home Secretary.)

Since a regional planning committee is only able to act in an advisory capacity, the devolution of responsibility for providing, managing, equipping and maintaining the various community homes must be settled by the authorities among themselves (s. 38).

It is intended that the children's regional planning committees will discuss with the managers of voluntary approved schools the future role and status of each establishment within the new system. It will also be open to a committee to agree with the managers of a voluntary home registered under section 29 of the Children Act 1948 that the home should provide regular facilities within the public system.

When agreement has been reached on the future role of each establishment, and the area development plan has been approved by the Secretary of State, formal steps will be taken to establish the new status of the voluntary home or school. Arrangements will be made to safeguard the interests of the staff, and of the managers of voluntary establishments, during the period of transition to the new system.

Many voluntary organisations, such as the Church of England homes and the Catholic establishments, may wish to co-operate, either in a semi-independent capacity, or fully to be integrated: the former will be legally described as "assisted"; the latter as "controlled". Appropriate "instruments of management" will be drafted by the Secretary of State, but the "general religious spirit and ethos of any particular home", will, as far as possible prevail (s. 39). Representation on the governing bodies of these homes follows a formula designed to secure that in the case of "assisted homes" the voluntary organisation is a two-thirds majority over the local authority, and vice-versa in the case of those which are controlled (ss. 39–41). Controlled homes are granted a fair degree of antonomy with regard to staffing and most forms of expenditure and assisted homes are considerably more independent (s. 42). Whatever its status, local authority, controlled or assisted, the safety and welfare of the occupants of the community home is paramount, and the Secretary of State is empowered to make regulations accordingly (s. 43). If a voluntary organisation comes within the aegis of the community home system its registration, which would of course be superfluous, is dispensed with (s. 44); and, in the matter of disputes, while the Secretary of State is given general powers to determine them, religious points may be referred to the appropriate ecclesiastical or denominational body (s. 45). As the regional plans get under way, the Secretary of State can direct that existing approved schools, remand homes, probation homes and hostels may cease legally to be designated as such, and may, as it were, "float into" the area scheme. Such a procedure may cause disturbances in staffing and the interests of such parties are protected under the provisions of Schedule 3.

Some of the voluntary organisations may wish, for various reasons, to discontinue certain establishments or to leave the community system: if they do, reasonable notice—usually two years—is required to be given to the local authority (s. 47) and, since public money has been spent on their establishments, any profits so arising must be repaid (s. 48).

Consequential modifications of the Children Act 1948, *ss.* 13 *and* 19 (*ss.* 49, 50)

These sections simply re-enact the relevant sections of the Children Act 1948 (see the notes to ss. 49, 50, *post*).

Foster children (*ss.* 51–57)

The introduction of the Children and Young Persons Bill also provided an opportunity to make much needed improvements in the law on private fostering, which is contained in the Children Act 1958. That enactment suffered in not being sufficiently all-inclusive, and the powers of local authorities to protect foster children were, in some respects, inadequate. The substance of ss. 51 to 57 (which relate to these matters) was not, as the Government admitted on second reading, exactly germane to the principal purposes of the new Act, but since it was largely directed to the interests of children, the opportunity was taken to amend the law on the fostering of children. The aim of the sections is to help local authorities to concentrate more effort on cases most requiring supervision; by bringing *de facto* adoption and similar arrangements within the scope of the law; by closing the gap which existed between the Children Act 1958 (which only covered arrangements lasting for more than a month, and the Nurseries and Child Minders Regulation Act 1948 (which controls daily minding and only covers arrangements lasting not more than six days). The defects have been remedied by extending the powers of local authorities to inspect premises and by imposing conditions about the keeping of foster children and other relevant matters.

The system adopted in the new Act has been to amend the relevant sections of the Children Act 1958 and to reprint them, as amended, in the form of a "Keeling Schedule" (*i.e.*, Sch. 7, *post*).

Section 51 re-enacts in more flexible terms s. 1 of the Children Act 1958 (which imposes a duty on local authorities to visit all foster children) so as to enable authorities to concentrate more effort on cases calling for special attention. Section 52 amends the definition of a foster child in s. 2 of the 1958 Act to include cases (such as *de facto* adoptions) in which the foster parent receives no reward; to reduce from one month to six days the maximum period for which a child can be kept by a regular foster parent without coming within the definition (to close the gap between the 1958 Act and the Nurseries and Child Minders Regulation Act 1948, which covers periods of up to six days); and to increase the protection accorded to children who are living on school premises but not being educated there. (There is a consequential amendment of the definition of a "protected child" in the Adoption Act 1958.) Section 53 amends s. 3 of the 1958 Act by providing for a notification to be given to the local authority by a person on his becoming or ceasing to be a foster parent, in place of the existing requirement for notifications to be given in respect of individual children; but authorities will have power under s. 55 (2) to require the giving of particulars in individual cases. Section 54 clarifies and strengthens existing powers to inspect

2—A.L.S. 189

premises in which foster children are kept. Section 55 extends the powers of local authorities to impose requirements in respect of premises where foster children are kept, and clarifies and extends their powers to prohibit the reception of a foster child by an unsuitable person or in unsuitable premises. Section 56 extends the classes of person specified in s. 6 of the 1958 Act who may not keep a foster child without the local authority's consent. Section 57 in certain cases protects from conviction a person who keeps foster children in unknowing contravention of s. 6; it also enables proceedings for failure to give any notice required by the 1958 Act to be brought at any time within six months of the discovery of the offence.

It should be noted that nothing has been done to remedy some of the extremely heart-breaking situations which are still possible under the present system—see s. 52. During Committee one Member said: "I have known cases in which parents showed not the slightest interest in the child, almost from the time of its birth until the time arrived at the age of 15, for it to earn some money. *That* is when they begin to show some interest. During all those years it is not uncommon for a parent to have shown not the slightest connection with that child, sending neither Birthday nor Christmas Card and certainly not visiting the child. At the age of 15, however, and this is a very important age in a young person's life, when school ceases and work begins, the child is faced with the traumatic experience of a parent coming along to tear him away from his foster parents. I am not so much concerned about the heartbreak of the foster parents, although it is dreadful when a child whom they look upon as theirs is taken arbitrarily from them. But I am concerned with the child. I can think of nothing worse for a child at that stage in life to be taken forcibly from the only home it has ever known." However the Government suggested that the matter was under active consideration and that to remedy the situation would call for more comprehensive treatment which could not conveniently be interpolated in the present enactment.

Inspection (ss. 58 and 59)

Sections 58 and 59 (which are based on the existing law) empower the Secretary of State to authorise officers to enter and inspect community homes and other premises and provide penalties for obstructing officers in the exercise of these functions.

PART III: MISCELLANEOUS AND GENERAL (ss. 60–73)

This Part of the Act makes the usual miscellaneous alterations in various enactments which cannot conveniently be accommodated in the other Parts of the Act.

Section 60 meets the case where a person has committed an offence against a child or young person and is now outside the jurisdiction of the English courts and s. 61 makes new arrangements for the appointment of juvenile court panels. Section 62 gives local authorities a yardstick whereby to measure the rates of contribution which the parents of children in care ought to make. The purpose of s. 63 is to arrange for the collection of statistical information.

Section 64 indicates that Parliament will "foot the bill" when it comes to providing highly specialised establishments for children in need of treatment and s. 65 makes a corresponding arrangement for voluntary homes. Section 66 is highly technical in content, but it means that local authorities will have their expenses under this Act taken into account when grants are being allocated in accordance with the Local Government Act 1966. Section 67 simply declares that other expenses will be met by Parliament.

Land may have to be subject to compulsory purchase, and s. 68 provides for this, while many rules and regulations will have to be made—some comprehensive, others temporary and local: for this, provision is made in s. 69. The meaning of certain words and phrases is given in s. 70 along with other declarations and s. 71 extends the Act to the Scilly Islands. The last two sections are concerned with temporary "change-over" problems and citation, commencement and extent, as to which see the notes to s. 73, *post.*

THE TATTOOING OF MINORS ACT 1969

This Act creates the new offence whereby a person who undertakes to tattoo a young person not yet of the age of 18 renders himself liable to a summary conviction which might, depending on circumstances, result in his being fined up to £50, or, in the case of a second or subsequent conviction, £100.

The Act was originally introduced into the House of Commons under the private members procedure, but was warmly welcomed by the Government. It is worth noting that the British Guild of Tattooing joined the medical profession in supporting the Act, the rationale of which was well expressed by its sponsors in these words:

> "When I became interested in the matter, not being tattooed myself but being quite used to seeing people who have been tattooed, I was surprised to find how much distress can be caused by a tattoo undertaken in a moment of exuberance, and this is so even with hard-baked people with wide experience of the world. A former colleague wrote to tell me how much he supported the Bill, having himself been unfortunate enough to have been tattooed when he was a young midshipman. It is not only those who are particularly sensitive who later find their tattoo an embarrassment. I can substantiate that by quoting examples which have been sent to me by the Director of the Manchester Youth Development Trust. He mentions a youth of 19 who says he wants his tattoo removed because 'People take one look at you—decent people like—and they don't want to know you'. He mentioned a boy aged 14 who had been tattooed for a dare and now regrets it; a boy aged 16 who thinks that his tattoo will prevent him ever getting a good job and a lad of 19 with tattoos on his hands which, he says 'make me look like a crook'. One can understand that people come to resent their tattoos." (780 H. of C. Official Report 1952.)
>
> "The purpose of the proposed legislation is not to interfere with the liberty of the subject but to protect a youngster from committing a folly which he or she will perhaps later bitterly regret. There is an additional

reason. A tattoo professionally executed can in most cases only be removed by a nasty operation of plastic surgery. Every year now hundreds
of young people apply for this help to get them out of their difficulties.
But surgeons are busy men and the applicant may be told to wait for a
year or several years." (300 H. of L. Official Report 645.)

During the Debates it was reported that at several hospitals between 100 and
200 skin-grafting operations were performed each year to remove tattoo marks,
and that the average age of the patients who had been tattooed was 17. The
cost of each operation was estimated to be £250. This was an expensive and
not very constructive burden on the Health Service and the measure was frequently described as an effective and useful device against what was threaten-
ing to be a social problem.

THE REPRESENTATION OF THE PEOPLE ACT 1969

(1969 c. 15)

PRELIMINARY NOTE

This Act received the Royal Assent on 17th April 1969 and came into operation in accordance with s. 27, *post.* So far as it relates to elections to the Parliament of the United Kingdom the Act applies to Great Britain and Northern Ireland; see in particular s. 1 (5), *post.* But the Act does not affect the law relating to the Parliament of Northern Ireland or to local government in Northern Ireland (see s. 26 (4), *post,* applying the Representation of the People Act 1949, s. 174 (2)). The Parliament of Northern Ireland is, however, empowered to repeal or amend such Parts of the Act as relate to matters in respect of which it has power to make laws (see s. 26 (4), *post,* applying s. 174 (3) of the Act of 1949).

ARRANGEMENT OF SECTIONS

The franchise and its exercise

An Act to amend the law about the qualification of electors at elections to the Parliament of the United Kingdom or at local government elections in Great Britain, and the qualification for election to and membership of local authorities in England and Wales, about the conduct of and manner of voting at those elections and about candidates' election expenses thereat, and otherwise to make provision about matters incidental to those elections, and for purposes connected therewith   [17th April 1969]

The franchise and its exercise

1. Voting age

(1) For purposes of the Representation of the People Acts a person shall be of voting age if he is of the age of eighteen years or over; and, if otherwise qualified, a person who is of voting age on the date of the poll at a parliamentary or local government election shall be entitled to vote as an elector, whether or not he is of voting age on the qualifying date.

(2) A person, if otherwise qualified, shall accordingly be entitled to be registered in a register of parliamentary electors or a register of local government electors if he will attain voting age before the end of the twelve months following the day by which the register is required to be published; but, if he will not be of voting age on the first day of those twelve months—

> (a) his entry in the register shall give the date on which he will attain that age; and
>
> (b) until the date given in the entry he shall not by virtue of the entry be treated as an elector for any purposes other than purposes of an election at which the day fixed for the poll is that or a later date.

(3) A person, if otherwise qualified, shall be capable of voting as proxy at parliamentary or local government elections at which he is of voting age on the date of the poll, and of being appointed proxy for that purpose before he is of voting age.

(4) A person shall be qualified under the parliamentary or local elections rules to assist a blind voter to vote if that person is one of the relatives specified in the relevant rule and is of voting age.

(5) For purposes of the Representation of the People Acts a person shall be deemed, according to the law in Northern Ireland as well as according to the law in other parts of the United Kingdom, not to have attained a given age until the commencement of the relevant anniversary of the day of his birth.

*   *   *   *   *

GENERAL NOTE
  See pp. 1–3, *ante.*

COMMENCEMENT
  See s. 27 (1), *post.*

CONSTRUCTION
  See s. 26 (1), *post.*

SUB-S. (1)
  This subsection corresponds in principle with the Family Law Reform Act 1969, s. 1, *post.*

  A person shall be of voting age
  Note that the expressions "voting age" and "full age" are not, in the context of electoral law, synonymous. Section 1 (1) of the Family Law Reform Act 1969, *post*, by which a person is to attain full age on reaching 18 is expressly excluded from application to the Representation of the People Acts (see s. 1 (4) of, and Sch. 2 to, that Act, *post*).

If he is
   Note that this includes "she"; see the Interpretation Act 1889, s. 1 (1) (*a*) (24 Halsbury's Statutes (2nd Edn.) 206).

Age of eighteen
   See sub-s. (5) of this section.   Cf. also the Family Law Reform Act 1969, s. 9, *post*. Note that a person can vote in an election that takes place on his birthday.

If otherwise qualified
   I.e., in accordance with the provisions of the Representation of the People Act 1949, ss. 1, 2 (11 Halsbury's Statutes, 3rd Edn., 547, 549).

Qualifying date
   The 10th October in any year is the qualifying date for a parliamentary or local government election at which the date fixed for the poll falls within the period of 12 months beginning with the 16th February in the next following year; see the Electoral Registers Act 1949, s. 1 (3) (11 Halsbury's Statutes (3rd Edn.) 801).

SUB-S. (2)
   By virtue of s. 26, Sch. 4, *post*, this subsection is authorised to be inserted as s. 8 (3) of the Representation of the People Act 1949.

Registers
   As to the preparation and publication of registers of parliamentary and local government electors, see the Electoral Registers Act 1949, s. 1 (11 Halsbury's Statutes (3rd Edn.) 801), and the London Government Act 1963, s. 8 (1), Sch. 3 (43 Halsbury's Statutes (2nd Edn.) 679, 788, 789).

Date of publication of register
   See the Electoral Registers Act 1949, s. 1 (2) (11 Halsbury's Statutes (3rd Edn.) 801).

Twelve months following, etc.
   The expression "months" means "calendar months"; see the Interpretation Act 1889, s. 3 (24 Halsbury's Statutes (2nd Edn.) 207).   In calculating this period the *dies a quo* is not to be reckoned; see *Goldsmiths' Co.* v. *West Metropolitan Rail. Co.*, [1904] 1 K.B. 1; [1900–3] All E.R. Rep. 667, C.A., and *Stewart* v. *Chapman*, [1951] 2 K.B. 792; [1951] 2 All E.R. 613.

SUB-S. (3)
   By virtue of s. 26, Sch. 4, *post*, this sub-s. is authorised to be inserted in the Representation of the People Act 1949 as s. 14 (2A) (omitting the words "or local government") and as an additional paragraph in s. 25 (3) (omitting the words "parliamentary or").

Voting as proxy; appointment of proxy
   As to the appointment of proxies for parliamentary and local government elections, see the Representation of the People Act 1949, ss. 14 and 25 (1)–(3) (11 Halsbury's Statutes (3rd Edn.) 563, 575).   As to the place and manner of voting as such proxies, see ss. 15 and 25 (4)–(6) of that Act, respectively (*ibid.*, pp. 565, 575).

SUB-S. (4): THE RELEVANT RULE
   As to parliamentary elections, see the Representation of the People Act 1949, Sch. 2, Rule 40 (3) (11 Halsbury's Statutes (3rd Edn.) 758).   As to local elections, see *ibid.*, Sch. 2, Rule 35 (England and Wales) (*ibid.*, p. 759) and Sch. 3, Rule 33 (3) (Scotland) (not printed in this work).
   Rule 40 (3), as amended by s. 24 (1) of, and Sch. 2, para. 28, to, this Act reads as follows:
   "For the purposes of this rule, a person shall be qualified to assist a blind voter to vote, if that person is either—
      (*a*) a person who is entitled to vote as an elector at the election; or
      (*b*) the father, mother, brother, sister, husband, wife, son or daughter of the blind voter and has attained the age of [eighteen years]."

SUB-S. (5)
   By virtue of s. 26, Sch. 4, *post*, this subsection is authorised to be inserted as s. 174 (1A) of the Representation of the People Act 1949.   It corresponds with the provisions of s. 9 of the Family Law Reform Act 1969 *post*, and is made necessary in this context

since that enactment did not extend to Northern Ireland (*ibid.*, s. 13), nor, more especially, since under s. 19 of the Government of Ireland Act 1920 (17 Halsbury's Statutes (2nd Edn.) 72) the Parliament of Northern Ireland may not alter the election laws relating to the qualifications of electors in relation to elections to the Parliament of the United Kingdom.

Other parts of the United Kingdom
   I.e., Great Britain; see the Royal and Parliamentary Titles Act 1927, s. 2 (2) (6 Halsbury's Statutes (3rd Edn.) 520). "Great Britain" means England, Wales and Scotland by virtue of the Union with Scotland Act 1706, preamble, Art. I (*ibid.*), pp. 501, 502, and the Wales and Berwick Act 1746, s. 3 (24 Halsbury's Statutes (2nd Edn.) 183).

REPRESENTATION OF THE PEOPLE ACTS
   The following Acts in force may be cited by this collective title:—The Representation of the People Act 1918 (11 Halsbury's Statutes (3rd Edn.) 464), the Representation of the People Act 1945 (*ibid.*, p. 469), the Representation of the People Act 1948 (*ibid.*, p. 471), the House of Commons (Redistribution of Seats) Act 1949 (*ibid.*, p. 534), the Representation of the People Act 1949 (*ibid.*, p. 543), the Electoral Registers Act 1949 (*ibid.*, p. 801), the Electoral Registers Act 1953 (*ibid.*, p. 806), the House of Commons (Redistribution of Seats) Act 1958 (*ibid.*, p. 809), the London Government Act 1963, Sch. 3 (43 Halsbury's Statutes (2nd Edn.) 788), the Elections (Welsh Forms) Act 1964 (11 Halsbury's Statutes (3rd Edn.) 812), and this Act (see s. 28, *post*).

26. Construction with Representation of the People Act 1949, and printing of that Act with insertions

(1) Expressions to which, for purposes of the Representation of the People Act 1949, a meaning is assigned by that Act or any Act amending it shall have the same meaning for purposes of this Act.

(2)–(3) (*Omitted.*)

(4) Section 174 (2) and (3) of the Representation of the People Act 1949 (which relate to the operation of the Act as regards Northern Ireland) shall apply to this Act as they apply to that.

(5) In any revised edition of the statutes published by authority the enactments mentioned in column 1 in Schedule 4 to this Act may be inserted in the Representation of the People Act 1949 as indicated in column 2 of that Schedule, with any adjustment which may be required of references in those enactments to that Act, and such further adaptations as are so indicated.

COMMENCEMENT
   See the note "Orders under this Section" to s. 27, *post*.

REPRESENTATION OF THE PEOPLE ACT 1949
   See 11 Halsbury's Statutes (3rd Edn.) 543. For s. 174 (2) and (3) of that Act, see *ibid.*, p. 703.

27. Commencement

(1) Subject to subsection (2) below, the following provisions of this Act, that is to say, sections 1, 2 and 3 and, so far as it relates to the qualification for voting at local government elections, section 15, shall come into force so as to have effect with respect to the registers of electors to be published in the year 1970 and the elections for which those registers are used; and to the extent to which it has effect for the purpose of those provisions any other provision of this Act (including any provision of Schedule 2 making an amendment consequential on or supplementary to those provisions) shall come into force in like manner.

(2) (*Omitted.*)

(3) Subject to subsections (1) and (2) above, the provisions of this Act shall come into force on such day as may be appointed by order of the Secretary of State, and different days may be appointed for different provisions and for different purposes of the same provision.

(4) The power of the Secretary of State to make orders under subsection (3) above shall be exercisable by statutory instrument which shall be laid before Parliament after being made.

CONSTRUCTION
See s. 26 (1), *ante.*

STATUTORY INSTRUMENT
As to statutory instruments generally, see the Statutory Instruments Act 1946, 24 Halsbury's Statutes (2nd Edn.) 440. See also the Laying of Documents before Parliament (Interpretation) Act 1948 (*ibid.*, p. 448).

ORDERS UNDER THIS SECTION
By the Representation of the People Act 1969 (Commencement) Order 1969, S.I. 1969 No. 630, ss. 26–28 of, and Sch. 4 to, this Act were brought into operation on 12th May 1969.

28. Citation

This Act may be cited as the Representation of the People Act 1969, and shall be included among the Acts that may be cited as the Representation of the People Acts.

REPRESENTATION OF THE PEOPLE ACTS
See the note to s. 1, *ante.*

SCHEDULES

SCHEDULE 4

Section 26

INSERTIONS AUTHORISED IN REPRESENTATION OF THE PEOPLE ACT 1949
IN REVISED EDITION OF STATUTES

Enactment			*Place and manner of insertion*		
*	*	*	*	*	*
This Act					
Section 1 (2) ..	..	..	As section 8 (3).		
Section 1 (3) ..	..	..	Both as section 14 (2A) (omitting the words "or local government") and as an additional paragraph in section 25 (3) (omitting the words "parliamentary or").		
Section 1 (5) ..	..	..	As section 174 (1A).		
*	*	*	*	*	*

THE FAMILY LAW REFORM
ACT 1969
(1969 c. 46)

PRELIMINARY NOTE

This Act received the Royal Assent on 25th July 1969 and, except for the provisions listed in s. 28 (4) (a)–(g), *post*, extends to England and Wales only. Parts I, II and IV of the Act were brought into force on the 1st January 1970 (see S.I. 1969 No. 1140, noted to s. 28, *post*), and Part III will be brought into force when the arrangements between the Government and the medical profession for the taking of blood samples have been completed. This is expected to be some time in 1970.

ARRANGEMENT OF SECTIONS

PART I

REDUCTION OF AGE OF MAJORITY AND RELATED PROVISIONS

PART II

PROPERTY RIGHTS OF ILLEGITIMATE CHILDREN

An Act to amend the law relating to the age of majority, to persons who have not attained that age and to the time when a particular age is attained; to amend the law relating to the property rights of illegitimate children and of other persons whose relationship is traced through an illegitimate link; to make provision for the use of blood tests for the purpose of determining the paternity of any person in civil proceedings; to make provision with respect to the evidence required to rebut a presumption of legitimacy and illegitimacy; to make further provision, in connection with the registration of the birth of an illegitimate child, for entering the name of the father; and for connected purposes   [25th July 1969]

PART I

REDUCTION OF AGE OF MAJORITY AND
RELATED PROVISIONS

1. Reduction of age of majority from 21 to 18

(1) As from the date on which this section comes into force a person shall attain full age on attaining the age of eighteen instead of on attaining the age of twenty-one; and a person shall attain full age on that date if he has then already attained the age of eighteen but not the age of twenty-one.

(2) The foregoing subsection applies for the purposes of any rule of law, and, in the absence of a definition or of any indication of a contrary intention, for the construction of "full age", "infant", "infancy", "minor", "minority" and similar expressions in—

> (a) any statutory provision, whether passed or made before, on or after the date on which this section comes into force; and
>
> (b) any deed, will or other instrument of whatever nature (not being a statutory provision) made on or after that date.

(3) In the statutory provisions specified in Schedule 1 to this Act for any reference to the age of twenty-one years there shall be substituted a reference to the age of eighteen years; but the amendment by this subsection of the provisions specified in Part II of that Schedule shall be without prejudice to any power of amending or revoking those provisions.

(4) This section does not affect the construction of any such expression as is referred to in subsection (2) of this section in any of the statutory provisions described in Schedule 2 to this Act, and the transitional provisions and savings contained in Schedule 3 to this Act shall have effect in relation to this section.

(5) The Lord Chancellor may by order made by statutory instrument amend any provision in any local enactment passed on or before the date on which this section comes into force (not being a provision described in paragraph 2 of Schedule 2 to this Act) by substituting a reference to the age of eighteen years for any reference therein to the age of twenty-one years; and any statutory instrument containing an order under this subsection shall be subject to annulment in pursuance of a resolution of either House of Parliament.

(6) In this section "statutory provision" means any enactment (including, except where the context otherwise requires, this Act) and any order, rule, regulation, byelaw or other instrument made in the exercise of a power conferred by any enactment.

(7) Notwithstanding any rule of law, a will or codicil executed before the date on which this section comes into force shall not be treated for the purposes of this section as made on or after that date by reason only that the will or codicil is confirmed by a codicil executed on or after that date.

GENERAL NOTE

This section implements the major recommendation of the Committee on the Age of Majority (Cmnd. 3342) which was that the age of full legal capacity should be lowered from 21 to 18, and may be compared with the Age of Majority (Scotland) Act 1969.

It should be noted that the new age of majority has no application to the criminal or penal laws.

See further, pp. 4, 5, *ante*.

SUB-S. (1)

This has been described as the most spectacular provision of the Act, inasmuch as it abrogates a rule of law which can be traced back as far even as Magna Carta. Nevertheless, it will not prove so overwhelming in its application as might at first appear, since, for many purposes, full age is already settling on 18—as, for example, in much industrial law and in national insurance.

For the historical background as to how the age of 21 evolved as the age of majority, see Appendix I, *post*.

As from the date on which this section comes into force

I.e., 1st January 1970; see s. 28 (3), *post*, and the note thereto.

Shall attain full age on attaining the age of eighteen
During the passage of the Act, it was repeatedly stressed that the expression "full age" was not synonymous with "adult". The purpose of this Act is to confer, at the age of 18, the right to hold property and to make binding contracts. Other points of law and the ages which are relevant to their application are not affected. See, for example, the special meanings given to "adult" in the Magistrates' Courts Act 1952, ss. 19 (1) and 126 (5) and the meaning of "statutory adult" in the Merchant Shipping Act 1894, s. 268 (2).
As to when a person attains a given age, see s. 9, *post.*

Instead of on attaining the age of twenty-one . . .
Thus Coke on Littleton (103)
"The Guardian shall have the Custody of the Land until the Heir come to his full Age of one and twenty Years Because by Intendment of the Law the Heir is not able to do Knights Service before that Age, which is grounded upon apparent Reason. There note, That the full Age of a Man or Woman to alien, demise, let contract, &c. is one and twenty years."

As to persons already 18 *but not yet* 21
The final words of this subsection were designed to confer full age upon such persons. Following the old rule at common law, those whose 18th birthdays coincided with the coming into force of this section would have attained that age the day previously. See s. 9, *post,* for further details. During the Parliamentary Debates it was estimated that this section emancipated some 2,265,000 young people—see "Annual Digest of Statistics" for current figures (H.M.S.O.).

If he has
"He" includes "she"; see the Interpretation Act 1889, s. 1 (1) (*a*) (24 Halsbury's Statutes (2nd Edn.) 205).

SUB-S. (2)
This subsection directs that wherever they may occur, words and phrases indicative of minority status, are to be interpreted so as to harmonise with the rule expounded in the preceding subsection. In the case of statutory provisions this rule has no limitations, but in the case of private dispositions, only if made after the coming into force of this section—*i.e.,* 1st January 1970.
This subsection is also designed to cover all future legislation as well as existing enactments and the effect will be that the words "minor" and "minority" will take upon themselves a fixed meaning and be used in preference to other expressions.

Any rule of law
It is not absolutely certain what matters are covered by this expression, as distinct from statutory rules, but most authorities are agreed that since a person at the age of 18 is no longer subject to parental suzerainty, it follows that he is not amenable to wardship jurisdiction. Authorities also concur that contractual capacity, including the power to give a valid receipt and discharge others from legal liabilities (21 Halsbury's Laws (3rd Edn.) 138); the acquisition of an independent domicil (7 Halsbury's Laws (3rd Edn.) 44) and the holding of certain public offices are included. Whether a minor was or was not able to change his name by simple adoption or by instrument was never settled. Certainly, if over 16, his consent to such an alteration was required if it was made by others on his behalf.

In the absence of a definition
See, for example, the Children and Young Persons Act 1933, s. 1 (2) (*b*), where an "infant" is a person under 3 years of age.

Any indication of a contrary intention
See, for example, the Matrimonial Causes Act 1965, s. 34 (153 Stats. Supp.), where the expression "child" may be understood, on the authority of *Le Mare* v. *Le Mare,* [1960] 2 All E.R. 280, as an appropriate description of a person well over the age of 21. Further, in *Milroy* v. *Milroy* (1844), 14 Sim. 48, a reference to "infancy" was construed in a sense different from the conventional one of being not yet 21.

Similar expressions
The range of possible expressions is not, as a matter of fact, particularly extensive: the number of words and phrases which indicate age and status is, even in current English, fairly limited (see Roget's "Thesaurus", paras. 127–131). Older enactments

certainly proliferate expressions including boy, girl, infant, junior, young person, minor, juvenile, minimum age, full age, senior, adult, man and woman, but the tendency has been, in recent years, to narrow the range upon the five examples actually given in the subsection: and, in the light of the special purposes of this Act, the selection provided in this subsection and the suggestion made in s. 12 (*post*), it is most unlikely that there will be any innovations or departure.

Any statutory provision
This is defined in sub-s. (6) of this section.

Any deed, will or other instrument
See sub-s. (7) of this section for wills made prior to the coming into force of this section.
As to when a will is "made", see 39 Halsbury's Laws (3rd Edn.) 907g.

SUB-S. (3): WITHOUT PREJUDICE TO ANY POWER
Since it might be thought that once Parliament had put its hand upon certain statutory instruments, no lesser power could interfere with them, this provision expressly permits them to remain subject to the ordinary administrative rules.

SUB-S. (4)
This subsection excludes from the general provisions of the section, enactments relating to the Sovereign—who in any case comes of full age on attaining 18; legislation as to voting age—which is covered by the Representation of the People Act 1969, s. 1, *ante*; and all statutory provisions affecting taxation.
The exceptions are individually noted in the Schedule.

SUB-S. (5)
Under this subsection the Lord Chancellor can make changes in local enactments. This is a common method of dealing with the extremely assorted collection of local Acts which exist and which are not very well indexed in some cases and not easy to "spot" and deal with in the Act itself.

Any statutory instrument . . . subject to annulment
For statutory instruments generally, see the Statutory Instruments Act 1946 (36 Statutes Supp. 95) and the Laying of Documents before Parliament (Interpretation) Act 1948 (56 Statutes Supp. 293).

SUB-S. (6)
This definition is more or less in standard form. Since the provisions of Part I of this Act (relating to the new age of majority) are intended to be virtually of universal application, the subsection is drawn somewhat more comprehensively than its counterparts in other enactments; *e.g.*, the Transport Act 1947, s. 125.

SUB-S. (7)
This subsection provides that the changes in the Act will not have any retrospective effect.

Any rule of law
The reference is to the "rule of republication" which lays down that "A codicil confirming a will brings the will down to the date of the codicil. As the codicil bears a certain date, so in effect does the will bear the same" (*Duffield* v. *Duffield*, [1824–34] All E.R. Rep. 704, *per* Alexander, C.B.).

Date on which this section comes into force
I.e., 1st January 1970; see s. 28 (3), *post*, and the note thereto.

By reason only
This point may be important in cases where a testator has drawn up a will before the passing of the Act and used expressions, such as "infant", subject to the old rules as to the age of majority and later, after its passing, has supplied a codicil using the like terminology. It is submitted that any apparent conflict may be resolved by recourse to the provision of sub-s. (2) of this section that such words need not be accorded their new meaning where there is "any indication of a contrary intention". Cf. *Re Heath's Will Trusts. Hamilton* v. *Lloyds Bank, Ltd.*, [1949] 1 All E.R. 199. It is, of course, still open to parties to claim that a will is to speak from the date of confirmation rather than that of the original execution.
A similar provision is made in s. 15 (8), *post*.

2. Provisions relating to marriage

(1) In the following enactments, that is to say—

- (a) section 7 (c) of the Foreign Marriage Act 1892 (persons under 21 intending to be married by a marriage officer to swear that necessary consents have been obtained);
- (b) paragraph 2 (c) of Part I of the Schedule to the Marriage with Foreigners Act 1906 (persons under 21 seeking certificate to swear that necessary consents have been obtained);
- (c) section 78 (1) of the Marriage Act 1949 (definition of "infant" as person under the age of 21),

for the words "twenty-one years" there shall be substituted the words "eighteen years".

(2) In subsection (5) of section 3 of the said Act of 1949 (which defines the courts having jurisdiction to consent to the marriage of an infant)—

- (a) for the words "the county court of the district in which any respondent resides" there shall be substituted the words "the county court of the district in which any applicant or respondent resides"; and
- (b) after the words "or a court of summary jurisdiction" there shall be inserted the words "having jurisdiction in the place in which any applicant or respondent resides".

(3) Where for the purpose of obtaining a certificate or licence for marriage under Part III of the said Act of 1949 a person declares that the consent of any person or persons whose consent to the marriage is required under the said section 3 has been obtained, the superintendent registrar may refuse to issue the certificate or licence for marriage unless satisfied by the production of written evidence that the consent of that person or of those persons has in fact been obtained.

(4) In this section any expression which is also used in the said Act of 1949 has the same meaning as in that Act.

GENERAL NOTE

This section is in accordance with several recommendations made by the Committee on the Age of Majority (Cmnd. 3342: 1967), viz. the need for parental or court consent to marry should cease at the age of eighteen; a magistrates' court should have jurisdiction to hear an application for permission to marry if either the applicant or a respondent resides in the area of the court; there should be statutory authority for the obtaining of written evidence of consent.

It may reasonably be anticipated that with the lowering of the age of "free marriage" from 21 to 18 the number of applications to the Courts for approval of the marriage of minors—now limited only to those whose ages lie between the two years spanning sixteen and seventeen—will substantially decline. This is supported by the statistics for 1965:

AGE	PER 1000 OF THE POPULATION	
(*Years*)	*Youths*	*Girls*
16–17	4	45
18–20	175	664
21	205	499

N.B. These figures cover all marriages under age and do not take into account whether parental consent was given or withheld.

COMMENCEMENT
This section came into force on 1st January 1970; see s. 28 (3), *post*, and the note thereto.

SUB-S. (1)
This subsection simply directs that for references to the age of 21 in enactments relating to marriage, there shall be substituted references to 18. The references to the Marriage Act 1949 are straightforward; those affecting the Acts of 1892 and 1906 are designed to extend the provisions to British subjects living abroad.

SUB-S (2): RESIDES
A person resides where in common parlance he lives, and a temporary absence is immaterial providing there is an intention to return and a house or lodging to which to return; see *R. v. St. Leonard's, Shoreditch (Inhabitants)* (1865), L.R. 1 Q.B. 21; *R. v. Glossop Union* (1866), L.R. 1 Q.B. 227. There is authority for saying that a person may be resident in more than one place at the same time; see *Levene* v. *Inland Revenue Comrs.*, [1928] All E.R. Rep. 746; [1928] A.C. 217, H.L., *per* Viscount Cave, L.C., at pp. 749 and 223, respectively, and *Langford Property Co., Ltd.* v. *Tureman*, [1949] 1 K.B. 29; *sub nom. Langford Property Co., Ltd.* v. *Athanassoglou*, [1948] 2 All E.R. 722, C.A.

Para (b)
This provision was inserted to obviate difficulties of the kind encountered in *R. v. Sandbach JJ., Ex parte Smith*, [1950] 2 All E.R. 781.

SUB-S. (3)
This refers to the production of written evidence and arises from the fact that no such requirement was contained in the Marriage Act 1949. Its omission was noted by the Committee on the Age of Majority as follows:

> "At present superintendent registrars, on the instructions of the Registrar General, always attempt to obtain written evidence of consent to the marriage of a minor but they have no power to require it. But even where a document is produced purporting to be the consent of the parents it is sometimes false and although the form of consent provided by the Registrar General calls for the signatures of the parents to be witnessed the witnesses' signatures are not always genuine.
> It is desirable that there should be statutory authority for obtaining written evidence of consent."

Note that the request for written evidence is discretionary. There is nothing in the subsection or in the principal Act to prevent a Superintendent Registrar from assuming from the conduct of those involved that the necessary consents have been given.
For the documents mentioned, see 10 Ency. Forms and Precedents (4th Edn.) 1124.

Written
For meaning, see the Interpretation Act 1889, s. 20 (24 Halsbury's Statutes (2nd Edn.) 222).

DEFINITION
By virtue of sub-s. (4) of this section, for meaning of "superintendent registrar", see the Marriage Act 1949, s. 78 (28 Halsbury's Statutes (2nd Edn.) 719).

FOREIGN MARRIAGE ACT 1892, S. 7 (C)
See 17 Halsbury's Statutes (3rd Edn.) 19.

MARRIAGE WITH FOREIGNERS ACT 1906, SCH., PART I, PARA. 2 (C)
See 17 Halsbury's Statutes (3rd Edn.) 34.

MARRIAGE ACT 1949, SS. 3, 78 (1), PART III
See 17 Halsbury's Statutes (3rd Edn.) 47, 96 and 66 *et seq.*, respectively.

3. Provisions relating to wills and intestacy

(1) In the following enactments, that is to say—

    (*a*) section 7 of the Wills Act 1837 (invalidity of wills made by persons under 21);

(b) sections 1 and 3 (1) of the Wills (Soldiers and Sailors) Act 1918 (soldier etc. eligible to make will and dispose of real property although under 21),

in their application to wills made after the coming into force of this section, for the words "twenty-one years" there shall be substituted the words "eighteen years".

(2) In section 47 (1) (i) of the Administration of Estates Act 1925 (statutory trusts on intestacy), in its application to the estate of an intestate dying after the coming into force of this section, for the words "twenty-one years" in both places where they occur there shall be substituted the words "eighteen years".

(3) Any will which—

(a) has been made, whether before or after the coming into force of this section, by a person under the age of eighteen; and

(b) is valid by virtue of the provisions of section 11 of the said Act of 1837 and the said Act of 1918,

may be revoked by that person notwithstanding that he is still under that age whether or not the circumstances are then such that he would be entitled to make a valid will under those provisions.

(4) In this section "will" has the same meaning as in the said Act of 1837 and "intestate" has the same meaning as in the said Act of 1925.

GENERAL NOTE

This section implements the 34th and 35th recommendations proposed by the Committee on the Age of Majority (Cmnd. 3342: 1967) which were to the following effect: full testamentary capacity should be granted to all persons at the age of 18; and a person should on attaining the age of 18 have full power to give valid receipts and discharges and otherwise deal with interests under trusts in all respects as he can now do on attaining the age of 21.

COMMENCEMENT

This section came into force on 1st January 1970; see s. 28 (3), *post*, and the note thereto.

SUB-S. (1)

This subsection simply declares that a person can make a valid will at the age of 18 instead of 21, as was formerly the case.

Wills Act 1837, *s*. 7

See 26 Halsbury's Statutes (2nd Edn.) 32. Section 7 now reads: "No will made by any person under the age of [eighteen] years shall be valid." It should be noted that this amendment applies only to formal wills and to those made by a person after the coming into force of this Part of the Act (*i.e.*, 1st January 1970; see s. 28 (3), *post*, and the note thereto). Since it is well established that a will made by a person under age is wholly invalid whether or not he survive into majority, this emendation should not be taken as implying that wills made by persons between 18 and 21—possibly in anticipation of this Act—will thereupon attract an automatic validity.

As to informal wills made by servicemen before the passing of this Act, see sub-s. (3) of this section.

Wills (Soldiers and Sailors) Act 1918 *ss*. 1, 3 (1)

See 26 Halsbury's Statutes (2nd Edn.) 1361. Section 1 now reads: "In order to remove doubts as to the construction of the Wills Act 1837, it is hereby declared and enacted that section eleven of that Act authorises and always has authorised any soldier being in actual military service, or any mariner or seaman at sea, to dispose of his personal estate as he might have done before the passing of this Act, though under the age of [eighteen years]."

Before s. 7 of the Wills Act 1837 had imposed the limits of 21, the old rule as to testamentary capacity was, in the case of a boy, the age of 14; and, in the case of a girl, 12. These ages therefore, mark the absolute limits of the privilege.

Section 3 (1) now reads: "A testamentary disposition of any real estate in England or Ireland made by a person to whom section eleven of the Wills Act 1837, applies, and who dies after the passing of this Act, shall, notwithstanding that the person making the disposition was at the time of making it under [eighteen years] of age or that the disposition has not been made in such manner or form as was at the passing of this Act required by law, be valid in any case where the person making the disposition was of such age and the disposition has been made in such manner and form that if the disposition had been a disposition of personal estate made by such a person domiciled in England or Ireland it would have been valid."

SUB-S. (2)

This is the reverse of the foregoing subsection in that the one permits the testamentary disposition of property at 18; the other allows it to be taken on intestacy. It would be illogical for young persons to be given full control over any property they might acquire except that due to them on another's failure to make a will. Furthermore, having at 18 full contractual capacity, the temptation to anticipate their expectations through ill-judged bargains is thus removed.

Note that under the provisions of s. 14, *post*, illegitimate children may take under Part IV of the Administration of Estates Act 1925.

Administration of Estates Act 1925, *s.* 47 (1) (*i*)

See 13 Halsbury's Statutes (3rd Edn.) 76; 77 Statutes Supp. (Intestates Estates Act 1952, s. 47). This Act was, so far as affects intestate succession, considerably amended by the Intestates' Estates Act 1952.

The relevant Part of s. 47 (1) of the Act of 1925 now reads:

"Where under this Part of this Act the residuary estate of an intestate, or any part thereof, is directed to be held on the statutory trusts for the issue of the intestate, the same shall be held upon the following trusts, namely:

(i) In trust, in equal shares if more than one, for all or any the children or child of the intestate, living at the death of the intestate, who attain the age of [eighteen years] or marry under that age, and for all or any of the issue living at the death of the intestate who attain the age of [eighteen years] or marry under that age of any child of the intestate who predeceases the intestate . . ."

The combined effect of this and the foregoing subsection is that young people of 18 not only secure full control of their property on an intestacy at that age, but at the same time can now arrange for its disposition entirely as they wish. Previously, were they to have died before reaching 21, their shares would have reverted automatically to the original estate, and parties, on whom they might have wished to confer a benefit were disregarded. Certainly married infants were able to take an absolutely vested interest, but, having no testamentary capacity, had to accept that, if they were to die, the ordinary rules of intestate succession would be applied. In most cases these conformed with what they would have wished, but there were exceptions.

SUB-S. (3)

This subsection simply provides the machinery whereby a "soldier's will" may conveniently be revoked. The rationale is to be found in the Report of the Committee on the Age of Majority (Cmnd. 3342: 1967), and is to the effect that servicemen have been known to make wills at an early age and frequently in favour of a fellow serviceman. Upon leaving the service they may completely forget all about it, and, upon their death, sometimes years later, their property has to pass to someone who they had completely forgotten and who may also be very difficult to trace. Of course, such a will would be automatically revoked on a subsequent marriage. It also clears up a slight ambiguity in the law relating to the revocation of such wills in that while the Wills Act 1837 is clear on the subject of the making of a privileged will, it is silent as to its revocation. The point was dealt with by the Court of Appeal in *Wood* v. *Gossage*, [1921] All E.R. Rep. 107, 109. It is expected that the appropriate authorities, responsible for the various services will direct the attention of servicemen to these provisions and advise accordingly.

Any will
For meaning see sub-s. (4) of this section.

Valid by virtue of the provisions of section 11 *of the* (*Acts of* 1837 *and* 1918)
The principal provision is that in order to make such a will, a serviceman should be "in actual military service" or that a sailor should be "at sea". Whatever the expressions may have meant in the 17th century, it is agreed that the conditions of modern warfare lend them an obscurity which it might be desirable to have clarified. The point was discussed by the Committee on the Age of Majority but no positive solution was reached. However, it is submitted that the judgments of the Court of Appeal in *Re Wingham*, [1948] 2 All E.R. 908—particularly that of Denning, L.J. (as he then was) more than adequately indicate that the Courts have a full understanding of what is involved, and no amplification in this Act was really needed.

SUB-S. (4)

Wills
This word is elaborately defined in s. 1 of the Wills Act 1837 (see 26 Halsbury's Statutes (2nd Edn.) 1327), and includes a will in the popular sense, a testament, a codicil, an appointment by will or by writing in the nature of a will and any other testamentary disposition. The words "any other testamentary disposition" are sufficient to extend the application of the new rules to wills now rendered valid under the Wills Act 1963 (143 Statutes Supp.).

Intestate
In ordinary language this means "dying without making a will", but the definition in s. 55 (vi) of the Administration of Estates Act 1925 is considerably wider in that it can include a partial intestacy. Since s. 9 of that Act provides for the vesting of estates in a Probate Judge between a death and the granting of administration it seems that the expression also means the failure to appoint by will any executor able or willing to act. The meaning is discussed in *Re Skeats, Thain* v. *Gibbs*, [1936] 2 All E.R. p. 302, *per* Clauson, J.

4. Maintenance for children under Guardianship of Infants Acts to continue to age of 21

(1) An order under section 3 (2), 5 (4) or 6 of the Guardianship of Infants Act 1925 for the payment of sums towards the maintenance or education of a minor may require such sums to continue to be paid in respect of any period after the date on which he ceases to be a minor but not extending beyond the date on which he attains the age of twenty-one; and any order which is made as aforesaid may provide that any sum which is payable thereunder for the benefit of a person who has ceased to be a minor shall be paid to that person himself.

(2) Subject to subsections (3) and (4) of this section, where a person who has ceased to be a minor but has not attained the age of twenty-one has, while a minor, been the subject of an order under any of the provisions of the Guardianship of Infants Acts 1886 and 1925, the court may, on the application of either parent of that person or of that person himself, make an order requiring either parent to pay to the other parent, to anyone else for the benefit of that person or to that person himself, in respect of any period not extending beyond the date when he attains the said age, such weekly or other periodical sums towards his maintenance or education as the court thinks reasonable having regard to the means of the person on whom the requirement is imposed.

(3) No order shall be made under subsection (2) of this section, and no liability under such an order shall accrue, at a time when the parents of the person in question are residing together, and if they so reside for a period of three months after such an order has been made it shall cease to have effect.

(4) No order shall be made under subsection (2) of this section requiring any person to pay any sum towards the maintenance or education of an illegitimate child of that person.

(5) Subsection (2) of this section shall be construed as one with the said Acts of 1886 and 1925, and—

    (*a*) any order under that subsection, or under any corresponding enactment of the Parliament of Northern Ireland, shall be included among the orders to which section 16 of the Maintenance Orders Act 1950 applies;

    (*b*) any order under that subsection shall be included among the orders mentioned in section 2 (1) (*d*) of the Reserve and Auxiliary Forces (Protection of Civil Interests) Act 1951 and be deemed to be a maintenance order within the meaning of the Maintenance Orders Act 1958.

GENERAL NOTE

This section preserves the law as it stands at present, and is, in fact, a compromise between the general principle of this Part of the Act—the lowering of full age to 18 and the recommendation of the Committee on the Age of Majority that the High Court and magistrates' courts should have power to make maintenance orders without age limit.

COMMENCEMENT

This section came into force on 1st January 1970; see s. 28 (3), *post*, and the note thereto.

SUB-S. (1)

This refers to existing orders or to orders to be made with respect to persons not yet 18.

The maintenance or education

Note that this proves an alternative: the word "maintenance" includes "education" but "education" may stand alone. Cf. the Children and Young Persons Act 1932, s. 79 (3)—"the expression 'maintenance' shall include education".

As to this point, the Report of the Committee on the Age of Majority said: "Education is largely a matter between the father and the mother. Disputes between parents as to education are often no more, in fact, than disputes about maintenance."

Minor

The actual word appearing in the Act of 1925 is "infant" and since this is to be construed in the new sense (*i.e.*, as a person not yet 18)—see s. 1 (2), *ante*—the need arises for the special terms of this section. For definition of "minor", see s. 12, *post*.

The date on which he ceases to be a minor; the date on which he attains the age of twenty-one

This is now the relevant anniversary of his date of birth; see s. 9 (1), *post*.

Any order which is made . . . to that person himself

This provision is directed towards students who may no longer be living at home.

SUB-S. (2)

This subsection enables the court to order maintenance to be paid by a parent for a minor aged 18 or over, provided that an order under the Guardianship of Infants Acts 1886 and 1925 has been made at some time during his minority. The condition precedent puts the minor of 18 or over in respect of whom no order has been made prior to 1st January 1970 in a worse position than he was in before, when an application could have been made under the Guardianship of Infants Acts until he attained 21. The Guardianship of Infants Act 1925, s. 7 (1) (*a*) is not repealed, so that a magistrates' court cannot entertain any application (other than for variation or discharge of an existing order) relating to a minor who has attained the age of 16 unless he is physically or mentally incapable of self-support. Thus an application under this subsection will (except in the case of a disabled minor) have to be made to the High Court (or county court—see the Guardianship of Infants Act 1886, s. 9, and the Guardianship and Maintenance of Infants Act 1951, s. 1).

To anyone else for the benefit of that person
This presumably is directed to a person appointed under s. 4 (2A) of the Act of 1925, to testamentary guardians and, it is submitted, since the age of free marriage is now set at 18, a wife or husband.

The court
In the case of a person over 16, who is physically or mentally handicapped, this could be a magistrates' court (see s. 7 (1) (a) of the 1925 Act), otherwise, it is the county court or the High Court.

SUB-S. (3)
This reproduces the substance of s. 3 (3) of the Guardianship of Infants Act 1925.

Residing together
For the meaning of this, see *Evans* v. *Evans*, [1946] 2 All E.R. 656; *Thomas* v. *Thomas*, [1948] 2 All E.R. 98; and *Harris* v. *Harris*, [1952] 1 All E.R. 401.

A period of three months
When the period prescribed is a calendar month running from any unspecified date, the period runs out on the day immediately preceding the corresponding day in the month following; see further 37 Halsbury's Laws (3rd Edn.) 143.

SUB-S. (4)
In Committee, a determined attempt was made to replace this subsection with provisions which conferred similar rights on the mother of an illegitimate child. But the Government resisted them on the grounds that "in affiliation proceedings the critical question is that of paternity. Once that is established, the provisions of the Affiliation Acts come into operation and protect the interests of illegitimate children to much the same extent as legitimate children are protected under the Guardianship Acts."

No order shall be made
The correct procedure to secure maintenance for an illegitimate child is to apply for an affiliation order under the Affiliation Proceedings Act 1957 (108 Statutes Supp. 39).

SUB-S. (5): CONSTRUED AS ONE
I.e., the enactments in question are to be construed as if they were contained in one Act unless there is a manifest discrepancy; see, *e.g.*, *Phillips* v. *Parnaby*, [1934] 2 K.B. 299; [1934] All E.R. Rep. 267, at p. 302 and p. 269, respectively, and the Preliminary Note to the title Statutes, 24 Halsbury's Statutes (2nd Edn.) 145. It follows, in particular, that definitions applicable to the earlier provisions may be relevant to the constructions of provisions of this Act; see *Solomons* v. *R. Gertzenstein, Ltd.*, [1954] 2 All E.R. 625; [1954] 2 Q.B. 243, C.A., and *Crowe (Valuation Officer)* v. *Lloyd's British Testing Co., Ltd.*, [1960] 1 All E.R. 411; [1960] 1 Q.B. 592, C.A. See also *Kirkness (Inspector of Taxes)* v. *John Hudson & Co., Ltd.*, [1955] 2 All E.R. 345; [1955] A.C. 696.

GUARDIANSHIP OF INFANTS ACTS 1886 AND 1925
I.e., the Guardianship of Infants Act 1886 and the Guardianship of Infants Act 1925 (17 Halsbury's Statutes (3rd Edn.) 415, 424); see s. 11 (2) of the Act of 1925. For ss. 3 (2), 5 (4), 6 of the Act of 1925, see *ibid.*, pp. 426, 427, 428.

MAINTENANCE ORDERS ACT 1950, S. 16
68 Statutes Supp. 70. That section provides that "Any order to which this section applies made by a court in any part of the United Kingdom may, if registered in accordance with the provisions of this Part of this Act in a court in another part of the United Kingdom, be enforced in accordance with those provisions in that other part of the United Kingdom."

RESERVE AND AUXILIARY FORCES (PROTECTION OF INTERESTS) ACT 1951, S. 2 (1) (D)
73 Statutes Supp. 24. That Act was designed to protect the civil interests of servicemen in that no person was allowed to proceed against them during their period of service for the payment of any money without first having obtained the leave of an appropriate court. To this general rule exceptions were made and listed, among which were orders made under the Guardianship of Infants Act 1925.

MAINTENANCE ORDERS ACT 1958
That Act provides for the registration, enforcement and variation of maintenance orders and sets forth the powers for attachment of earnings. For definition of "maintenance order" in that Act, see s. 21 thereof (110 Statutes Supp. 40).

5. Modification of other enactments relating to maintenance of children so as to preserve benefits up to age of 21

(1) For the purposes of the Inheritance (Family Provision) Act 1938, the dependants of a deceased person shall continue to include any son who has not attained the age of twenty-one; and accordingly—

    (*a*) in subsection (1) (*c*) of that Act for the words "infant son" there shall be substituted the words "a son who has not attained the age of twenty-one years";

    (*b*) in subsection (2) (*c*) of that Act for the words "in the case of an infant son, his attaining the age of twenty-one years" there shall be substituted the words "in the case of a son who has not attained the age of twenty-one years, his attaining that age".

(2) Where a child in respect of whom an affiliation order has been made under the Affiliation Proceedings Act 1957 has attained the age of eighteen and his mother is dead, of unsound mind or in prison—

    (*a*) any application for an order under subsection (2) or (3) of section 7 of that Act directing that payments shall be made under the affiliation order for any period after he has attained that age may be made by the child himself; and

    (*b*) the child himself shall be the person entitled to any payments directed by an order under that section to be so made for any such period as aforesaid.

(3) Section 22 of the Matrimonial Causes Act 1965 (power to order maintenance for infant children in cases of wilful neglect) shall continue to apply to children up to the age of twenty-one, but not so as to enable an order for custody to be made under section 35 (1) of that Act (custody of children where maintenance is ordered under section 22) in respect of any child who has attained the age of eighteen; and accordingly—

    (*a*) in subsection (2) of the said section 22 for the words "any infant child of the marriage in question and any infant illegitimate child of both parties to the marriage" there shall be substituted the words "any child of the marriage who is under twenty-one and any illegitimate child of both parties to the marriage who is under that age";

    (*b*) in the said section 35 (1) after the words "any child to whom that subsection applies" there shall be inserted the words "who is under eighteen", and at the end there shall be added the words "and the child is under that age".

COMMENCEMENT

This section came into force on 1st January 1970; see s. 28 (3), *post*, and the note thereto.

SUB-S. (1)

This subsection preserves the right of a son who is under 21 to apply for reasonable provision to be made for him out of his parent's estate. Periodical payments ordered for such a son may continue up to 21, but not beyond (unless the son is under a disability).

The Inheritance (Family Provision) Act 1938 (13 Halsbury's Statutes (3rd Edn.) 118) requires that a testator should have made "reasonable provision" and not to have bestowed legacies. Whether such provision has or has not been made is for the court to decide; see *Re Goodwin, Goodwin* v. *Goodwin*, [1968] 3 All E.R. 12.
See, generally, 16 Halsbury's Laws (3rd Edn.) 913, 923.

Attained the age; attaining that age
A person attains a given age on the relevant anniversary of his date of birth; see s. 9 (1), *post*.

SUB-S. (2)
This subsection permits a child who has attained the age of 18 to make an application for payments under an affiliation order, and to receive benefits, where his mother is dead, of unsound mind or in prison. It therefore does no more than adjust the existing law to the new circumstances brought about by the Act.
Under s. 7 (2) and (3) of the Affiliation Proceedings Act 1957, payments made under an order can be directed to continue beyond the age of 16 and up to 21 so as to enable the child to pursue a course of training or further education—but only upon the application of the mother. If she is unable to do so, either from being dead, mentally incapable or in prison, the court may, under s. 5 (4) of the Act, nominate a guardian to act on behalf of the child. This power is inappropriate under the new law which confers independence at 18, and so the child, if of full age may make application himself. The obvious anomaly created by this arrangement is that if a child has a mother incapable of acting, he can put forward his own claims, but if a child has a mother who simply will not take any steps on his behalf, he can do nothing about it.

SUB-S. (3)
This subsection removes from the courts the authority to make an order for the custody of a child after the age of 18, but preserves their power to award maintenance for wilful neglect until 21.

INHERITANCE (FAMILY PROVISION) ACT 1938
13 Halsbury's Statutes (3rd Edn.) 118.

AFFILIATION PROCEEDINGS ACT 1957
See 108 Statutes Supp.

MATRIMONIAL CAUSES ACT 1965
See 153 Statutes Supp.

6. Maintenance for wards of court

(1) In this section "the court" means any of the following courts in the exercise of its jurisdiction relating to the wardship of children, that is to say, the High Court, the Court of Chancery of the County Palatine of Lancaster and the Court of Chancery of the County Palatine of Durham, and "ward of court" means a ward of the court in question.

(2) Subject to the provisions of this section, the court may make an order—

    (*a*) requiring either parent of a ward of court to pay to the other parent; or

    (*b*) requiring either parent or both parents of a ward of court to pay to any other person having the care and control of the ward,

such weekly or other periodical sums towards the maintenance and education of the ward as the court thinks reasonable having regard to the means of the person or persons on whom the requirement is imposed.

(3) An order under subsection (2) of this section may require such sums as are mentioned in that subsection to continue to be paid in respect of any period after the date on which the person for whose benefit the payments are to be

made ceases to be a minor but not beyond the date on which he attains the age of twenty-one, and any order made as aforesaid may provide that any sum which is payable thereunder for the benefit of that person after he has ceased to be a minor shall be paid to that person himself.

(4) Subject to the provisions of this section, where a person who has ceased to be a minor but has not attained the age of twenty-one has at any time been the subject of an order making him a ward of court, the court may, on the application of either parent of that person or of that person himself, make an order requiring either parent to pay to the other parent, to anyone else for the benefit of that person or to that person himself, in respect of any period not extending beyond the date when he attains the said age, such weekly or other periodical sums towards his maintenance or education as the court thinks reasonable having regard to the means of the person on whom the requirement in question is imposed.

(5) No order shall be made under this section, and no liability under such an order shall accrue, at a time when the parents of the ward or former ward, as the case may be, are residing together, and if they so reside for a period of three months after such an order has been made it shall cease to have effect; but the foregoing provisions of this subsection shall not apply to any order made by virtue of subsection (2) (*b*) of this section.

(6) No order shall be made under this section requiring any person to pay any sum towards the maintenance or education of an illegitimate child of that person.

(7) Any order under this section, or under any corresponding enactment of the Parliament of Northern Ireland, shall be included among the orders to which section 16 of the Maintenance Orders Act 1950 applies; and any order under this section shall be included among the orders mentioned in section 2 (1) (*d*) of the Reserve and Auxiliary Forces (Protection of Civil Interests) Act 1951 and be deemed to be a maintenance order within the meaning of the Maintenance Orders Act 1958.

(8) The court shall have power from time to time by an order under this section to vary or discharge any previous order thereunder.

GENERAL NOTE

   This section arises from the 18th recommendation of the Committee of Inquiry on the Age of Majority (Cmnd. 3342: 1967) that "the Chancery Division should be given power to make maintenance orders in wardship proceedings". See generally, pp. 6, 7, *ante*.

COMMENCEMENT

   This section came into force on 1st January 1970; see s. 28 (3), *post*, and the note thereto.

SUB-S. (1)

   This declares which courts shall, in future, enjoy the power to award maintenance.

High Court

   I.e., Her Majesty's High Court of Justice in England; see the Interpretation Act 1889, s. 13 (24 Halsbury's Statutes (2nd Edn.) 213). By virtue of the Supreme Court of Judicature (Consolidation) Act 1925, s. 56 (18 Halsbury's Statutes (2nd Edn.) 490) jurisdiction relating to the wardship of children is vested in the Chancery Division of the High Court.

Court of Chancery of the County Palatine of Lancaster

For the jurisdiction of, and the general provisions relating to, that Court, see the Chancery of Lancaster Acts 1850 to 1961 (7 Halsbury's Statutes (3rd Edn.) 484, 499, 544, 669, 733), and 9 Halsbury's Laws (3rd Edn.) 473 *et seq.*

Court of Chancery of the County Palatine of Durham

For the jurisdiction of, and the general provisions relating to, that Court, see the Durham (County Palatine) Act 1836 and the Palatine Court of Durham Act 1889 (7 Halsbury's Statutes (3rd Edn.) 461, 539), and 9 Halsbury's Laws (3rd Edn.) 478 *et seq.*

SUB-S. (2)

This corresponds in terms with the provisions of s. 5 of the Guardianship of Infants Act 1886, as extended by s. 3 of the Act of 1925 and s. 16 of the Administration of Justice Act 1928.

SUB-SS. (3), (4)

These provisions correspond with s. 4 (1), (2), *ante.*

SUB-S. (5)

This subsection largely corresponds with s. 4 (3), *ante*, but, unlike the guardianship rule, the fact that the parents are residing together does not affect orders to make payments to a person other than the parent.

Any order made by virtue of sub-s. 2 (b)

This refers to orders payable to third parties. It is an obvious exception, and is directed to situations such as those wherein an anxious father and mother find wardship proceedings the only means of curbing the rebellious disposition of their child.

SUB-SS. (6), (7)

These provisions correspond with s. 4 (4), (5) *ante.*

SUB-S. (8)

The power to revoke, vary or discharge orders is generally conferred under circumstances analogous with this section; see, for example, the Guardianship of Infants Act 1925, s. 3 (4).

MAINTENANCE ORDERS ACT 1950, S. 16

68 Statutes Supp. 70.

RESERVE AND AUXILIARY FORCES (PROTECTION OF CIVIL INTERESTS) ACT 1951, S. 2 (1) (*d*)

73 Statutes Supp. 24.

MAINTENANCE ORDERS ACT 1958

For definition of "maintenance order" in that Act, see s. 21 thereof (110 Statutes Supp. 40).

7. Committal of wards of court to care of local authority and supervision of wards of court

(1) In this section "the court" means any of the following courts in the exercise of its jurisdiction relating to the wardship of children, that is to say, the High Court, the Court of Chancery of the County Palatine of Lancaster and the Court of Chancery of the County Palatine of Durham, and "ward of court" means a ward of the court in question.

(2) Where it appears to the court that there are exceptional circumstances making it impracticable or undesirable for a ward of court to be, or to continue

to be, under the care of either of his parents or of any other individual the court may, if it thinks fit, make an order committing the care of the ward to a local authority; and thereupon Part II of the Children Act 1948 (which relates to the treatment of children in the care of a local authority) shall, subject to the next following subsection, apply as if the child had been received by the local authority into their care under section 1 of that Act.

(3) In subsection (2) of this section "local authority" means one of the local authorities referred to in subsection (1) of section 36 of the Matrimonial Causes Act 1965 (under which a child may be committed to the care of a local authority by a court having jurisdiction to make an order for its custody); and subsections (2) to (6) of that section (ancillary provisions) shall have effect as if any reference therein to that section included a reference to subsection (2) of this section.

(4) Where it appears to the court that there are exceptional circumstances making it desirable that a ward of court (not being a ward who in pursuance of an order under subsection (2) of this section is in the care of a local authority) should be under the supervision of an independent person, the court may, as respects such period as the court thinks fit, order that the ward be under the supervision of a welfare officer or of a local authority; and subsections (2) and (3) of section 37 of the said Act of 1965 (ancillary provisions where a child is placed under supervision by a court having jurisdiction to make an order for its custody) shall have effect as if any reference therein to that section included a reference to this subsection.

(5) The court shall have power from time to time by an order under this section to vary or discharge any previous order thereunder.

GENERAL NOTE

This section confers a new power upon the Chancery judges and one similar to that enjoyed by those in the Divorce Court. It follows the 22nd recommendation of the Committee of Inquiry on the Age of Majority (Cmnd. 3342: 1967) that "the Chancery Division should be invested with power to commit children to the care of a local authority or order that they be placed under the supervision of a welfare officer or local authority".

COMMENCEMENT

This section came into force on 1st January 1970; see s. 28 (3), *post*, and the note thereto.

SUB-S. (1)

This is identical to s. 6 (1), *ante*.

SUB-S. (2)

This corresponds with s. 36 (1) of the Matrimonial Causes Act 1965 (153 Statutes Supp. 194).

Exceptional circumstances

See, for example, *F. v. F.*, [1959] 3 All E.R. 180 and *G. v. G.*, [1962] C.L.Y. 1557.

A local authority

For meaning, see sub-s. (3) of this section.

Child

This is defined in the Children Act 1948 as a person under 18.

SUB-S. (4)
This corresponds with s. 37 (1) of the Matrimonial Causes Act 1965.

CHILDREN ACT 1948, S. 1, PART II
17 Halsbury's Statutes (3rd Edn.) 539, 549 *et seq.*

MATRIMONIAL CAUSES ACT 1965, SS. 36 (1)–(6), 37 (2), (3)
See 153 Statutes Supp.

8. Consent by persons over 16 to surgical, medical and dental treatment

(1) The consent of a minor who has attained the age of sixteen years to any surgical, medical or dental treatment which, in the absence of consent, would constitute a trespass to his person, shall be as effective as it would be if he were of full age; and where a minor has by virtue of this section given an effective consent to any treatment it shall not be necessary to obtain any consent for it from his parent or guardian.

(2) In this section "surgical, medical or dental treatment" includes any procedure undertaken for the purposes of diagnosis, and this section applies to any procedure (including, in particular, the administration of an anaesthetic) which is ancillary to any treatment as it applies to that treatment.

(3) Nothing in this section shall be construed as making ineffective any consent which would have been effective if this section had not been enacted.

GENERAL NOTE
This section, which implements the 44th recommendation of the Committee on the Age of Majority (Cmnd. 3342: 1967), provides that, without prejudice to any assent that might otherwise be lawful, the consent of persons aged 16 and over to surgical, medical and dental treatment is to be as valid as the consent of a person of full age.
The Committee chose 16 as the right age for consent to medical treatment, for the following reasons: (1) A person over 16 may choose his own doctor (see the National Health Service (General, Medical and Pharmaceutical Services) Regulations 1966, S.I. 1966 No. 1210, reg. 30); (2) a person of 16 or over may decide to admit himself as a voluntary patient to a mental hospital and may apply to a Mental Health Review Tribunal (see the Mental Health Act 1959, s. 5 (2)); (3) 16 is the age of consent to sexual intercourse; and (4) the practice of accepting consent to medical treatment at 16 has been widely used for a considerable period. See further p. 7, *ante.*
In a memorandum circulated among the staff of a large Midlands hospital, the following matters were mentioned:

"It is no longer legally necessary to seek *parental consent* to surgical procedures upon patients over 16 years of age but in many cases the prospective treatment of a young person (*e.g.*, whether or not to operate) will be discussed with parents and great weight attached to their views and wishes. This is however a social and professional matter, and not a *legal* requirement.
Indeed the last portion of subsection (1) emphasises that the consent of a young person over the age of 16 is 'effective' and does *not* require parental endorsement.
Thus where such a young person clearly wishes to give a sole consent and does not wish his parents to be consulted, it would be administratively inadvisable to consult the parents as well as legally unnecessary."

COMMENCEMENT
This section came into force on 1st January 1970; see s. 28 (3), *post*, and the note thereto.

SUB-S. (1)
Consent
An example of such a consent is reproduced in Appendix II, *post*.

Minor
   For meaning, see s. 12, *post.*

Attained the age of sixteen years
   See s. 9 (1), *post.*

The absence of consent . . . trespass to his person . . .
   See 38 Halsbury's Laws (3rd Edn.) 760–762.

As effective
   That is to say, it will be "as effective" as any consent would be if obtained freely and with a full understanding of all it implies.
   In criminal cases consent is no defence to an unlawful act: therefore the acquiescence of a minor to any illegal operation or submission to any process which is represented to him as being of a medical nature will not avail; see *R.* v. *Williams,* [1922] All E.R. Rep. 433. Otherwise a trespass is committed if the practitioner should either secure the consent of the patient by fraud (as in the foregoing) or be negligent in failing to inform the patient of any risks involved; and particularly if it could be shown that the patient, having been so informed, would have withheld consent—see *Bolam* v. *Friern Hospital Management Committee,* [1957] 2 All E.R. 118. It would certainly be a trespass were the doctor to proceed against his patient's wishes.
   The high level to which the practice of medicine has been elevated is reflected in the current opinion that in the majority of cases the implied consent of any patient to submit to the superior understanding of his medical advisers is taken for granted.
   Cf. s. 21, *post.*

Of full age
   I.e., the age of 18; see s. 1 (1), *ante.*

Parent or guardian
   See 21 Halsbury's Laws (3rd Edn.) 204–213.

SUB-S. (2)
   This subsection is largely definition. It should be noted that consent cannot be given for blood donation. See further, p. 7, *ante.*

Surgical, medical or dental treatment
   These terms are not defined as such. However the provisions of the Medical Act 1957, s. 31, and the Dentists Act 1957, s. 34 (1), are intended to protect the public against imposters and there is not much likelihood of young people falling into their hands. It may be noted that there are extensive prohibitions against the unauthorised advertising of matters relating to such hazards as cancer, venereal disease, etc. (see 26 Halsbury's Laws (3rd Edn.) 303). See also 1 Ency. Forms and Precedents (4th Edn.) 163, for the British Code of Standards relating to advertisements of a medical nature.
   For the Abortion Act 1967, see 164 Statutes Supp. 272.
   Note that the section does not apply to "mental treatment", as this is already covered by the Mental Health Act 1959, s. 5 (2) (119 Statutes Supp. 122).

The purposes of diagnosis
   This is generally taken to mean the recognition of a particular ailment from the history, symptoms, physical signs and any tests which may have been made. It includes the taking of blood samples—cf. the provisions of Part III of this Act, particularly s. 21, *post.*

In particular, the administration of an anaesthetic
   Apart from the removal of doubts this provision has been specially inserted with regard to a point made by the Committee in its Report (Cmnd. 3342). According to the Report, a particularly difficult situation often arose in the case of girls who were sent to hospital in need of a therapeutic abortion, and refused point blank to enter the hospital unless a guarantee was given that their parents should not be told about it. The Church of England Board for Social Responsibility mentioned a similar situation occurring in many of their mother and baby homes, where a young unmarried pregnant girl might be required to produce a parental consent to an anaesthetic before being allowed to enter the home. Many of these girls, living away from their families expressly to avoid their parents knowing of their plight, would be prepared to suffer any

extremes, rather than that should happen. The refusal to produce a consent form, duly signed often kept them from receiving the help that reputable establishments were able to offer.

Ancillary to any treatment
"Ancillary" has been defined as being subordinate or subservient. It is derived from the Latin "ancilla" meaning a "servant girl" and is thus appropriate to describe activities which go to serve a greater purpose. In this context it can, *inter alia*, include the administration of drugs to relieve pain, induce sleep, etc.; injections; enemata; and the application of plasters and poultices.
Note: treatment by hypnotism is permitted under s. 5 of the Hypnotism Act 1952 (77 Statutes Supp. 189).

SUB-S. (3)
The provisions of this subsection are designed to implement a suggestion, made by several medical associations that from 16 to 18 the patient should be able to consent to medical treatment but that a refusal could be overridden by parents. It would be useful, presumably, in cases where a young person had become some form of addict and refused treatment.

9. Time at which a person attains a particular age

(1) The time at which a person attains a particular age expressed in years shall be the commencement of the relevant anniversary of the date of his birth.

(2) This section applies only where the relevant anniversary falls on a date after that on which this section comes into force, and, in relation to any enactment, deed, will or other instrument, has effect subject to any provision therein.

GENERAL NOTE
This section implements the 51st recommendation of the Committee on the Age of Majority (Cmnd. 3342: 1967) that the moment of attaining an age in law should be the commencement of the relevant anniversary of the day of the person's birth, instead of the commencement of the day preceding the relevant anniversary. The old rule was expounded in *Re Shurey, Savory* v. *Shurey*, [1918] 1 Ch. 263.
As to the time when a child is deemed to attain a given age for the purposes of child relief, etc., see the Finance Act 1969, s. 11 (4) which excludes this section.

COMMENCEMENT
See the note to sub-s. (2) below.

SUB-S. (1)
As to proof of age, see 15 Halsbury's Laws (3rd Edn.), para. 522. For some practical examples involving the interpretation of the expression "the time at which a person attains a particular age", consult Digest of Commissioners' Decisions (National Insurance, etc. Acts) (H.M.S.O.) under the heading "Age"—in particular Decision R (G) 3/62 which is digested in that volume and fully reported in Vol. IV of the Reported Decisions.

A particular age
Note that the section is directed to the attainment of any age and not simply to that of majority.

SUB-S. (2)
This subsection provides for the fact that those whose birthdays fell on the same day as this section came into force—*i.e.*, 1st January 1970 (see s. 28 (3), *post* and the note thereto), had already attained a given age the day before under the common law rule.

In relation to any enactment
This, among other things, involves the application of the Calendar (New Style) Act 1750, s. 2 (25 Halsbury's Statutes (2nd Edn.) 137) which makes provision for what is popularly called "leap year". The question as to what would happen to people born on 29th February was raised during the Committee proceedings of the Bill. The reply

was that in a leap year, everybody must live for 366 days to complete an anniversary. This piece of learning is derived from the case of *R.* v. *Worminghall (Inhabitants)* (1817), 6 M. & S. 350. In that case, service for a period from 13th October to 11th October—a period which included 29th February—was held not to be a service for one year, though it had lasted for 365 days. A child born on 29th February must live until 1st March the following year to complete one year and thereafter his "relevant anniversary" will be, in ordinary years, the 1st March and in leap years, the 29th February. See 37 Halsbury's Laws (3rd Edn.) 79 (*f*) and 84 (1).

10. Modification of enactments relating to Duke of Cornwall and other children of Her Majesty

(1) Section 1 (1) of this Act shall apply for the construction of the expression "minor" in section 2 (2) of the Civil List Act 1952 (which relates to the amount payable for the Queen's Civil List while the Duke of Cornwall is for the time being a minor) and accordingly—

> (a) section 2 (2) (b) of that Act (which relates to the three years during which the Duke is over 18 but under 21); and
>
> (b) in section 2 (2) (a) of that Act the words "for each year whilst he is under the age of eighteen years",

are hereby repealed except in relation to any period falling before section 1 of this Act comes into force.

(2) In section 4 (1) (a) of the said Act of 1952 (under which benefits are provided for the children of Her Majesty, other than the Duke of Cornwall, who attain the age of 21 or marry) for the words "twenty-one years" there shall be substituted the words "eighteen years" but no sum shall be payable by virtue of this subsection in respect of any period falling before section 1 of this Act comes into force.

(3) In section 38 of the Duchy of Cornwall Management Act 1863 (under which certain rights and powers of the Duke of Cornwall may, while he is under 21, be exercised on his behalf by the Sovereign or persons acting under Her authority) for the words "twenty-one years" wherever they occur there shall be substituted the words "eighteen years".

GENERAL NOTE
> See p. 8, *ante.*

COMMENCEMENT
> This section came into force on 1st January 1970; see s. 28 (3), *post*, and the note thereto.

SUB-S. (1)
> The Civil List Act 1952 made financial provision "for the honour and dignity of the Crown and the Royal Family". Following a practice initiated upon the accession of George III in 1760, the hereditary revenues of the Sovereign were surrendered to the nation in return for a fixed annual income. In the case of Her Present Majesty, this was £475,000, with an off-set from the revenues of the Duchy of Cornwall. Up to the Duke of Cornwall attaining the age of 18, all but one-ninth of this was paid into the Treasury, and for the last three years of his minority, all but £30,000. The amendment cancels the references to 18 (now superfluous) and allows the Duke of Cornwall— who is always the Heir-Apparent—to retain the aforesaid £30,000 by virtue of being of full age.
>
> As to the Revenues of the Crown, see 7 Halsbury's Laws (3rd Edn.) paras. 944–48.

Before section 1 of this Act comes into force
> *I.e.*, before 1st January 1970; see s. 28 (3), *post*, and the note thereto.

SUB-S. (2)
> The wording of this subsection reflects the provisions of s. 3 (2) *ante*, and also several items in Schedule 1, particularly that referring to s. 31 (2) (i) (*a*) of the Trustee Act 1925. Its practical effect is that the incomes paid to the younger children of Her Majesty (other than the Duke of Cornwall) may be taken at 18 instead of 21.

CIVIL LIST ACT 1952, SS. 2 (2), 4 (1) (a)
> See 6 Halsbury's Statutes (3rd Edn.) 549, 550.

DUCHY OF CORNWALL MANAGEMENT ACT 1863
> 26 & 27 Vict. c. 49; not printed in this work.

11. Repeal of certain enactments relating to minors

The following enactments are hereby repealed—

> (*a*) the Infant Settlements Act 1855 (which enables a male infant over 20 and a female infant over 17 to make a marriage settlement), together with section 27 (3) of the Settled Land Act 1925, except in relation to anything done before the coming into force of this section;
>
> (*b*) in section 6 of the Employers and Workmen Act 1875 (powers of justices in respect of apprentices)—
>
> > (i) the paragraph numbered (1) (power to direct apprentice to perform his duties), and
> >
> > (ii) the sentence following the paragraph numbered (2) (power to order imprisonment of an apprentice who fails to comply with direction);
>
> (*c*) in the Sexual Offences Act 1956, section 18 and paragraph 5 of Schedule 2 (fraudulent abduction of heiress).

GENERAL NOTE
> This section is in accordance with recommendations made by the Committee on the Age of Majority (Cmnd. 3342: 1967) that the minimum age for the making of settlements should be 18 for both sexes and that the Infant Settlements Act 1855 should be repealed; that so much of s. 6 of the Employers and Workmen Act 1875 as enables the court to imprison an apprentice should be repealed; and that s. 18 of the Sexual Offences Act 1956 should be repealed. See further p. 8, *ante*.

COMMENCEMENT
> This section came into force on 1st January 1970; see s. 28 (3), *post*, and the note thereto.

PARAGRAPH (*b*)
> The Employers and Workmen Act 1875, s. 6, as amended, now reads:
>
> > **"6. Powers of justices in respect of apprentices**
> > In a proceeding before a court of summary jurisdiction in relation to a dispute under this Act between a master and an apprentice, the court shall have the same powers as if the dispute were between an employer and a workman, and the master were the employer and the apprentice the workman, and the instrument of apprenticeship a contract between an employer and a workman, and shall also have the following power: If it rescinds the instrument of apprenticeship it may, if it thinks it just to do so, order the whole or any part of the premium paid on the binding of the apprentice to be repaid."

PARAGRAPH (c)
Note that girls under 18 are adequately protected by ss. 19 and 20 of the Sexual Offences Act 1956 (102 Statutes Supp.), which make it an offence to take girls out of the possession of their parents or guardian against their wishes. For the law relating to abduction in general, see 10 Halsbury's Laws (3rd Edn.), paras. 1462–1467.

INFANT SETTLEMENTS ACT 1855
17 Halsbury's Statutes (3rd Edn.) 410.

SETTLED LAND ACT 1925, S. 27 (3)
23 Halsbury's Statutes (2nd Edn.) 77.

EMPLOYERS AND WORKMEN ACT 1875, S. 6
12 Halsbury's Statutes (3rd Edn.) 26

SEXUAL OFFENCES ACT 1956, S. 18, SCH. 2, PARA. 5
102 Statutes Supp. 36, 62.

12. Persons under full age may be described as minors instead of infants

A person who is not of full age may be described as a minor instead of as an infant, and accordingly in this Act "minor" means such a person as aforesaid.

GENERAL NOTE
This section implements the 52nd recommendation of the Committee on the Age of Majority (Cmnd. 3342: 1967). See further p. 9, *ante*.

COMMENCEMENT
This section came into force on 1st January 1970; see s. 28 (3), *post*, and the note thereto.

FULL AGE
As to "full age", see s. 1 (1), *ante*.

MAY BE DESCRIBED
Note that the section is permissive, not mandatory and so it will be in order still to employ the former expression.

13. Powers of Parliament of Northern Ireland

Notwithstanding anything in the Government of Ireland Act 1920 the Parliament of Northern Ireland shall have power to make laws for purposes similar to any of the purposes of this Part of this Act [as amended by the Finance Act 1969].

GENERAL NOTE
A convenient summary of the law of Northern Ireland relating to minors is to be found at Appendix 6 of the Report of the Committee on the Age of Majority (Cmnd. 3342: 1967).

COMMENCEMENT
This section came into force on 1st January 1970; see s. 28 (3), *post*, and the note thereto.

AS AMENDED BY THE FINANCE ACT 1969
These words were added by Finance Act 1969, s. 16 (2) (181 Statutes Supp. 38).

GOVERNMENT OF IRELAND ACT 1920
17 Halsbury's Statutes (2nd Edn.) 56.

PART II

PROPERTY RIGHTS OF ILLEGITIMATE CHILDREN

14. Right of illegitimate child to succeed on intestacy of parents, and of parents to succeed on intestacy of illegitimate child

(1) Where either parent of an illegitimate child dies intestate as respects all or any of his or her real or personal property, the illegitimate child or, if he is dead, his issue, shall be entitled to take any interest therein to which he or such issue would have been entitled if he had been born legitimate.

(2) Where an illegitimate child dies intestate in respect of all or any of his real or personal property, each of his parents, if surviving, shall be entitled to take any interest therein to which that parent would have been entitled if the child had been born legitimate.

(3) In accordance with the foregoing provisions of this section, Part IV of the Administration of Estates Act 1925 (which deals with the distribution of the estate of an intestate) shall have effect as if—

    (a) any reference to the issue of the intestate included a reference to any illegitimate child of his and to the issue of any such child;

    (b) any reference to the child or children of the intestate included a reference to any illegitimate child or children of his; and

    (c) in relation to an intestate who is an illegitimate child, any reference to the parent, parents, father or mother of the intestate were a reference to his natural parent, parents, father or mother.

(4) For the purposes of subsection (2) of this section and of the provisions amended by subsection (3) (c) thereof, an illegitimate child shall be presumed not to have been survived by his father unless the contrary is shown.

(5) This section does not apply to or affect the right of any person to take any entailed interest in real or personal property.

(6) The reference in section 50 (1) of the said Act of 1925 (which relates to the construction of documents) to Part IV of that Act, or to the foregoing provisions of that Part, shall in relation to an instrument inter vivos made, or a will or codicil coming into operation, after the coming into force of this section (but not in relation to instruments inter vivos made or wills or codicils coming into operation earlier) be construed as including references to this section.

(7) Section 9 of the Legitimacy Act 1926 (under which an illegitimate child and his issue are entitled to succeed on the intestacy of his mother if she leaves no legitimate issue, and the mother of an illegitimate child is entitled to succeed on his intestacy as if she were the only surviving parent) is hereby repealed.

(8) In this section "illegitimate child" does not include an illegitimate child who is—

    (a) a legitimated person within the meaning of the said Act of 1926 or a person recognised by virtue of that Act or at common law as having been legitimated; or

3—A.L.S. 189

(*b*) an adopted person under an adoption order made in any part of the United Kingdom, the Isle of Man or the Channel Islands or under an overseas adoption as defined in section 4 (3) of the Adoption Act 1968.

(9) This section does not affect any rights under the intestacy of a person dying before the coming into force of this section.

GENERAL NOTE

This section implements recommendations made by the Russell Committee in its Report on the Law of Succession in Relation to Illegitimate Persons (Cmnd. 3051: 1966). These were: (1) The rights of a bastard (and his *legitimate* issue in his place if he predeceases) to share on his mother's intestacy should be extended to cases where the mother leaves legitimate issue, and on the basis of equality. (2) The rights of a bastard (and his *legitimate* issue in his place if he predeceases) to share on his father's intestacy should be the same as in the case of a mother as so extended. (3) The rights of a father on the intestacy of his bastard should be equal to those of the mother but subject to the rule that he shall be presumed not to have survived his child unless the contrary is shown.

The section may usefully be compared with s. 1 of the Law Reform (Miscellaneous Provisions) (Scotland) Act 1968 in which the same recommendations were implemented with regard to Scotland—thus bringing the law of the two countries into line.

The section draws no distinction between illegitimate children who have been recognised by their natural parents and others; it will be a matter for proof in each case that the claimant is the child of the intestate (but see sub-s. (4) of this section and the note thereto).

The section does not do away with the distinction between legitimate and illegitimate birth for purposes of intestate succession: the principle is that an illegitimate child's relationship with each of his natural parents is equated with that of a legitimate child, but this recognition does not extend to permit participation by an illegitimate person in the estate of ancestors more remote than parents (*e.g.*, grandparents) or in the estate of collaterals (*e.g.*, brothers and sisters, whether of the whole or the half blood). Nor does it extend to permit participation by any person in the estate of an illegitimate person who dies intestate if the latter dies without leaving issue, a surviving spouse, or either of his parents.

SUB-S. (1)

Either parent

This means parents by blood relationship only and not by process of law; see sub-s. (8).

An illegitimate child

This expression seems to have displaced the original designation "bastard". After the Bastardy Act of 1923, the use of the less offensive "illegitimate person" seems to have been found preferable, though "bastard" remains a correct legal description.

Intestate

This term is defined by s. 55 (1) (vi) of the Administration of Estates Act 1925 (13 Halsbury's Statutes (3rd Edn.) 87) as including "a person who leaves a will but dies intestate as to some beneficial interest in his real or personal estate".

All or any of his real or personal property

This expression is designed to cover cases of partial intestacy—for which see s. 49 of the Administration of Estates Act 1925 (13 Halsbury's Statutes (3rd Edn.) 82).

His issue

This word is confined to *legitimate* issue who attain an absolutely vested interest, which, by virtue of the provisions of s. 3 (2), *ante*, are those who attain 18 or marry. "Issue" means "legitimate issue". "The law does not contemplate illegitimacy. The proper description of a legitimate child is 'child'," (*R. v. Totley* (Inhabitants) (1845), 7 Q.B. 596, *per* Lord Denman, at p. 600), and this rule of construction in statutes is not affected by s. 15, *post*, which relates only to "dispositions". Thus where a bastard dies during the lifetime of either of his parents, and would, had he survived either of them, have been beneficially interested in their estates on intestacy, only his legitimate issue are able to stand in his shoes. The distinction between legitimate and illegitimate births still remains: the only innovation is that a bastard is put on terms of equality with the legitimate offspring of either of his parents. Beyond this mutual blood-bond of parent and child, the laws of intestate succession do not extend to participation in the estates of grandparents or of brothers and sisters whether of whole or half blood.

Note: this limitation applies only to *Statutes*: a wider interpretation is permissible under s. 15 (1), *post*, which applies to *Dispositions*. See also s. 16, *post*.

Shall be entitled to take any interest therein

For the nature of the interests which may be taken, see the Administration of Estates Act 1925, Part IV (13 Halsbury's Statutes (3rd Edn.) 70 *et seq.*; the Intestates' Estates Act 1952, Sch. 1 (77 Statutes Supp. 62) and the Family Provision Act 1966 (158 Statutes Supp. 62).

The Russell Committee appreciated that the terms of this section might operate severely against the interests of some illegitimate persons and the following example was implied: M. and F. were an engaged couple who anticipated matrimony and pro-created C. and P., twin brothers. M. and F. were shortly afterwards killed in an accident and C. and P. were taken into the home of M.'s parents and brought up as their own children. C. suffers from a permanent disability and has to remain at home, being supported by his twin brother P. and his "grandfather" and "grandmother". He wins a large sum of money in a competition and expresses his determination to share it among the four of them but dies before having been able to do anything about it. Under the terms of the present section, neither his twin brother nor his "grandparents" could take. However his estate would pass as *bona vacantia*, and the interest that would actually fall to the survivors would be as indicated in s. 46 (1) (vi) of the Act of 1925 which is that the Crown or the Duchy of Cornwall may distribute the estate among persons for whom the intestate might reasonably have been expected to make provision.

SUB-S. (2)

The provisions of this subsection were criticised in Parliament on the grounds that it seems wrong that a father who, in effect, has disowned his child, has gone away and taken no interest in it, should be able to come forward—possibly after the child has made a name for himself in the world and has perhaps left quite a large amount of money and property. But it was held up as a matter of principle: "The son succeeds by virtue of blood and not behaviour. A father is entitled to succeed on intestacy to the property of an illegitimate son and equally this does not depend on what the father's conduct has been." Note, however, the presumption in sub-s. (4) of this section.

The provisions of sub-s. (2) correspond with s. 9 (2) of the Legitimacy Act 1926 (repealed by sub-s. (7) of this section).

SUB-S. (4)

Referring to this, the Government spokesman in the House of Lords said: "I should imagine that the court is going to be very jealous to make certain that he really is the father; and the worse he has treated his son, the more difficult, from a practical point of view it will be for him to prove that he is the father." (298 H. of L. Official Report 764.) The subsection is almost identical with s. 1 of the Law Reform (Miscellaneous Provisions) (Scotland) Act 1968.

As to rebuttable presumptions, see 15 Halsbury's Laws (3rd Edn.), paras. 618 *et seq.* By virtue of sub-s. (4), it is open to parties to act as if the father of the illegitimate child were dead and the burden of showing that he is both the father and that he is alive rests squarely upon the shoulders of those who choose to assert it. In practice, therefore, persons responsible for the distribution of the estate of a deceased illegitimate individual are under no obligation to ascertain whether or not the father has survived his child (see s. 17, *post*): should a man come forward with a claim, the trustees have two courses of action open to them—either to admit the claim, in which case the concurrence of all other interested parties must be obtained; or seek the advice of the court.

Unless the contrary is shown

The *onus probandi* lies upon those who seek to displace the presumption that the father of an illegitimate child did not survive him. In effect there are two matters of evidence: first, is the person claiming to be the father actually alive?—this can usually be proved without any difficulty; and, second, is that person the father of the deceased illegitimate child? How the second may be proved depends very much upon the facts of the case and the Russell Committee made the following observations:

As to affiliation orders. "We cannot regard affiliation orders as sufficiently reliable to be taken as conclusive proof, for the purposes of succession, of the fact of paternity. Such orders cover but a small proportion of the field of illegitimacy: and even so there are grounds for supposing that there are cases in which the mother successfully selects the man who is the best prospect. We think that greater weight could be attributed in the field of succession to affiliation orders—and certainly to their refusal—if mothers were compelled to submit to blood tests." Since Part III of the present Act now directs the taking of blood tests in the cases of disputed paternity, it is submitted that a man claiming to be the father of a bastard child and able to support his claim by reference to such a test would be held to have rebutted the presumption. In a way no harm would be done because it is more than likely that as a result of the blood test, he would have been obliged to make contribution to the maintenance of the child and so there would be no "unjust enrichment".

As to a declaratory judgment. The Committee rejected the idea that, following the practice of Danish law, it should be made the responsibility of the local authority or the State or a court official to investigate the birth of every bastard and secure either express recognition by the father of paternity or bring the matter before a court for a declaration.

As to statutory declarations. The Committee also declined to lay down that some particular act of recognition should conclusively establish paternity for purposes of succession: for example, execution of a declaration of parenthood in a statutory form by both parents deposited with some appropriate authority.

(Note, however, that under the provisions of s. 27, *post*, entry of father's name on registration of birth of illegitimate child is possible.)

Under all the foregoing conditions, unless there has been some voluntary recognition on the part of the father as to the parentage of the child, it would appear that very few cases would be admissible. It will be for the court before which the problem falls to be decided, to estimate whether the claimant has, on a balance of probabilities, established the fact of paternity. There may of course be many factors pointing towards or away from paternity, of greater or less weight depending upon the circumstances of the particular case. There may have been an affiliation order, contested or not: or an application for one may have failed. A man may have contributed to a greater or lesser degree to the support of the child as his child: he may have recognised the child as his in a number of ways by statements formal or informal and he might have signed the birth register under the conditions indicated in s. 27, *post*.

SUB-S. (5)

This reproduces the terms of s. 9 (3) of the Legitimacy Act 1926 (repealed by sub-s. (7) of this section).

SUB-S. (6)

The Administration of Estates Act 1925, s. 50, reads as follows: "References to any Statutes of Distribution in an instrument *inter vivos* made or in a will coming into operation after the commencement of this Act, shall be construed as references to this Part [*i.e.*, Part IV] of this Act; and references in such an instrument or will to statutory next of kin shall be construed, unless the context otherwise requires, as referring to the persons who would take beneficially on an intestacy under the foregoing provisions of this Part of this Act." The effect of this subsection is, therefore, that references to any Statutes of Distribution in an instrument *inter vivos* made, or in a will coming into operation, after this section comes into force are to be construed as references to the extended rules of intestate succession created by this section.

After the coming into force of this section

I.e., after 1st January 1970; see s. 28 (3), *post*, and the note thereto.

SUB-S. (7)

The power contained in this section expands upon that originally permitted under the Act of 1926 and its separate existence is no longer necessary.

SUB-S. (8)

This provision is necessary otherwise the limitations imposed by sub-s. (4) of this section might create inconveniences.

Legitimated persons
    Note that under s. 3 of the Act of 1926 such persons are empowered to take interests in property which might be more extensive than those permitted under the present Act—particularly with regard to entailed interests (see Legitimacy Act 1926, s. 3 (1) (c), 2 Halsbury's Statutes (2nd Edn.) 495).

At common law
    This expression was inserted during the final stages of the passing of the Act through the House of Lords, its purpose being explained as follows: "The object of [s. 14 (8)] is to ensure that no person born illegitimate and subsequently legitimated or adopted should be treated less favourably than he would be if the section had never been enacted. It is necessary, therefore, to exclude from [s. 14] all classes of legitimated persons—thus preserving for them rights already conferred by various statutes—and the insertion of these words ensures that persons recognised at common law as having been legitimated are also protected." (298 H. of L. Official Report 908.) The necessity for this specific provision arises from the fact that the provisions of the Legitimacy Act of 1926 extend only to persons who are legitimated by that Act (see ss. 8 (2) and 11 thereof). There are cases where persons have not been held to be legitimated under that measure although legitimated at common law; see *Re Hurll. Angelini* v. *Dick and Others*, [1952] 2 All E.R. 322.

Adopted persons
    Note that the rights of such persons to take under intestacy are set out in s. 16 of the Adoption Act 1958 (115 Statutes Supp. 83).

ADMINISTRATION OF ESTATES ACT 1925, PART IV, S. 50 (1)
    13 Halsbury's Statutes (3rd Edn.) 70 *et seq.*, 83.

LEGITIMACY ACT 1926
    1 Halsbury's Statutes (3rd Edn.) 62. For s. 9 of that Act, see *ibid.*, p. 67.

ADOPTION ACT 1968, S. 4 (3)
    See 177 Statutes Supp.

15. Presumption that in dispositions of property references to children and other relatives include references to, and to persons related through, illegitimate children

(1) In any disposition made after the coming into force of this section—

    (a) any reference (whether express or implied) to the child or children of any person shall, unless the contrary intention appears, be construed as, or as including, a reference to any illegitimate child of that person; and

    (b) any reference (whether express or implied) to a person or persons related in some other manner to any person shall, unless the contrary intention appears, be construed as, or as including, a reference to anyone who would be so related if he, or some other person through whom the relationship is deduced, had been born legitimate.

(2) The foregoing subsection applies only where the reference in question is to a person who is to benefit or to be capable of benefiting under the disposition or, for the purpose of designating such a person, to someone else to or through whom that person is related; but that subsection does not affect the construction of the word "heir" or "heirs" or of any expression which is used to create an entailed interest in real or personal property.

(3) In relation to any disposition made after the coming into force of this section, section 33 of the Trustee Act 1925 (which specifies the trusts implied

by a direction that income is to be held on protective trusts for the benefit of any person) shall have effect as if—

 (*a*) the reference to the children or more remote issue of the principal beneficiary included a reference to any illegitimate child of the principal beneficiary and to anyone who would rank as such issue if he, or some other person through whom he is descended from the principal beneficiary, had been born legitimate; and

 (*b*) the reference to the issue of the principal beneficiary included a reference to anyone who would rank as such issue if he, or some other person through whom he is descended from the principal beneficiary, had been born legitimate.

(4) In this section references to an illegitimate child include references to an illegitimate child who is or becomes a legitimated person within the meaning of the Legitimacy Act 1926 or a person recognised by virtue of that Act or at common law as having been legitimated; and in section 3 of that Act—

 (*a*) subsection (1) (*b*) (which relates to the effect of dispositions where a person has been legitimated) shall not apply to a disposition made after the coming into force of this section except as respects any interest in relation to which the disposition refers only to persons who are, or whose relationship is deduced through, legitimate persons; and

 (*b*) subsection (2) (which provides that, where the right to any property depends on the relative seniority of the children of any person, legitimated persons shall rank as if born on the date of legitimation) shall not apply in relation to any right conferred by a disposition made after the coming into force of this section unless the terms of the disposition are such that the children whose relative seniority is in question cannot include any illegitimate children who are not either legitimated persons within the meaning of that Act or persons recognised by virtue of that Act as having been legitimated.

(5) Where under any disposition any real or personal property or any interest in such property is limited (whether subject to any preceding limitation or charge or not) in such a way that it would, apart from this section, devolve (as nearly as the law permits) along with a dignity or title of honour, then, whether or not the disposition contains an express reference to the dignity or title of honour, and whether or not the property or some interest in the property may in some event become severed therefrom, nothing in this section shall operate to sever the property or any interest therein from the dignity or title, but the property or interest shall devolve in all respects as if this section had not been enacted.

(6) This section is without prejudice to sections 16 and 17 of the Adoption Act 1958 (which relate to the construction of dispositions in cases of adoption).

(7) There is hereby abolished, as respects dispositions made after the coming into force of this section, any rule of law that a disposition in favour of illegitimate children not in being when the disposition takes effect is void as contrary to public policy.

(8) In this section "disposition" means a disposition, including an oral disposition, of real or personal property whether inter vivos or by will or codicil; and, notwithstanding any rule of law, a disposition made by will or codicil executed before the date on which this section comes into force shall not be treated for the purposes of this section as made on or after that date by reason only that the will or codicil is confirmed by a codicil executed on or after that date.

GENERAL NOTE

This section is designed to carry the intention of Part II of this Act still further forward in that whereas the previous section confers equality upon both legitimate and illegitimate children following an intestacy, this directs that references to children in any disposition shall no longer be confined to those who are legitimate, but shall be extended also to include those who are not. Furthermore, unlike s. 14, *ante*, this section extends to the whole range of relationships and not simply those of parent and child (see sub-s. (1) (*b*)).

The old law, which still holds good with regard to dispositions made before 1st January 1970 was clearly stated in *Hill* v. *Crook*, [1874–80] All E.R. Rep. 62, by Lord Cairns: "The principle which may fairly be extracted from the cases upon this subject is this—the term "children" in a will *prima facie* means legitimate children, and if there is nothing more in the will the circumstance that the person whose children are referred to has illegitimate children will not entitle those illegitimate children to take." See further pp. 11–14, *ante*.

Many life policies provide that on the death there should be payment out at the trustees' discretion. It may be payment out to a very wide class, including relatives and children. Since by nature of this section the word "children" now includes those who are illegitimate and their relatives as well, the trustees cannot be expected to review the whole class of beneficiaries. Many life offices expressed fears that such a trust would be void for uncertainty under the rule stated in *Inland Revenue Commissioners* v. *Broadway Cottages Trust*, [1954] 3 All E.R. 120, in which it was held that a trust of income for such members of a class as the trustees should select was, if the whole range of members of the class were not ascertainable, void for uncertainty, although certain members of the class were ascertainable. The Attorney-General, discussing this point in the House of Commons on report drew attention to *Re Baden's Deed Trusts*, [1969] 1 All E.R. 1016, in which Harman, L.J. observed (at p. 1020): ". . . this doctrine about the certainty of the objects of a discretionary trust which has been applied to a number of large quasi-charitable gifts seems never to have been applied to the ordinary case of a family settlement in which there are discretionary trusts expressed to be for the benefit of the family and (say) their wives and issue. It has never, so far as I know, been suggested that such a trust is invalidated because (say) one of the grandchildren had disappeared and it is not known whether he is in existence and has a wife or wives and children or issue. Many discretionary trusts have been and are being administered without complete certainty in this respect."

If the learned judge's doubts are well-founded—and it is to be borne in mind the observation is *obiter*—the danger against which the life offices sought to be protected may be exaggerated. "Since" said the Attorney-General, "in practice, the only settlements likely to be drawn up without professional advice are those resulting from a 'home-made will', it is . . . most unlikely that [the section] will ever cause such uncertainty as will invalidate a trust. . . . It is the case that one of the consequences of [s. 15] is that those making settlements hereafter will have to be careful to ensure that in using expressions denoting relationships without qualification they do not extend the possible range of objects too widely. However in practice these settlements are invariably drafted with professional assistance from solicitors and others who will have the section well in mind." (H. of C. Official Report 1437.)

SUB-S. (1)

This is the key to the whole section: it reverses that long-standing rule expressed in *Wilkinson* v. *Adam* (1813), 1 V. & B. 422, *per* Lord Eldon, "the description 'child', 'son', 'issue', every word of that species must be taken *prima facie* to mean legitimate child, son, or issue".

In any disposition

For definition, see sub-s. (8) of this section. Note that the presumption dealt with in this section is not extended to statutes. Consequently the expression "issue" as used in s. 14, *ante*, does not extend to the illegitimate issue of a bastard.

After the coming into force of this section

I.e., after 1st January 1970; see s. 28 (3), *post*, and the note thereto.

Of any person

Hence these words are sufficient to expand the law to include not only the illegitimate children of an unnamed female, the identity of whom is rarely in dispute, but also the illegitimate children of a man procreated by him through a woman to whom he is not married—and the identity of which man may not be certain. In his respect, the words of Maugham, J. are apposite: "the court declines to inquire into the actual parentage of a man's alleged offspring. The most that can be done in the case of a gift to the illegitimate children of a male in a will describing the children in that way is—in a proper case —to construe it as a gift to children who have acquired, before the date when the will becomes effective, the reputation of being the children of the supposed father. There is no objection to the court's inquiry, not into the parentage, but into the reputation of persons described as 'the reputed children of' a particular male . . . there is no difficulty in ascertaining who are the reputed illegitimate children of a particular person, and there is never any difficulty in inquiring who are the illegitimate children of an unmarried female." *Re Hyde*, [1931] All E.R. Rep., 52, at p. 53.

Shall

The rule of construction is mandatory in its application.

Unless the contrary intention appears

It is submitted that in cases of dispute, the burden of proving that such an intention is expressed lies upon those who assert it. "The burden of proof in any particular case depends on the circumstances in which the claim arises. In general the rule which applies is *ei qui affirmat non ei qui negat incumbit probatio*. It is an ancient rule founded on considerations of good sense, and it should not be departed from without good reasons,"—*per* Lord Maugham in *Constantine Line* v. *Imperial Smelting Corporation*, [1941] All E.R., p. 179.

A reference to any illegitimate child

It is submitted that *Caller* v. *Caller*, [1966] 2 All E.R. 754, is authority to support the contention that this expression may include a child not yet born. "In my view a man can accept as a child of the family his wife's unborn child just as readily as he can accept her born child" *per* Latey, J., at p. 758. Note also sub-s. (7) of this section.

Person or persons related

In deducing relationships for the purposes of this section, there is nothing to limit the reference simply to descendants, but that ascendants and collaterals may be included where appropriate. "Where one devises the rest of his personal estate to his relations, or to be divided among his relations, without saying what relations, it shall go among all such relations as are capable of taking within the Statute of Distribution [see, now, the Administration of Estates Act 1925]; else it would be uncertain; for the relation may be infinite." Anon (1716), 1 P Wms. 326, *per* Jekyll, M.R., at pp. 326, 327.

For a comprehensive discussion of the meaning of "relations" see *Sydall* v. *Castings*, [1966] 3 All E.R. 772.

SUB-S. (2)

This subsection makes it quite clear that the new rule is designed only to expand any class of beneficiaries so as to include those whose illegitimacy would otherwise have excluded them and is not to apply in cases where parties are designated, not as beneficiaries, but for some other purpose—*e.g.*, as an executor.

At first sight it may seem odd that a gift "to my eldest son" (B.) (who is illegitimate) will be effective against the second son (L.) (who is not); yet the appointment of "my eldest son as executor" will operate so as to confer that office upon the second (L.). However, it may be that the Act has in contemplation situations such as this:

As a young man, T has procreated an illegitimate son B through a casual relationship with F, but, following some agreement or other, has taken no interest in the child and more or less lost sight of him. Several years later he marries W and rears a family, including two sons X and Y—none of which family know anything of B. T dies, and in his will he appoints his "eldest son" as his executor. It is obvious that he expects X to carry out the duties of executorship, but if the rule as set out in sub-s. (1) of this section were to prevail, X might find himself superseded by B.

In practice, this difference in interpretation is not likely to cause any difficulties.

No doubt practitioners engaged in the drafting of dispositions will recommend that their clients clearly designate by name—and possibly other particulars, if parties bear the same name—those whom they wish to act in the capacities indicated in this subsection.

Heir or heirs

This provision is only reasonable since the essential feature of an entailed interest is that succession is usually limited to a certain class of descendants—generally "to A and the heirs male of his body", so that only male descendants of A who trace an unbroken descent from him may inherit. The intention of a grantor would be frustrated if a tenant, finding that he would die without a legitimate successor, were empowered, as it were, to procreate bastards so as to defeat a reversion.

For the meaning of "heir" generally, see "Words and Phrases Legally Defined" (2nd Edn.), Vol. 2, p. 352; 39 Halsbury's Laws (3rd Edn.), 3588. For entailed interests generally, see 32 Halsbury's Laws (3rd Edn.) 274 *et seq.*

SUB-S. (3)

This subsection extends the principles of this section to the provisions of the Trustee Act 1925 which direct that upon the failure of a beneficiary's interest, the trustees have a discretion to pay the money elsewhere. A very common form of disposition is one wherein a trustee is given a discretion to pay the income arising out of a fund to a beneficiary until he dies or becomes bankrupt or alienates his interest in some way: in which cases the trustees may apply the income elsewhere for the benefit of his wife or issue or any other indicated persons. Such dispositions may be made simply by designating the trusts as being held "on protective trusts". See 38 Halsbury's Laws (3rd Edn.), para. 1773. For the effect of a maintenance order on a protective trust income, see *Re Richardson's Will Trusts*, [1958] 1 All E.R. 538.

SUB-S. (4)

This subsection was described in Committee as being extremely complicated and, although drawn with remarkable precision, even those members who were legally qualified declared that the language was puzzling and ambiguous. The purport was explained as follows:

Para. (*a*) refers to s. 3 (1) (*b*) of the Legitimacy Act 1926 in which it is enacted that a legitimated person shall be entitled to take any interest under any disposition coming into operation after the date of his legitimation. A donor would naturally wish to know whether any illegitimate child he had in contemplation, would be able to benefit, and, in the case of a gift executed, for example, on 1st January 1970 in favour of A's children, the following problem might present itself. A has a child who is illegitimate B, but, following A's marriage to his mother in the February, automatically becomes a "legitimated person". In this capacity he falls outside the provisions of this Act, and must appeal to those of 1926: but these would only give him an interest under a disposition that came into operation on a date following his legitimation. Since his legitimation occurred in February and the disposition was effective in the preceding January, he would be positively prejudiced by now being legitimate. This situation is obviated by the terms of this para. which ensures that rights which would otherwise accrue to, or be traced through a person born illegitimate are not lost through that person subsequently being legitimated.

Of course, if the disposition is so worded as to exclude persons who are illegitimate, no problem arises.

Para. (*b*) refers to s. 3 (2) of the Legitimacy Act 1926 which, as applied to the provisions of this Act, could create the following situation. A has an illegitimate child B, born to him by a woman F. He marries S who bears him L. Subsequently S dies and A marries F, thereby legitimating B. Under s. 3 (2) of the Act of 1926, the question of the relative seniority of L and B is settled by reference to the date of legitimation and not the date of birth: therefore in this example, L, although the younger in years will legally be regarded as "the elder child of A", and B, though older, will rank as "the second child". If a disposition were made after this section had come into force, making a gift to "the eldest child of A", as matters stood, it would be taken to refer to L. However, suppose that A had not married F and B had remained illegitimate: in this case the rules of nature would prevail and, under s. 15 (1), he would be simply regarded as A's child and the question of legitimacy, illegitimacy or legitimation would not arise, and being obviously older, would thereupon exclude L. Such a capricious situation is intolerable: it is absurd that a child who is illegitimate can be put at a disadvantage by being legitimated or be able to score an advantage over one who is legitimate through his parents remaining unmarried.   The purpose of this paragraph is to obviate this state of affairs by setting aside the artificial rule in the Act of 1926 and declaring that simple chronology is to prevail.

At common law
See corresponding note at s. 14 (8) (*a*), *ante.*

SUB-S. (5)
This section is in common form, appearing, for example in the Legitimacy Act 1926, s. 3 (3) and the Legitimacy Act 1959, s. 2 (5).   A similar provision is made in s. 5 (5) of the Scottish enactment of 1968.   Attention is drawn to the fact that children of void or voidable marriages who are deemed to be legitimate by virtue of s. 2 of the Legitimacy Act 1959 (119 Statutes Supp.) or of s. 11 of the Matrimonial Causes Act 1965 (153 Statutes Supp.) are not debarred from succeeding to a title or dignity.

SUB-S. (6)
The effect of the Adoption Act 1958, s. 16 (115 Statutes Supp.) is to put an adopted child in the same position with regard to testamentary dispositions, settlements, intestacy, etc., as if it were the legitimate child of its adoptive parents.   The effect of s. 17 of that Act is to give to adopted children the status of being brother or sister to other children involved.

SUB-S. (7)
This subsection was introduced during the report stage (Commons) in order to clear up doubts as to the survival of the old rule that "where a man, *by deed*, creates a trust in favour of illegitimate children (neither born nor *en ventre sa mere*) at the date of the deed then, apart from the objection as to want of certainty in the beneficiaries, the trust will be void as being contrary to public policy and conducive to immorality.   Similarly, a trust *by will* in favour of the illegitimate children *of another* not begotten at the death of the testator will be void as encouraging illicit intercourse." (*Underhill's Law of Trusts and Trustees*, 11th Edn., p. 91.)   See also *Hill* v. *Crook*, [1874–80] All E.R. Rep. 62.
   This section by necessary implication overrides these old authorities, and this subsection now puts the matter beyond doubt.

SUB-S. (8)
Not withstanding any rule of law
The rule of law to which reference is made is that of "re-publication", for which, in general, see 39 Halsbury's Laws (3rd Edn.) 904 *et seq.*   The matter may arise under circumstances wherein the validity of a disposition has to be referred to a codicil or the originating will: see, for example, *Re Sebag-Montefiore, Sebag-Montefiore* v. *Alliance Assurance Co. Ltd.*, [1944] 1 All E.R. 672.   The matter may also be of importance in cases where a confirmatory document exists and expressions are used such as "my eldest son" or "full age" and it is not clear whether they are to be interpreted in the old sense or the new.   As to effect where words are ambiguous in context, see 29 Halsbury's Laws (3rd Edn.), para. 1478.   See also a similar provision in s. 1 (7), *ante.*

TRUSTEE ACT 1925, S. 33
26 Halsbury's Statutes (2nd Edn.) 102.

LEGITIMACY ACT 1926
1 Halsbury's Statutes (3rd Edn.) 62.   For s. 3 of that Act, see *ibid.*, p. 64.

ADOPTION ACT 1958, SS. 16, 17
See 115 Statutes Supp.

16. Meaning of "child" and "issue" in s. 33 of Wills Act 1837

(1) In relation to a testator who dies after the coming into force of this section, section 33 of the Wills Act 1837 (gift to children or other issue of testator not to lapse if they predecease him but themselves leave issue) shall have effect as if—

   (*a*) the reference to a child or other issue of the testator (that is, the intended beneficiary) included a reference to any illegitimate child of the testator and to anyone who would rank as such issue if he, or some other person through whom he is descended from the testator, had been born legitimate; and

(b) the reference to the issue of the intended beneficiary included a reference to anyone who would rank as such issue if he, or some other person through whom he is descended from the intended beneficiary, had been born legitimate.

(2) In this section "illegitimate child" includes an illegitimate child who is a legitimated person within the meaning of the Legitimacy Act 1926 or a person recognised by virtue of that Act or at common law as having been legitimated.

GENERAL NOTE

The purpose of this section is to expand the meaning of the expression "child or other issue of the testator" in the Wills Act 1837, s. 33, so as to include illegitimate relationships. Like s. 15, it applies to descendants to any degree.

SUB-S. (1)

A testator who dies after the coming into force of this section
I.e., after 1st January 1970; see s. 28 (3), *post*, and the note thereto. Note that the section is directed to when the testator dies and not to when the will was made.

The intended beneficiary
Note that the effect of the Act of 1837 is not to *substitute* the children or other issue of the predeceased beneficiary, but merely to confirm that during the subsistence of the will he had what almost amounted to a *vested interest*, capable of passing to his descendants. Since the testator is still alive when his intended donee dies, it is open to him to amend his will, but if for any reason he does not do this, it may fairly be taken that he intended the gift to be passed on and was prepared to accept that if the donee failed to make provision, the gift would ultimately devolve according to the prescribed rules following intestacy.

SUB-S. (2)

This is the converse of s. 14 (8) (*a*), *ante*. Note that an adopted person is considered to be the child of his adopter and not of his natural parents for the purposes of dispositions by will; see the Adoption Act 1958, s. 16 (115 Statutes Supp. 83).

WILLS ACT 1837, S. 33

26 Halsbury's Statutes (2nd Edn.) 1352.

LEGITIMACY ACT 1926

1 Halsbury's Statutes (3rd Edn.) 62.

17. Protection of trustees and personal representatives

Notwithstanding the foregoing provisions of this Part of this Act, trustees or personal representatives may convey or distribute any real or personal property to or among the persons entitled thereto without having ascertained that there is no person who is or may be entitled to any interest therein by virtue of—

(a) section 14 of this Act so far as it confers any interest on illegitimate children or their issue or on the father of an illegitimate child; or

(b) section 15 or 16 of this Act,

and shall not be liable to any such person of whose claim they have not had notice at the time of the conveyance or distribution; but nothing in this section shall prejudice the right of any such person to follow the property, or any property representing it, into the hands of any person, other than a purchaser, who may have received it.

GENERAL NOTE

This section is modelled on s. 27 (2) of the Trustee Act 1925 and s. 17 (3) of the Adoption Act 1958.

COMMENCEMENT

This section came into force on 1st January 1970; see s. 28 (3), *post*, and the note thereto.

Trustees and personal representatives

During the passing of the Act it was strenuously argued that the protection afforded by this section ought to be extended to life offices. The reason advanced was that it is the practice of many life offices in small cases, on the death of the policy holder, to make payment to the widow or to the next of kin without the production of the grant of representation. Nevertheless an amendment which sought to extend this section to them was rejected: in the words of the Attorney-General: "Insurers are not the only people affected by this problem. Bankers also in practice allow close relatives to draw cheques on the deceased's current account on the Manager's being satisfied that they are entitled to succeed. The problem facing the life companies is one which faces any debtor of the estate who is prepared to take a chance on paying the right person. One of the inevitable consequences of accepting the policy in [s. 15] is that the risk of making a mistake is greater. . . .

Trustees and personal representatives, however, are in a different position from that of insurers, bankers and other debtors. They are obliged to pay out to the persons entitled, whereas insurers and bankers are not; and they can, in a doubtful case, insist on representation being taken out. If [this section] were extended beyond the class of persons obliged to pay out, it is difficult to see where to draw the line. In practice, the . . . problem is not likely to be as great as [many Associations] fear. The need for ready cash usually occurs where the assured was a man who dies leaving a widow. If he dies intestate she is absolutely entitled to the first £8,750 of his estate. So in the case of an estate worth less than that sum the insurance companies are safe in paying the widow. If the estate is worth more, she will certainly have to take out representation and, even in this case, the underwriters are safe if they pay her and take out an indemnity. It must be borne in mind that the greater the protection given to those paying out, the greater the risk that the person entitled in law will be deprived of his rights. A balance has to be struck between attempting on the one hand, to help the underwriters and the legitimate family, and, on the other hand, protecting the interests of the illegitimate child." (786 H. of C. Official Report 1438.)

Convey or distribute; conveyance or distribution

This covers the case where property is appropriated by personal representatives and is retained by them *qua* trustees or beneficiaries. Cf. *Clegg* v. *Rowland* (1866), L.R. 3 Eq 368.

Section 14 of this Act

Note that the interests conferred by s. 14, *ante*, are, in relation to parents, upon the children; and, in relation to the children, upon *both* parents. It was specifically mentioned, during the debates, that this section does not, in spite of the particular reference to a father in para. (*a*), affect any duty of the personal representative of an illegitimate person who dies intestate to ascertain whether the deceased's mother may be entitled to an interest in his estate by virtue of s. 14, *ante*. Survival of the mother will in most cases be readily ascertainable, save where a child has been adopted, in which case it is irrelevant.

Notice

During the committee stages an attempt was made to gloss this word along lines similar to s. 199 of the Law of Property Act 1925 (*i.e.*, "actual notice"). It was firmly rejected by the Attorney-General who expanded upon the matter thus:

"The purpose of the amendment is to cut down the operation of constructive notice in relation to claims arising under Part II. The main objection to the amendment is that the Act is not intended to, and as drafted does not, attract the doctrine of constructive notice in any event. . . . There is nothing in this section to suggest that notice has any other meaning than its natural meaning. If it were glossed in any way, the implication would be that without the gloss, 'notice' would have an artificial meaning. But there is no reason to suppose that this would be so. Both s. 27 of the Trustee Act 1925 and s. 17 (3)—on which this section is modelled—employ the word without qualification. Were there to be put on this word the interpretation implied in this amendment, it could be taken that in these other enactments 'notice' includes 'constructive notice'. But there is no reason to suggest that this is so, and it would be undesirable to raise such an implication . . .

Apart from these considerations, the Amendment might have an unfortunate effect. By requiring actual notice to the trustee or personal representative it might be held to imply that it was permissible for him to shut his eyes to facts which were obvious and from which the existence of a relevant claim should have been inferred." (H. of C. Official Report S.C.B. 29th April, 1969, Col. 136.)

Purchaser
This does not bear the meaning which it sometimes bears in real property legislation—*i.e.*, a person who takes otherwise than by descent—but means somebody who buys or gives valuable consideration for property—as, for example in s. 27 (2) of the Trustee Act 1925 and s. 17 (3) of the Adoption Act 1958. A suggestion to add the words "for value" was rejected on the grounds that it might then be implied that the word in the Acts of 1925 and 1958 had a wider meaning.

18. Illegitimate children to count as dependants under Inheritance (Family Provision) Act 1938

(1) For the purposes of the Inheritance (Family Provision) Act 1938, a person's illegitimate son or daughter shall be treated as his dependant in any case in which a legitimate son or daughter of that person would be so treated, and accordingly in the definition of the expressions "son" and "daughter" in section 5 (1) of that Act, as amended by the Family Provision Act 1966, after the words "respectively include" there shall be inserted the words "an illegitimate son or daughter of the deceased".

(2) In section 26 (6) of the Matrimonial Causes Act 1965 (which provides, among other things, for the word "dependant" to have the same meaning as in the said Act of 1938 as amended by the said Act of 1966), after the words "as amended by the Family Provision Act 1966" there shall be inserted the words "and the Family Law Reform Act 1969".

(3) This section does not affect the operation of the said Acts of 1938 and 1965 in relation to a person dying before the coming into force of this section.

GENERAL NOTE
This section implements the recommendation of the Committee on the Law of Succession in Relation to Illegitimate Persons (Cmnd. 3051: 1966) that an illegitimate child should have the same right as a legitimate child to apply in the estate of either parent under the Inheritance (Family Provision) Act 1938. That Act confers a power on the court to make reasonable provision for a dependant in cases where the court considers that in all the circumstances it should have been made and it has not been made.

SUB-S. (1)
The effect of this subsection is to displace the authority of *Re Makein*, [1955] 1 All E.R. 57—in which a considerable number of authorities were quoted and discussed as to the meaning of "child" and "dependant". The factors which led Harman, J. to rule that the words "son" or "daughter" did not include illegitimate offspring, are worthy to be quoted in that the difficulties he indicated have not been met by this section: *i.e.* that there is no standard against which the claims of illegitimate children are to be measured. "I cannot think that the legislature contemplated applications by illegitimate offspring competing with the claims, whether under a will, an intestacy or under the Act, of the legitimate dependants. The task of the courts in those circumstances would be not only odious but impossible to carry out, for who could know what other dependants might enter the lists to make further claims to a share? It would indeed be visiting the sins of the fathers on the children."

Of course his objection is in some way met in that the burden of showing that a party has a claim arising through an illegitimate link lies pretty firmly upon the shoulders of those asserting it—see, especially, s. 17, *ante.*

Son and daughter
The definition in the Inheritance Family Provision Act 1938, as amended, now reads: "'son' and 'daughter' respectively include an illegitimate son or daughter of the deceased, a male or female child adopted by the deceased in pursuance of adoption proceedings taken in any part of the United Kingdom, the Isle of Man and the Channel Islands, and also the son or daughter of the deceased *en ventre sa mere* at the date of the death of the deceased."

SUB-S. (3)
Coming into force of this section
I.e., 1st January 1970; see s. 28 (3), *post,* and the note thereto.

WILLS ACT 1837, S. 33
26 Halsbury's Statutes (2nd Edn.) 1352.

LEGITIMACY ACT 1926
1 Halsbury's Statutes (3rd Edn.) 62.

19. Policies of assurance and property in industrial and provident societies

(1) In section 11 of the Married Women's Property Act 1882 and section 2 of the Married Women's Policies of Assurance (Scotland) Act 1880 (policies of asssurance effected for the benefit of children) the expression "children" shall include illegitimate children.

(2) In section 25 (2) of the Industrial and Provident Societies Act 1965 (application of property in registered society where member was illegitimate and is not survived by certain specified relatives) for the words "and leaves no widow, widower or issue, and his mother does not survive him" there shall be substituted the words "and leaves no widow, widower or issue (including any illegitimate child of the member) and neither of his parents survives him".

(3) Subsection (1) of this section does not affect the operation of the said Acts of 1882 and 1880 in relation to a policy effected before the coming into force of that subsection; and subsection (2) of this section does not affect the operation of the said Act of 1965 in relation to a member of a registered society who dies before the coming into force of the said subsection (2).

GENERAL NOTE
There are two arms to this section, which may be taken in order. Sub-s. (1) extends s. 11 of the Married Women's Property Act 1882 and s. 2 of the Married Women's Policies of Assurance (Scotland) Act 1880, so as to cover insurance policies taken out on the life of the assured in favour of his or her illegitimate children. Under s. 11 of the 1882 Act and s. 2 of that of 1880, an insurance policy effected on the assured's life for the benefit of a partner or children creates a trust in their favour and does not form part of the estate—there is an exception under the Scottish Act. Such policies have two main advantages; the policy money cannot, except in unusual circumstances, be made over to satisfy creditors, nor, if taken out before 10th March 1968, be aggregated for estate duty. Since the Revenue has always taken the view that references to "children" in these policies referred only to those who were born in lawful wedlock, illegitimate children got a poor innings. As it is, the express inclusion of these enactments in this Act will now ensure equality.
Sub-s. (2) makes an amendment to s. 25 (2) of the Industrial and Provident Societies Act 1965, which is consequential on s. 14, *ante.* Section 25 of the 1965 Act makes provision for a case where a member of a registered society dies leaving in the society shares and so on, not exceeding £500, and enables the society to pay the money to persons appearing to be entitled to it, without any need for a grant of representation.

Sub-s. (2) of that section provides for the situation where the member is illegitimate and leaves no relatives falling within a specified class: the Treasury may give directions to the committee of the society as to the disposal of his shares, and since the class of persons who may take on intestacy has been extended by s. 14 of this Act, an appropriate alteration has been made.

COMMENCEMENT

This section came into force on 1st January 1970; see s. 28 (3), *post*, and the note thereto. Note, however, that the provisions of this section do not affect the interpretation of existing policies.

SUB-S. (1)

Policies of assurance effected for the benefit of children
It has been held that a policy can extend to a second wife and subsequent children (*Re Browne's Policy, Browne* v. *Browne*, [1903] 1 Ch. 188)—thus a widow and child shared jointly with children of first marriage.

Example
P effects a policy as from 1st January 1970 in favour of his wife W and two children (A and B). W dies, and P has an affair with J who bears him an illegitimate child (I). P subsequently marries F who bears him two children (C) and (D). On P's death, the widowed F takes jointly with A, B, I, C and D.
In a case where F had also effected a policy for the benefit of her husband and children and had died shortly after P's death, would the provisions of s. 15 extend to I? It is suggested that they would not. The reason for this is that the provisions of s. 15 (1) (*b*) are designed to cover, in general, those beneficiaries belonging to a "second generation" and whose relationship with the person making the disposition can be traced through a union of which one of the parties was related, by blood, to that person. In the example, no such relationship exists between F and I. Nor would it avail to invoke the provisions (as amended) of the Married Women's Property Act 1882. This enactment refers unequivocally to "her children" and, although by marrying a widower with legitimate children, F would, in law, make them "hers" for the purposes of the 1882 enactment, her marriage to P cannot in any way make I "her child", who therefore would be excluded.

SUB-S. (2)
The Industrial and Provident Societies Act 1965, s. 25 now reads:

"25. Provision for intestacy

(1) If any member of a registered society dies intestate and at his death his property in the society in respect of shares, loans or deposits does not exceed in the whole [£500] and is not the subject of any nomination under section 23 of this Act, then, subject to subsection (2) of this section, the committee of the society may, without letters of administration [or probate of any will] or, in Scotland, without confirmation having been obtained, distribute that property among such persons as appear to the committee on such evidence as they deem satisfactory to be entitled by law to receive it.
(2) If the member aforesaid was illegitimate [and leaves no widow, widower or issue (including any illegitimate child of the member) and neither of his parents survives him] the committee shall deal with his property in the society as the Treasury shall direct."

The committee of the society may . . . distribute that property
Note that this power is discretionary. This indicates that if the Committee have any doubts as to who should receive any money, they are entitled to refuse payment, and let the matter go forward under the provisions of s. 60 of the Act (decision of disputes).

Entitled by law to receive it
The rights to succession on intestacy are as set out in the Administration of Estates Act 1925, as amended by the Intestates' Estates Act 1952, Sch. 1, and the Family Provision Act 1966. It is important to remember that illegitimate children are now "entitled by law" to benefit under these provisions (s. 14, *ante*).
For the relevant provisions on intestacy, see the Intestates Estates Act 1952 (77 Statutes Supp. 62–69).

Neither of his parents

This is to give effect to s. 14 (2), *ante*. The original words (reproduced in the subsection) were described as not entirely apt for the purposes of the new rules of distribution.

For the law as to Industrial and Provident Societies with respect to this matter, see 21 Halsbury's Laws (3rd Edn.), paras. 99–100.

SUB-S. (3)

This was described as a drafting amendment and was introduced during report in the Commons. It derives from a point raised in Committee that the effect of the section on existing policies was not clearly indicated. Referring to the subsection, the Attorney-General said: "As to the construction of an existing policy, sub-s. (1) cannot have any effect. Section 15, which embodies the new rule of construction, does not affect existing dispositions and any reference in an existing policy to children will be *prima facie* construed as a reference to legitimate children."

Moreover, since s. 11 of the 1882 Act and its Scottish counterpart as they now stand, operate on policies for the benefit of legitimate children, any reference in an existing policy to either of these enactments will be the strongest possible evidence that the *prima facie* construction is the construction intended. The ultimate effect of sub-s. (3) is to prevent the section from affecting, in retrospect any existing policy of life assurance or the operation of s. 25 (2) of the Industrial and Provident Societies Act 1965 in respect of a person dying before it came into force.

Coming into force of that subsection

I.e., 1st January 1970; see s. 28 (3), *post*, and the note thereto.

SCOTLAND

This section also extends to Scotland (see s. 28 (4) (*g*), *post*). The Industrial and Provident Societies Act 1965 applies to Scotland without modification and since s. 1 of the Law Reform (Miscellaneous Provisions) (Scotland) Act 1968 enacted for that country a rule corresponding with that in section 14 of the present Act, the incorporation of a reference to Scotland in respect of these enactments is appropriate.

MARRIED WOMEN'S PROPERTY ACT 1882, S. 11

17 Halsbury's Statutes (3rd Edn.) 118.

MARRIED WOMEN'S POLICIES OF ASSURANCE (SCOTLAND) ACT 1880

43 & 44 Vict. c. 26; not printed in this work.

INDUSTRIAL AND PROVIDENT SOCIETIES ACT 1965, S. 25 (2).

17 Halsbury's Statutes (3rd Edn.) 354.

PART III

PROVISIONS FOR USE OF BLOOD TESTS IN DETERMINING
PATERNITY

20. Power of court to require use of blood tests

(1) In any civil proceedings in which the paternity of any person falls to be determined by the court hearing the proceedings, the court may, on an application by any party to the proceedings, give a direction for the use of blood tests to ascertain whether such tests show that a party to the proceedings is or is not thereby excluded from being the father of that person and for the taking, within a period to be specified in the direction, of blood samples from that person, the mother of that person and any party alleged to be the father of that person or from any, or any two, of those persons.

A court may at any time revoke or vary a direction previously given by it under this section.

(2) The person responsible for carrying out blood tests taken for the purpose of giving effect to a direction under this section shall make to the court by which the direction was given a report in which he shall state—

(*a*) the results of the tests;

(*b*) whether the party to whom the report relates is or is not excluded by the results from being the father of the person whose paternity is to be determined; and

(*c*) if that party is not so excluded, the value, if any, of the results in determining whether that party is that person's father;

and the report shall be received by the court as evidence in the proceedings of the matters stated therein.

(3) A report under subsection (2) of this section shall be in the form prescribed by regulations made under section 22 of this Act.

(4) Where a report has been made to a court under subsection (2) of this section, any party may, with the leave of the court, or shall, if the court so directs, obtain from the person who made the report a written statement explaining or amplifying any statement made in the report, and that statement shall be deemed for the purposes of this section (except subsection (3) thereof) to form part of the report made to the court.

(5) Where a direction is given under this section in any proceedings, a party to the proceedings, unless the court otherwise directs, shall not be entitled to call as a witness the person responsible for carrying out the tests taken for the purpose of giving effect to the direction, or any person by whom any thing necessary for the purpose of enabling those tests to be carried out was done, unless within fourteen days after receiving a copy of the report he serves notice on the other parties to the proceedings, or on such of them as the court may direct, of his intention to call that person; and where any such person is called as a witness the party who called him shall be entitled to cross-examine him.

(6) Where a direction is given under this section the party on whose application the direction is given shall pay the cost of taking and testing blood samples for the purpose of giving effect to the direction (including any expenses reasonably incurred by any person in taking any steps required of him for the purpose), and of making a report to the court under this section, but the amount paid shall be treated as costs incurred by him in the proceedings.

GENERAL NOTE

This section implements the following proposals made by the Law Commission in its Report on Blood Tests and the Proof of Paternity in Civil Proceedings (Law Com. No. 16: 1968): (1) that in all civil proceedings in which the court has to determine the paternity of any child it should have the power to direct that the parties to the action, the child concerned and its mother submit to blood tests; (2) that any party to the proceedings should be entitled to apply for a direction; (3) that both exclusion and non-exclusion results should be admissible in evidence; (4) that the results of blood tests should be capable of proof by a certificate from the serologist responsible for the tests; and (5) that provision should be made so that any party can call the serologist concerned to give evidence in person and can cross-examine him.

See further pp. 16, 17, *ante.*

COMMENCEMENT

This section had not been brought into force up to 17th April 1970.

SUB-S. (I)

In any civil proceedings
 Note that criminal proceedings are not covered by the section. While proof of paternity is in rare cases an issue in criminal law, *e.g.*, in incest cases, the criminal courts have special powers for meeting the situation. See corresponding note under s. 26, *post*.

In which the paternity of any person falls to be determined
 This would include affiliation proceedings; petitions for divorce on the grounds of adultery; nullity proceedings; appeals against maintenance and applications for the custody of a minor.
 During the Committee Stages in the Commons the point was raised as to whether it was desirable to limit the application of the section only to "paternity" since it was also possible for "maternity" to be at issue. The Government decided that the circumstances were so rare as to need no express provision.

By the court hearing the proceedings
 The expression "court" is not defined but its direct relationship with the words "In any civil proceedings" clearly implies that the new power is conferred upon any court within whose competence such proceedings lie—cf. s. 6 (1), *ante*. It is submitted that there is nothing in this Act to extend the power to order a blood test to anywhere other than the ordinary courts of law, excluding, therefore, as an example, the "determining authority" described in the National Insurance (Guardian's Allowance) Regulations, S.I. 1948 No. 2687, reg. 3 (*a*) (15 Halsbury's Statutory Instruments, title National Insurance (Part 1)).

The court may
 It should be noted that the exercise of this new power is discretionary. If a party were able to demand a blood test as of right, it might encourage petitions for divorce, based on flimsy allegations of misconduct and in the hope that a blood test might simply prove fortuitous in its results. It can safely be postulated that if the courts have reason to suspect that accusations, say, of adultery are not really substantiated and that the demand for a blood test is more to prove a wife's fidelity rather than a child's parentage, the direction will be withheld.

On an application
 It is proposed that in affiliation proceedings a summons served under the Affiliation Proceedings Act 1957 shall be accompanied with an application form, and, possibly an explanatory leaflet. The defendant will be invited to state whether he intends to apply for the test. In other proceedings, unless agreed beforehand, the matter will be the subject of a preliminary hearing.

By any party to the proceedings
 The court does not itself take the initiative. This must come from a party to the proceedings. In divorce or nullity proceedings the petitioner is most likely to make the application. In affiliation proceedings, however, applications are likely to be demanded as often by the man as by the mother.

Give a direction for the use of blood tests
 See s. 21, *post*, for matters relating to the testing of blood. Note that there is no power to exert physical compulsion in order to obtain blood samples from uncooperative parties or to impose sanctions. As the court's power to put whatever construction it sees fit upon a refusal to take a blood test, see s. 23, *post*.

To ascertain whether such tests show that a party to the proceedings is or is not thereby excluded from being the father of that person
 The curious wording of this portion of the section, particularly the words "is or is not thereby excluded" should be noted. As medical knowledge stands at present, the only conclusive blood test for paternity is "negative": that is, a particular man simply cannot be the father of a particular child. No other test is conclusive—that is, it cannot be made to yield a result which states positively that a given man is, indisputably, the father of a given child: the most it can do is to demonstrate, with varying degrees of conviction, that he might be. This level of probability varies according to what factors are found in the blood samples. If, for example, both the father and the child share some uncommon feature, the degree of probability rises almost to certainty:

if there are no special characteristics, the degree of probability can sink to as low as 50 per cent. in which case the court will have to look for supporting evidence elsewhere. These factors, therefore, give rise to the special terminology used in this subsection which is, that tests going conclusively to show that a man is not the father of a certain child are said to provide an "exclusion result"; while those which can indicate, with varying odds, only that he might be the father, are said to yield a "non-exclusion result".

This distinction is not always easily grasped and the point may need careful explaining to parties. Results which fall in the "non-exclusion" category should be acted upon cautiously—especially if the possibility of the man being the father is set on a low ratio. This accounts for the special directions given in sub-s. (4) of the section.

The "person" referred to, is, of course, the child of which the paternity is in issue. For the necessary approval or consents to the taking of a blood sample from such a person, see s. 21 (2) and (3), *post*.

See further Appendix III, paras. 9 and 10, *post*.

Any party alleged to be the father of that person
The expression "any party alleged to be the father of that person" is not to be construed in any number other than the singular. Apart from the natural law that a child may have only one father, the wording is deliberately directed against the citing of joint defendants in affiliation proceedings. Where a woman knows that the father of her child must be one, say, of two men, but does not know which of the two it is, then a blood test would tell her. Equally so, a man against whom such a claim is made might have reasonable cause to know that other men have been involved, and, were they to be joined with him in a blood test, a fairer judgment would follow. The Law Commission considered the attractiveness of this reasoning, but decided against it on the grounds that if it proved impossible to serve process on one of the defendants, or if one defendant failed to attend the hearing, the whole issue would be stultified since no blood test could be ordered on the absent party. Furthermore, if both results yielded a non-exclusion factor, the courts would be left with the insoluble problem of deciding, who, of two possible fathers, is to bear the responsibility. Apart from that, the two defendants might conspire to refuse to be tested. Were they to do so, the provision contained in s. 23, *post*, that the court may interpret such refusal as it sees fit, is rendered nugatory, since it is impossible to draw any conclusions which might operate against two people.

Or from any, or any two, of those persons
These words, which were added during the Committee stage (Commons), allow the court in the very rare case where it seems desirable, to order a two-way test—on the child and alleged father alone—or even a one-way test on either the child or the alleged father alone, where there are in existence records concerning the blood group of the other against which the sample tested can be checked.

Explaining the significance of the words, the Attorney-General said:

"When the Law Commission's Report, on which Part III of the Bill is based, was prepared, it was thought that for blood tests to yield any useful evidence it was necessary in every case to test all three parties [see Appendix III, para. 7, *post*]. It was known that it was possible to get an exclusion result from a test on the child and the alleged father alone, but it was then thought that the chances of obtaining such a result were so small as to be insignificant.

I am told, however, that medical science is advancing continuously and rapidly in this interesting sphere. After the Report was published and the Bill introduced it emerged that there was a better than 50 per cent. chance of obtaining an exclusion result from a two-way test—on the child and the alleged father alone. Moreover, the chances of success in such two-way tests are likely to increase as new blood groups are discovered.

It should be made clear that the chance of an exclusion result will probably never be as good from a two-way as from a three-way test and that no "inclusion" result of any significance can be obtained from a two-way test alone. It should also be made clear that the circumstances in which a court might want to direct a one-way test are at present barely conceivable; such a thing is merely a remote theoretical possibility. Thus, it is apparent that in the vast majority of cases the court will direct the ordinary three-way test; and especially so in affiliation proceedings, which will be the main type of case where the new power will be used.

Parliament does not legislate often in this sphere and, as science is advancing fast it would clearly be wrong for the Bill to insist rigidly on three-way tests if any possible cases can be envisaged where other kinds might be useful. To give some examples, which are admittedly rare cases, where two-way tests might be appropriate, I could cite, first, the case of where the mother is dead, is abroad or cannot be traced but where the issue of paternity arises in proceedings in which the child and the alleged father are involved. A second case is where the mother refuses to be tested but does not, or for some reason cannot properly, refuse for the child. Here the court can draw the appropriate inference from her refusal, but blood test evidence is preferable to mere inference. I am told that there may be other cases which cannot now be foreseen."

Revoke or vary
This automatically follows upon the preceding paragraph, and it is anticipated that it can usefully be exercised where the parties come to some agreement, or subsequent evidence indicates that there is something undesirable in the proceedings, *e.g.*, that it is merely a speculative action. It would also prove convenient should one of the parties be unable to be tested (*i.e.*, dies, falls ill or disappears) thus relieving the other parties from the obligation to be tested to no purpose and obviating unnecessary expense. The power to "vary" a direction may be used, for example, to deal with the case—unlikely, but made possible by the power to order two, or even one-way tests—where a mother has refused for herself but not for the child, and the court decides to order a test.

SUB-S. (2)
The person responsible
I.e., a person appointed by the Secretary of State under s. 22 (1) (*e*), *post*, who is expected to be a properly qualified serologist.

Shall . . . make a report
I.e., a report in the form prescribed under s. 22 (1) (*i*), *post*; see sub-s. (3) of this section.
It is anticipated that the results of blood tests will be set out in the form of a standard certificate, which will specify, together with reasons, whether the results exclude a putative father or go to support the presumption or the allegation that he could be (see para. (*b*) of this subsection). In the case of a non-exclusion result, there should be quoted statistics as to the incidence of other men who could equally as well be the father, were they also to be tested. The serologist will certainly be expected to suggest what weight ought to be attached to his findings—but see sub-s. (4) of this section. (See further Appendix III, para. 10, *post*.)

The report shall be received as evidence
It should be noted that while there is no discretion conferred upon the court as to whether the report should or should not be made admissible, its contents serve only as supporting and not conclusive evidence.

SUB-S. (4)
With the leave of the court
This is to prevent the persons responsible for carrying out the tests from being importuned for additional statements in circumstances where the standard report is quite adequate for the purposes of the proceedings.

Or shall
This will be useful in cases where the court itself feels that further and better particulars would assist it to come to a decision. Apart from that it may have some value in dealing with parties who are unnecessarily unco-operative, obstructive and parade a real or simulated inability to understand the evidence.

SUB-S. (5)
The special nature of the proceedings in which the issue of paternity is to be decided, and in which the results of blood tests are a vital factor, calls for a modification of established procedure. Since the physical presence of the court expert is, in most cases, neither convenient nor necessary, this Act contemplates the presentation of his evidence in written form only. In most instances this should be quite adequate, but where there are genuine doubts as to the certainty of his findings or as to what construction can safely be put upon them, it is only reasonable that the expert should be made available for oral examination. This is provided for in this subsection and the rules of evidence modified appropriately.
Cf. R.S.C. Ord. 40, r. 4.

Any person by whom anything necessary . . . was done
    In most cases, this would be the medical practitioner whom the Secretary of State is required to appoint for taking blood-samples. Evidence from such person might be required if doubts were cast upon the validity of the test on the grounds that the donor was ill or possibly suffering from a mental disability or even that the results of the tests were related to the wrong samples.

Shall be entitled to cross-examine him
    This removes the difficulty which would confront parties who might wish to challenge the validity of the blood tests. Since the serologist is not required automatically to appear in court (see sub-s. (2) of this section), the responsibility for securing his presence lies upon whichever party wishes to challenge his evidence. It is well-established however that a witness (other than a hostile witness) ought not to be cross-examined by the party calling him, yet this is exactly why he is to be called. A party may cross-examine his own witness should he prove hostile, but only if the judge gives permission, This would definitely be withheld on the grounds, for which there is ample authority that a hostile animus is not to be imputed to a witness simply because his evidence is unfavourable.

SUB-S. (6)
    This subsection provides that costs are to be borne by the party who asks the court to give the direction. The words "the amount paid shall be treated as costs incurred by him in the proceedings" are designed to exclude an application for a blood test from those matters which it is necessary to refer to an Area Committee for approval in legal aid proceedings; see the Legal Aid (General Regulations) 1962, S.I. 1962 No. 148, reg. 15 (5) as amended by S.I. 1962 No. 1714 (5 Halsbury's Statutory Instruments, title Courts (Part 1)).

DEFINITIONS
    For "blood sample", "blood tests" and "excluded", see s. 25, *post*.

21. Consents, etc., required for taking of blood samples

(1) Subject to the provisions of subsections (3) and (4) of this section, a blood sample which is required to be taken from any person for the purpose of giving effect to a direction under section 20 of this Act shall not be taken from that person except with his consent.

(2) The consent of a minor who has attained the age of sixteen years to the taking from himself of a blood sample shall be as effective as it would be if he were of full age; and where a minor has by virtue of this subsection given an effective consent to the taking of a blood sample it shall not be necessary to obtain any consent for it from any other person.

(3) A blood sample may be taken from a person under the age of sixteen years, not being such a person as is referred to in subsection (4) of this section, if the person who has the care and control of him consents.

(4) A blood sample may be taken from a person who is suffering from mental disorder within the meaning of the Mental Health Act 1959 and is incapable of understanding the nature and purpose of blood tests if the person who has the care and control of him consents and the medical practitioner in whose care he is has certified that the taking of a blood sample from him will not be prejudicial to his proper care and treatment.

(5) The foregoing provisions of this section are without prejudice to the provisions of section 23 of this Act.

GENERAL NOTE

This section preserves the right of an adult to refuse to give a blood sample in spite of a direction by the court under s. 20, *ante*. However, as to the inferences which may be drawn from such a refusal, see s. 23, *post*.

Some doubt has been expressed as to whether this subsection has removed from the court the power to order a minor aged 16 or over to undergo a test. It is not saved by the provisions of s. 8 (3), *ante*, because that section does not cover blood tests.

It is suggested that the power has, in fact, been removed. This is only reasonable since, in the case of affiliation proceedings, if the age of consent to sexual intercourse is 16, parties, if they refuse to give a blood sample must be prepared for all the consequences that follow—*i.e.*, the inferences derived under s. 23, *post*. In other cases, the most likely ground for resisting an order is to preserve the claims arising on the presumption of legitimacy and these are effectively dealt with in s. 23 (2), *post*.

COMMENCEMENT

This section had not been brought into force up to 17th April 1970.

SUB-S. (1)

His consent

The provisions of the Interpretation Act 1889, s. 1, apply and the consent of the mother or any female party is to be obtained. There is nothing in the provisions of s. 22 (1), *post*, suggesting that the consent is to take any special form. As to the consequences of a refusal of consent, see s. 23, *post*.

SUB-S. (2)

Attained the age of sixteen

As to when a person attains a given age, see s. 9, *ante*.

It shall not be necessary to obtain consent for it from any other person

This provision is necessary since the taking of blood samples for the purpose of determining paternity is not "any surgical, medical or dental treatment" within the meaning of s. 8, *ante*.

SUB-S. (3)

A child under the age of 16 cannot furnish an effective consent to a blood test: this must be made on its behalf by a parent or guardian.

The person who has the care and control

This will usually be the mother, but the expression can include a local authority, acting under the various powers conferred upon it by the Children and Young Person Acts—*e.g.*, the Children Act 1948, s. 2 (17 Halsbury's Statutes, 3rd Edn., 542). For the duties of a guardian *ad litem* in this respect, see *Re L.*, [1968] 1 All E.R. 20, C.A.

Cf. s. 23 (3), *post*.

SUB-S. (4)

The purpose of this subsection is to give practitioners clear guidance as to how they may act if one of the parties proves to be mentally handicapped. If the doctor taking the actual sample of blood becomes aware of the person's mental disorder and that he cannot give a valid consent, he can thereupon insist that those having responsibilities towards the patient act appropriately. If they refuse consent, this can be taken into account under the provisions of s. 23, *post*, which are expressly saved by sub-s. (5) of this section.

MENTAL HEALTH ACT 1959

119 Statutes Supp. For the meaning of "mental disorder" in that Act, see s. 4 thereof.

22. Power to provide for manner of giving effect to direction for use of blood tests

(1) The Secretary of State may by regulations make provision as to the manner of giving effect to directions under section 20 of this Act and, in particular, any such regulations may—

    (a) provide that blood samples shall not be taken except by such medical practitioners as may be appointed by the Secretary of State;

(b) regulate the taking, identification and transport of blood samples;

(c) require the production at the time when a blood sample is to be taken of such evidence of the identity of the person from whom it is to be taken as may be prescribed by the regulations;

(d) require any person from whom a blood sample is to be taken, or, in such cases as may be prescribed by the regulations, such other person as may be so prescribed, to state in writing whether he or the person from whom the sample is to be taken, as the case may be, has during such period as may be specified in the regulations suffered from any such illness as may be so specified or received a transfusion of blood;

(e) provide that blood tests shall not be carried out except by such persons, and at such places, as may be appointed by the Secretary of State;

(f) prescribe the blood tests to be carried out and the manner in which they are to be carried out;

(g) regulate the charges that may be made for the taking and testing of blood samples and for the making of a report to a court under section 20 of this Act;

(h) make provision for securing that so far as practicable the blood samples to be tested for the purpose of giving effect to a direction under section 20 of this Act are tested by the same person;

(i) prescribe the form of the report to be made to a court under section 20 of this Act.

(2) The power to make regulations under this section shall be exercisable by statutory instrument which shall be subject to annulment in pursuance of a resolution of either House of Parliament.

COMMENCEMENT
This section had not been brought into force up to 17th April 1970.

SUB-S. (1)

Secretary of State
Although this Act emanates from the Lord Chancellor's Office and is subject, in most cases, to his directions—see *e.g.*, s. 1 (5), *ante,* and s. 26 (3), *post,* these regulations are to be made by the Home Secretary. This is because the procedures will relate to proceedings in the magistrates' courts in respect of which responsibility lies on the Home Secretary rather than on the Lord Chancellor.

Paras. (a) and (b)
It is extremely important, not only that samples of blood should be correctly labelled and properly packed when being sent for testing, but also that equipment be sterile. For these reasons it is intended to set up panels of medical practitioners on a regional basis to one of whom parties would be referred by the court making the order which could at the same time arrange for him to be supplied with standard equipment. This would ensure uniform and accurate labelling and the use of the vital sterile apparatus. Hence a convenient service could be maintained without an excessive number of panels or practitioners.

Blood samples
For meaning, see s. 25, *post.*

Para. (c)

For the purposes of identification in the case of blood tests it will be necessary to provide for a careful check on identity, particularly as far as the child is concerned. It is anticipated that the parties, if not accompanied by their solicitors, will have to produce a photograph and this will ultimately be attached to the report. In the case of very young children, of whom photographs are not very reliable, some additional identification will be called for—possibly a footprint as well as a dated photograph. See s. 24, *post*, for the offence of impersonation under this Act.

Para. (d)

In rare cases the accuracy of some blood group tests can be affected if the person being tested has suffered from certain illnesses or received a blood transfusion—though this can usually be detected during the course of the tests. The declarations which are to be made under the regulations will be sent to the expert carrying out the tests who can then declare to what extent, if any, the validity of his findings is affected.

Paras. (e), (f), (h) and (i)

Regulations made under these paragraphs will ensure that blood testing in connection with paternity disputes will be undertaken at properly equipped centres and that competent parties will be responsible for them. They will also ensure uniformity in technique and procedure and that every source of error is eliminated as far as possible. See further Appendix III, para. 6, *post*.

SUB-S. (2): STATUTORY INSTRUMENT; SUBJECT TO ANNULMENT
See the note to s. 1, *ante*.

REGULATIONS UNDER THIS SECTION
No regulations had been made under this section up to 17th April 1970.

23. Failure to comply with direction for taking blood tests

(1) Where a court gives a direction under section 20 of this Act and any person fails to take any step required of him for the purpose of giving effect to the direction, the court may draw such inferences, if any, from that fact as appear proper in the circumstances.

(2) Where in any proceedings in which the paternity of any person falls to be determined by the court hearing the proceedings there is a presumption of law that that person is legitimate, then if—

(a) a direction is given under section 20 of this Act in those proceedings, and

(b) any party who is claiming any relief in the proceedings and who for the purpose of obtaining that relief is entitled to rely on the presumption fails to take any step required of him for the purpose of giving effect to the direction,

the court may adjourn the hearing for such period as it thinks fit to enable that party to take that step, and if at the end of that period he has failed without reasonable cause to take it the court may, without prejudice to subsection (1) of this section, dismiss his claim for relief notwithstanding the absence of evidence to rebut the presumption.

(3) Where any person named in a direction under section 20 of this Act fails to consent to the taking of a blood sample from himself or from any person named in the direction of whom he has the care and control, he shall be deemed for the purposes of this section to have failed to take a step required of him for the purpose of giving effect to the direction.

GENERAL NOTE
This section is in accordance with the recommendations of the Law Commission (Law Com. No. 16, paras. 39–47) that where a person refuses to comply with the court's direction the court should be entitled to draw whatever inferences it thinks appropriate from the refusal; and that where a person is applying for relief and is relying on the presumption of legitimacy, if he refuses to comply with the court's direction to submit to a blood test the court should have power to dismiss the application notwithstanding the presumption.

COMMENCEMENT
This section had not been brought into force up to 17th April 1970.

SUB-S. (1)
It should be noted that the power to draw inferences and act upon them as appears "proper" represents the limits of the sanction. This follows upon s. 20 (1), *ante,* whereby the court is authorised only to give "directions" and not make "orders". Consequently the penalties attached for disobedience to any order are not applicable. As to the penalties for impersonation and other frauds, see s. 24, *post.*

Any person fails to take any step required
There do not seem to be any religious bodies which object to blood samples being taken from their members. The texts most frequently quoted in this respect are Leviticus VII:27 and XIX:26; also Acts XV:29. It is suggested that at the most, they can be interpreted only as prohibitions against blood transfusion and are quite inapplicable to the taking of blood samples.
The only persons who are likely to object on medical grounds are those with blood disorders such as haemophilia. Even so, the taking of a blood sample is hardly likely to present any great hazard and it may be assumed that the person taking the sample as indicated in s. 22 (1) (*a*) would take all the necessary precautions.
See further sub-s. (3) of this section.

The court may draw
Note that the power to draw inferences is permissive, not mandatory. There will, no doubt be cases like *B.* v. *B.* and *E.* (*B. intervening*), [1969] All E.R. 1108, in which Lord Denning said: "I think that the husband can quite reasonably say that the established position is not to be put at hazard by a blood test. He is entitled to rely on the presumption of legitimacy. His refusal is quite reasonable. No adverse inference should be drawn against him by reason of it."

SUB-S. (2)
The purpose of this subsection is to prevent one of the parties to any dispute within the contemplation of this Part of the Act from enjoying a tactical advantage. Its effect is to suspend the presumption of legitimacy until the court's direction is complied with. See further p. 18, *ante.*

Presumption of law that that person is legitimate
See further, s. 26, *post.*

Para. (*b*)
It should be noted that the power to set aside the presumption of legitimacy, without supporting evidence, arises only if a party is seeking to rely on it for the purposes of maintenance or similar relief. Note also, that as in the previous subsection, the power is discretionary.
The topic was very fully discussed in the Report of the Law Com. No. 16; paras. 42–47.

SUB-S. (3)
This subsection was inserted during the Committee stage of the Bill to remove the possibility that a person who refuses to have a blood sample taken may contest that he has not refused to take any step required of him because he is only exercising a statutory right conferred on him by s. 21, *ante.*

Person
This includes a body corporate, *e.g.*, a local authority. Cf. s. 21 (3), *ante.*

Blood sample
For meaning, see s. 25, *post.*

24. Penalty for personating another, etc., for purpose of providing blood sample

If for the purpose of providing a blood sample for a test required to give effect to a direction under section 20 of this Act any person personates another, or proffers a child knowing that it is not the child named in the direction, he shall be liable—

    (*a*) on conviction on indictment, to imprisonment for a term not exceeding two years, or

    (*b*) on summary conviction, to a fine not exceeding £400.

COMMENCEMENT
    This section had not been brought into force up to 17th April 1970.

KNOWING
    There is authority for saying that, where a person deliberately refrains from making inquiries the results of which he might not care to have, this constitutes in law actual knowledge of the facts in question; see *Knox* v. *Boyd*, 1941 S.C. (J.) 82, at p. 86, and *Taylor's Central Garages (Exeter), Ltd.* v. *Roper* (1951), 115 J.P. 445, at pp. 449, 450, *per* Devlin, J.; and see also, in particular, *Mallon* v. *Allon*, [1963] 3 All E.R. 843; [1964] 1 Q.B. 385, at p. 847 and p. 394, respectively. However, mere neglect to ascertain what would have been found out by making reasonable enquiries is not tantamount to knowledge; see *Taylor's Central Garages (Exeter), Ltd.* v. *Roper, ubi supra, per* Devlin, J.; and cf. *London Computator, Ltd.* v. *Seymour*, [1944] 2 All E.R. 11; but see also *Mallon* v. *Allon, ubi supra,* and *Wallworth* v. *Balmer,* [1965] 3 All E.R. 721.

INDICTMENT
    The offence is triable in England and Wales by courts of quarter sessions; see the Criminal Law Act 1967, s. 8 (2) (163 Statutes Supp. 28).
    Note that there is no alternative of a fine. For appeal against sentence, see the Criminal Appeal Act 1968, s. 9 (172 Statutes Supp. 47). Since the sentence cannot exceed two years, the provisions of the Criminal Justice Act 1967 apply with regard to suspended sentences; see in particular s. 39 of that Act (163 Statutes Supp. 156–158).

SUMMARY CONVICTION
    Summary jurisdiction and procedure in England and Wales are now mainly governed by the Magistrates' Courts Act 1952 (32 Halsbury's Statutes, 2nd Edn., 416), and the Magistrates' Courts Act 1957 (37 Halsbury's Statutes, 2nd Edn., 626), and provisions in the Criminal Justice Act 1967 (163 Statutes Supp.).

DEFINITION
    For "blood sample", see s. 25, *post.*

25. Interpretation of Part III

In this Part of this Act the following expressions have the meanings hereby respectively assigned to them, that is to say—

    "blood samples" means blood taken for the purpose of blood tests;

    "blood tests" means blood tests carried out under this Part of this Act and includes any test made with the object of ascertaining the inheritable characteristics of blood;

    "excluded" means excluded subject to the occurrence of mutation.

COMMENCEMENT
    This section had not been brought into force up to 17th April 1970.

BLOOD TESTS
    See, generally, Appendix III, paras. 11–14, *post.*

EXCLUDED

This is very much a term of art which can be appreciated by referring to Appendix III, para. 4, *post*, and, in particular, to *F.* v. *F.*, [1968] 1 All E.R. 242.

PART IV

MISCELLANEOUS AND GENERAL

26. Rebuttal of presumption as to legitimacy and illegitimacy

Any presumption of law as to the legitimacy or illegitimacy of any person may in any civil proceedings be rebutted by evidence which shows that it is more probable than not that that person is illegitimate or legitimate, as the case may be, and it shall not be necessary to prove that fact beyond reasonable doubt in order to rebut the presumption.

GENERAL NOTE

This section implements the recommendations of the Law Commission (Law Com. No. 16, para. 69 (*a*)) that the presumption of legitimacy should be made rebuttable by proof on a balance of probabilities.

It is important to note that this section does not reverse the presumption. It only provides that the party seeking to displace the presumption does not have to prove his case, as it were, "beyond a shadow of doubt".

COMMENCEMENT

This section came into force on 1st January 1970; see s. 28 (3), *post*, and the note thereto.

ANY PRESUMPTION OF LAW

The presumption is that every child born of a married woman during the subsistence of the marriage is *prima facie* the child of her husband; and the presumption also extends to a child born to a widow or divorcee provided the period of conception falls within the possible limits. For cases on the presumption of legitimacy decided on the old strict standard of proof, see *R.* v. *Luffe*, [1803–13] All E.R. Rep. 726; *Banbury Peerage Case*, [1803–13] All E.R. Rep. 171; *Morris* v. *Davies*, [1835–42] All E.R. Rep. 270; *Piers* v. *Piers*, [1843–60] All E.R. Rep. 159; *Re Bromage*, [1935] All E.R. Rep. 80; *Re Jenion*, [1952] 1 All E.R. 1228; *W.* v. *W.*, [1953] 2 All E.R. 1013; *Cotton* v. *Cotton*, [1954] All E.R. 105; *Francis* v. *Francis*, [1959] 3 All E.R. 206; *Knowles* v. *Knowles*, [1962] 1 All E.R. 659; *Re L*, [1968] 1 All E.R. 20, C.A.

LEGITIMACY OR ILLEGITIMACY

This choice of words arises from the fact that while the presumption of legitimacy applies even where a husband and wife are living apart during the possible period of conception, a presumption of *illegitimacy* has to be made if they are living apart under a valid decree of judicial separation or a separation order and it is clear that the child must have been conceived after the decree or order was made.

REBUTTED BY EVIDENCE

In practice this means that the burden of proof lies upon those who claim that the presumptions of legitimacy or otherwise must be displaced. It is important to remember that the presumption is still a subsisting rule of law and that it is only the degree of proof which has been permitted to be set at a lower level than formerly. While it is predicted that the new standards implied in this section would prevail in a case such as that of *Watson* v. *Watson*, [1953] 2 All E.R. 1013, and in that of *Ah Chuck* v. *Needham*, [1931] N.Z.L.R. 559, the merits of the proof adduced in each case must be measured against the particular circumstances.

MORE PROBABLE THAN NOT

What constitutes "probability" is a matter of fact not of law: the case most frequently quoted when the "balance of probabilities" is under discussion is *Lancaster* v. *Blackwell Colliery Co.*, 12 B.W.C.C. 400 in which Lord Birkenhead said:

"If the facts which are proved give rise to conflicting inferences of equal degree of probability, so that the choice between them is a mere matter of conjecture, then

of course the applicant fails to prove his case, because it is plain that in these matters the onus is on the applicant. But where the known facts are not equally consistent, where there is ground for comparing and balancing probabilities as to their
respective value, and where a reasonable man might hold that the more probable
conclusion is that for which the applicant contends, then the arbitrator is justified
in drawing an inference in his favour."

IT SHALL NOT BE NECESSARY TO PROVE THAT FACT BEYOND REASONABLE
DOUBT
      It is submitted that a refusal by one of the parties to proceedings as are contem-
plated by this section to submit to a blood test as indicated in Part III, *ante*, would go.
a very long way to removing any doubts as to the legitimacy or illegitimacy of a person.
In cases where such evidence could not be taken—*e.g.*, where parties have died, a
greater reliance must be placed upon circumstantial evidence. Much of this, in the
past, has not measured up to the strict standards which were demanded, but it is submitted that this section would bring decisions different from those actually given in
cases such as *Bowen* v. *Norman*, [1938] 2 All E.R. 776 and *Cotton* v. *Cotton*, [1954] 2 All
E.R. 105.

27. Entry of father's name on registration of birth of illegitimate child

(1) In section 10 of the Births and Deaths Registration Act 1953 (which provides that the registrar shall not enter the name of any person as the father of
an illegitimate child except at the joint request of the mother and the person
acknowledging himself to be the father and requires that person to sign the
register together with the mother) for the words from "except" onwards there
shall be substituted the words "except—

> (*a*) at the joint request of the mother and the person acknowledging him-
> self to be the father of the child (in which case that person shall sign
> the register together with the mother) ; or
> (*b*) at the request of the mother on production of—
> > (i) a declaration in the prescribed form made by the mother stating
> > that the said person is the father of the child; and
> > (ii) a statutory declaration made by that person acknowledging him-
> > self to be the father of the child."

(2) If on the registration under Part I of the said Act of 1953 of the birth of
an illegitimate child no person has been entered in the register as the father,
the registrar may re-register the birth so as to show a person as the father—

> (*a*) at the joint request of the mother and of that person (in which case
> the mother and that person shall both sign the register in the presence
> of the registrar) ; or
> (*b*) at the request of the mother on production of—
> > (i) a declaration in the prescribed form made by the mother stating
> > that the person in question is the father of the child; and
> > (ii) a statutory declaration made by that person acknowledging him-
> > self to be the father of the child;

but no birth shall be re-registered as aforesaid except with the authority of the
Registrar General and any such re-registration shall be effected in such manner
as may be prescribed.

(3) A request under paragraph (*a*) or (*b*) of section 10 of the said Act of 1953
as amended by subsection (1) of this section may be included in a declaration
under section 9 of that Act (registration of birth pursuant to a declaration made

in another district) and, if a request under the said paragraph (*b*) is included in such a declaration, the documents mentioned in that paragraph shall be produced to the officer in whose presence the declaration is made and sent by him, together with the declaration, to the registrar.

(4) A request under paragraph (*a*) or (*b*) of subsection (2) of this section may, instead of being made to the registrar, be made by making and signing in the presence of and delivering to such officer as may be prescribed a written statement in the prescribed form and, in the case of a request under the said paragraph (*b*), producing to that officer the documents mentioned in that paragraph, and the officer shall send the statement together with the documents, if any, to the registrar; and thereupon that subsection shall have effect as if the request had been made to the registrar and, if the birth is re-registered pursuant to the request, the person or persons who signed the statement shall be treated as having signed the register as required by that subsection.

(5) This section shall be construed as one with the said Act of 1953; and in section 14 (1) (*a*) of that Act (re-registration of birth of legitimated person) the reference to section 10 of that Act shall include a reference to subsection (2) of this section.

GENERAL NOTE

This section enables the name of the father of an illegitimate child to be entered on the register of births, first, without the need for his attending personally to sign the register on the occasion of first registration, and secondly, also without his having to attend in person, on the occasion of the re-registration of a birth that has already been registered.

Cf. the Registration of Births, Deaths and Marriages (Scotland) Act 1965, s. 18; not printed in this work.

COMMENCEMENT

This section came into force on 1st January 1970; see s. 28 (2), *post*, and the note thereto.

SUB-S. (1)

Prior to the passing of this Act, there was no provision for a "late entry" of a father's name unless the child's birth was re-registered on legitimation. The present subsection now permits a registrar to enter up a father's name at any time and without the necessity for the father to attend in person. The limited provisions originally made were thought sometimes to prevent a father from acknowledging his child in this way and that if the two parents now wished the father's name to appear, its inclusion might certainly benefit the child.

Joint request

If the mother is dead this requirement cannot be met and no provision is made for a father wishing to acknowledge himself as the parent of his child under these conditions.

Shall sign the register

If both parents attend together, the person acknowledging himself to be the father is to sign before the mother does so; see the Registration of Births, Deaths and Marriages (Amendment) Regulations 1969, S.I. 1969 No. 1811, reg. 8.

Prescribed form

See the Registration of Births, Deaths and Marriages (Amendment) Regulations 1969, S.I. 1969 No. 1811, Sch. 2.

Statutory declaration

For statutory declarations in general, see the Statutory Declarations Act 1835 (12 Halsbury's Statutes, 3rd Edn., 804); and Interpretation Act 1889, s. 21 (24 Halsbury's Statutes, 2nd Edn., 222).

SUB-S. (2)

This subsection provides for the re-registration of the birth of an illegitimate child. The subsection differs from its Scottish counterpart in providing directly for re-registration and not for prior amendment of the original entry. The disadvantage of operating by way of amendment is that the method of correction laid down by the Registration Acts would give more than normal emphasis to the circumstances of the child's birth.

So as to show a person as the father

Note that the words are ". . . to show *a* person as the father . . ." and not ". . . *the* person . . .". This emphasises the fact that although a certain man's name is entered upon a register as the father of a given child, it indicates only that he acknowledges himself to be the father of the child and is not to be taken as conclusive proof of the fact that he actually procreated it. Thus, in *Re Stollery*, [1926] All E.R. Rep. 67, Lord Hanworth (quoting McCardie, J. in *Re Goodrich*, [1918] P. at p. 260) said: "I desire to add that neither the register nor the certificate are in any way conclusive, but only *prima facie* evidence of the facts to be established. . . . Evidence, however, can clearly be given to contradict them, and in a proper case, corroboration of them may be required."

Joint request

See the note to sub-s. (1) above.

Shall . . . sign the register

See the note to sub-s. (1) above.

Prescribed form

See the note to sub-s. (1) above.

Re-registration shall be effected in such manner as may be prescribed

See the Registration of Births, Deaths and Marriages (Amendment) Regulations 1969, S.I. 1969 No. 1811, regs. 4, 5.

SUB-S. (3)

Section 9 of the Act of 1953 provides the means whereby a qualified informant, unable to attend the office of the Registrar for the region in which the child was born, may remit the necessary particulars in writing.

SUB-S. (4)

This subsection provides the means whereby the father and mother of an illegitimate child, who perhaps are no longer living in the region in which the child was born, can arrange for the necessary information to be remitted in writing.

Delivering to such officer as may be prescribed

See the Registration of Births, Deaths and Marriages (Amendment) Regulations 1969, S.I. 1969 No. 1811, reg. 3.

28. Short title, interpretation, commencement and extent

(1) This Act may be cited as the Family Law Reform Act 1969.

(2) Except where the context otherwise requires, any reference in this Act to any enactment shall be construed as a reference to that enactment as amended, extended or applied by or under any other enactment, including this Act.

(3) This Act shall come into force on such date as the Lord Chancellor may appoint by order made by statutory instrument, and different dates may be appointed for the coming into force of different provisions.

(4) In this Act—

(*a*) section 1 and Schedule 1, so far as they amend the British Nationality Act 1948, have the same extent as that Act and are hereby declared for the purposes of section 3 (3) of the West Indies Act 1967 to extend to all the associated states;

(*b*) section 2, so far as it amends any provision of the Foreign Marriage Act 1892 or the Marriage with Foreigners Act 1906, has the same extent as that provision;

(*c*) sections 4 (5) and 6 (6), so far as they affect Part II of the Maintenance Orders Act 1950, extend to Scotland and Northern Ireland;

(*d*) section 10, so far as it relates to the Civil List Act 1952, extends to Scotland and Northern Ireland;

(*e*) section 11, so far as it relates to the Employers and Workmen Act 1875, extends to Scotland;

(*f*) section 13 extends to Northern Ireland;

(*g*) section 19 extends to Scotland;

but, save as aforesaid, this Act shall extend to England and Wales only.

SUB-S. (1)
    Family Law Reform Act 1969
      See Introduction, p. 20, *ante.*

SUB-S. (3)
    This Act shall come into force, etc.
      See the note "Orders under this section" below.

    Statutory Instrument
      For provisions as to statutory instruments generally, see the Statutory Instruments Act 1946 (36 Statutes Supp.).

BRITISH NATIONALITY ACT 1948
    1 Halsbury's Statutes (3rd Edn.) 861.

WEST INDIES ACT 1967, S. 3 (3)
    4 Halsbury's Statutes (3rd Edn.) 613.

FOREIGN MARRIAGE ACT 1892
    17 Halsbury's Statutes (3rd Edn.) 16.

MARRIAGE WITH FOREIGNERS ACT 1906
    17 Halsbury's Statutes (3rd Edn.) 31.

MAINTENANCE ORDERS ACT 1950, PART II
    125 Statutes Supp.

CIVIL LIST ACT 1952
    6 Halsbury's Statutes (3rd Edn.) 547.

EMPLOYERS AND WORKMEN ACT 1875
    12 Halsbury's Statutes (3rd Edn.) 23.

ORDERS UNDER THIS SECTION
    By the Family Law Reform Act 1969 (Commencement No. 1) Order 1969, S.I. 1969 No. 1140, Parts I, II and IV of, and the Schedules to, this Act came into force on 1st January 1970. It is anticipated that Part III will be brought into force sometime in 1970.

SCHEDULES

SCHEDULE 1

Section 1 (3)

STATUTORY PROVISIONS AMENDED BY SUBSTITUTING 18 FOR 21 YEARS

PART I

ENACTMENTS

	Short title	*Section*	*Subject matter*
c. 24.	The Tenures Abolition Act 1660.	Sections 8 and 9.	Custody of children under 21.
c. 22.	The Trade Union Act Amendment Act 1876.	Section 9.	Persons under 21 but above 16 eligible as members of trade union but not of committee of management etc.
c. 25.	The Friendly Societies Act 1896.	Section 36.	Persons under 21 eligible as members of society and branches but not of committee etc.
c. 18.	The Settled Land Act 1925.	Section 102 (5).	Management of land during minority.
c. 19.	The Trustee Act 1925.	Section 31 (1) (ii), (2) (i) (a) and (b).	Power to apply income for maintenance and to accumulate surplus income during a minority.
c. 20.	The Law of Property Act 1925.	Section 134 (1).	Restriction on executory limitations.
c. 49.	The Supreme Court of Judicature (Consolidation) Act 1925.	Section 165 (1).	Probate not to be granted to infant if appointed sole executor until he attains the age of 21 years.
c. 56.	The British Nationality Act 1948.	Section 32 (1) and (9).	Definition of "minor" and "full age" by reference to age of 21.
c. 44.	The Customs and Excise Act 1952.	Section 244 (2) (a).	Entry invalid unless made by person over 21.
c. 46.	The Hypnotism Act 1952.	Section 3.	Persons under 21 not to be hypnotised at public entertainment.
c. 63.	The Trustee Savings Banks Act 1954.	Section 23.	Payments to persons under 21.
c. 69.	The Sexual Offences Act 1956.	Section 38.	Power of court where person convicted of incest with girl under 21.
c. 5.	The Adoption Act 1958.	Section 57 (1).	Definition of "infant" by reference to age of 21.

Short title	Section	Subject matter
c. 22. The County Courts Act 1959.	Section 80.	Persons under 21 may sue for wages in same manner as if of full age.
c. 72. The Mental Health Act 1959.	Section 49 (4) (*c*).	Provision where nearest relative of patient is under 21.
	Section 51 (1).	Meaning of "nearest relative" of patient who has not attained the age of 21.
	Section 127 (2).	Rescinding order under s. 38 of Sexual Offences Act 1956 in case of girl under 21 who is a defective.
c. 37. The Building Societies Act 1962.	Section 9.	Persons under 21 eligible as members of building society but cannot vote or hold office.
	Section 47.	Receipts given to building society by persons under 21 to be valid.
c. 2. The Betting, Gaming and Lotteries Act 1963.	Section 22 (1) and (3).	Offence of sending betting advertisements to persons under 21.
c. 12. The Industrial and Provident Societies Act 1965.	Section 20.	Persons under 21 but above 16 eligible as members of society but not of committee etc.

Part II

Rules, Regulations etc.

Title	Provision	Subject matter
1927 S.R. & O. 1184; 1953 S.I. 264. The Supreme Court Funds Rules 1927 as amended by the Supreme Court Funds Rules 1953.	Rule 97 (1) (i).	Unclaimed moneys in court.
1929 S.R. & O. 1048. The Trustee Savings Banks Regulations 1929.	Regulation 28 (2).	Payments to persons under 21.
1933 S.R. & O. 1149. The Savings Certificates Regulations 1933.	Regulation 2 (1) (*a*).	Persons entitled to purchase and hold certificates.
	Regulation 21 (2).	Persons under disability.
1946 S.R. & O. 1156. The North of Scotland Hydro-Electric Board (Borrowing and Stock) Regulations 1946.	Regulation 36 (1) and (2).	Stock held by persons under 21.

Title	Provision	Subject matter
1949 S.I. 751. The Gas (Stock) Regulations 1949.	Regulation 19 (1) and (2).	Stock held by persons under 21.
1954 S.I. 796. The Non-Contentious Probate Rules 1954.	Rules 31 and 32.	Grants of probate on behalf of infant and where infant is co-executor.
1955 S.I. 1752. The South of Scotland Electricity Board (Borrowing and Stock) Regulations 1955.	Regulation 30 (1) and (2).	Stock held by persons under 21.
1956 S.I. 1657. The Premium Savings Bonds Regulations 1956.	Regulation 2 (1).	Persons entitled to purchase and hold bonds.
	Regulation 12 (2).	Persons under disability.
1957 S.I. 2228. The Electricity (Stock) Regulations 1957.	Regulation 22 (1) and (2).	Stock held by persons under 21.
1963 S.I. 935. The Exchange of Securities (General) Rules 1963.	Rule 1 (1).	Definition of "minor".
1965 S.I. 1420. The Government Stock Regulations 1965.	Regulation 14 (1), (2), (3) and (5).	Stock held by persons under 21.
1965 S.I. 1500. The County Court Funds Rules 1965.	Rule 36 (1) (b).	Unclaimed moneys in court.
1965 S.I. 1707. The Mayor's and City of London Court Funds Rules 1965.	Rule 25 (1) (b).	Unclaimed moneys in court.
1968 S.I. 2049. The Registration of Births, Deaths and Marriages Regulations 1968.	Regulation 63 and, in Schedule 1, Forms 15 to 18.	Forms of notice of marriage.

SCHEDULE 2

Section 1 (4)

Statutory Provisions Unaffected by Section 1

1. The Regency Acts 1937 to 1953.

2. The Representation of the People Acts (and any regulations, rules or other instruments thereunder), section 7 of the Parliamentary Elections Act 1695, section 57 of the Local Government Act 1933 and any statutory provision relating to muni-

cipal elections in the City of London within the meaning of section 167 (1) (a) of the Representation of the People Act 1949.

3. (*Repealed by the Finance Act* 1969, *Sch.* 21, *Pt. IV.*)

GENERAL NOTE
 Note that the Representation of the People Act 1969, s. 1, *ante*, has conferred the right to vote upon 18-year-olds; while the Finance Act 1969 (181 Statutes Supp.) has made the appropriate financial adjustments—as a consequence of which, para. (3) of this Schedule was repealed by s. 16 (1) of that Act.

SCHEDULE 3

Section 1 (4)

TRANSITIONAL PROVISIONS AND SAVINGS

Interpretation

1.—(1) In this Schedule "the principal section" means section 1 of this Act and "the commencement date" means the date on which that section comes into force.

(2) Subsection (7) of the principal section shall apply for the purposes of this Schedule as it applies for the purposes of that section.

Funds in court

2. Any order or directions in force immediately before the commencement date by virtue of—

(a) any rules of court or other statutory provision (including, in particular, section 174 of the County Courts Act 1959) relating to the control of money recovered by or otherwise payable to an infant in any proceedings; or

(b) section 19 of the Administration of Justice Act 1965 (control of money recovered by widow in fatal accident proceedings which are also brought for the benefit of an infant),

shall have effect as if any reference therein to the infant's attaining the age of twenty-one were a reference to his attaining the age of eighteen or, in relation to a person who by virtue of the principal section attains full age on the commencement date, to that date.

Wardship and custody orders

3.—(1) Any order in force immediately before the commencement date—

(a) making a person a ward of court; or

(b) under the Guardianship of Infants Acts 1886 and 1925, or under the Matrimonial Causes Act 1965 or any enactment repealed by that Act, for the custody of, or access to, any person,

which is expressed to continue in force until the person who is the subject of the order attains the age of twenty-one, or any age between eighteen and twenty-one, shall have effect as if the reference to his attaining that age were a reference to his attaining the age of eighteen or, in relation to a person who by virtue of the principal section attains full age on the commencement date, to that date.

(2) This paragraph is without prejudice to so much of any order as makes provision for the maintenance or education of a person after he has attained the age of eighteen.

Adoption orders

4. The principal section shall not prevent the making of an adoption order or provisional adoption order under the Adoption Act 1958 in respect of a person who has attained the age of eighteen if the application for the order was made before the commencement date, and in relation to any such case that Act shall have effect as if the principal section had not been enacted.

Power of trustees to apply income for maintenance of minor

5.—(1) The principal section shall not affect section 31 of the Trustee Act 1925—

    (a) in its application to any interest under an instrument made before the commencement date; or

    (b) in its application, by virtue of section 47 (1) (ii) of the Administration of Estates Act 1925, to the estate of an intestate (within the meaning of that Act) dying before that date.

(2) In any case in which (whether by virtue of this paragraph or paragraph 9 of this Schedule) trustees have power under subsection (1) (i) of the said section 31 to pay income to the parent or guardian of any person who has attained the age of eighteen, or to apply it for or towards the maintenance, education or benefit of any such person, they shall also have power to pay it to that person himself.

Personal representatives' powers during minority of beneficiary

6. The principal section shall not affect the meaning of "minority" in sections 33 (3) and 39 (1) of the Administration of Estates Act 1925 in the case of a beneficiary whose interest arises under a will or codicil made before the commencement date or on the death before that date of an intestate (within the meaning of that Act).

Accumulation periods

7. The change, by virtue of the principal section, in the construction of—

    (a) sections 164 to 166 of the Law of Property Act 1925;

    (b) section 13 (1) of the Perpetuities and Accumulations Act 1964,

(which lay down permissible periods for the accumulation of income under settlements and other dispositions) shall not invalidate any direction for accumulation in a settlement or other disposition made by a deed, will or other instrument which was made before the commencement date.

Limitation of actions

8. The change, by virtue of the principal section, in the construction of section 31 (2) of the Limitation Act 1939 (limitation in case of person under disability) shall not affect the time for bringing proceedings in respect of a cause of action which arose before the commencement date.

Statutory provisions incorporated in deeds, wills, etc.

9. The principal section shall not affect the construction of any statutory provision where it is incorporated in and has effect as part of any deed, will or other instrument the construction of which is not affected by that section.

THE CHILDREN AND YOUNG PERSONS ACT 1969

(1969 c. 54)

PRELIMINARY NOTE

This Act received the Royal Assent on 22nd October 1969, but is only partly in force. Orders under s. 73, *post* (see S.I. 1969 Nos. 1552, 1565, noted to that section) have so far brought into force most of the provisions of Part II of the Act, which provides the legal basis for the establishment of the new community home system and makes various amendments dealing with the fostering of children.

As for Part I of the Act, which relates to care proceedings, the abolition of approved schools, fit person orders, and the introduction of the new system of supervision, it was announced that it is intended to bring most of that Part into force on 1st October 1970 (see 790 H. of C. Official Report 188). However, only after close consultation with the police and the local authorities will ss. 4, 5 and 7 (1) (which relate to the prosecution of children and young persons and the minimum age for borstal training) be brought into operation. The date could be the same as for the remainder of Part I and in any case s. 4 will at first be made applicable only to children aged 10 and 11.

Only for intermediate treatment will there be made any provision for implementation on a local basis: otherwise the Act will be brought into force generally for the whole country.

In general, the Act applies only to England and Wales, but detailed provisions for the application of certain parts of the Act to Scotland, Northern Ireland, the Channel Islands and the Isle of Man are made by s. 73 (4)–(7), *post*.

ARRANGEMENT OF SECTIONS

Part I

CARE AND OTHER TREATMENT OF JUVENILES THROUGH COURT PROCEEDINGS

Care of children and young persons through juvenile courts

An Act to amend the law relating to children and young persons; and for purposes connected therewith   [22nd October 1969]

PART I

CARE AND OTHER TREATMENT OF JUVENILES THROUGH COURT PROCEEDINGS

Care of children and young persons through juvenile courts

1. Care proceedings in juvenile courts

(1) Any local authority, constable or authorised person who reasonably believes that there are grounds for making an order under this section in respect of a child or young person may, subject to section 2 (3) and (8) of this Act, bring him before a juvenile court.

(2) If the court before which a child or young person is brought under this section is of opinion that any of the following conditions is satisfied with respect to him, that is to say—

(a) his proper development is being avoidably prevented or neglected or his health is being avoidably impaired or neglected or he is being ill-treated; or

(b) it is probable that the condition set out in the preceding paragraph will be satisfied in his case, having regard to the fact that the court or another court has found that that condition is or was satisfied in the case of another child or young person who is or was a member of the household to which he belongs; or

(c) he is exposed to moral danger; or

(d) he is beyond the control of his parent or guardian; or

(e) he is of compulsory school age within the meaning of the Education Act 1944 and is not receiving efficient full-time education suitable to his age, ability and aptitude; or

(f) he is guilty of an offence, excluding homicide,

and also that he is in need of care or control which he is unlikely to receive unless the court makes an order under this section in respect of him, then, subject to the following provisions of this section and sections 2 and 3 of this Act, the court may if it thinks fit make such an order.

(3) The order which a court may make under this section in respect of a child or young person is—

(a) an order requiring his parent or guardian to enter into a recognisance to take proper care of him and exercise proper control over him; or

(b) a supervision order; or

(c) a care order (other than an interim order); or

(d) a hospital order within the meaning of Part V of the Mental Health Act 1959; or

(e) a guardianship order within the meaning of that Act.

(4) In any proceedings under this section the court may make orders in pursuance of paragraphs (c) and (d) of the preceding subsection but subject to

that shall not make more than one of the orders mentioned in the preceding subsection, without prejudice to any power to make a further order in subsequent proceedings of any description; and if in proceedings under this section the court makes one of those orders and an order so mentioned is already in force in respect of the child or young person in question, the court may discharge the earlier order unless it is a hospital or guardianship order.

(5) An order under this section shall not be made in respect of a child or young person—

> (*a*) in pursuance of paragraph (*a*) of subsection (3) of this section unless the parent or guardian in question consents;
>
> (*b*) in pursuance of paragraph (*d*) or (*e*) of that subsection unless the conditions which, under section 60 of the said Act of 1959, are required to be satisfied for the making of a hospital or guardianship order in respect of a person convicted as mentioned in that section are satisfied in his case so far as they are applicable;
>
> (*c*) if he has attained the age of sixteen and is or has been married.

(6) In this section "authorised person" means a person authorised by order of the Secretary of State to bring proceedings in pursuance of this section and any officer of a society which is so authorised, and in sections 2 and 3 of this Act "care proceedings" means proceedings in pursuance of this section and "relevant infant" means the child or young person in respect of whom such proceedings are brought or proposed to be brought.

GENERAL NOTE

> The whole heart of the Act is contained in this section, which provides that a court may make an order in respect of a child only if it is satisfied that one of the conditions specified in sub-s. (2) is present; and that the child or young person is in need of care and control which it is unlikely to receive unless the court makes the order.
>
> During the passage of the Act through Parliament, this section attracted more attention than any other. During the Committee proceedings in the Lords an amendment which cancelled the words "and also that he is in need of care and control which he is unlikely to receive unless the court makes an order under this section in respect of him" was carried by 68 votes to 28, but the deleted words were restored by the Commons.

COMMENCEMENT OF THIS SECTION

> See s. 73 (2), *post*, and the note thereto.

SUB-S. (1)

> This subsection replaces s. 62 (2) of the Children and Young Persons Act 1933 (repealed by s. 72 (4), Sch. 6, *post*).

> *Local authority*
>
> For meaning, see s. 70 (1), *post*; but note that in relation to sub-s. (2) (*e*) above, any reference to a local authority in this section is, by s. 2 (8), *post*, to be construed as a reference to a local education authority.

> *Constable*
>
> This means, of course, not a person holding the rank of constable in a police force, but a person holding the office of constable; cf. 30 Halsbury's Laws (3rd Edn.) 97. The hallmark of a constable is his attestation as such before a justice of the peace, or, in the case of the metropolitan police district, before the Commissioner or an Assistant Commissioner of Police of the Metropolis.
>
> Of present day constables, the member of a police force is the most important; see, generally, the Police Act 1964, ss. 7, 18, 19, Sch. 2 (148 Statutes Supp.). Other persons holding the office of constable are special constables appointed by the chief

officers of police of each police area in accordance with regulations (see the Police Act 1964, ss. 16, 18, 34, Sch. 2 (*ibid.*)); constables appointed by justices on the application of various bodies for the purpose of providing special protection for the interests of such bodies (30 Halsbury's Laws (3rd Edn.) 49); special constables appointed by justices on the nomination of the Defence Council or the Atomic Energy Authority (*ibid.*, p. 50); transport constables appointed by justices on the application of the British Transport Commission (*ibid.*); canal constables appointed by justices or the watch committee on the application of canals or navigable rivers (*i.e.*, usually the British Waterways Board) (*ibid.*, p. 51); harbour constables appointed by justices on the nomination of harbour, dock and pier authorities (*ibid.*); civil aviation constables appointed on the nomination of the Board of Trade (*ibid.*, p. 52); park constables appointed by local authorities and attested as constables before justices (*ibid.*); and university constables appointed by and attested before the chancellor or vice-chancellor of the universities of Oxford or Cambridge (*ibid.*).

Contrast the provision of sub-s. (1) of this section with s. 5 (9), *post*, by which the expression "qualified informant" in relation to the laying of informations against young persons includes not constables generally, but only "a police officer and a member of a designated police force acting in his capacity as such . . . officer or member".

Authorised person

For meaning, see sub-s. (6) of this section. Referring to this expression, the Government said, "As far as is known, no individual has ever been authorised to institute proceedings under s. 62 of the 1933 enactment, from which this provision is derived, and the only society authorised so far is the National Society for the Prevention of Cruelty to Children". The reference to the N.S.P.C.C. in fact includes three societies: the National Society, the Liverpool, and the Birkenhead and Wirral Societies for the Prevention of Cruelty to Children. At the time of the passing of the Act, it was indicated that it would be very unlikely for any other body to be so authorised.

Who reasonably believes

It is well-established that a belief may be supported by facts not only within the informant's own knowledge but also on information supplied by another—so long, of course, as it comes in such a way as to give it credibility: cf. *McArdle* v. *Egan*, [1933] All E.R. Rep. 611.

Order under this section

Note that generally only one order may subsist at a time—see sub-s. (4) of this section. Note the restrictions in sub-s. (5) of this section. For appeals, see s. 2 (12), *post*. For alternative proceedings, see s. 3 (7), *post*.

Child or young person

For meaning, see s. 70 (1), *post*. Note that, by virtue of sub-s. (5) (*c*) of this section, a young person who has attained the age of sixteen who is or has been married may not be brought or dealt with by a juvenile court under this section.

Subject to section 2 (3)

The reference to s. 2 (3) of this Act includes a reference to s. 34 (2), *post*, in the circumstances they specified.

Juvenile court

Juvenile courts in England and Wales are specially constituted magistrates' courts sitting for the purpose of hearing a charge against a child or young person or for the purpose of exercising any other jurisdiction conferred on them by or under any statute; see the Children and Young Persons Act 1933, s. 45 (17 Halsbury's Statutes (3rd Edn.) 468), in conjunction with the Children and Young Persons Act 1963, s. 17 (1), Sch. 2 (139 Statutes Supp.). As to juvenile courts generally, see 21 Halsbury's Laws (3rd Edn.) 330 *et seq.*, and as to their constitution, see the Juvenile Courts (Constitution) Rules 1954, S.I. 1954 No. 1711 and, in relation to London, the Juvenile Courts (London) Order 1965, S.I. 1965 No. 584, as amended by S.I. 1965 No. 1362 and S.I. 1968 No. 592. As to possible modifications to their constitution etc., see s. 61, *post*.

SUB-S. (2)

This subsection replaces the Children and Young Persons Act 1963, s. 2 (repealed by s. 72 (4), Sch. 6, *post*).

Any of the following conditions
Note that by the last leg of sub-s. (2), it is necessary not only that one of the conditions mentioned in paras. (a)–(e) is satisfied, but also that the child or young person is in need of care or control which he is unlikely to receive unless the court makes an order.

The court is satisfied
As care proceedings are civil proceedings, the standard of proof required is normally that of a preponderance of probabilities but note the exception in the case of condition (f) (the "offence condition") where, by virtue of s. 3 (3), *post*, the standard of proof required of the person bringing the proceedings is that required for criminal proceedings, viz., proof "beyond a reasonable doubt".

Para. (a)
This paragraph replaces s. 2 (2) (b) of the Act of 1963.
Avoidably. This expression was inserted to cover, for example, the situation where a child was suffering from a degenerate disease and could expect no proper development and nothing could be done to avoid it.
Health. This word is wide enough to include mental health and any affliction, impediment or disability and anything else calling for medical, surgical or dental treatment or nursing.
Ill-treated. This expression is new in this context although it appears in s. 1 (1) and s. 40 (1) (a) of the 1933 enactment. It may be taken that any course of conduct likely to cause injury to a child, whether such injury be mental or physical, would constitute "ill-treatment". It should be noted that both parents are equally culpable: it is no longer held that a wife is subservient to her husband and can take no blame for any neglect to her children. See *R.* v. *Watson and Watson*, [1959] Crim. L.R. 785.
It is submitted that this provision is wide enough to cover cases in which parents, because of their religious beliefs or from other prejudices refuse to consent to their children receiving certain forms of medical treatment: *e.g.*, injections, blood-transfusions—but see the Family Law Reform Act 1969, s. 8, *ante*.

Para. (b)
This was inserted during Report in the Lords. It may be compared with s. 2 (2) (d) and (e) of the 1963 Act (repealed). It was originally thought that paras. (a) and (c) of this subsection would be adequate, but it was pointed out that there were limitations. Situations wherein ill-treatment of one child presented a palpable hazard to other children in the household were not directly covered and it was decided that it ought to be made possible for the court to be able to make an order in respect of them as a preventive measure. In particular, there are some "battered baby" cases where, if something is not done there will be a very real danger that the same thing might happen to another baby in the household.
See also s. 2 (7), *post*.

Para. (c)
It is thought that the expression "moral danger "does not have an exclusively sexual connotation, but that it includes the danger of stealing, the danger of violence and other dangers of that kind. See *e.g., Bowers* v. *Smith*, [1953] 1 All E.R. 320, *per* Lord Goddard, C.J. "To say that, because three young adolescents who have just come to puberty have had intercourse with a disreputable girl when they were sexually excited and, perhaps, tempted by the girl, their parents have been guilty of not exercising proper care and attention seems to me to be going a great deal too far."
See also *Mohamed* v. *Knott*, [1968] 2 All E.R. 563 (way of life in which parties to the marriage had been brought up abroad should have been taken into account when considering whether wife was in moral danger).

Para. (d)
"Control" includes discipline; see s. 70 (1), *post*. "That word 'control' is to be construed as meaning capable of giving the child a proper upbringing, among other things." *per* Manson, J. in *Re Jepson* (1960), 32 W.W.R.—a Canadian case.
See also *Bowers* v. *Smith*, supra.

Parent
This expression is not defined. It is certainly apt to cover the father and mother of a legitimate child. It is also apt to include the mother of an illegitimate child; cf., in particular, *Re G. (an infant)*, [1956] 2 All E.R. 876, C.A., at p. 879, *per* Lord Evershed, M.R. The position of the natural father of an illegitimate child is more doubtful. Until 1959, unless the context otherwise required, he could not be regarded as a "parent" within the meaning of an Act of Parliament applying to England and Wales, for he had there no rights at all in relation to the child; see, in particular, *Re M. (an*

infant), [1955] 2 All E.R. 911; [1955] 2 Q.B. 479, C.A., at pp. 912, 913 and pp. 488, 489, respectively, *per* Denning, L.J. Now, however, by virtue of the Legitimacy Act 1959, s. 3 (119 Statutes Supp.), he has such rights and may be given the custody of the child. By the Family Law Reform Act 1969, s. 14 (see *ante*), an illegitimate child and his parents have the same right to share in each other's estates on intestacy as if the child were legitimate. In these circumstances it would seem that at least the natural father of an illegitimate child entitled to his custody may have to be regarded as a "parent" within the meaning of the Act.

It is plain that both the father and the mother of a juvenile can at the same time come within the statutory meaning of "parent". This being so, it is believed that, where there is a reference to the parent of a person or his parent and he has two parents, either parent alone constitutes "the parent" or "his parent" within the meaning of the Act. In fact such an interpretation seems to be required by the principle of equality between father and mother enunciated in the Guardianship of Infants Act 1925, s. 1 (17 Halsbury's Statutes (3rd Edn.) 424); cf. *Re Collins*, [1950] 1 All E.R. 1057; [1950] Ch. 498, C.A. It is also in accordance with the Interpretation Act 1889, s. 1 (1) (24 Halsbury's Statutes (2nd Edn.) 206) (under which unless the contrary intention appears, words in the singular include the plural and words in the plural include the singular) (cf., in particular, *Plunkett* v. *Alker*, [1954] 1 All E.R. 396; [1954] 1 Q.B. 420).

Guardian

By virtue of s. 70 (1), *post*, for meaning, see the Children and Young Persons Act 1933, s. 107 (1) (17 Halsbury's Statutes (3rd Edn.) 515).

Para. (*e*)

This paragraph was especially welcomed by several speakers who indicated that the entries on a class register of a child's absence could often be interpreted as clear signs of impending trouble.

Compulsory school age. By the Education Act 1944, s. 35 (11 Halsbury's Statutes (3rd Edn.) 194) compulsory school age is defined as "any age between five years and fifteen years", but provision is made for the upper age limit to be revised to sixteen by Order in Council (*ibid.*).

Efficient full-time education. This phrase is reproduced from the Education Act 1944, s. 40 (2) (11 Halsbury's Statutes (3rd Edn.) 200) which relates to the enforcement of school attendance. Sub-ss. (2)–(5) of that section are substituted by s. 72 (3), Sch. 5, para. 13, *post*, as from a day to be appointed.

The word "efficient" refers to the actual content of a child's education and not to the establishment providing it. Apart from wilful truancy on the part of a child the expression would be relevant in a case where a parent contended that he is providing the child with an education at home. If this is to be allowed to continue, it must be shown to be efficient. What the standard of efficiency is in such cases depends on facts and since usually only the education service can really decide, it follows that proceedings under this paragraph may be brought only by them—see s. 2 (8), *post*. See also *Bevan* v. *Shears*, [1911] 2 K.B. 936, for a commentary on "efficient".

Para. (*f*)

The provisions of s. 50 of the 1933 Act, as amended by that of 1963 provide that a child under the age of 10 in law cannot commit an offence. The word "offence" in this paragraph thus covers offences committed by children aged 10 upwards and by young persons.

By virtue of s. 4, *post*, no child (*i.e.*, a person aged 10 but under 14) may be *charged* with an offence. But s. 4 only removes certain consequences which would otherwise arise from the committing of an offence. The child's capacity to commit an offence is unaffected—he remains *doli capax*, and may still, for example, be arrested (see s. 28 (4), *post*).

For provisions supplementary to this para. see s. 3, *post*.

For the powers of a court upon a finding of guilt, see s. 7 (7), *post*.

As to the restrictions upon criminal proceedings in respect of young persons, see s. 5, *post*.

Offence

This is not defined and during Committee several expressions were mooted as alternatives. It was contended that the term was so wide that the most trivial offence could be used as a means of bringing a child to court so as to get him into the hands of the local authority. It was suggested, for example, that riding a bicycle on the pavement or bilking the railways of a small fare, could be utilised by an over-officious and too zealous child care officer as the means of making an order. However, a safeguard against such a possibility is provided by the second condition—that the child must be in need of care and control.

SUB-S. (3)

Referring to this subsection, the Home Secretary said that it gives the court three basic options which are available in all care and criminal proceedings. These options apply to all children up to the age of 17. The first option is to bind over parents. This is regarded as appropriate in cases where the court judges that the parents have grown slack and need pulling up. It is part of the principle and philosophy of this Act that where possible the responsibility should be put upon the family. It was hoped, said the Home Secretary, that the courts would use this option wherever they believed it to be the right treatment. Binding over is something like a conditional discharge or a suspended fine and he regarded it as important in that it brought the parents fully into the picture. The second option is the supervision order which is to take the place of probation orders and the present supervision orders. The third option is the care order which is very similar to the present so-called "fit person order". Both will be extremely flexible and embrace a wide range of possibilities. In addition, a hospital order or a guardianship order may be made in the case of a person suffering from mental disorder.

The cardinal principle behind the making of any order is that it should reflect the needs of the party in respect of whom it is made. Another principle is that it is for the court to decide the nature and the extent of the compulsory powers to be exercised and that, within well specified limits, the responsibility for decisions on treatment in individual cases should be placed on those who undertake the treatment. But in all cases there is the safeguard of appeal to quarter sessions (see s. 2 (12), *post*), and throughout the life of a care or a supervision order the Act provides a right to apply to the juvenile court for a revocation or variation of an order, with, again, an appeal to quarter sessions against a refusal of an application (see ss. 16 (8), 21 (4), *post*). The courts retain powers in criminal cases to fine (see ss. 6 (3), 34 (5), *post*), to order a conditional discharge or one that is absolute (see the Criminal Justice Act 1948, s. 7 (8 Halsbury's Statutes (3rd Edn.) 346), and (in the case of persons old enough to hold a licence) to order a disqualification or endorsement in motor vehicle cases (see the Road Traffic Act 1962, ss. 5, 7 (135 Statutes Supp.). Cf. also s. 7 (8), *post* (power of magistrates' court to make certain orders without remitting case to juvenile court).

Para. (a): Enter into a recognisance

This is derived largely from s. 62 (1) (c) of the 1933 Act (repealed) and s. 6 (1) (a) of that of 1963 (repealed). Note that there is a double duty imposed on the recognisant: to "take proper care" and also to "exercise proper control".

Note that the recognisance may not stipulate for more than £50; see s. 2 (13), *post*; nor may it be entered into without the consent of the recognisant. Its duration is for three years only or until the offender is 18, whichever is the earlier; see s. 2 (13), *post*.

See, generally, the Magistrates' Courts Act 1952, ss. 91 (1), (3), 92, 96, 98 (5) (14 Halsbury's Statutes (2nd Edn.) 493–495, 497); see further, the Magistrates' Courts Rules 1968, S.I. 1968 No. 1920, rr. 69 *et seq.*, and the Magistrates' Courts (Forms) Rules 1968, S.I. 1968 No. 1919, Sch., Forms 116 *et seq.*

Para. (b): Supervision order

This is derived from s. 62 (1) (d) of the 1933 Act (repealed). It was generally welcomed and described as one of the most imaginative parts of the Act. "Under the new arrangements the supervisor can direct the person supervised to engage in certain activities—it is wide open (see s. 12, *post*). And here is opportunity, of course, for a very imaginative kind of treatment. History tells us that very often new and imaginative proposals about the treatment of offenders begin in the juvenile courts and creep up into the adult courts. Those who are engaged in considering non-custodial treatment of adult offenders may have something to learn from what the supervisors are able to invent." (302 H. of L. Official Report 1186.)

For meaning of "supervision order" see s. 11, *post*, and for the general rules appertaining to them, see ss. 12 to 19, *post*.

Para. (c): care order

This replaces s. 57 of the Act of 1933 (power to send juvenile offenders to approved schools or to commit them to fit persons) and along with that section are repealed all the provisions contained in ss. 58 and 62 to 85 of that Act dealing with remand homes, approved schools, etc. (see s. 72 (4), Sch. 6, *post*).

The purpose of the new order is to put the child or young person entirely into the hands of the local authority which will then decide what is the best course to follow. The emphasis is thus on welfare and not on punishment. Under the old system, the court stipulated that an offender had to be sent to a specifically designated establishment—which then sometimes led to the undignified situation wherein a court was left with the magistrates' clerk telephoning seven or eight places to find out where there was accommodation.

For the meaning of "care order" see s. 20, *post*, and see generally ss. 20 to 24, *post*.

As to the "community home" system, which will play so important a part in this new development, see Part II(ss. 35–59), *post*.

Paras. (d) and (e) : *Hospital and guardianship orders*

These paragraphs enable a court, if satisfied on the written or oral evidence of two medical practitioners that the child or young person is suffering from mental illness, psychopathic disorder, subnormality or severe subnormality and that the disorders are of such a degree as to justify the person's detention in a hospital for treatment or being placed under the guardianship of a local authority to make orders accordingly.

Note that a person having attained the age of 16 and capable of expressing his own wishes may apply for admission to an institution as a "voluntary patient", see s. 5 of the Act of 1959.

Note also sub-s. (5) (b) of this section.

SUB-S. (4)

This subsection in general provides that the courts are not to make more than one of the orders mentioned in sub-s. (3) of this section. However, an exception is made for a care order and a hospital order to run concurrently. The court might rightly consider that a hospital order is appropriate but the child may have no parents or no effective parents so there will be nobody to visit him while in hospital or to receive him on discharge. The hospital order will naturally prevail over the care order as regards the place where the youngster is to reside for so long as the order is in force.

For the consequential amendments to the Mental Health Act 1959, see Sch. 5, paras. 37 to 41, *post*.

Earlier order

In addition to the orders mentioned in sub-s. (3) of this section, fit person orders (other than those committing a child or young person to a local authority), supervision orders and orders to enter into a recognisance, made under the Children and Young Persons Act 1933 (17 Halsbury's Statutes (3rd Edn.) 435) are deemed to be earlier orders within the meaning of sub-s. (4), by virtue of s. 72 (1), Sch. 4, para. 1, *post*.

SUB-S. (5)

This subsection qualifies the powers of the court in the case of recognisances, hospital orders and married persons.

Para. (a)

This paragraph replaces *inter alia*, s. 7 (2) of the Act of 1963. It is important to note that unless the parent or guardian consents—in other words, is willing to co-operate with the authorities—the order may not be made. For the terms of a recognisance, see Magistrates' Courts Act 1952, s. 54 (1) and (2). The consent, it is thought, should be included in the recitals: see *R* v. *Darlington Corpn. Juvenile Court, Ex parte Hartlepool Corpn.*, [1957] 1 All E.R. 398.

Para. (b) : *Unless the conditions . . . under s. 60 of the Act of* 1959 *. . . are satisfied*

These conditions are, in the case of a hospital order (i) that the court is satisfied that arrangements have been made for the admission of the person to the hospital in the event of the order being made and for his admission thereto within a period of 28 days beginning with the date of the making of the order (Mental Health Act 1959, s. 60 (3), 39 Halsbury's Statutes, 2nd Edn., 1014); and (ii) that the person is described by each of the practitioners whose evidence is taken into account as suffering from the same one form of mental disorder, whether or not he is also described by either of them as suffering from another form of disorder (*ibid.*, s. 60 (5), *ibid.*). In the case of a guardianship order the conditions are (i) that the court is satisfied that the local health authority or approved person is willing to receive the person into guardianship (*ibid.*, s. 60 (4) *ibid.*); and (ii) that the practitioners concur as in the case of a hospital order.

Para. (c)

There was a suggestion during the Committee proceedings in the Lords that this requirement was inconsistent with the purposes of the Act and that the words "or has been married" should be deleted. By so doing it was pointed out that cover would then, for example, be available to a girl who had been married at 16 and then almost immediately afterwards become widowed. She could not, of course, fall again beneath parental control, because it would be absurd to hold that marriage at 16 released the girl from parental control and widowhood revived it. The Government explained that in such tragic circumstances the local authorities had powers to give a girl advice, assistance and guidance and to arrange accommodation for her under s. 1 of the Children and Young Persons Act 1963. It was suggested that a girl who had married at 16 then was obliged to initiate divorce proceedings might be in some sort of moral danger: the Government submitted that such circumstances would be so unusual and would attract other aspects of the law, and in any case a petition for divorce could be presented within three years, only by leave of the court. Para. (c) is derived from s. 64 (1) of the 1963 Act (repealed).

Attained the age. By the Family Law Reform Act 1969, s. 9 (p. 61, *ante*) as from the coming into force of that section on 1st January 1970, a person is deemed to attain a given age at the commencement of the relevant anniversary of his birth.

Is or has been married. A void marriage is regarded as never having taken place; see, in particular, *De Reneville* v. *De Reneville*, [1948] 1 All E.R. 56; [1948] P. 100, at p. 60 and p. 111, respectively, *per* Lord Greene, M.R. On the other hand a voidable marriage is valid unless and until it is annulled; see, in particular, *De Reneville* v. *De Reneville, supra,* and *R.* v. *Algar*, [1953] 2 All E.R. 1381; [1954] 1 Q.B. 279. *Quaere* whether a person whose voidable marriage has been annulled "has been married"; cf., in particular, on the one hand, *G.* v. *M.* (1885), 10 A.C. 171, and *Newbould* v. *Attorney-General*, [1931] P. 75; [1931] All E.R. Rep. 377, and, on the other hand, *R.* v. *Algar, supra.*

DEFINITIONS
For "local authority", "child" and "young person", see s. 70 (1), *post.*

TRANSITIONAL PROVISIONS
As to the making of an order under this section where criminal proceedings were begun before the commencement of s. 4, *post,* and the person was found guilty of an offence, and by reason of that section could not have been charged with the offence on the date of the finding, see s. 72 (1) and Sch. 4, paras. 1, 2 (1), *post.*
See also the note "Earlier order" on p. 110.

EDUCATION ACT 1944
See 11 Halsbury's Statutes (3rd Edn.) 153 *et seq.*

MENTAL HEALTH ACT 1959, PART V, S. 60
See 39 Halsbury's Statutes (2nd Edn.) 1013–1034, 1013, 1014. Sub-s. (6) of s. 60 of that Act is amended, and, in part, repealed, by s. 72 (3), (4), Sch. 5, para. 40, Sch. 6, *post,* as from a day to be appointed.

ORDER OF THE SECRETARY OF STATE
See, generally, as to orders under this Act, s. 69, *post.* Note, in particular, as to orders made under sub-s. (6) of this section, sub-s. (1) of that section.
No orders had been made under sub-s. (5) of this section up to 1st May 1970.

2. Provisions supplementary to s. 1

(1) If a local authority receive information suggesting that there are grounds for bringing care proceedings in respect of a child or young person who resides or is found in their area, it shall be the duty of the authority to cause enquiries to be made into the case unless they are satisfied that such enquiries are unnecessary.

(2) If it appears to a local authority that there are grounds for bringing care proceedings in respect of a child or young person who resides or is found in their area, it shall be the duty of the authority to exercise their power under the preceding section to bring care proceedings in respect of him unless they are satisfied that it is neither in his interest nor the public interest to do so or that some other person is about to do so or to charge him with an offence.

(3) No care proceedings shall be begun by any person unless that person has given notice of the proceedings to the local authority for the area in which it appears to him that the relevant infant resides or, if it appears to him that the relevant infant does not reside in the area of a local authority, to the local authority for any area in which it appears to him that any circumstances giving rise to the proceedings arose; but the preceding provisions of this subsection shall not apply where the person by whom the notice would fall to be given is the local authority in question.

(4) Without prejudice to any power to issue a summons or warrant apart from this subsection, a justice may issue a summons or warrant for the purpose of securing the attendance of the relevant infant before the court in which care proceedings are brought or proposed to be brought in respect of him; but subsections (3) and (4) of section 47 of the Magistrates' Courts Act 1952 (which among other things restrict the circumstances in which a warrant may be issued) shall apply with the necessary modifications to a warrant under this subsection as they apply to a warrant under that section and as if in subsection (3) after the word "summons" there were inserted the words "cannot be served or".

(5) Where the relevant infant is arrested in pursuance of a warrant issued by virtue of the preceding subsection and cannot be brought immediately before the court aforesaid, the person in whose custody he is—

(a) may make arrangements for his detention in a place of safety for a period of not more than seventy-two hours from the time of the arrest (and it shall be lawful for him to be detained in pursuance of the arrangements); and

(b) shall within that period, unless within it the relevant infant is brought before the court aforesaid, bring him before a justice;

and the justice shall either make an interim order in respect of him or direct that he be released forthwith.

(6) Section 77 of the Magistrates' Courts Act 1952 (under which a summons or warrant may be issued to secure the attendance of a witness) shall apply to care proceedings as it applies to the hearing of a complaint.

(7) In determining whether the condition set out in subsection (2) (b) of the preceding section is satisfied in respect of the relevant infant, it shall be assumed that no order under that section is to be made in respect of him.

(8) In relation to the condition set out in subsection (2) (e) of the preceding section the references to a local authority in that section and subsections (1), (2) and (11) (b) of this section shall be construed as references to a local education authority; and in any care proceedings—

(a) the court shall not entertain an allegation that that condition is satisfied unless the proceedings are brought by a local education authority; and

(b) the said condition shall be deemed to be satisfied if the relevant infant is of the age mentioned in that condition and it is proved that he—

(i) is the subject of a school attendance order which is in force under section 37 of the Education Act 1944 and has not been complied with, or

(ii) is a registered pupil at a school which he is not attending regularly within the meaning of section 39 of that Act, or

(iii) is a person whom another person habitually wandering from place to place takes with him,

unless it is also proved that he is receiving the education mentioned in that condition;

but nothing in paragraph (*a*) of this subsection shall prevent any evidence from being considered in care proceedings for any purpose other than that of determining whether that condition is satisfied in respect of the relevant infant.

(9) If on application under this subsection to the court in which it is proposed to bring care proceedings in respect of a relevant infant who is not present before the court it appears to the court that he is under the age of five and either—

(*a*) it is proved to the satisfaction of the court, on oath or in such other manner as may be prescribed by rules under section 15 of the Justices of the Peace Act 1949, that notice of the proposal to bring the proceedings at the time and place at which the application is made was served on the parent or guardian of the relevant infant at what appears to the court to be a reasonable time before the making of the application; or

(*b*) it appears to the court that his parent or guardian is present before the court

the court may if it thinks fit, after giving the parent or guardian if he is present an opportunity to be heard, give a direction under this subsection in respect of the relevant infant; and a relevant infant in respect of whom such a direction is given by a court shall be deemed to have been brought before the court under section 1 of this Act at the time of the direction, and care proceedings in respect of him may be continued accordingly.

(10) If the court before which the relevant infant is brought in care proceedings is not in a position to decide what order, if any, ought to be made under the preceding section in respect of him, the court may make an interim order in respect of him.

(11) If it appears to the court before which the relevant infant is brought in care proceedings that he resides in a petty sessions area other than that for which the court acts, the court shall, unless it dismisses the case and subject to subsection (5) of the following section, direct that he be brought under the preceding section before a juvenile court acting for the petty sessions area in which he resides; and where the court so directs—

(*a*) it may make an interim order in respect of him and, if it does so, shall cause the clerk of the court to which the direction relates to be informed of the case;

(*b*) if the court does not make such an order it shall cause the local authority in whose area it appears to the court that the relevant infant resides to be informed of the case, and it shall be the duty of that authority to give effect to the direction within twenty-one days.

(12) The relevant infant may appeal to quarter sessions against any order made in respect of him under the preceding section except such an order as is mentioned in subsection (3) (*a*) of that section.

(13) Such an order as is mentioned in subsection (3) (*a*) of the preceding section shall not require the parent or guardian in question to enter into a recognisance for an amount exceeding fifty pounds or for a period exceeding three years or, where the relevant infant will attain the age of eighteen in a period shorter than three years, for a period exceeding that shorter period; and section 96 of the Magistrates' Courts Act 1952 (which relates to the forfeiture of recognisances) shall apply to a recognisance entered into in pursuance of such an order as it applies to a recognisance to keep the peace.

(14) For the purposes of this Act, care proceedings in respect of a relevant infant are begun when he is first brought before a juvenile court in pursuance of the preceding section in connection with the matter to which the proceedings relate.

GENERAL NOTE
> Except for the arrangements made in sub-s. (8) with regard to the "education cases", and in sub-ss. (6) (powers to secure the attendance of a witness) and (9) (proceedings in respect of a child under the age of five), the substance of the section is similar to existing law.

COMMENCEMENT OF THIS SECTION
> See s. 73 (2), *post*, and the note thereto.

SUB-S. (1)
> This corresponds with s. 2 of the Children and Young Persons (Amendment) Act 1952 (repealed by s. 72 (4), Sch. 6, *post*).

> *Resides*
> A person resides where in common parlance he lives, and a temporary absence is immaterial providing there is an intention to return and a house or lodging to which to return; see *R.* v. *St. Leonard's, Shoreditch (Inhabitants)* (1865), L.R. 1 Q.B. 21; *R.* v. *Glossop Union* (1866), L.R. 1 Q.B. 227. There is authority for saying that a person may be resident in more than one place at the same time; see *Levene* v. *Inland Revenue Comrs.*, [1928] All E.R. Rep. 746; [1928] A.C. 217, H.L., *per* Viscount Cave, L.C., at pp. 749 and 223, respectively, and *Langford Property Co., Ltd.* v. *Tureman*, [1949] 1 K.B. 29; *sub nom. Langford Property Co., Ltd.* v. *Athanassoglou*, [1948] 2 All E.R. 722, C.A.

> *Local authority*
> For meaning, see s. 70 (1), *post*; and note also sub-s. (8) of this section.

> *Information*
> *I.e.*, knowledge. This should not be confused with "an information" laid under the Magistrates' Courts Act 1952, s. 1 (1) (32 Halsbury's Statutes (2nd Edn.) 421).

> *Grounds*
> The grounds for bringing the proceedings in respect of a child or young person are set out in s. 1 (2), *ante*.

SUB-S. (2)
> This corresponds with s. 62 (2) of the Children and Young Persons Act 1933 (repealed by s. 72 (4), Sch. 6, *post*).

> *Neither in his interest nor the public interest*
> This expression was inserted on Report to meet a Committee suggestion that while "the interests of a child are paramount it nevertheless seems that if one has reached the stage when local authorities decide that there are grounds for bringing these proceedings, then they should not merely reject them on the basis that they do not consider that it is in the child's interests to take them, without considering, at the same time, the interest of the public as a whole."

Or to charge him with an offence
"It would be inappropriate to lay upon a local authority a duty to bring care proceedings in a case where the authority knew that the police intended to prosecute, and this additional phrase makes it clear that the local authority has no such duty in that case" (*per* the Home Secretary: 784 H. of C. Offical Report 1058).

By s. 4, *post*, a *child* may not be charged with any offence except homicide. For restrictions on bringing criminal proceedings against *young persons*, see s. 5, *post*.

SUB-S. (3)
This subsection incorporates material from s. 35 of the Children and Young Persons Act 1933 (repealed by s. 72 (4), Sch. 6, *post*).

Person
The persons who may bring care proceedings are defined by s. 1 (1), (6), *ante*, as any local authority or constable or any person authorised by order of the Secretary of State and any officer of a society which is so authorised.

Notice of proceedings
No form of notice is specified in this Act.

SUB-S. (4)
This subsection empowers a justice to issue a summons or warrant for the purpose of securing the attendance of a child or young person before the court in care proceedings. It applies, subject to appropriate modifications, sub-ss. (3) and (4) of s. 47 of the Magistrates' Courts Act 1952 to such a warrant. The effect is that a warrant may be issued only if the court is satisfied, by a statement on oath, that a summons cannot be served—for example, because the whereabouts of the supervised person are not known—or, in a case where the supervised person fails to attend the hearing, that a summons was served a reasonable time before the hearing.

Cf. s. 16 (2), *post*, which enacts similar provisions in relation to the variation or discharge of a supervision order.

SUB-S. (5)
This subsection deals with the situation where a child or young person is arrested in pursuance of such a warrant as is mentioned in sub-s. (4) of this section and cannot be brought immediately before the court. It requires him to be brought within 72 hours before a justice who has power to make an interim order or direct he be released.

Cannot be brought immediately before the court
Cf. s. 16 (3), *post*, which enacts a similar provision in relation to the variation or discharge of a supervision order.

Seventy-two hours
Juvenile courts do not sit daily and it may be some days before a person can be brought before it: it is only reasonable therefore that the warrant should constitute authority for the detention during a reasonable period before appearance can be arranged. It should specify where the person is to be detained during that period.

SUB-S. (7)
This is directly consequential upon s. 1 (2) (*b*), *ante*, and makes it clear that since the condition rests on a finding of probability this probability must be assessed in the light of what the court thinks would be more than likely to happen to the child if no order were made.

SUB-S. (8)
This replaces s. 40A of the Education Act 1944. S. 40 (2)–(5) of that Act are consequentially substituted by s. 72 (3), Sch. 5, para. 13, *post*.

Local education authority
For meaning, see the Education Act 1944, s. 114 (1) (11 Halsbury's Statutes (3rd Edn.) 257). By the London Government Act 1963, s. 30 (43 Halsbury's Statutes (2nd Edn.) 709) as from 1st April 1965 any reference in the Education Acts 1944 to 1968 or in any other Act to the local education authority is to be construed in relation to any outer London Borough (as defined by s. 1 (1) (*b*) of the Act of 1963 (43 Halsbury's Statutes (2nd Edn.) 670) as a reference to the Council of that Borough, and, subject

to *ibid.*, s. 30 (6), (7), *ibid.*, p. 711, in relation to the remainder of Greater London (as defined by *ibid.*, s. 2 (1)), *ibid.*, 672) as a reference to the Greater London Council acting by means of a special committee known as the Inner London Education Authority constituted as mentioned in *ibid.*, s. 30 (2), *ibid.*, p. 710.

Age mentioned in that condition
I.e., between the age of five and fifteen years. Cf. the notes "compulsory school age" and "attained the age" to s. 1, *ante.*

Not been complied with
For the effect of non-compliance with a school attendance order, see the Education Act 1944, s. 37 (5) (11 Halsbury's Statutes (3rd Edn.) 196).

Registered pupil
For meaning, see the Education Act 1944, s. 114 (1) (11 Halsbury's Statutes (3rd Edn.) 257).

School
By the Education Act 1944, s. 114 (1), (2) (11 Halsbury's Statutes (3rd Edn.) 258), "school" in that Act, in effect, means an institution for providing primary or secondary education or both, being a maintained school, an aided school, a special agreement school, an independent school or a direct grant school.

Person habitually wandering
This phrase refers to vagrants and is reproduced from the Education Act 1944, s. 40A, which was inserted in that Act by the Children and Young Persons Act 1963, s. 64, Sch. 3, para. 36 (139 Statutes Supp.). S. 40A of the 1944 Act is repealed by s. 72 (4), Sch. 6, *post*, as from a day to be appointed.
Cf. the Children and Young Persons Act 1933, s. 10 (17 Halsbury's Statutes (3rd Edn.) 443). A new sub-s. (1A) is inserted after sub-s. (1) of s. 10 of that Act, and sub-s. (2) of s. 10 thereof is, in part, repealed by, s. 72 (3), (4), Sch. 5, para. 2, Sch. 6, *post*. As to vagrants generally, see 10 Halsbury's Laws (3rd Edn.) 697 *et seq.*

Evidence
As to evidence in court proceedings, see the Evidence Act 1938 (125 Statutes Supp.); and the Civil Evidence Act 1968 (174 Statutes Supp.).

SUB-S. (9)
This subsection enables care proceedings to be brought in the case of a child under the age of five without his actually being present in court. The court is empowered to give a direction, the effect of which will be that a child less than five years old and not before the court during care proceedings on its behalf will be deemed to have been brought before it. The direction may only be given if the parents are present or, if they are not present, if it is proved that notice of the proceedings was served on them at a reasonable time before the making of the application for the direction. The parents, if they are present, are to be given the opportunity to be heard.
Note: the power is permissive, not mandatory. There is no question of the court being obliged to deal with the case in the child's absence unless it is satisfied that it would be proper to do so. There could be cases where it is alleged that the child is being ill-treated and the court might well decide that its physical presence would be essential.

Parent or guardian
See the notes to s. 1, *ante.*

SUB-S. (10)
This reproduces in part s. 67 (2) of the Children and Young Persons Act 1933 (repealed).

Interim order
For special provisions relating to interim orders, see s. 22, *post.*

SUB-S. (11)
This corresponds with ss. 35 (rep.) and 56 of the Children and Young Persons Act 1933.

Juvenile court
See the note to s. 1, *ante.*

Cause . . . to be informed
So much of sub-s. (11) (*a*) as requires the clerk to be informed applies also to a warrant issued pursuant to s. 22 (5), *post*; see s. 22 (6), *post*.

Clerk of the court
See the Magistrates' Courts Act 1952, s. 118 (32 Halsbury's Statutes (2nd Edn.) 513), in conjunction with the Administration of Justice Act 1964, s. 39 (2), Sch. III, para. 22 (4) (147 Statutes Supp.).
Cf. also the definition "justices' clerk" in the Justices of the Peace Act 1949, s. 15 (10) (64 Statutes Supp.), in conjunction with the Justices of the Peace Act 1968, s. 5 (180 Statutes Supp.), and note the Criminal Justice Act 1967, s. 104 (1) (163 Statutes Supp.).

Within twenty-one days
In calculating this period the *dies a quo* is not to be reckoned, see, in particular, *Goldsmiths' Co.* v. *West Metropolitan Rail. Co.*, [1904] 1 K.B. 1; [1900–3] All E.R. Rep. 667, C.A., and *Stewart* v. *Chapman*, [1951] 2 K.B. 792; [1951] 2 All E.R. 613 (and contrast *Hare* v. *Gocher*, [1962] 2 Q.B. 641; [1962] 2 All E.R. 763, and *Trow* v. *Ind Coope (West Midlands), Ltd.*, [1967] 2 Q.B. 899; [1967] 2 All E.R. 900, C.A.).
Note that under s. 3 (5), *post*, a finding that the offence condition is satisfied is binding upon the court to which the case is remitted.

SUB-S. 12: QUARTER SESSIONS
This expression is defined by the Interpretation Act 1889, s. 13 (14) (24 Halsbury's Statutes (2nd Edn.) 215), in conjunction with the Criminal Justice Administration Act 1956 (94 Statutes Supp.), and the Administration of Justice Act 1964, s. 2 (3) (147 Statutes Supp.). Note also s. 3 (7), *post*. Provision for appeal to quarter sessions is also made in relation to care proceedings by s. 16 (6), *post*. For provisions as to procedure on appeal, see the Magistrates' Courts Act 1952, ss. 83 *et seq.* (32 Halsbury's Statutes (2nd Edn.) 484 *et seq.*) and the Magistrates' Courts Rules 1968, S.I. 1968 No. 1920, rr. 62–64.

SUB-S. (13)
This corresponds with s. 55 of the Children and Young Persons Act 1933 (repealed in part by s. 72 (4), Sch. 6, *post*).

Fifty pounds
It is unusual for an Act of Parliament to set a limit to the amount of recognisance: normally it is left to the discretion of the court. The Government was induced to set a fixed sum as maximum.

"When we are discussing the power of the court to bind over parents we must remember that it will do so in an attempt to bring home to parents the need to exercise responsibility over their children. But any court, let alone any parent, knows that parents cannot be with their children all the time. For example, if a child were to commit an offence on the way to or from school, the court could not properly consider that a parent had failed to exercise due care and control to an extent that would require him to forfeit the recognisance into which he had entered at the request of the court, and with his own consent." (303 H. of L. Official Report 830.)

Enter into a recognisance
See the note to s. 1, *ante*.

Attain the age
Cf. the note "attained the age" to s. 1, *ante*.

SUB-S. (14)
This subsection establishes a convenient point from which to date care proceedings. It will be useful when considering such things as the time from which certain orders are deemed to run or whether time spent in a community home before proceedings are begun is to be taken into account—see, *e.g.* s. 3 (1) (*b*), *post*.

DEFINITIONS
For "local authority", "child", "young person", "resides", "petty sessions area", see s. 70 (1), *post*; for "interim order", see s. 20 (1), *post*; for "relevant infant" and "care proceedings", see s. 1 (6), *ante*.

MAGISTRATES' COURTS ACT 1952, SS. 47, 77, 96
See 32 Halsbury's Statutes (2nd Edn.) 459, 480, 497.

EDUCATION ACT 1944, SS. 37, 39
See 11 Halsbury's Statutes (3rd Edn.) 196–199.

3. Further supplementary provisions relating to s. 1 (2) (f)

(1) In any care proceedings, no account shall be taken for the purposes of the condition set out in paragraph (*f*) of subsection (2) of section 1 of this Act (hereafter in this section referred to as "the offence condition") of an offence alleged to have been committed by the relevant infant if—

    (*a*) in any previous care proceedings in respect of him it was alleged that the offence condition was satisfied in consequence of the offence; or

    (*b*) the offence is a summary offence within the meaning of the Magistrates' Courts Act 1952 and, disregarding section 4 of this Act, the period for beginning summary proceedings in respect of it expired before the care proceedings were begun; or

    (*c*) disregarding section 4 of this Act, he would if charged with the offence be entitled to be discharged under any rule of law relating to previous acquittal or conviction.

(2) In any care proceedings the court shall not entertain an allegation that the offence condition is satisfied in respect of the relevant infant unless the proceedings are brought by a local authority or a constable; but nothing in this or the preceding subsection shall prevent any evidence from being considered in care proceedings for any purpose other than that of determining whether the offence condition is satisfied in respect of the relevant infant.

(3) If in any care proceedings the relevant infant is alleged to have committed an offence in consequence of which the offence condition is satisfied with respect to him, the court shall not find the offence condition satisfied in consequence of the offence unless, disregarding section 4 of this Act, it would have found him guilty of the offence if the proceedings had been in pursuance of an information duly charging him with the offence and the court had had jurisdiction to try the information; and without prejudice to the preceding provisions of this subsection the same proof shall be required to substantiate or refute an allegation that the offence condition is satisfied in consequence of an offence as is required to warrant a finding of guilty, or as the case may be, of not guilty of the offence.

(4) A person shall not be charged with an offence if in care proceedings previously brought in respect of him it was alleged that the offence condition was satisfied in consequence of that offence.

(5) If in any care proceedings in which it is alleged that the offence condition is satisfied in respect of the relevant infant it appears to the court that the case falls to be remitted to another court in pursuance of subsection (11) of the preceding section but that it is appropriate to determine whether the condition is satisfied before remitting the case, the court may determine accordingly; and any determination under this subsection shall be binding on the court to which the case is remitted.

(6) Where in any care proceedings the court finds the offence condition satisfied with respect to the relevant infant in consequence of an indictable offence within the meaning of the Magistrates' Courts Act 1952 then, whether or not the court makes an order under section 1 of this Act—

(a) section 34 of that Act (which relates to compensation for loss of property or damage to it) shall apply as if the finding were a finding of guilty of the offence and as if the maximum amount of an award under that section were one hundred pounds; and

(b) the court shall if the relevant infant is a child, and may if he is not, order any sum awarded by virtue of this subsection to be paid by his parent or guardian instead of by him unless it is satisfied that the parent or guardian cannot be found or has not conduced to the commission of the offence by neglecting to exercise due care or control of him, so however that an order shall not be made in pursuance of this paragraph unless the parent or guardian has been given an opportunity of being heard or has been required to attend the proceedings and failed to do so; and

(c) any sum payable by a parent or guardian by virtue of the preceding paragraph may be recovered from him in like manner as if he had been convicted of the offence in question;

but where the finding in question is made in pursuance of the preceding subsection, the powers conferred by this subsection shall be exercisable by the court to which the case is remitted instead of by the court which made the finding.

For the purposes of this subsection an offence under section 14 (1) of the Criminal Justice Administration Act 1914 (which provides for damage committed wilfully or maliciously to be punishable on summary conviction) shall be treated as an indictable offence within the meaning of the said Act of 1952.

(7) Where in any care proceedings the court finds the offence condition satisfied with respect to the relevant infant and he is a young person, the court may if it thinks fit and he consents, instead of making such an order as is mentioned in section 1 (3) of this Act, order him to enter into a recognisance for an amount not exceeding twenty-five pounds and for a period not exceeding one year to keep the peace or to be of good behaviour; and such an order shall be deemed to be an order under section 1 of this Act but no appeal to quarter sessions may be brought against an order under this subsection.

(8) Where in any care proceedings the court finds the offence condition satisfied with respect to the relevant infant in consequence of an offence which was not admitted by him before the court, then—

(a) if the finding is made in pursuance of subsection (5) of this section and the court to which the case is remitted decides not to make any order under section 1 of this Act in respect of the relevant infant; or

(b) if the finding is not made in pursuance of that subsection and the court decides as aforesaid.

the relevant infant may appeal to quarter sessions against the finding, and in a case falling within paragraph (a) of this subsection any notice of appeal shall be given within fourteen days after the date of the decision mentioned in that paragraph; and a person ordered to pay compensation by virtue of subsection (6) of this section may appeal to quarter sessions against the order.

(9) An appeal in pursuance of the preceding subsection or subsection (12) of the preceding section against an order made by a court in consequence of a finding made by another court by virtue of subsection (5) of this section shall lie to the same quarter sessions as would have had jurisdiction to entertain an appeal under subsection (8) of this section against the finding if the court had decided not to make any order.

GENERAL NOTE
It should be noted that there is no provision in this section limiting the time within which proceedings must be brought against a child after the identity of the alleged offender first comes to the knowledge of the prosecutor.

It should also be noted that the court which finds the "offence condition" satisfied need not necessarily make the appropriate order (see sub-s. (5)).

COMMENCEMENT OF THIS SECTION
See s. 73 (2), *post*, and the note thereto.

SUB-S. (1)
Care proceedings
For meaning, see s. 1 (6), *ante*.

Summary offence
By virtue of sub-s. (1) (*b*) of this section, for meaning, see the Magistrates' Courts Act 1952, s. 125 (1) (32 Halsbury's Statutes (2nd Edn.) 518). "Offence" means, in the words of Macnaghten, J., in *Horsfield* v. *Brown*, [1932] 1 K.B. 355, at p. 367, "an act or omission punishable under the criminal law".

Period . . . expired
As to the time limit for commencing summary proceedings, see the Magistrates' Courts Act 1952, s. 104 (125 Statutes Supp.).

Summary proceedings
Summary jurisdiction and procedure in England and Wales are now mainly governed by the Magistrates' Courts Acts, 1952 and 1957, *i.e.*, the Magistrates' Courts Act 1952 (125 Statutes Supp.) and the Magistrates' Courts Act 1957 (104 Statutes Supp.), though amendments are made by provisions in the Criminal Justice Act 1967 (163 Statutes Supp.).

Begun
As to when care proceedings are deemed to have begun, see s. 2 (14), *ante*.

Rule of law relating to previous acquittal or conviction
For the grounds on which pleas of *autrefois acquit* and *autrefois convict* can succeed, see 10 Halsbury's Laws (3rd Edn.) 406.

SUB-S. (2)
This subsection provides that only a local authority or a constable can bring care proceedings on the grounds that the "offence condition" is satisfied. However, the N.S.P.C.C. are not precluded from bringing evidence of transgressions which would be relevant to any of the considerations mentioned in paras. (*a*) to (*e*) of s. 1 (2).

Note that neither an "authorised person" as defined in s. 1 (6), *ante*, nor a "local education authority" (see s. 2 (5), *ante*) may bring care proceedings on the ground that the "offence condition" is satisfied. For meaning of "local authority" see s. 70 (1), *post*, and for "constable", see the note to s. 1, *ante*.

Evidence
See the note to s. 2, *ante*.

SUB-S. (3)
This subsection provides that for the offence condition to be satisfied the burden of proof is to be the same as in criminal proceedings, and that the law of evidence in this con-

nection will operate in exactly the same way as in criminal proceedings. However, except in relation to the allegation of an offence, the law applicable to the proceedings will be the same as that applicable in civil proceedings generally.

Guilty of an offence
Cf. the note "guilty of an offence" to s. 1, *ante*.

Information
See the note "Laying an information" to s. 5, *post*.

Jurisdiction
Jurisdiction may be given by a statute by implication; see *Cullen* v. *Trimble* (1872), L.R. 7 Q.B. 416, and *Johnson* v. *Colam* (1875), L.R. 10 Q.B. 544.

Proof
As care proceedings are civil proceedings, the standard of proof required of the person bringing the proceedings is normally that of a preponderance of probabilities, but by sub-s. (3) of this section, the standard required to prove the "offence condition" is to be the standard required for criminal proceedings, viz., proof "beyond reasonable doubt".

SUB-S. (4)
A person
I.e., a "relevant infant" as defined in s. 1 (6), *ante*.

Any determination
As to the right of appeal to quarter sessions where a finding (*i.e.*, a determination) is made in pursuance of this subsection and the court to which the case is remitted decides not to make any order under s. 1, *ante*, see sub-ss. (8), (9) of this section. As to the right to appeal against an order made as a result of such a finding, see s. 2 (12), *ante*, in conjunction with sub-s. (9) of this section.

SUB-S. (5)
Note also sub-s. (9) of this section.

SUB-SS. (6) AND (7)
These subsections provide that where the offence condition is satisfied in care proceedings and the offence is an indictable one, s. 34 of the Magistrates' Courts Act 1952 (which enables magistrates to make compensation orders in criminal proceedings) is to apply, subject to a maximum of £100. The maximum in the Act of 1952 is £400, but since in the great majority of cases the compensation ordered by the court would have to be paid by the parents, the limit is fixed at £100.

Parent or guardian
See the note to s. 1, *ante*.

Enter into a recognisance
See the note to s. 1, *ante*.

Quarter sessions
See the note to s. 2, *ante*.

SUB-S. (8): WITHIN FOURTEEN DAYS
Cf. the note "within twenty-one days" to s. 2, *ante*.

SUB-S. (9)
This subsection provides that where one court finds the offence proved by virtue of sub-s. (5) of this section and the case is remitted to another court which makes an order, any appeal against the order is to quarter sessions for the area of the court proving the offence and not of the court making the order.

DEFINITION
For "child", see s. 70 (1), *post*; for "relevant infant", see s. 1 (6), *ante*.

MAGISTRATES' COURTS ACT 1952
See 32 Halsbury's Statutes (2nd Edn.) 416 *et seq*. For the meaning of "indictable offence" in that Act, see s. 125 thereof, *ibid.*, 518.

CRIMINAL JUSTICE ADMINISTRATION ACT 1914, S. 14 (1)
See 32 Halsbury's Statutes (2nd Edn.) 912.

Consequential changes in criminal proceedings etc.

4. Prohibition of criminal proceedings for offences by children

A person shall not be charged with an offence, except homicide, by reason of anything done or omitted while he was a child.

GENERAL NOTE

This section, one of the most imortant in the Act, reflects the philosophy that children who commit crimes are more in need of care and protection than punishment and that the procedure that is followed with regard to children who are neglected or badly treated is just as appropriate for those who commit offences.

As from the coming into force of this section, criminal proceedings will not be possible (except in the case of homicide) against a child, and no criminal act by a child will be recorded against him as a "finding of guilt", since by s. 72 (4), Sch. 6, *post*, the Children and Young Persons Act 1933, s. 59 (1) (17 Halsbury's Statutes (3rd Edn.) 476) is to be repealed in relation to children. However, it will still be possible to arrest a child (see s. 28 (4), *post*).

It is recognised that to bring this provision into operation immediately would throw far too heavy a burden on the local authorities and so the implementation will be carefully phased. It is intended initially to apply it to children aged 10 and 11, and to postpone the full implementation of the section until the local authorities have all the manpower and resources needed to cope with the new system. See the Under-Secretary's statement on p. 24, *ante*.

Note that s. 34 (7), *post*, provides that an order applying this section to children of 12 or 13 will require an affirmative resolution of both Houses of Parliament. "There is no intention", said the Government, "of rushing these provisions into operation before the necessary resources are available."

COMMENCEMENT OF THIS SECTION

See s. 73 (2), *post*, and the note thereto.

EXCEPT HOMICIDE

Homicide is a crime rarely committed by children and on an average, the numbers are less than one a year. Its commission is invariably indicative of a severely disturbed personality. This might require the child to be kept in detention for a very long period—extending, possibly, beyond its 19th birthday, which is the latest possible date upon which a care order may expire. This is certainly not a matter which can be left to a magistrates' court; it is appropriate for trial by judge and jury.

The expression "homicide" includes murder, manslaughter and infanticide; see 10 Halsbury's Laws (3rd Edn.) 704 *et seq.*

CHILD

I.e., a person under the age of 14; see s. 70 (1), *post*.

Note, however, that by s. 34 (1), (4), *post*, the Secretary of State may by order provide that "child" in this section shall be construed as excluding a child who has attained such age as may be specified in the order, not being under ten. Note also s. 34 (7), *post*.

SAVING

Note that by Sch. 4, para. 2 (2), *post*, nothing in this section is to be construed as preventing any act or omission which occurred abroad from being a civil offence under the Army Act 1955 (35 Halsbury's Statutes (2nd Edn.) 443), the Air Force Act 1955 (35 Halsbury's Statutes (2nd Edn.) 608, or the Naval Discipline Act 1957 (37 Halsbury's Statutes (2nd Edn.) 948).

TRANSITIONAL PROVISIONS

As to the position where proceedings were commenced before the commencement of this section, and the date of the finding occurred after its commencement, see Sch. 4, para. 2 (1), *post*.

See also the second para. of the note "Child" above.

5. Restrictions on criminal proceedings for offences by young persons

(1) A person other than a qualified informant shall not lay an information in respect of an offence if the alleged offender is a young person.

(2) A qualified informant shall not lay an information in respect of an offence if the alleged offender is a young person unless the informant is of opinion that the case is of a description prescribed in pursuance of subsection (4) of this section and that it would not be adequate for the case to be dealt with by a parent, teacher or other person or by means of a caution from a constable or through an exercise of the powers of a local authority or other body not involving court proceedings or by means of proceedings under section 1 of this Act.

(3) A qualified informant shall not come to a decision in pursuance of the preceding subsection to lay an information unless—

    (a) he has told the appropriate local authority that the laying of the information is being considered and has asked for any observations which the authority may wish to make on the case to the informant; and

    (b) the authority either have notified the informant that they do not wish to make such observations or have not made any during the period or extended period indicated by the informant as that which in the circumstances he considers reasonable for the purpose or the informant has considered the observations made by the authority during that period;

but the informant shall be entitled to disregard the foregoing provisions of this subsection in any case in which it appears to him that the requirements of the preceding subsection are satisfied and will continue to be satisfied notwithstanding any observations which might be made in pursuance of this subsection.

(4) The Secretary of State may make regulations specifying, by reference to such considerations as he thinks fit, the descriptions of cases in which a qualified informant may lay an information in respect of an offence if the alleged offender is a young person; but no regulations shall be made under this subsection unless a draft of the regulations has been approved by a resolution of each House of Parliament.

(5) An information laid by a qualified informant in a case where the informant has reason to believe that the alleged offender is a young person shall be in writing and shall—

    (a) state the alleged offender's age to the best of the informant's knowledge; and

    (b) contain a certificate signed by the informant stating that the requirements of subsections (2) and (3) of this section are satisfied with respect to the case or that the case is one in which the requirements of the said subsection (2) are satisfied and the informant is entitled to disregard the requirements of the said subsection (3).

(6) If at the time when justices begin to inquire into a case, either as examining justices or on the trial of an information, they have reason to believe that the alleged offender is a young person and either—

    (a) it appears to them that the person who laid the information in question was not a qualified informant when he laid it; or (*b*) the information is not in writing or does not contain such a certificate as is mentioned in subsection (5) (*b*) of this section,

it shall be their duty to quash the information, without prejudice to the laying of a further information in respect of the matter in question; but no proceedings shall be invalidated by reason of a contravention of any provision of this section and no action shall lie, by reason only of such a contravention, in respect of proceedings in respect of which such a contravention has occurred.

(7) Nothing in the preceding provisions of this section applies to an information laid with the consent of the Attorney General or laid by or on behalf or with the consent of the Director of Public Prosecutions.

(8) It shall be the duty of a person who decides to lay an information in respect of an offence in a case where he has reason to believe that the alleged offender is a young person to give notice of the decision to the appropriate local authority unless he is himself that authority.

(9) In this section—

"the appropriate local authority", in relation to a young person, means the local authority for the area in which it appears to the informant in question that the young person resides or, if the young person appears to the informant not to reside in the area of a local authority, the local authority in whose area it is alleged that the relevant offence or one of the relevant offences was committed; and

"qualified informant" means a servant of the Crown, a police officer and a member of a designated police force acting in his capacity as such a servant, officer or member, a local authority, the Greater London Council, the council of a county district and any body designated as a public body for the purposes of this section;

and in this subsection "designated" means designated by an order made by the Secretary of State; but nothing in this section shall be construed as preventing any council or other body from acting by an agent for the purposes of this section.

GENERAL NOTE

The essential object of this section is to establish the principle that offenders aged 14 and under 17 should be dealt with outside the court as far as it is reasonably possible and to provide the necessary criteria to assist the authorities coming to a decision whether or not to prosecute in each case. There is no requirement that the consent of a juvenile court magistrate must be secured before prosecuting any young person. Instead, decisions on the prosecution of young persons are left with the police, after consultation with the local authority.

COMMENCEMENT OF THIS SECTION

See s. 73 (2), *post*, and the note thereto.

SUB-S. (1)

This should be read in conjunction with sub-s. (9). It provides that no one except a "qualified informant" may lay an information against a young person. While a decision on prosecution will, in the great majority of cases, rest with the police, it would be too restrictive to confine it strictly to members of police forces within the meaning of the Police Act 1964.

Qualified informant

For meaning see sub-s. (9) of this section.

Lay an information

For provisions as to procedure for laying an information, see the Magistrates' Courts Act 1952, s. 1 (32 Halsbury's Statutes (2nd Edn.) 421) and the Magistrates' Courts Rules 1968, S.I. 1968 No. 1920, rr. 1, 12. An "information" is nothing more than "the statement by which the magistrate is informed of the offence for which a summons or warrant is required"; see *R.* v. *Hughes* (1879), 4 Q.B.D. 614, at p. 633, *per* Huddleston, B.

Young person

I.e., a person who has attained the age of 14 and is under the age of 17; see s. 70 (1), *post*.

Note, however, that by s. 34 (1) (*b*), (4), *post*, the Secretary of State may by order provide that any reference to a young person in this section (except sub-s. (8) thereof) shall be construed as including a child of or over the age of ten, or excluding a young person who has attained such age as may be specified.

SUB-S. (2)

This lays down the tests which a qualified informant is to apply in deciding whether to prosecute a young person. These tests are of two kinds: first the informant must be satisfied that the case is of a description prescribed in sub-s. (4); secondly, the qualified informant must also be satisfied that it would not be adequate for the case to be dealt within any of the other ways set out in the second half of that subsection.

The case is of a description prescribed in pursuance of sub-s. (4) *of this section*

It is intended to issue regulations which will give guidance to qualified informants on the exercise of their discretion in deciding whether or not the case is, in fact, one contemplated by sub-s. (4) of this section.

Constable

See the note to s. 1, *ante.*

Or through an exercise of the powers of a local authority

See, for example, the Children and Young Persons Act 1963, s. 1, which requires the local authority to make available ". . . such advice, guidance and assistance as may promote the welfare of children by diminishing the need to bring children before a juvenile court". See also the Children Act 1948, s. 1, which places upon the local authority a duty, in defined circumstances, to receive a child into care.

SUB-S. (3)

Note that a local authority has a complete discretion as to whether it wishes to make any observations prior to the laying of an information. However, once a decision has been made to bring proceedings, and the authority has been so informed by virtue of sub-s. (8) of this section, the authority is then *obliged* to make investigation unless it is of the opinion that it is unnecessary to do so.

The appropriate local authority

For meaning see sub-s. (9) of this section.

SUB-S. (4)

The regulations which are to be made under this section are intended to help the police to establish some uniformity in approach. The Government did not pretend that this provision would bring about a perfect consistency, but thought that the public must at least be given some assurance that the police do not exercise their discretion in an arbitrary or capricious manner. In this way it is hoped to rectify such gross discrepancies are as found, for example, in the use of the caution which at present varies from 2 per cent. to 70 per cent. throughout the country.

By reference to such considerations as he thinks fit

The criteria envisaged were originally set out in the White Paper "Children in Trouble" (Cmd. 3601: 1968).

SUB-S. (5)

Writing

Expressions referring to writing are to be construed as including references to printing, lithography, photography and other modes of representing or reproducing words in visible form; see the Interpretation Act 1889, s. 20 (24 Halsbury's Statutes (2nd Edn.) 222).

SUB-S (6)
Examining justices
The expression is not defined for the purposes of this Act. But cf. the Criminal Justice Act 1925, s. 49 (2) (14 Halsbury's Statutes (2nd Edn.) 960), where they are defined as "the justices before whom a charge is made against any person for an indictable offence".

Trial of an information
As to summary trial of a young person, see (as from the coming into force of this and the next following section), s. 6, *post*, and the Magistrates' Courts Act 1952, ss. 18, 25 (1) (32 Halsbury's Statutes (2nd Edn.) 437, 443), as amended by s. 6 (2), *post*.

SUB-S. (8)
This requires a qualified informant to notify the local authority when he decides to prosecute a young person. As to the duty of the local authority to carry out investigations when it has been notified under this subsection, see s. 9, *post*.

Young person
I.e., a person who has attained the age of 14 and is under the age of 17; see s. 70 (1), *post*.
Note, however, that the Secretary of State is empowered by order to provide that the expression "young person" in this subsection shall be construed as including a child of such age as may be specified, but not being under ten; see s. 34 (1) (*c*), (4), *post*.

SUB-S. (9)
Note that although the informant will normally be a police officer, who is defined in s. 70 (1), *post*, as a member of a police force within the meaning of the Police Act (148 Statutes Supp.), it is desirable on practical grounds to include certain other police forces—*e.g.*, the British Transport Police. (Police forces attached to docks and harbours and certain statutory undertakings are also likely to be "designated" for the purpose of this section.) Local authorities, in bye-law cases, Government departments—*e.g.*, Customs and Excise; and other responsible public bodies which may have regular occasion to prosecute juveniles—*e.g.*, the Post Office—are also to be included.

Local authority
For meaning, see s. 70 (1), *post*.

Resides
I.e., habitually resides; see s. 70 (1), *post*, and the note thereto.

Servant of the Crown
I.e., All those officers of state and their subordinates who now perform, pursuant to statutory authority, such functions of public government as were formerly the peculiar prerogatives of the Crown; see 7 Halsbury's Laws (3rd Edn.) 252n.

Greater London Council
I.e., the chairman and councillors of Greater London; see the London Government Act 1963, s. 2 (2) (43 Halsbury's Statutes (2nd Edn.) 677).

County district
I.e., a non-county borough, urban district or rural district; see the Local Government Act 1933, s. 1 (1) (14 Halsbury's Statutes (2nd Edn.) 361).

DEFINITIONS
For "local authority", "police officer" and "reside", see s. 70, *post*.

TRANSITIONAL PROVISIONS
See the second paras. of the notes "Young person" to sub-ss. (1), (8) above.

REGULATIONS
See generally as to regulations under this Act, s. 69, *post*. Note, in particular, as to regulations made under sub-s. (4) of this section, sub-s. (2) of that section.
No regulations had been made under sub-s. (4) of this section up to 1st May 1970.

ORDERS
See generally as to orders under this Act, s. 69 (1), (3), (4), *post*.
No orders had been made under sub-s. (9) of this section up to 1st May 1970.

6. Summary trial of young persons

(1) Where a person under the age of seventeen appears or is brought before a magistrates' court on an information charging him with an offence, other than homicide, which is an indictable offence within the meaning of the Magistrates' Courts Act 1952, he shall be tried summarily unless—

(*a*) he is a young person and the offence is such as is mentioned in subsection (2) of section 53 of the Act of 1933 (under which young persons convicted on indictment of certain grave crimes may be sentenced to be detained for long periods) and the court considers that if he is found guilty of the offence it ought to be possible to sentence him in pursuance of that subsection; or

(*b*) he is charged jointly with a person who has attained the age of seventeen and the court considers it necessary in the interests of justice to commit them both for trial;

and accordingly in a case falling within paragraph (*a*) or paragraph (*b*) of this subsection the court shall, if it is of opinion that there is sufficient evidence to put the accused on trial, commit him for trial.

(2) In sections 18 (1) and 25 (1) of the said Act of 1952 (which provide for the trial on indictment of persons aged fourteen or over who are charged with certain summary offences within the meaning of that Act) for the word "fourteen" there shall be substituted the word "seventeen".

(3) If on trying a person summarily in pursuance of subsection (1) of this section the court finds him guilty, it may impose a fine of an amount not exceeding fifty pounds or may exercise the same powers as it could have exercised if he had been found guilty of an offence for which, but for section 107 (2) of the said Act of 1952, it could have sentenced him to imprisonment for a term not exceeding three months.

GENERAL NOTE
Some concern was expressed during Committee that the age-old right to claim trial by jury was not being accorded to young persons under this Act. The Government agreed that a young person, found guilty on summary conviction, might have been acquitted by a jury and that while "in most instances the penalty involved would not be severe, nevertheless it would be a stigma which would attach itself to the reputation of the young person for the whole of his life". But the Government stood by the provision and advanced the following reasons for its decision: Jury trial for children under 14, except for homicide, disappeared with the abolition of imprisonment for children under that age (see the Magistrates' Courts Act 1952, s. 21). Now that imprisonment has been abolished for those under 17, there is no reason to retain jury trial for young persons except in the circumstances either where the young offender is liable to an exceptional sentence under an order under the Children and Young Persons Act 1933, s. 53, or where his trial is one held jointly with an adult, and it is necessary, in the interests of justice that the case should go before a jury.

COMMENCEMENT OF THIS SECTION
See s. 73 (2), *post*, and the note thereto.

PERSON UNDER THE AGE OF SEVENTEEN
I.e., either a "child" or "young person". But note that as from the coming into force of s. 4, *ante*, a child may not be charged with an offence except homicide. It must be envisaged, therefore, that this section will come into operation before s. 4, *ante*, is brought fully into operation.

Note that by sub-s. (5) of s. 34, *post* (transitional modifications of Part I for persons of specified ages), where a child is tried summarily in pursuance of this section, for the words "fifty pounds" in sub-s. (3) of this section the words "ten pounds" are to be substituted.

As to the time when a person attains a given age, see the note "Attained the age" to s. 1, *ante*.

APPEARS

See as to appearance by counsel or solicitor, the Magistrates' Courts Act 1952, s. 99 (32 Halsbury's Statutes (2nd Edn.) 500). But cf. s. 16 (1), *post*.

INFORMATION

Cf. the note "laying an information" to s. 5, *ante*.

HOMICIDE

See the note to s. 4, *ante*.

INDICTABLE OFFENCE

The expression "indictable offence" is defined by s. 125 (2) of the Magistrates' Courts Act 1952 (32 Halsbury's Statutes (2nd Edn.) 518).

TRIED SUMMARILY

For special provisions as to procedure, see the Summary Jurisdiction (Children and Young Persons) Rules 1933, S.R. & O. 1933 No. 819 (as amended by S.R. & O. 1938 No. 1201, S.I. 1950 No. 827, S.I. 1963 No. 2120, S.I. 1967 No. 1660 and S.I. 1969 No. 259) and the Magistrates' Courts Rules 1968, S.I. 1968 No. 1920, r. 90.

ATTAINED THE AGE

See the note to s. 1, *ante*.

INTERESTS OF JUSTICE

Cf. the note "ends of justice" to s. 29, *post*.

COMMIT . . . FOR TRIAL

As to committal for trial, see the Magistrates' Courts Act 1952, ss. 7 *et seq.* (32 Halsbury's Statutes (2nd Edn.) 428 *et seq.*) and as to procedure generally, see the Magistrates' Courts Rules 1968, S.I. 1968 No. 1920.

FINE

For meaning, see the Magistrates' Courts Act 1952, s. 126 (1) (32 Halsbury's Statutes (2nd Edn.) 519) as amended by the Criminal Justice Act 1961, s. 41 (1) (127 Statutes Supp.), and *ibid.*, Sch. 4 (*ibid.*). By proviso (ii) to s. 6 (1) of the Costs in Criminal Cases Act 1952 (32 Halsbury's Statutes (2nd Edn.) 414), when the accused is under seventeen, the amount of the cost ordered to be paid by himself under that subsection is not to exceed the amount of any fine so to be paid. See also as to the case where the fine does not exceed 5s., proviso (i) to the same subsection.

FIFTY POUNDS

When a child is tried summarily under this section (*i.e.*, before the commencement of s. 4, *ante*), for the words "fifty pounds" are substituted the words "ten pounds", by s. 34 (5), *post*.

SAME POWERS

I.e., until the coming into force of s. 4, *ante*, and s. 7, *post*, in the case of a child, absolute discharge, conditional discharge, approved school order, attendance centre order, fit person order, guardianship order, hospital order, committal to remand home, or probation order; in the case of a young person, magistrates also have power to commit to a detention centre, and in the case of a young person aged fifteen or over they also have power to order borstal training. See, generally, Stone's Justices' Manual, 1970.

TRANSITIONAL PROVISION

See the note "Fifty pounds" above.

SAVING

By Sch. 4, para. 4, *post*, where a person is committed for trial by a jury before sub-s. (1) of this section comes into force, or chooses to be tried by a jury before sub-s. (2) of this section comes into force, proceedings in respect of the offence are not affected by the coming into force of that subsection.

MAGISTRATES' COURTS ACT 1952, SS. 18 (1), 25 (1), 107 (2)

See 32 Halsbury's Statutes (2nd Edn.) 437, 433, 507.

ACT OF 1933

I.e., the Children and Young Persons Act 1933 (17 Halsbury's Statutes (3rd Edn.) 435 *et seq.*); see s. 70 (1), *post*. S. 53 of the Act of 1933 is extended by s. 30, *post*.

7. Alterations in treatment of young offenders etc.

(1) The minimum age at conviction which qualifies for a sentence of borstal training under section 20 of the Criminal Justice Act 1948 shall be seventeen instead of fifteen years; and accordingly in subsection (1) of that section and section 28 (1) of the Magistrates' Courts Act 1952, for the word "fifteen" there shall be substituted the word "seventeen".

(2) In section 3 (1) of the said Act of 1948 (which authorises the court by or before which a person is convicted of an offence to make a probation order in respect of him) after the word "person" there shall be inserted the words "who has attained the age of seventeen".

(3) If a court having power to order children or young persons of any class or description to be detained in a detention centre in pursuance of section 4 of the Criminal Justice Act 1961 or to attend at an attendance centre in pursuance of section 19 of the said Act of 1948 is notified in pursuance of this subsection by the Secretary of State that a detention centre or, as the case may be, an attendance centre will not be available for the reception from that court of children or young persons of that class or description after a date specified in the notification, the power in question shall not be exercisable by that court after that date; and the Secretary of State shall cause a copy of any notification under this subsection to be published in the London Gazette before the date specified in the notification.

(4) Section 5 of the said Act of 1961 (which provides for detention for defaults) shall cease to apply to young persons.

(5) An order sending a person to an approved school shall not be made after such day as the Secretary of State may by order specify for the purposes of this subsection.

(6) Sections 54 and 57 of the Act of 1933 (which among other things enable a child or young person found guilty of an offence to be sent to a remand home or committed to the care of a fit person) shall cease to have effect.

(7) Subject to the enactments requiring cases to be remitted to juvenile courts and to section 53 (1) of the Act of 1933 (which provides for detention for certain grave crimes), where a child is found guilty of homicide or a young person is found guilty of any offence by or before any court, that court or the court to which his case is remitted shall have power—

(*a*) if the offence is punishable in the case of an adult with imprisonment,

5—A.L.S. 189

to make a care order (other than an interim order) in respect of him;
or

(*b*) to make a supervision order in respect of him; or

(*c*) with the consent of his parent or guardian, to order the parent or
guardian to enter into a recognisance to take proper care of him and
exercise proper control over him,

and, if it makes such an order as is mentioned in this subsection while another
such order made by any court is in force in respect of the child or young person,
shall also have power to discharge the earlier order; and subsection (13) of
section 2 of this Act shall apply to an order under paragraph (*c*) of this subsection as it applies to such an order as is mentioned in that subsection.

(8) Without prejudice to the power to remit any case to a juvenile court
which is conferred on a magistrates' court other than a juvenile court by section
56 (1) of the Act of 1933, in a case where such a magistrates' court finds a person
guilty of an offence and either he is a young person or was a young person when
the proceedings in question were begun it shall be the duty of the court to exercise that power unless the court decides to deal with the case by exercising a
power to make one or more of the following orders, that is to say, an order discharging him absolutely or conditionally, an order for the payment of a fine,
damages or costs, an order requiring his parent or guardian to enter into a recognisance to take proper care of him and exercise proper control over him
or an order under section 5 or 7 of the Road Traffic Act 1962 (which relate re-
pectively to the disqualification of drivers and the endorsement of licences).

GENERAL NOTE

This section was discussed exhaustively both in Committee and on Report, particularly
in connection with the new provision to raise the age at which a person is liable for
borstal training from 15 to 17. An examination of the objections raised seems to confirm
a view, several times put forward by the supporters of the measure, that probation
orders contained valuable and important features which were not to be included in the
new supervision orders. This the Government simply did not accept and gained strong
support for their action from the National Association of Probation Officers itself,
which accepted the new proposals. In a letter to the Home Secretary, the Central
Council of Probation and After-Care Committees, which is composed mainly of magistrates, suggested that the probation order ought still to remain possible from the age of
14 upwards on the grounds that it made the offender aware of his responsibilities to
society; that its formality would impress the young person more than the alternative
and that the generalised decisions possible under the supervision order could hardly be
explained, let alone carried out. To this the spokesman in the Lords said: "Each of
these reasons clearly rests on the assumption that a probation order is markedly different
from a supervision order, and, as I have said, it is not." (303 H. of L. Official Report
862.)

As the Home Secretary had said in the Commons: "It is not very sensible to have
two almost identical systems running side by side, and the probation system and the
supervision system are almost identical. I claim for the supervision system that it is
more flexible and more all-embracing than the system of probation and will be of more
value to the children concerned than even the system of probation has been in recent
years." (748 H. of C. Official Report 1095.)

See, further, pp. 25, 26, *ante.*

COMMENCEMENT OF THIS SECTION

See s. 73 (2), *post*, and the note thereto.

SUB-S. (1): SEVENTEEN YEARS

Note that by s. 34 (1) (*d*), *post*, the Secretary of State is empowered by order to provide
that sub-s. (1) of this section shall have effect as if for "seventeen years" there were
substituted "sixteen years".

SUB-S. (2): ATTAINED THE AGE
See the note to s. 1, *ante*.

SUB-S. (3)

Detention centre
Detention centres are places in which persons of not less than fourteen but under twenty-one years of age who are ordered to be detained in such centres may be kept for short periods under discipline suitable to persons of their age and description; see the Prisons Act 1952, s. 43 (1) (*b*) (32 Halsbury's Statutes (2nd Edn.) 649), as amended by the Criminal Justice Act 1961, s. 41 (1) (127 Statutes Supp.), and *ibid.*, Sch. 4 (*ibid.*).

Attendance centre
For meaning, see the Criminal Justice Act 1948, s. 48 (2) (18 Halsbury's Statutes (2nd Edn.) 649).

SUB-S. (5): APPROVED SCHOOL ORDER
By virtue of s. 20 (1), *post*, for meaning, see the Children and Young Persons Act 1933, s. 107 (1) (17 Halsbury's Statutes (3rd Edn.) 515). That definition together with the definition of "approved school", is repealed by s. 72 (4), Sch. 6, *post*, as from a day to be appointed.
As to the discontinuance of approved schools on the establishment of community homes, see s. 46, Sch. 3, *post*.
For transitional provisions relating to the discontinuance of approved schools, see Sch. 4, para. 7, *post*.

SUB-S. (7)

Juvenile court
See the note to s. 1, *ante*.

Young person
I.e., a person who has attained the age of 14 and is under 17; see s. 70 (1), *post*.
Note, however, that by s. 34 (1) (*c*), (4), *post*, the Secretary of State is empowered by order to provide that the references to a young person in sub-ss (7) and (8) of this section shall be construed as including a child of such age as may be specified, not being under ten.

Adult
I.e., not a child or young person.

Care order; interim order
For meaning, see s. 20, *post*.

Supervision order
For meaning, see s. 11, *post*.

Consent
See the note to s. 1, *ante*.

Parent or guardian
See the notes to s. 1, *ante*.

Enter a recognisance
See the note to s. 1, *ante*.

Earlier order
In addition to the orders mentioned in sub-s. (7), fit person orders (other than those committing a child or young person to the care of a local authority), supervision orders and orders to enter into recognisances, made under provisions of the Children and Young Persons Act 1933 (17 Halsbury's Statutes (3rd Edn.) 435 *et seq.*), are deemed to be earlier orders within the meaning of sub-s. (7), by virtue of s. 72 (1), Sch. 4, para. 1, *post*.
A fit person order committing a child to a local authority which is in force on the coming into operation of sub-s. (6) of this section, is to be deemed on and after that date to be a care order committing him to the care of the authority; see Sch. 4, para. 8, *post*.

SUB-S. (8)

Is a young person or was a young person when the proceedings in question were begun
    These words remove the difficulty created by *Hamlyn* v. *Pearce*, [1962] 2 All E.R.
436, in which the Divisional court held, with some reluctance that there was no power
to make an approved school order or a fit person order after the party had attained
the age of 17. In that case a youth, just under the age of 17 was found guilty of an
offence which in the case of an adult was punishable by imprisonment. He was
remanded for 21 days, in order that a medical report could be effected, and on re-
appearing in court, it was discovered that during that time he had attained 17 years and
so an approved school order could not be made on his behalf. This new provision ties
up with s. 29 (1) of the Children and Young Persons Act 1963 which provides that where
care, protection or control proceedings in respect of a young person are begun in a
juvenile court and the young person attains the age of 17 before the conclusion of the
proceedings, the court may deal with the case and make any order which it could have
made if he had not attained that age.

Magistrates' court
    See the note to s. 5, *ante*.

Fine, damages or costs
    Cf. the note "fine" to s. 6, *ante*. The parent or guardian of a young person may be
ordered to pay the fine, damages or costs; see the Children and Young Persons Act
1933, s. 55 (17 Halsbury's Statutes (3rd Edn.) 473). Sub-s. (1) of s. 55 of that Act is
amended by s. 72 (3), Sch. 5, para. 5, *post*, and sub-ss. (1), (2), and (4) thereof are, in
part, repealed by s. 72 (4), Sch. 6, *post*, as from a day to be appointed.

An order under s. 5 or s. 7 of the Road Traffic Act 1962
    This is to obviate the need for a magistrates' court to remit a young person to the
juvenile court, merely to secure an endorsement of his licence, etc. The principle is also
applicable to cases where a young person is jointly charged with an adult in a traffic
offence and the court considers that as well as a fine, endorsement or disqualification
might be appropriate.

DEFINITIONS
    For "child" and "young person", see s. 70 (1), *post*.

TRANSITIONAL PROVISIONS
    See the notes "seventeen years", and "earlier order" and the second para. of the note
"Young person" above.

SAVINGS
    By Sch. 4, para. 5 (1), *post*, the coming into force of sub-s. (1) of this section does not
affect (1) any sentence of borstal training passed before its coming into force; or (2) any
committal for sentence before that date under the Magistrates' Courts Act 1952, s. 28 (1)
(32 Halsbury's Statutes (2nd Edn.) 447). But a sentence of borstal training may not
be passed on any person if on the date of the relevant conviction he had not attained
the minimum age specified in the Criminal Justice Act 1948, s. 20 (1) (8 Halsbury's
Statutes (3rd Edn.) 355).
    By Sch. 4, para. 5 (2), *post*, nothing in sub-s. (2) of this section affects a probation
order made before the coming into force of sub-s. (2).
    As to the saving of fit person orders in force on the coming into operation of sub-s.
(6) of this section, see Sch. 4, para. 9, *post*.

CRIMINAL JUSTICE ACT 1948, SS. 3 (1), 19, 20 (1)
    For ss. 3 (1) and 20 (1), see 8 Halsbury's Statutes (3rd Edn.) 339–340, 355. For s. 19,
see 14 Halsbury's Statutes (2nd Edn.) 1003–1005.
    Sub-s. (1) of s. 3 of that Act, and sub-ss. (1) of ss. 19, 20 thereof, are amended by
sub-ss. (1), (2) of this section, and s. 72 (3), Sch. 5, para. 23, *post*, as from a day to be
appointed.

MAGISTRATES' COURTS ACT 1952, S. 28 (1)
    See 32 Halsbury's Statutes (2nd Edn.) 447. Sub-s. (1) of s. 28 of that Act is amended
by sub-s. (1) of this section from a day to be appointed.

CRIMINAL JUSTICE ACT 1961, SS. 4, 5, 6
  See 8 Halsbury's Statutes (3rd Edn.) 504–506. S. 5 (2) (*a*), the words following s. 5 (2)
(*b*), and s. 5 (3) of that Act, are consequentially repealed by s. 72 (4), Sch. 6, *post*;
s. 5 (1) of that Act is substituted, and s. 5 (6) added, by s. 72 (3), Sch. 5, para. 44, *post*;
s. 6 (1), (2) and (3) in part, are repealed by s. 72 (4), Sch. 6, *post*; and s. 6 (3), thereof
is renumbered s. 5 (6) thereof, by s. 72 (3), Sch. 5, para. 44, *post*, all as from a day to be
appointed.

ACT OF 1933
  I.e., the Children and Young Persons Act 1933 (17 Halsbury's Statutes (3rd Edn.)
435 *et seq.*); see s. 70 (1), *post*. S. 56 (1) of that Act is amended and in part repealed,
and ss. 54, 57 are repealed by s. 72 (3), (4), Sch. 5, para. 6, Sch. 6, *post*, as from a day to
be appointed.

ROAD TRAFFIC ACT 1962, SS. 5, 7
  See 135 Statutes Supp.

ORDERS UNDER THIS SECTION
  See, generally, as to orders under this Act, s. 69, *post*. Note, in particular as to orders
under sub-s. (5) of this section, sub-s. (3) of that section.
  No orders had been made under sub-s. (5) of this section up to 1st May 1970.

8. Finger-printing of suspected young persons

(1) If a police officer not below the rank of inspector makes an application on
oath to a justice stating—

  (*a*) that there is evidence sufficient to justify the laying of an information
      that a young person has or is suspected of having committed an offence
      punishable with imprisonment in the case of an adult; and

  (*b*) that with a view to deciding, in accordance with section 5 of this Act,
      whether the information should be laid it is appropriate in the opinion
      of the officer for an order under subsection (2) of this section to be
      made in respect of the young person,

the justice may if he thinks fit issue a summons or warrant for the purpose of
securing the attendance of the young person before a magistrates' court with a
view to the making of such an order in respect of him.

  (2) The court before which a young person appears in pursuance of a summons or warrant under the preceding subsection may if it thinks fit order his
finger and palm prints to be taken by a constable.

  (3) Subsections (2) and (4) of section 40 of the Magistrates' Courts Act 1952
(which respectively relate to the taking and destruction of finger and palm
prints) shall have effect as if references to an order under that section included
references to an order under the preceding subsection and, in relation to an order
under the preceding subsection, as if for the words from "remanded" to "committed" in subsection (2) there were substituted the words "lawfully detained
at any place, at that place" and as if the reference to acquittal in subsection
(4) included a reference to a finding of a court that the condition set out in
section 1 (2) (*f*) of this Act is not satisfied in consequence of the offence specified
in the application mentioned in subsection (1) of this section.

GENERAL NOTE
  This section substantially widens the power to take finger-prints from people under 17—
far wider than that which exists against anybody in the country at the moment.
The Government reported that while finger-prints may be obtained under this section
as a preliminary to a decision by the police whether or not to use informal methods of

dealing with the offender, it was more than likely that they would be obtained in the early stages of an extremely serious case where there would certainly be a prosecution. The cardinal principle of this Act was that wherever possible a young person should not be brought to court if there were other ways of dealing with him and therefore the fullest possible information should be collected, including whether he has been involved in another offence to which his fingerprints might refer. In spite of strong representations that provision should be made for the destruction of prints, it was suggested that it would be wrong for the police to be deprived, say after 10 years, of an aid to detection: "No man has anything to fear on account of his finger-prints being kept by the Police save, and only, in the event of his committing a further offence."

COMMENCEMENT OF THIS SECTION
See s. 73 (2), *post*, and the note thereto.

SUB-S. (1)

Rank of inspector
See the Police Act 1964 (148 Statutes Supp.).

Laying an information
See the note to s. 5, *ante*.

Adult
See the note to s. 7, *ante*.

Magistrates' court
See the note to s. 5, *ante*.

SUB-S. (2)

Order
For the form for taking finger and palm prints, see the Magistrates' Courts (Forms) Rules 1968, S.I. 1968 No. 1919, Schedule, Form 6.

Constable
See the note to s. 1, *ante*.

DEFINITIONS
For "young person", "police officer", see s. 70 (1), *post*.

MAGISTRATES' COURTS ACT 1952, S. 40 (2), (4)
See 32 Halsbury's Statutes (2nd Edn.) 455.

9. Investigations by local authorities

(1) Where a local authority or a local education authority brings proceedings under section 1 of this Act or proceedings for an offence alleged to have been committed by a young person or are notified that any such proceedings are being brought, it shall be the duty of the authority, unless they are of opinion that it is unnecessary to do so, to make such investigations and provide the court before which the proceedings are heard with such information relating to the home surroundings, school record, health and character of the person in respect of whom the proceedings are brought as appear to the authority likely to assist the court.

(2) If the court mentioned in subsection (1) of this section requests the authority aforesaid to make investigations and provide information or to make further investigations and provide further information relating to the matters aforesaid, it shall be the duty of the authority to comply with the request.

GENERAL NOTE
This section replaces s. 35 of the Children and Young Persons Act 1933. It was suggested that the present section was defective in that it did not make provision for the probation service. The objection was that "there is a grave danger that people will feel that the local authority, through its children's officer, is to be the prosecuting authority, the reporting authority to the court and, at the same time, the treatment agency

to which the court eventually consigns the person." The Government agreed that the probation officers had been brought into the 1933 enactment for this purpose because at that time there was no children's service, but since then several statutes have required the local authority to make reports about the school records, the health and the character of the children. "It would be an unnecessary bifurcation if we said that, the local authority having provided all these reports through its children's service, it was for the probation officer to tell the court about the child's background."

COMMENCEMENT OF THIS SECTION
See s. 73 (2), *post*, and the note thereto.

SUB-S. (I)
Local education authority
See the note to s. 2, *ante*.

Young person
I.e., a person who has attained the age of 14 and is under 17; see s. 70 (1), *post*.
Note, however, that by s. 34 (1) (c), (4), *post*, the Secretary of State is empowered by order to provide that references to a young person in sub-s. (1) of this section shall be construed as including a child of such age or may be specified, not being under ten.

Notified
I.e., in accordance with s. 2 (3) or s. 5 (8), *ante*.

Make such investigations
For the circumstances in which a local authority is not required to make any investigations, see s. 34 (3), *post*.

TRANSITIONAL PROVISION
See the second para. of the note "Young person" and the note "Make such investigations" above.

DEFINITIONS
For "local authority" and "child" see s. 70 (1), *post*.

10. Further limitations on publication of particulars of children and young persons etc.

(1) In subsection (1) of section 49 of the Act of 1933 which (among other things imposes restrictions on reports of certain court proceedings concerning children or young persons but authorises the court or the Secretary of State, if satisfied that it is in the interests of justice to do so, to dispense with the requirements of that section)—

(a) the references to a young person concerned in the proceedings as the person in respect of whom they are taken shall be construed as including references to any person who has attained the age of seventeen but not eighteen and against or in respect of whom the proceedings are taken and, in the case of proceedings under Part I of this Act, any other person in respect of whom those proceedings are taken; and

(b) the references to a juvenile court shall, in relation to proceedings in pursuance of the provisions of sections 15 and 16 of this Act or on appeal from such proceedings, be construed as including a reference to any other magistrates' court or, as the case may be, the court in which the appeal is brought; and

(c) for the words "in the interests of justice so to do" there shall be substituted the words "appropriate to do so for the purpose of avoiding injustice to a child or young person" and after the word "section" there shall be inserted the words "in relation to him".

(2) Where by virtue of paragraph (*b*) of the preceding subsection the said section 49 applies to any proceedings, it shall be the duty of the court in which the proceedings are taken to announce in the course of the proceedings that that section applies to them; and if the court fails to do so that section shall not apply to the proceedings in question.

(3) A notice displayed in pursuance of section 4 of the Criminal Justice Act 1967 (which requires the publication of a notice stating the result of proceedings before examining justices and containing particulars of the person to whom the proceedings related) shall not contain the name or address of any child or young person unless the justices in question have stated that in their opinion he would be mentioned in the notice apart from the foregoing provisions of this subsection and should be mentioned in it for the purpose of avoiding injustice to him.

GENERAL NOTE

The rationale of this section arises out of the desire to protect from publicity any person whose subsequent appearance in an adult court arises solely in connection with the variation or discharge of a supervision order made when under 18. It was thought that it would only be fair to extend the protection afforded by the 1933 enactment—which imposes restrictions upon reporting proceedings in juvenile courts—to a young adult whose appearance in court, under s. 15 of the present Act, arose simply to secure the variation or discharge of an order, the terms and conditions of which he had satisfactorily carried out. It was intimated that it might be prejudicial to him if it were made public that he had, at some time been the subject of an order.

COMMENCEMENT OF THIS SECTION

See s. 73 (2), *post*, and the note thereto.

DEFINITIONS

For "child" and "young person", see s. 70 (1), *post*.

ACT OF 1933

I.e., the Children and Young Persons Act 1933 (17 Halsbury's Statutes (3rd Edn.) 435 *et seq.*); see s. 70 (1), *post*.

CRIMINAL JUSTICE ACT 1967, S. 4

See 163 Statutes Supp.

SUB-S. (1)

Para (*a*)

This applies the existing restrictions on publicity to all persons aged 17 to 18 against whom or in respect of whom proceedings are brought in a juvenile court and to all persons in respect of whom proceedings are so brought under Part I of this Act.

Para. (*b*)

This applies the juvenile court restrictions to all proceedings in the adult court relating to supervision orders. If this over-all provision were not made, it would be necessary to incorporate a special restrictive subsection in s. 15, and this would lead to complicated administrative proceedings on the part of the clerks of the court: they would first have to announce that these were proceedings to which the restrictions applied, and then, at the close of the proceedings, whether the restrictions did in fact apply. This was felt to be too much with regard to a minor point of law—the proceedings to which it is directed are seldom worthy of report.

SUB-S. (2)

This places on the adult court a duty to announce the fact that s. 49 of the Children and Young Persons Act 1933 applies to supervision proceedings in that court. The words, "and if the court fails . . . . etc." are necessary because it would be wrong for a newspaper to be liable to prosecution simply for publishing the name of a person appearing before an adult court if the court failed to fulfil this requirement.

Supervision

11. Supervision orders

Any provision of this Act authorising a court to make a supervision order in respect of any person shall be construed as authorising the court to make an order placing him under the supervision of a local authority designated by the order or of a probation officer; and in this Act "supervision order" shall be construed accordingly and "supervised person" and "supervisor", in relation to a supervision order, mean respectively the person placed or to be placed under supervision by the order and the person under whose supervision he is placed or to be placed by the order.

GENERAL NOTE

This section provides that a supervision order is to place a person either (*a*) under the supervision of a local authority designated by the order, or (*b*) under the supervision of a probation officer. Where the order places a person under the care of the local authority, it is not to specify any officer by name.

COMMENCEMENT OF THIS SECTION

See s. 73 (2), *post*, and the note thereto.

SUPERVISION ORDER

As to the requirements which may be included in a supervision order, see s. 12, *post*; as to the variation and discharge of supervision orders, see ss. 15, 16, *post*; as to termination of such orders, see s. 17, *post*; as to contents of such orders, see s. 18 (2), *post*.

LOCAL AUTHORITY DESIGNATED, ETC.

For meaning of "local authority", see s. 70 (1), *post*. As to the designation of a local authority as a supervisor, see s. 13 (1), *post*.

PROBATION OFFICER

As to the placing of a person under the supervision of a probation officer, see s. 13 (2), (3), *post*. Provisions as to the appointment, etc., of probation officers are contained in the Criminal Justice Act 1948, s. 45, Sch. 4, paras. 3 and 7 (8 Halsbury's Statutes (3rd Edn.) 362–363, 376–378).

TRANSITIONAL PROVISIONS

As to supervision orders in force before the coming into force of ss. 11–19 of this Act, see Sch. 4, para. 12, *post*.

12. Power to include requirements in supervision orders

(1) A supervision order may require the supervised person to reside with an individual named in the order who agrees to the requirement, but a requirement imposed by a supervision order in pursuance of this subsection shall be subject to any such requirement of the order as is authorised by the following provisions of this section.

(2) Subject to section 19 (6) of this Act, a supervision order may require the supervised person to comply with such directions of the supervisor as are mentioned in paragraph (*a*) or (*b*) or paragraphs (*a*) and (*b*) of this subsection, that is to say—

(*a*) directions requiring the supervised person to live for a single period specified in the directions at a place so specified;

(b) directions given from time to time requiring him to do all or any of the following things—

   (i) to live at a place or places specified in the directions for a period or periods so specified,

   (ii) to present himself to a person or persons specified in the directions at a place or places and on a day or days so specified,

   (iii) to participate in activities specified in the directions on a day or days so specified;

but it shall be for the supervisor to decide whether and to what extent he exercises any power to give directions conferred on him by virtue of the preceding provisions of this subsection and to decide the form of any directions; and a requirement imposed by a supervision order in pursuance of this subsection shall be subject to any such requirement of the order as is authorised by subsection (4) of this section.

(3) The periods specified in directions given by virtue of subsection (2) of this section in pursuance of a supervision order shall be in accordance with the following provisions, that is to say—

   (a) the aggregate of the periods specified in directions given by virtue of paragraph (a) and paragraph (b) of that subsection shall not exceed ninety days;

   (b) the period specified in directions given by virtue of the said paragraph (a) shall not exceed ninety days and subject to paragraph (e) below shall not begin after the expiration of one year beginning with the date of the order or, if the directions are authorised solely by a variation of the order, with the date of the variation;

   (c) the aggregate of the periods specified in directions given by virtue of the said paragraph (b) shall not exceed thirty days in the year beginning with the date aforesaid and thirty days in any year beginning with an anniversary of that date;

   (d) if the order provides that any of the preceding paragraphs of this subsection is to have effect in relation to the order as if for a reference to ninety days or thirty days there were substituted a reference to a shorter period specified in the order, the paragraph in question shall have effect accordingly;

   (e) for the purpose of calculating the period or periods in respect of which directions may be given in pursuance of the order—

      (i) the supervisor shall be entitled to disregard any day in respect of which directions were previously given in pursuance of the order and on which the directions were not complied with;

      (ii) a direction given in respect of one or more parts of a day shall be treated as given in respect of the whole of the day,

and if during the year mentioned in paragraph (b) of this subsection the supervised person is given such directions as are there mentioned specifying a period beginning in that year but does not begin to comply with the directions during that year, the supervisor shall be entitled to disregard so much of that paragraph as prevents that period from beginning after the expiration of that year.

(4) Where a court which proposes to make a supervision order is satisfied, on the evidence of a medical practitioner approved for the purposes of section 28 of the Mental Health Act 1959, that the mental condition of a supervised person is such as requires and may be susceptible to treatment but is not such as to warrant his detention in pursuance of a hospital order under Part V of that Act, the court may include in the supervision order a requirement that the supervised person shall, for a period specified in the order, submit to treatment of one of the following descriptions so specified, that is to say—

(*a*) treatment by or under the direction of a fully registered medical practitioner specified in the order;

(*b*) treatment as a non-resident patient at a place specified in the order; or

(*c*) treatment as a resident patient in a hospital or mental nursing home within the meaning of the said Act of 1959, but not a special hospital within the meaning of that Act.

(5) A requirement shall not be included in a supervision order in pursuance of the preceding subsection—

(*a*) in any case, unless the court is satisfied that arrangements have been or can be made for the treatment in question and, in the case of treatment as a resident patient, for the reception of the patient;

(*b*) in the case of an order made or to be made in respect of a person who has attained the age of fourteen, unless he consents to its inclusion;

and a requirement so included shall not in any case continue in force after the supervised person becomes eighteen.

GENERAL NOTE

This has been held by some to be one of the most important provisions of the Act—at least with respect to the contents of sub-ss. (2) and (3). They deal with what, in the White Paper "Children in Trouble" (Cmnd. 3601: 1968), was described as "intermediate treatment" and which was enthusiastically received by a wide section of the community concerned with child welfare. The actual arrangements will have to be planned and built up locally in each area, with the maximum participation from all the statutory and voluntary services, not only the children's services but also the other local services—the probation officers, the magistrates, the police, the churches and the multitude of voluntary organisations. "The Home Office", said the Secretary of State during the second Reading, "will mount development projects with the aim of gaining experience of how local schemes can be worked out." One Member spoke of the establishment of adventure training schools on the North Yorkshire moors "where youngsters could stay for perhaps a month at a time, and operating on 'Outward Bound' lines."

See, further, pp. 26, 27, *ante*.

COMMENCEMENT OF THIS SECTION

See s. 73 (2), *post*, and the note thereto.

SUB-S. (1)

Note that the supervision order itself may not make provision as to where a supervised person is to reside—only as to with whom he is to live. (In cases where it becomes necessary to specify a place, *i.e.*, a hostel, then usually the circumstances are such that a care order is called for.) However, as to the supervisor's power to direct the supervised person to reside at a particular place, see sub-s. (2) (*a*), (*b*) of this section.

Reside with
Notwithstanding, in particular, *Evans* v. *Evans*, [1947] 2 All E.R. 656; [1948] 1 K.B. 175, it would seem that a person does not "reside with" another person merely because both are living under the same roof; see, in particular, *Naylor* v. *Naylor*, [1961] 2 All E.R. 129; [1962] P. 253.

SUB-S. (2)
This subsection was strongly attacked in Committee on the grounds that it put almost limitless power into the hands of a supervisor and the point was even raised that supervisors might refuse to carry out the purposes of an order. Attempts to curb this power were resisted by the Government which put its case as follows: the boundaries within which the supervisor exercises his responsibility are set by the terms of the supervision order. Within those boundaries it is right that the supervisor should be regarded as a responsible person whose judgment as to the way in which he deals with a supervised person can and should be trusted. No responsible supervisor would simply disregard the wishes of the court and before he had the opportunity of gaining a closer knowledge of the child and his problems, announce, for example, that he would give no directions whatsoever.
The Opposition put its case as follows: It is appreciated that a supervisor needs a degree of flexibility. But it does derogate from the authority of the court, if, when it makes a decision to put a young person under supervision, at the end of the day the supervisor can either ignore the court's decision or radically modify it.
As to the statutory duty of a supervisor, see s. 14, *post.*
Note that an order may not be made under this subsection until the court is satisfied that a scheme under this section is actually in operation for the planning area in which the party lives; see s. 19 (6), *post.*

Para (b)
Referring to this, the Home Secretary said: "The function is to bring youngsters in trouble into contact with others taking part in the normal constructive activities of young people of their own age—social, educational, recreational, helping others. These activities may take place in the evenings or at the weekend and the children may go away under supervision, perhaps for longer periods. They may involve going away, for instance for adventure training or to a harvest camp. In some cases a supervision order might involve spending as much as three months away from home. For example, a period might be spent in a community home or a term at a boarding school."
Directions. As to the provision of facilities for carrying out the directions of a supervisor, see s. 19, *post.*
Live . . . at a place. As to restrictions on the power to impose this requirement on the variation of a supervision order, see ss. 15 (1), 16 (6) (a), *post.*
Exercise any power. For restrictions on the exercise of the supervisor's powers, see s. 19 (6), *post.* For a supervisor's duties, see s. 14, *post.*

SUB-S. (3)
It should be noted that there is nothing in this subsection to suggest that an order should begin "forthwith"—in fact there is no indication as to when an order is to start. The Government explained that the reason for this is that summary removal to any place where an immediate vacancy can be found and without the parents and the child having had time to collect their wits or the child its belongings, would be alien to the spirit and intention of a supervision order. It is unconstructive and could be damaging. If the period of residence is to do any good, time must be allowed for the necessary preparations. These are likely to take at least a day or two even if everybody agrees that the period of residence ought to start as soon as possible. Apart from this, an immediate order would be quite inappropriate in cases, say, where a child was at school, and an important examination was pending.

Beginning with etc.
In calculating the period of one year the *dies a quo* must be included (see *Hare* v. *Cocher*, [1962] 2 All E.R. 763; [1962] 2 Q.B. 641), but certain intervening days may be excluded in accordance with the provisions of para. (e) of this subsection.

SUB-S. (4)
The provisions of this subsection are largely derived from the Criminal Justice Act 1948, s. 3 (5), (6), s. 4 (4), s. 80 and Sch. 1, para. 7 and the Mental Health Act 1959, Sch. 7. There are several limitations upon them which are set out in sub-s. (5) of this section.

Court is satisfied
   Cf. the note to s. 1, *ante.*

Medical practitioner
   I.e., a registered medical practitioner within the meaning of the Medical Act 1956 (36 Halsbury's Statutes (2nd Edn.) 567); see the Mental Health Act 1959, s. 147 (119 Statutes Supp.).

Approved for the purposes of s. 28 *of the Mental Health Act* 1959
   See the Mental Health (Hospital and Guardianship) Regulations 1960, S.I. 1960 No. 1241, reg. 5.

Mental condition
   Cf. the definition "mental disorder" in the Mental Health Act 1959, s. 4 (1) (119 Statutes Supp.).

Treatment
   Cf. the definition "medical treatment" in the Mental Health Act, s. 147 (1) (119 Statutes Supp.), and see paras. (*a*), (*b*), (*c*) of this subsection.

Hospital order under Part V
   See the note "hospital order" to s. 1, *ante.*

The court may include
   It should be noted that a requirement to submit to treatment under this subsection may not be included in a supervision order unless: (*a*) the court is satisfied that arrangements for such treatment have been, or can be made, and (*b*) in the case of a young person, his consent is first obtained; see sub-s. (5) (*a*), (*b*) of this section. The requirement may not, in any case, continue after the supervised person becomes 18; see sub-s. (5).
   As to restrictions on the power to impose a requirement under sub-s. (4) on the variation of a supervision order, see ss. 15 (1), 16 (6), (*c*), (7), *post.*
   As to the cancellation or variation of a requirement under this section where the medical practitioner giving the treatment is unlikely to continue to treat or direct the treatment of the supervised person, or thinks that the treatment should be extended, changed or discontinued, see s. 15 (5), *post.*

Fully registered medical practitioner
   This means a person for the time being registered under the Medical Act 1956, ss. 7 or 18 (36 Halsbury's Statutes (2nd Edn.) 575, 587), as a fully registered medical practitioner (including a person whose registration has effect as if so made, and include in certain cases a person who is provisionally or temporarily registered; see s. 52 (2) of that Act, in conjunction with ss. 54 (1) and 57 (2) thereof. There is, however, room for doubt whether a person who is provisionally or temporarily registered can ever be a fully registered medical practitioner for the purposes of this section.

Patient
   For meaning, see the Mental Health Act 1959, s. 147 (1) (119 Statutes Supp.).

Resident patient
   As to the care of resident patients generally, see the Mental Health Act 1959, s. 6 (2) (39 Halsbury's Statutes (2nd Edn.) 968).

Hospital; mental nursing home
   These expressions are defined in s. 147 (1) of the Mental Health Act 1959 (119 Statutes Supp.).

Special hospital
   This expression is defined in s. 147 (1) of the Mental Health Act 1959 (119 Statutes Supp.).

SUB-S. (5)
   Note that there is no provision for a person confined under the terms of this and the foregoing subsection to have his case periodically reviewed. The Government pointed out that the provisions in this section with regard to mental cases were the same as those contained in s. 4 of the Criminal Justice Act 1948 and the Children and Young Persons Act 1963, Sch. 1, under which no right to apply to a Mental Health Tribunal existed and had, in fact, never been found necessary. "There is nothing to prevent a child or young person from walking out of the hospital or mental nursing home or failing to attend the clinic. If he does so he cannot be apprehended and taken back as in the

case of a hospital order. Parental rights are not over-ridden, as in the case of a guardianship order. All that can happen, as is the case with any other failure to comply with any other requirement in a supervision order is that a supervisor can again take the child or young person before the court. The court could then make a care order, but it is unlikely to do so to enforce treatment for a mental condition on an unwilling child, bearing in mind that before inserting such a requirement in a supervision order the court has to be satisfied that his mental condition is not such as to warrant his detention under a hospital order in the first place."

Becomes eighteen
    Cf. the note "attained the age" to s. 1, *ante*.

DEFINITIONS
    For "supervision order", "supervised person" and "supervisor", see s. 11, *ante*; for "young person", see s. 70 (1), *post*.

MENTAL HEALTH ACT 1959, S. 28, PART V
    See 39 Halsbury's Statutes (2nd Edn.) 984, 985, 1013, 1014.

13. Selection of supervisor

(1) A court shall not designate a local authority as the supervisor by a provision of a supervision order unless the authority agree or it appears to the court that the supervised person resides or will reside in the area of the authority.

(2) A court shall not insert in a supervision order a provision placing a child under the supervision of a probation officer unless the local authority of which the area is named or to be named in the order in pursuance of section 18 (2) (*a*) of this Act so request and a probation officer is already exercising or has exercised, in relation to another member of the household to which the child belongs, duties imposed by paragraph 3 (5) of Schedule 5 to the Criminal Justice Act 1948 or by rules under paragraph 6 (*b*) of that Schedule.

(3) Where a provision of a supervision order places a person under the supervision of a probation officer, the supervisor shall be a probation officer appointed for or assigned to the petty sessions area named in the order in pursuance of section 18 (2) (*a*) of this Act and selected under arrangements made by the probation and after-care committee; but if the probation officer selected as aforesaid dies or is unable to carry out his duties or if the case committee dealing with the case think it desirable that another officer should take his place, another probation officer shall be selected as aforesaid for the purposes of the order.

GENERAL NOTE
    Much of this section is derived from the Children and Young Persons Act 1963, s. 5 and Sch. 1, paras. 11 and 12—all of which are repealed by this Act. The main object of this section is contained in sub-s. (2) which draws the boundary between the work of the probation service with children and that of the children's service. Obviously this is a very difficult boundary to draw if every party is to be satisfied. The section recognises the primary responsibility of the children's service for working with children under 14, but gives the courts complete discretion to use either the children's service or the probation service between the ages of 14 and 17. There is also provision for probation officers to supervise children under 14 in families with which they are already working or have worked previously. It is anticipated that with the growth of the after-care service, including parole and the possibility of added duties in respect of non-custodial penalties, probation officers cannot but look forward to a new form of service, steadily increasing in variety and volume.

COMMENCEMENT OF THIS SECTION
    See s. 73 (2), *post*, and the note thereto.

SUB-S. (1)
This replaces s. 5 (3) of the Act of 1963.

Resides
This expression has frequently been a point of contention. As early as 1825, Bayley, J. in *R.* v. *North Curry (Inhabitants)* (1825), 4 B.C. 953 said that "where there is nothing more to show that it is used in a more extensive sense, it denotes the place where an individual eats, drinks and sleeps". See also *Stoke on Trent Borough Council* v. *Cheshire C.C.*, [1914–15] All E.R. 441; *Levene* v. *I.R.C.*, [1928] All E.R. Rep. 746 and *I.R.C.* v. *Lysaght*, [1928] All E.R. Rep. 575 and *Re Adoption Application* 52/1951, [1951] All E.R. 931.

SUB-S. (2)
See the General Note on p. 142, *ante.*

Child
I.e., a person under the age of 14; see s. 70 (1), *post.*
Note, however, that by s. 34 (1) (*a*), *post*, the Secretary of State is empowered by order to provide that the reference to a child in this section shall be construed as excluding a child who has attained such age as may be specified.

Probation Officer
See the note to s. 11, *ante.*

Or has exercised
These words were inserted during Report (Commons) to clear up any doubts that where a probation officer had already made contact with a family, he should be selected in preference to a stranger. It would be regrettable that "the bond of trust and respect that the probation officer has probably built up with the family" should not be recognised and if there is such a probation officer who has in the past worked with a family in relation to another member of it, then it was only sensible to give him the opportunity of putting his detailed knowledge to advantage.

Household
This word is capable of wide interpretation.—"The 'household' in the broad sense of a family, is a collective group living in a house, acknowledging the authority of a head the members of which, with few exceptions, are bound by marriage, blood affinity or other bond, between whom there is an intimacy and by whom there is felt a concern with and an interest in the life of all that gives it a unity." (*Wawanesa Mutual Ins. Co.* v. *Bell*, [1957] S.C.R. 581.)
It was argued during Committee that this made no provision for such cases where there were parties living together in the same street, sometimes as neighbours, and where the same probation officer was obviously called for—particularly if the parties were jointly involved in trouble. The Government indicated that the word would be given, in practice, a very wide interpretation, and there would be difficulties of definition if exceptional conditions were to be provided for. Such factors would certainly come to light in enquiries and proceedings and appropriate selections could be made in any case.

SUB-S. (3)
This replaces the provisions of s. 5 (2) and Sch. 1, para. 12 to the Act of 1963.

Person
I.e., a child or young person; see ss. 1 (3), 11, *ante.*
By virtue of the Criminal Justice Act 1967, s. 55 (163 Statutes Supp.), a probation officer under whose supervision a woman or a girl is placed may now be a man or a woman.

Probation and after-care committee; care committee
These committees are constituted under the Criminal Justice Act 1948, Sch. 5 para. 2 (8 Halsbury's Statutes (3rd Edn.) 376).

TRANSITIONAL PROVISION
See the second para. of the note "Child" above.

DEFINITIONS
    For "local authority", "reside", "petty sessions area", see s. 70 (1), *post*; for "super-visor", "supervision order", "supervised person", see s. 11, *ante*.

CRIMINAL JUSTICE ACT 1948, SCH. 5, PARAS. 3 (5), 6 (*b*)
    See 8 Halsbury's Statutes (3rd Edn.) 377, 378. The rules made under para. 6 (*b*) are the Probation (Allowances) Rules 1964, S.I. 1964 No. 904, as amended by S.I. 1965 No. 1521; the Probation (Conditions of Service) Rules 1965; S.I. 1965 No. 722, as amended by S.I. 1965 No. 1239, 1520, S.I. 1966 No. 273, S.I. 1967 No. 869, S.I. 1968 Nos. 386, 2003; the Probation Rules 1965, S.I. 1965 No. 723, as amended by S.I. 1967 No. 1884.

14. Duty of supervisor

While a supervision order is in force it shall be the duty of the supervisor to advise, assist and befriend the supervised person.

GENERAL NOTE
    See p. 27, *ante*. Cf. also s. 12, *ante*.

COMMENCEMENT OF THIS SECTION
    See s. 73 (2), *post*, and the note thereto.

ORDER IS IN FORCE
    As to when a supervision order ceases to be in force, see s. 17, *post*.

ADVISE, ASSIST AND BEFRIEND
    The same form of words is used, in relation to the duties of probation officers, in the Criminal Justice Act 1948, Sch. 5, para. 3 (5), 3rd Edn., Vol. 8, p. 377. Probation officers, however, also have additional duties to perform, as to which, see also *ibid.*, para. 6 (*b*), *ibid.*, p. 378.

DEFINITIONS
    For "supervision order", "supervisor" and "supervised person", see s. 11, *ante*.

15. Variation and discharge of supervision orders

(1) If while a supervision order is in force in respect of a supervised person who has not attained the age of eighteen it appears to a juvenile court, on the application of the supervisor or the supervised person, that it is appropriate to make an order under this subsection, the court may make an order discharging the supervision order or varying it by—

  (*a*) cancelling any requirement included in it in pursuance of section 12 or section 18 (2) (*b*) of this Act; or

  (*b*) inserting in it (either in addition to or in substitution for any of its provisions) any provision which could have been included in the order if the court had then had power to make it and were exercising the power,

and may on discharging the supervision order make a care order (other than an interim order) in respect of the supervised person; but the powers of variation conferred by this subsection do not include power to insert in the supervision order, after the expiration of twelve months beginning with the date when the order was originally made, a requirement in pursuance of section 12 (2) (*a*) of this Act or, after the expiration of three months beginning with that date, a require-ment in pursuance of section 12 (4) of this Act, unless in either case it is in substitution for such a requirement already included in the order.

(2) If on an application in pursuance of the preceding subsection, in a case where the supervised person has attained the age of seventeen and the supervision order was not made by virtue of section 1 of this Act or on the occasion of the discharge of a care order, it appears to the court appropriate to do so it may proceed as if the application were in pursuance of subsection (3) or, if it is made by the supervisor, in pursuance of subsections (3) and (4) of this section and as if in that subsection or those subsections, as the case may be, the word "seventeen" were substituted for the word "eighteen" and the words "a magistrates' court other than" were omitted.

(3) If while a supervision order is in force in respect of a supervised person who has attained the age of eighteen it appears to a magistrates' court other than a juvenile court, on the application of the supervisor or the supervised person, that it is appropriate to make an order under this subsection, the court may make an order discharging the supervision order or varying it by—

(a) inserting in it a provision specifying the duration of the order or altering or cancelling such a provision already included in it; or

(b) substituting for the provisions of the order by which the supervisor is designated or by virtue of which he is selected such other provisions in that behalf as could have been included in the order if the court had then had power to make it and were exercising the power; or

(c) substituting for the name of an area included in the order in pursuance of section 18 (2) (a) of this Act the name of any other area of a local authority or petty sessions area, as the case may be, in which it appears to the court that the supervised person resides or will reside; or

(d) cancelling any provision included in the order by virtue of section 18 (2) (b) of this Act or inserting in it any provision prescribed for the purposes of that paragraph; or

(e) cancelling any requirement included in the order in pursuance of section 12 (2) or (2) of this Act.

(4) If while a supervision order is in force in respect of a supervised person who has attained the age of eighteen it is proved to the satisfaction of a magistrates' court other than a juvenile court, on the application of the supervisor, that the supervised person has failed to comply with any requirement included in the supervision order in pursuance of section 12 or section 18 (2) (v) of this Act, the court may—

(a) whether or not it also makes an order under subsection (3) of this section, order him to pay a fine of an amount not exceeding twenty pounds or, subject to subsection (10) of the following section, make an attendance centre order in respect of him;

(b) if it also discharges the supervision order, make an order imposing on him any punishment which it could have imposed on him if it had then had power to try him for the offence in consequence of which the supervision order was made and had convicted him in the exercise of that power;

and in the case where the offence in question is of a kind which the court has no power to try or has no power to try without appropriate consents, the punishment imposed by virtue of paragraph (*b*) of this subsection shall not exceed that which any court having power to try such an offence could have imposed in respect of it and shall not in any event exceed imprisonment for a term of six months and a fine of four hundred pounds.

(5) If a medical practitioner by whom or under whose direction a supervised person is being treated for his mental condition in pursuance of a requirement included in a supervision order by virtue of section 12 (4) of this Act is unwilling to continue to treat or direct the treatment of the supervised person or is of opinion—

    (*a*) that the treatment should be continued beyond the period specified in that behalf in the order; or

    (*b*) that the supervised person needs different treatment; or

    (*c*) that he is not susceptible to treatment; or

    (*d*) that he does not require further treatment,

the practitioner shall make a report in writing to that effect to the supervisor; and on receiving a report under this subsection the supervisor shall refer it to a juvenile court, and on such a reference the court may make an order cancelling or varying the requirement.

(6) The preceding provisions of this section shall have effect subject to the provisions of the following section.

GENERAL NOTE

In substance, this section is derived from corresponding provisions in the Criminal Justice Act 1967.

The Act provides for a unified code of supervision which operates up to a person's 18th birthday. All the provisions about supervision orders are the same, whether the order was made in care proceedings (*i.e.*, under s. 1, *ante*) or in criminal proceedings (*i.e.*, s. 7 (7), *ante*), except as provided by sub-s. (2) of this section.

COMMENCEMENT OF THIS SECTION

See s. 73 (2), *post*, and the note thereto.

SUB-S. (1)

This subsection enables the court, while a supervised person is under the age of 18:

    (1) to discharge the supervision order—in which case it may make a care order;

    (2) to vary the supervision order by cancelling existing requirements or adding or substituting requirements permitted under s. 12, *ante* (but a limitation is imposed on the power to vary a requirement that the supervised person must live at a specified place for a single period).

The subsection does not, however, include powers to punish for the breach of an order (or for the original offence, if there was one). The reason for this is that it is thought that as long as a supervised person is young enough to benefit from the kinds of constructive treatment which can be rendered under this subsection, it is better to rely upon them rather than to start imposing sanctions. It is thought that fining a supervised young person for not conforming to the terms of his order is not likely to inspire his confidence in the supervisor or to induce willing co-operation, and is almost a recognition that the procedure has failed. In any case, a breach of an order is usually indicative that the youngster is not receiving the care and control that those belonging to him ought to be giving him and another order might obviously be called for.

In force

As to the termination of a supervision order, see s. 17, *post*.

Attained the age
    See the note to s. 1, *ante*.

Juvenile court
    For meaning, see s. 16 (11), *post*.

On the application of the supervisor
    See further, s. 16, *post*.

Or the supervised person
    The power of the supervised person to make an application under this section is also exercisable by his parent or guardian; see s. 70 (2), *post*.

May make an order
    As to appeals from such orders, see s. 16 (8), *post*. As to dismissal of an application to discharge a supervision order, see s. 16 (9), *post*.

On discharging the supervision order may make a care order
    For the converse situation, see s. 21 (2), (*post*).

Powers of variation . . . do not include
    For further restrictions on the powers of variation, see s. 16 (6), *post* (restrictions on variation of a requirement under s. 12, *ante*) and s. 16 (7), *post* (restriction on insertion or variation of a requirement under s. 12 (4), *ante*, where supervised person is over 14).

Months
    I.e., calendar months, see the Interpretation Act 1889, s. 3 (24 Halsbury's Statutes (2nd Edn.) 207).

Beginning with, etc.
    See the note to s. 12, *ante*.

SUB-S. (2)
    This gives the court power to impose a sanction upon a person aged 17 for breach of a supervision order originally made as a result of some offence (and not arising out of care proceedings). It arises from the difficulty that sub-s. (4) of this section cannot be made applicable to all cases occurring after the 17th birthday: it would, for instance, be inappropriate in conditions where the supervision order had been made for reasons other than an offence. The simple application of that subsection would exclude the possibilities of substituting a care order or of adding intermediate treatment. The rationale of the provision is that while it is not right to impose a fine on a child aged 14 or 15 who is still at school, where the offender is aged 17 and earning his own living, there is no reason why he should be treated differently from an 18-year-old.

Supervision order was not made by virtue of s. 1
    E.g., where it was made under s. 7 (7) (*b*), *ante*.

Supervision order . . . made . . . on the occasion of the discharge of a care order
    See s. 21 (2), *post*.

SUB-SS. (3) AND (4)
    The powers available to a juvenile court under sub-s. (1) are not appropriate in the case of supervised persons aged 18 or 19. A supervision order made in care proceedings cannot last beyond the 18th birthday (see s. 17, *post*). It is only *offenders* who can remain under supervision while 18 or 19 years old. Sub-ss. (3) and (4) are together designed to apply the provisions of the existing law relating to breaches of probation orders to supervised persons aged 18 or 19. These subsections enable a court, where the supervised person is 18 (or 17 in the circumstances laid down in sub-s. (2)):

    (1) to discharge the order—in which case, if it is proved that the supervised person has failed to comply with a requirement of the supervision order, it may also—

        (*a*) impose a fine of up to £20; or
        (*b*) make an attendance centre order; or
        (*c*) impose the punishment it could originally have imposed, or (if it had no such power) which a court of competent jurisdiction could have imposed; but the punishment is not, in any event to exceed imprisonment for a term of 6 months and a fine of £400; or

(2) to vary the order in any of the ways listed in paras. (*a*)–(*e*)—in which case, if it is proved that the supervised person has failed to comply with a requirement of the supervision order, it may also—

    (*a*) impose a fine of up to £20; or
    (*b*) make an attendance centre order.

Age of eighteen
    Note the provisions of sub-s. (2) of this section.

Magistrates' court
    For meaning, see s. 16 (11), *post*. Note also the provisions of sub-s. (2) of this section.

Supervisor is designated
    As to the designation and selection of a supervisor, see s. 13, *ante*.

SUB-S. (4)
    Proved
    I.e., on a balance of probabilities, since this is a civil process begun on an application. If the order imposes a punishment under the terms of para. (*b*), the offence for which the supervision order was originally imposed will already have been proved "beyond a reasonable doubt".

Attendance centre order
    For meaning, see s. 16 (10), *post*.

Term of six months, etc.
    Note that the maximum punishment which may be imposed under sub-s. (4) is six months' imprisonment *plus* a fine of £400.

SUB-S. (5)
    This is a substantial reproduction of the provisions of the Children and Young Persons Act 1963, Sch. 1, para. 10.

Medical practitioner
    Cf. the note "fully registered medical practitioner" to s. 12, *ante*.

Being treated
    Cf. the note "treatment" to s. 12, *ante*. As to types of treatment, see s. 12 (4) (*a*), (*b*), (*c*), *ante*.

Mental condition
    See the note to s. 12, *ante*.

Writing
    See the note to s. 5, *ante*.

DEFINITIONS
    For "supervision order", "supervised person" and "supervisor", see s. 11, *ante*; for "care order" and "interim order", see s. 20 (1), *post*; for "local authority", "petty sessions area" and "reside", see s. 70 (1), *post*.

16. Provisions supplementary to s. 15

(1) Where the supervisor makes an application or reference under the preceding section to a court he may bring the supervised person before the court, and subject to subsection (5) of this section a court shall not make an order under that section unless the supervised person is present before the court.

(2) Without prejudice to any power to issue a summons or warrant apart from this subsection, a justice may issue a summons or warrant for the purpose of securing the attendance of a supervised person before the court to which any application or reference in respect of him is made under the preceding section; but subsections (3) and (4) of section 47 of the Magistrates' Courts Act 1952

(which among other things restrict the circumstances in which a warrant may be issued) shall apply with the necessary modifications to a warrant under this subsection as they apply to a warrant under that section and as if in subsection (3) after the word "summons" there were inserted the words "cannot be served or".

(3) Where the supervised person is arrested in pursuance of a warrant issued by virtue of the preceding subsection and cannot be brought immediately before the court referred to in that subsection, the person in whose custody he is—

(a) may make arrangements for his detention in a place of safety for a period of not more than seventy-two hours from the time of the arrest (and it shall be lawful for him to be detained in pursuance of the arrangements); and

(b) shall within that period, unless within it the relevant infant is brought before the court aforesaid, bring him before a justice;

and the justice shall either direct that he be released forthwith or—

(i) if he has not attained the age of eighteen, make an interim order in respect of him;

(ii) if he has attained that age, remand him.

(4) If on an application to a court under subsection (1) of the preceding section—

(a) the supervised person is brought before the court under a warrant issued or an interim order made by virtue of the preceding provisions of this section; or

(b) the court considers that it is likely to exercise its powers under that subsection to make an order in respect of the supervised person but, before deciding whether to do so, seeks information with respect to him which it considers is unlikely to be obtained unless the court makes an interim order in respect of him,

the court may make an interim order in respect of the supervised person.

(5) A court may make an order under the preceding section in the absence of the supervised person if the effect of the order is confined to one or more of the following, that is to say—

(a) discharging the supervision order;

(b) cancelling a provision included in the supervision order in pursuance of section 12 or section 18 (2) (b) of this Act;

(c) reducing the duration of the supervision order or any provision included in it in pursuance of the said section 12;

(d) altering in the supervision order the name of any area;

(e) changing the supervisor.

(6) A juvenile court shall not—

(a) exercise its powers under subsection (1) of the preceding section to make a care order or an order discharging a supervision order or inserting in it a requirement authorised by section 12 of this Act or varying or cancelling such a requirement except in a case where the court is satisfied that the supervised person either is unlikely to receive the care or control he needs unless the court makes the order or is likely to receive it notwithstanding the order;

(*b*) exercise its powers to make an order under subsection (5) of the preceding section except in such a case as is mentioned in paragraph (*a*) of this subsection;

(*c*) exercise its powers under the said subsection (1) to make an order inserting a requirement authorised by section 12 (4) of this Act in a supervision order which does not already contain such a requirement unless the court is satisfied as mentioned in the said section 12 (4) on such evidence as is there mentioned.

(7) Where the supervised person has attained the age of fourteen, then except with his consent a court shall not make an order under the preceding section containing provisions which insert in the supervision order a requirement authorised by section 12 (4) of this Act or which alter such a requirement already included in the supervision order otherwise than by removing it or reducing its duration.

(8) The supervised person may appeal to quarter sessions against—

(*a*) any order under the preceding section, except an order made or which could have been made in the absence of the supervised person and an order containing only provisions to which he consented in pursuance of the preceding subsection;

(*b*) the dismissal of an application under that section to discharge a supervision order.

(9) Where an application under the preceding section for the discharge of a supervision order is dismissed, no further application for its discharge shall be made under that section by any person during the period of three months beginning with the date of the dismissal except with the consent of a court having jurisdiction to entertain such an application.

(10) In paragraph (*a*) of subsection (4) of the preceding section "attendance centre order" means such an order to attend an attendance centre as is mentioned in subsection (1) of section 19 of the Criminal Justice Act 1948; and the provisions of that section shall accordingly apply for the purposes of that paragraph as if the words from "has power" to "probation order" in subsection (1) there were substituted the words "considers it appropriate to make an attendance centre order in respect of any person in pursuance of section 15 (4) of the Children and Young Persons Act 1969" and for references to an offender there were substituted references to the supervised person and as if subsection (5) were omitted.

(11) In this and the preceding section references to a juvenile court or any other magistrates' court, in relation to a supervision order, are references to such a court acting for the petty sessions area for the time being named in the order in pursuance of section 18 (2) (*a*) of this Act; and if while an application to a juvenile court in pursuance of the preceding section is pending the supervised person to whom it relates attains the age of seventeen or eighteen, the court shall deal with the application as if he had not attained the age in question.

COMMENCEMENT OF THIS SECTION
    See. s. 73 (2), *post*, and the note thereto.

SUB-S. (1)

    Application or reference
        I.e., an application under s. 15 (1), (3) and (4), *ante*, or a reference under s. 15 (5), *ante*.

    A court; a justice
        See sub-s. (11) of this section.

    Is present
        This is another exception to the general rule contained in the Magistrates' Courts Act 1952, s. 99 (32 Halsbury's Statutes (2nd Edn.) 500) that a party to proceedings before a magistrates' court may be represented by counsel or solicitor.
        Presence of the supervised person is not, however, required in the circumstances specified in sub-s. (5) of this section.

SUB-S. (2): SUMMONS OR WARRANT
    Cf. s. 2 (4), *ante*, which enacts similar provisions in relation to the making of an order on the bringing of care proceedings.

SUB-S. (3)

    Cannot be brought immediately before the court
        Cf. s. 2 (5), *ante*, which enacts similar provisions in relation to the notifying of an order on the bringing of care proceedings.

    Attained the age
        See the note to s. 1, *ante*.

    Interim order
        As to the making of such orders, see s. 22, *post*.

SUB-S. (5)

    Reducing the duration, etc.
        As to the maximum duration of a supervision order, see s. 17, *post*.

    Any area
        I.e., the local authority area or the petty sessions area named in the order in accordance with s. 18 (2),(*a*), *post*.

    Changing the supervisor
        As to the selection of a supervisor, see s. 13, *ante*.

SUB-S. (6): CARE OR CONTROL
    For meaning, see the last leg of s. 70 (1), *post*.

SUB-S. (7): CONSENT
    Cf. the note "Consents" to s. 1, *ante*.

SUB-S. (8)

    Appeal to quarter sessions
        See the note "Quarter sessions" to s. 2, *ante*.

    Made in absence of, etc.
        I.e., an order made by virtue of sub-s. (5) of this section.

SUB-S. (9)

    Months
        See the note to s. 15, *ante*.

    Beginning with, etc.
        See the note to s. 12, *ante*.

Court having jurisdiction

I.e., a juvenile court having jurisdiction in accordance with s. 15 (1) or (5), *ante*, or s. 15 (3) or (4), *ante*, as modified by s. 15 (2), *ante*; or a magistrates' court having jurisdiction in accordance with s. 15 (3) or (4), *ante*.

DEFINITIONS

For "supervisor", "supervised person" and "supervision order". see s. 11, *ante*; for "young person" and "petty sessions area', see s. 70 (1), *post*; for "care order" see s. 20 (1), *post*.

MAGISTRATES' COURTS ACT 1952, s. 47 (3), (4)

See 125 Statutes Supp.

CRIMINAL JUSTICE ACT 1948, S. 19 (1), (5)

See 14 Halsbury's Statutes (2nd Edn.) 1003–1005. Sub-s. (1) of s. 19 of that Act is amended by s. 72 (3), Sch. 5, para. 23, *post*, as from a day to be appointed.

17. Termination of supervision

A supervision order shall, unless it has previously been discharged, cease to have effect—

(a) in any case, on the expiration of the period of three years, or such shorter period as may be specified in the order, beginning with the date on which the order was originally made;

(b) if the order was made by virtue of section 1 of this Act or on the occasion of the discharge of a care order and the supervised person attains the age of eighteen on a day earlier than that on which the order would expire under paragraph (a) above, on that earlier day.

GENERAL NOTE

The provisions contained in this section may be compared with ss. 62 (2) (d) and 75 (3) of the Children and Young Persons Act 1933 (repealed by s. 72 (4), Sch. 6, *post*).

COMMENCEMENT OF THIS SECTION

See s. 73 (2), *post*, and the note thereto.

HAS PREVIOUSLY BEEN DISCHARGED

I.e., by virtue of ss. 1 (4), 15 (1), (3), *ante*. See also as to the discharge of an order, s. 16 (5) (a), (6) (a), *ante*, and as to the dismissal of an application for discharge, s. 16 (8) (b), (9), *ante*.

BEGINNING WITH, ETC.

See the note to s. 12, *ante*.

OR THE DISCHARGE OF A CARE ORDER

I.e., in accordance with s. 1 (4), *ante*, or s. 21 (2), *post*. For meaning of "care order", see s. 20 (1), *post*.

ATTAINS THE AGE

See the note "attained the age" to s. 1, *ante*.

DEFINITIONS

For "supervision order" and "supervised person", see s. 11, *ante*.

18. Supplementary provisions relating to supervision orders

(1) A court shall not make a supervision order unless it is satisfied that the supervised person resides or will reside in the area of a local authority; and a court shall be entitled to be satisfied that the supervised person will so reside if he is to be required to so reside by a provision to be included in the order in pursuance of section 12 (1) of this Act.

(2) A supervision order—

(*a*) shall name the area of the local authority and the petty sessions area in which it appears to the court making the order, or to the court varying any provision included in the order in pursuance of this paragraph, that the supervised person resides or will reside; and

(*b*) may contain such prescribed provisions as the court aforesaid considers appropriate for facilitating the performance by the supervisor of his functions under section 14 of this Act, including any prescribed provisions for requiring visits to be made by the supervised person to the supervisor.

and in paragraph (*b*) of this subsection "prescribed" means prescribed by rules under section 15 of the Justices of the Peace Act 1949.

(3) A court which makes a supervision order or an order varying or discharging a supervision order shall forthwith send a copy of its order—

(*a*) to the supervised person, and if the supervised person is a child, to his parent or guardian; and

(*b*) to the supervisor and any person who has ceased to be the supervisor by virtue of the order; and

(*c*) to any local authority who is not entitled by virtue of the preceding paragraph to such a copy and whose area is named in the supervision order in pursuance of the preceding subsection or has ceased to be so named by virtue of the court's order; and

(*d*) where the supervised person is required by the order, or was required by the supervision order before it was varied or discharged, to reside with an individual or to undergo treatment by or under the direction of an individual or at any place, to the individual or the person in charge of that place; and

(*e*) where a petty sessions area named in the order or discharged order in pursuance of subsection (2) of this section is not that for which the court acts, to the clerk to the justices for the petty sessions area so named;

and, in a case falling within paragraph (*e*) of this subsection, shall also send to the clerk to the justices in question such documents and information relating to the case as the court considers likely to be of assistance to them.

(4) Where a supervision order requires compliance with such directions as are mentioned in section 12 (2) of this Act, any expenditure incurred by the supervisor for the purposes of the directions shall be defrayed by the local authority of which the area is named in the order in pursuance of subsection (2) of this section.

GENERAL NOTE

This section corresponds largely with provisions contained in the Criminal Justice Act 1948, s. 3 (repealed in part) and the Children and Young Persons Act 1963, s. 5, Sch. 1, para. 14 (repealed).

COMMENCEMENT OF THIS SECTION

See s. 73 (2), *post*, and the note thereto.

SUB-S. (2): PRESCRIBED

No rules had been made under the Justices of the Peace Act 1949, s. 15, prescribing matters for the purpose of sub-s. (2) (*b*) of this section up to 1st May 1970.

SUB-S. (3)

Forthwith

On the meaning of this expression, see *Re Southam, Ex parte Lamb* (1881), 19 Ch. D. 169, C.A., at p. 173; *Re Muscovitch, Ex parte Muscovitch*, [1939] 1 All E.R. 135; [1939] Ch. 694, C.A., at p. 139 and pp. 697, 698, respectively; and *Sameen* v. *Abeywickerma*, [1963] 3 All E.R. 382; [1963] A.C. 597, P.C.

And if the supervised person is a child, to his parent or guardian

This provision ensures that those to whom the child belongs are kept informed. Supervision orders are to play an important part in the new arrangements for children and it is very important that the parents should know, in black and white, what is expected of them.

As to meaning of "parent or guardian", see the note to s. 1, *ante*.

Para. (c)

This provision ensures that where, for example, the supervision order has appointed a probation officer as supervisor, and the court includes in the order powers for the supervisor to give directions under s. 12 (2), *ante*, the local authority, which has to meet the cost of giving effect to any such directions should be informed of the making and contents of the order.

Reside with

See the note to s. 12, *ante*.

Undergo treatment, etc.

See s. 12 (4), *ante*.

Clerk to the justices

Cf. the note "clerk of the court" to s. 2, *ante*.

DEFINITIONS

For "supervision order", "supervised person" and "supervisor", see s. 11, *ante*; for "reside", "local authority" and "petty sessions area", see s. 70 (1), *post*.

JUSTICES OF THE PEACE ACT 1949, S. 15

See 28 Halsbury's Statutes (2nd Edn.) 856–857.

19. Facilities for the carrying out of supervisors' directions

(1) It shall be the duty of the children's regional planning committee for each planning area (hereafter in this section referred to as "the committee") to make arrangements, with such persons as the committee thinks fit, for the provision by those persons of facilities for enabling directions given by virtue of section 12 (2) of this Act to persons resident in the area to be carried out effectively.

(2) The committee shall specify the arrangements made in pursuance of the preceding subsection in a scheme and shall submit the scheme to the Secretary of State for him to determine the date on which it is to come into force; and the Secretary of State shall, after consultation with the committee and the relevant authorities, determine that date and notify his determination to the committee.

(3) On receiving a notification in pursuance of subsection (2) of this section in respect of a scheme, the committee shall send copies of the scheme and notification to each of the relevant authorities and to the clerk to the justices for each petty sessions area of which any part is included in the planning area in question; and each of the relevant authorities shall, as soon as practicable after

receiving those documents, keep a copy of them available at their principal offices for inspection by members of the public at all reasonable hours and on demand by any person furnish him with a copy of them free of charge.

(4) If, after the scheme prepared by the committee under this section has come into force, any arrangements specified in it are cancelled or the committee makes arrangements for the purposes of this section other than arrangements so specified, the committee shall send notice of the cancellations or other arrangements, stating the date on which they are to come into force and the alterations in the scheme which they entail, to the Secretary of State and the authorities and clerks mentioned in subsection (3) of this section; and on and after that date the scheme shall have effect subject to those alterations and the relevant authorities shall have, in relation to the notice, the same duty as is imposed on them by that subsection in relation to the scheme.

(5) Arrangements in pursuance of this section shall not be made for any facilities unless the facilities are approved or are of a kind approved by the Secretary of State for the purposes of this section; but where arrangements in pursuance of this section are made by the committee with any of the relevant authorities for the provision of facilities by the authority it shall be the duty of the authority to provide those facilities while the scheme is in force and those arrangements are specified in it.

(6) A court shall not include in a supervision order any such requirements as are mentioned in section 12 (2) of this Act unless the court is satisfied that a scheme under this section is in force for the planning area in which the supervised person resides or will reside or that the date on which such a scheme is to come into force has been determined; and a supervisor authorised to give directions by virtue of any such requirements shall not, in pursuance of those requirements, give directions involving the use of facilities which are not for the time being specified in a scheme in force under this section for the planning area aforesaid.

GENERAL NOTE

This important section places upon the local authorities the responsibility for deciding what facilities it will include in its scheme. This is largely because the central Government does not have the necessary detailed knowledge of what is available in each area.

"Here is a challenge to the Local Authorities to make full and imaginative use of these new powers. The Government hope and expect that they will work in the closest co-operation with the local magistrates, the police, the probation service and any voluntary organisations, including the religious bodies—indeed all societies, bodies, groups and movements which are willing to make facilities available. The main function of the Home Office will be to act as a clearing-house for ideas and as a stimulating influence. The Department will collect all the available material about what is being done or tried out in this field, both in Britain and overseas and will disseminate this information to the local authorities."

(*per* Under-Secretary of State for the Home Department, H. of C. Official Report, S.C.G., 29th April 1969, col. 394.)

COMMENCEMENT OF THIS SECTION

See s. 73 (2), *post*, and the note thereto.

SUB-S. (1)

Children's regional planning committee

As to the establishment of such committees, see s. 35 (3), (4), Sch. 2, *post*.

Persons

In the absence of any contrary intention, this expression includes any body of persons corporate or incorporate; see the Interpretation Act 1889, s. 19 (24 Halsbury's Statutes (2nd Edn.) 222).

During Committee it was indicated that it must be "made clear to the public that these are new means and new methods of dealing with juvenile crime which it is believed will be more successful than the methods at present sought to prevent it", and that "it is essential that they be sold to the public if we are not to have public resentment against them, and it is important, as a means of selling them to that public, that as many people as possible are brought into the circle such as the round table, the rotary and organisations of that nature who are already doing a lot of work among young people and in youth clubs" (H. of C. Official Report, S.C.G., 29th April 1969, col. 399).

SUB-S. (2)

Scheme

Schemes made under this section are not required to be made by statutory instrument, and will not be noted in this work.

Consultation

On what constitutes consultation, see, in particular, *Rollo* v. *Minister of Town and Country Planning*, [1948] 1 All E.R. 13, and *Re Union of Whippingham and East Cowes Benefices, Derham* v. *Church Comrs. of England*, [1954] 2 All E.R. 22; [1954] A.C. 245, P.C.

SUB-S. (3)

Clerk to the justices

Cf. the note "Clerk of the court" to s. 2, *ante*.

Practicable

It should be noted that "practicable" is not the same as "reasonably practicable"; cf., in particular, *Marshall* v. *Gotham, Ltd.*, [1954] 1 All E.R. 937; [1954] A.C. 360, at p. 942 and p. 373, respectively, *per* Lord Reid.　See also as to the meaning of "practicable" in particular, *Lee* v. *Nursery Furnishings, Ltd.*, [1945] 1 All E.R. 387, at p. 389; *Adsett* v. *K. & L. Steelfounders & Engineers, Ltd.*, [1953] 2 All E.R. 320, C.A.; *Moorcroft* v. *Thomas Powles & Sons, Ltd.*, [1962] 3 All E.R. 741, at p. 746; and *Jayne* v. *National Coal Board*, [1963] 2 All E.R. 220.

Members of the public

For a discussion on the meaning of this expression, see *Director of Public Prosecutions* v. *Milbanke Tours, Ltd.*, [1960] 2 All E.R. 467, at p. 471.

Reasonable hours

For construction of this expression, see 37 Halsbury's Laws (3rd Edn.) 102.

DEFINITIONS

For "planning area", see s. 35 (1), *post*; for "relevant authorities", "petty sessions area" and "reside", see s. 70 (1), *post*; for "supervision order", "supervised person" and "supervisor", see s. 11, *ante*.

Committal to care of local authorities

20. Orders for committal to care of local authorities

(1) Any provision of this Act authorising the making of a care order in respect of any person shall be construed as authorising the making of an order committing him to the care of a local authority; and in this Act "care order" shall be construed accordingly and "interim order" means a care order containing provision for the order to expire with the expiration of twenty-eight days, or of a shorter period specified in the order, beginning—

　　(*a*) if the order is made by a court, with the date of the making of the order; and (*b*) if it is made by a justice, with the date when the person to whom it relates was first in legal custody in connection with the matter in consequence of which the order is made.

(2) The local authority to whose care a person is committed by a care order shall be—

(*a*) except in the case of an interim order, the local authority in whose area it appears to the court making the order that that person resides or, if it does not appear to the court that he resides in the area of a local authority, any local authority in whose area it appears to the court that any offence was committed or any circumstances arose in consequence of which the order is made; and

(*b*) in the case of an interim order, such one of the local authorities mentioned in paragraph (*a*) of this subsection as the court or justice making the order thinks fit (whether or not the person in question appears to reside in their area).

(3) Subject to the provisions of the following section, a care order other than an interim order shall cease to have effect—

(*a*) if the person to whom it relates had attained the age of sixteen when the order was originally made, when he attains the age of nineteen; and

(*b*) in any other case, when that person attains the age of eighteen.

(4) A care order shall be sufficient authority for the detention by any local authority or constable of the person to whom the order relates until he is received into the care of the authority to whose care he is committed by the order.

GENERAL NOTE

Much of this section is consequential upon the abolition of the "fit person order" and the "approved school order". One problem arising out of this was that the approved school order ran until the young person was 19 whereas the fit person order ended upon his attaining 18. The section adopts the approved school approach, thus enabling a young person to remain in the care of a local authority until he is 19—a decision which drew the comment from one opponent that it was now absurd "to give a young man the vote but to put him in the care of the local authority." Whatever justification there might be in these criticisms, the Government took exactly the opposite view, saying: "It has been suggested that the period under a care order is, potentially at least, longer than the term of an approved school order and that is a disadvantage over the old. I submit to the Committee that it is a marked advantage. One of the reasons for the general support expressed in comments on both White Papers (*i.e.*, "The Child, The Family and The Young Offender" and "Children in Trouble") for the idea of abolishing the approved school order was the fact that this order has a fixed maximum term and a normal minimum one as well. Provided that there are adequate safeguards—and the Government believe that there are—the more flexible care order is much to be preferred, allowing not only a longer period of care, where necessary, but also an earlier return home where that is appropriate." (*per* the Under-Secretary of State for the Home Office.)

It should be noted that s. 1 of the Children Act 1948 (duty of local authority to provide for orphans, deserted children, etc.) (17 Halsbury's Statutes (3rd Edn.) 539, 540) and s. 2 of that Act (assumption by local authority of parental rights) (*ibid.*, p. 542) are not repealed by this Act. A local authority may therefore either assume care of a child or young person under the Act of 1948 or have such a person committed to its care under this Act.

COMMENCEMENT OF THIS SECTION
> See s. 73 (2), *post*, and the note thereto.

SUB-S. (1)

Any provision . . . authorising the making of a care order
> *I.e.*, ss. 1 (3) (*c*), 7 (7) (*a*), 15 (1), *ante*.
> As to the variation and discharge of care orders, see s. 21, *post*.

Any person
> *I.e.*, any child or young person; see s. 1 (1), (3), *ante*, for the meanings of "child" and "young person", see s. 70 (1), *post*.

Local authority
> As to the powers and duties of local authorities with respect to persons committed to their care, see s. 24, *post*.

Interim order
> For special provisions relating to such orders, see s. 22, *post*. As to the making of interim orders where a child or young person is detained in a place of safety, see s. 28 (6), *post*.

Beginning with, etc.
> See the note to s. 12, *ante*.

Any circumstances arose
> *I.e.*, any of the circumstances specified in s. 1 (2) (*a*)–(*d*), *ante*.

SUB-S. (3)
> This subsection attracted a great deal of criticism: mostly based upon two issues. First that there seemed to be an anomaly between para. (*a*), which referred to an order persisting until the person was 19 and *para*. (*b*), which directed it to cease when he was 18. To this the answer was given that a care order is not a sentence. Its object is care, treatment and control. This fact is basic to all the provisions of the Act about care orders, including those mentioned in this section. Consequently the length of time for which care, treatment or control under a care order is required is bound to vary from one case to another. This cannot be anticipated at the time the order is made. It is essential therefore that the law should allow sufficient time for treatment and sufficient flexibility to vary the actual length of each order according to the circumstances of the individual child—to whose interests the whole of this Act is geared. A court is not a treatment agency: its proper function is judicial—that is, to decide whether the circumstances justify the making of a care order in the first place and to decide whether to revoke the order if an application is made by the child, his parents or the local authority. If the Act provided only for orders to last until 18, then in many cases this would result in a young person, just over 17, for example, being in care for barely one year. This would often not be long enough for the treatment which was desirable. The length of treatment does not automatically diminish as a young person approaches his 17th birthday, and if the aim of the care order is to provide the treatment required and that aim is to be achieved, the law must allow at least two years in all cases.
> The second objection taken was that there seemed to be no provision for limiting the time under which a child or young person might be kept in the care of the authorities. The general impression was that "under these new arrangements, they just bung them anywhere." Several strong pleas were made that there should be a review of every case at least every three years. But the Government replied that to impose a three-year review would make a radical change in a system which has been operating very successfully for the past 36 years. A care order under the Act corresponds to the fit person order under the old enactments. Of the several thousands of children in care under fit person orders, there are included a substantial number of offenders. Many are children with difficult behavioural problems and a larger number are committed to care for their own protection. There is nothing out of this experience over 36 years to justify restricting the fit person order to three years at a time. The effect of the proposal would be to parade all children in care—which means from the age of nought to 18; infants in arms to youths in crash-helmets—before the courts every three years. Furthermore, there are already quite adequate safeguards in that under s. 21 (2), (3), *post*, it is open to the child, young person or parents or guardian to lodge appeals at three-monthly intervals. In addition there is the great openness of the community home system which would ensure that any sinister moves against a child would soon be

detected and the resulting publicity and scandal, as has well been illustrated in the past when the isolated case has been brought to light, should act as a spur to the authorities to see that right is done. A further check on any abuse in this respect would arise out of the provisions of s. 43 (2), *post*, which empowers the Home Secretary to make regulations relevant to the care, custody and control of persons in care.

Attained the age
See the note to s. 1, *ante*.

SUB-S. (4)

Detention
As to the detention of a child or young person *prior* to the making of an order, see s. 28, *post*.

Constable
See the note to s. 1, *ante*.

TRANSFERS
For modifications of this section in relation to transfers between England or Wales and Northern Ireland, see s. 25 (1), *post*; and between England or Wales and the Channel Islands or the Isle of Man, see s. 26 (3), *post*.

DEFINITIONS
For "local authority" and "reside", see s. 70 (1), *post*.

21. Variation and discharge of care orders

(1) If it appears to a juvenile court, on the application of a local authority to whose care a person is committed by a care order which would cease to have effect by virtue of subsection (3) (*b*) of the preceding section, that he is accommodated in a community home or a home provided by the Secretary of State and that by reason of his mental condition or behaviour it is in his interest or the public interest for him to continue to be so accommodated after he attains the age of eighteen, the court may order that the care order shall continue in force until he attains the age of nineteen; but the court shall not make an order under this subsection unless the person in question is present before the court.

(2) If it appears to a juvenile court, on the application of a local authority to whose care a person is committed by a care order or on the application of that person, that it is appropriate to discharge the order, the court may discharge it and on discharging it may, unless it was an interim order and unless the person to whom the discharged order related has attained the age of eighteen, make a supervision order in respect of him.

(3) Where an application under the preceding subsection for the discharge of a care order is dismissed, then—

(*a*) in the case of an interim order, no further application for its discharge shall be made under that subsection except with the consent of a juvenile court (without prejudice to the power to make an application under subsection (4) of the following section); and

(*b*) in any other case, no further application for its discharge shall be made under this subsection by any person during the period of three months beginning with the date of the dismissal except with the consent of a juvenile court.

(4) The person to whom the relevant care order relates or related may appeal to quarter sessions against an order under subsection (1) of this section or a supervision order made in pursuance of subsection (2) of this section or the dismissal of an application under the said subsection (2) for the discharge of the care order.

(5) The local authority to whose care a person is committed by a care order (other than an interim order) may, within the period of three months beginning with the date of the order, appeal to quarter sessions against the provision of the order naming their area on the ground that at the time the order was made the person aforesaid resided in the area of another local authority named in the notice of appeal; but no appeal shall be brought by a local authority under this subsection unless they give notice in writing of the proposal to bring it to the other local authority in question before giving notice of appeal.

(6) References in this section to a juvenile court, in relation to a care order, are references to a juvenile court acting for any part of the area of the local authority to whose care a person is committed by the order or for the place where that person resides.

COMMENCEMENT OF THIS SECTION
    See s. 73 (2), *post*, and the note thereto.

SUB-S. (1)

Juvenile court
    See sub-s. (6) of this section, see also the note to s. 1, *ante*.

Accommodated in a community home
    See also s. 50, *post*.

Community home
    As to the establishment of such homes, see ss. 35–45, *post*.

Attains the age
    See the note "attained the age" to s. 1, *ante*.

The court may order
    As to an appeal from such order, see sub-s. (4) of this section.

Is present
    See the note to s. 16, *ante*.

SUB-SS. (2)–(4)
    These subsections apply also to a warrant issued pursuant to s. 22 (5), *post*; see s. 22 (6), *post*.

Application of that person
    The application may be made by his parent or guardian; see s. 70 (2), *post*.
    The Government promised by means either of a circular to local authorities or of rules of court to ensure that the child, if he is old enough to understand, and his parents, are made fully aware of the nature of a care order and of their right to apply at any time for its revocation.

On discharging it may . . . make a supervision order
    For the converse situation, see s. 15 (1), *ante*.

Months
    See the note to s. 15, *ante*.

Beginning with, etc.
    See the note to s. 12, *ante*.

Quarter sessions
    See the note to s. 2, *ante*.

SUB-S. (5): WRITING
    See the note to s. 5, *ante*.

TRANSFERS
    For modification of this section in relation to a transfer between England or Wales and Northern Ireland, see s. 25 (1), *post*. The section is omitted in relation to a transfer between England or Wales and the Channel Islands or the Isle of Man by virtue of s. 26 (3), *post*.

DEFINITIONS
    For "local authority" and "reside", see s. 70 (1), *post*; for "care order", "interim order", see s. 20 (1), *ante*; for "supervision order", see s. 11, *ante*.

22. Special provisions relating to interim orders

(1) A juvenile court or a justice shall not make an interim order in respect of any person unless either—

    (*a*) that person is present before the court or justice; or

    (*b*) the court or justice is satisfied that he is under the age of five or cannot be present as aforesaid by reason of illness or accident.

(2) An interim order shall contain provision requiring the local authority to whose care a person is committed by the order to bring that person before a court specified in the order on the expiration of the order or at such earlier time as the specified court may require, so however that the said provision shall, if the court making the order considers it appropriate so to direct by reason of the fact that that person is under the age of five or by reason of illness or accident, require the local authority to bring him before the specified court on the expiration of the order only if the specified court so requires.

(3) A juvenile court acting for the same area as a juvenile court by which or a justice by whom an interim order has been made in respect of any person may, at any time before the expiration of the order, make a further interim order in respect of him; and the power to make an interim order conferred by this subsection is without prejudice to any other power to make such an order.

(4) The High Court may, on the application of a person to whom an interim order relates, discharge the order on such terms as the court thinks fit; but if on such an application the discharge of the order is refused, the local authority to whose care he is committed by the order shall not exercise in his case their powers under section 13 (2) of the Children Act 1948 (which enables them to allow a parent or other person to be in charge of him) except with the consent and in accordance with any directions of the High Court.

(5) If a court which has made or, apart from this subsection, would make an interim order in respect of a person who has attained the age of fourteen certifies that he is of so unruly a character that he cannot safely be committed to the care of a local authority and has been notified by the Secretary of State that a remand centre is available for the reception from the court of persons of his class or description, then, subject to the following provisions of this section, the court shall commit him to a remand centre for twenty-eight days or such shorter period as may be specified in the warrant; but in a case where an interim order is in force in respect of the person in question, a warrant under this subsection

6—A.L.S. 189

shall not be issued in respect of him except on the application of the local authority to whose care he is committed by the order and shall not be issued for a period extending beyond the date fixed for the expiration of the order, and on the issue of a warrant under this subsection in such a case the interim order shall cease to have effect.

In this subsection "court" includes a justice.

(6) Subsections (1), (3) and (4) of this section, so much of section 2 (11) (*a*) as requires the clerk to be informed and section 21 (2) to (4) of this Act shall apply to a warrant under subsection (5) of this section as they apply to an interim order but as if the words "is under the age of five or" in subsection (1) of this section were omitted.

COMMENCEMENT OF THIS SECTION
See s. 73 (2), *post*, and the note thereto.

SUB-S. (1)
Juvenile court
See the note to s. 1, *ante*.

Is present
Cf. the note to s. 16, *ante*.

Under the age of five
Cf. the note "attained the age" to s. 1, *ante*.

Accident
An accident in the popular and ordinary sense of the word denotes, in the words of Lord Macnaghten in *Fenton* v. *Thorley & Co., Ltd.*, [1903] A.C. 443, at p. 448, "an unlooked-for mishap or an untoward event which is not expected or designed".

SUB-S. (4)
High court
I.e., Her Majesty's High Court of Justice in England; see the Interpretation Act 1889, s. 13 (24 Halsbury's Statutes (2nd Edn.) 213).

Application
An application may also be made by a parent or guardian; see s. 70 (2), *post*.

Consent
Cf. the note "consents" to s. 1, *ante*.

SUB-S. (5)
Court
Note the last line of this subsection.

Person who has attained the age of 14
Note that the Secretary of State may by order provide that sub-s. (5) shall have effect as if for the reference to the age of 14 there were substituted a reference to such greater age as may be specified; see s. 34 (1) (*f*), *post*.

Remand centre
I.e., a place for the detention of persons not less than 14 but under 21 years of age; see the Prisons Act 1952, s. 43 (1) (32 Halsbury's Statutes (2nd Edn.) 648).

SUB-S. (6)
Clerk
I.e., clerk of the court; see the note to s. 2, *ante*.

DEFINITIONS

For "interim order", see s. 20 (1), *ante*; for "local authority" see s. 70 (1), *post*.

TRANSITIONAL PROVISION

See the note "Person who has attained the age of 14" above.

CHILDREN ACT 1948, S. 13 (2)

See 17 Halsbury's Statutes (2nd Edn.) 550. Section 13 of that Act is substituted by s. 49, *post*, as from a day to be appointed.

23. Remand to care of local authorities etc.

(1) Where a court—

    (*a*) remands or commits for trial a child charged with homicide or remands a child convicted of homicide; or

    (*b*) remands a young person charged with or convicted of one or more offences or commits him for trial or sentence,

and he is not released on bail, then, subject to the following provisions of this section, the court shall commit him to the care of a local authority in whose area it appears to the court that he resides or that the offence or one of the offences was committed.

(2) If the court aforesaid certifies that a young person is of so unruly a character that he cannot safely be committed to the care of a local authority under the preceding subsection, then if the court has been notified by the Secretary of State that a remand centre is available for the reception from the court of persons of his class or description, it shall commit him to a remand centre and, if it has not been so notified, it shall commit him to a prison.

(3) If, on the application of the local authority to whose care a young person is committed by a warrant under subsection (1) of this section, the court by which he was so committed or any magistrates' court having jurisdiction in the place where he is for the time being certifies as mentioned in subsection (2) of this section, the provisions of the said subsection (2) relating to committal shall apply in relation to him and he shall cease to be committed in pursuance of the said subsection (1).

(4) The preceding provisions of this section shall have effect subject to the provisions of section 28 of the Magistrates' Courts Act 1952 (which relates to committal to quarter sessions with a view to a borstal sentence).

(5) In this section "court" and "magistrates' court" include a justice; and notwithstanding anything in the preceding provisions of this section, section 105 (5) of the said Act of 1952 (which provides for remands to the custody of a constable for periods not exceeding three clear days) shall have effect in relation to a child or young person as if for the reference to three clear days there were substituted a reference to twenty-four hours.

GENERAL NOTE

This section is mostly derived from subsisting law.

It should be noted that s. 7 (1), *ante*, raises the age at which a young person can be sent to borstal from 15 to 17 and so it is still possible for young persons to be kept in custody in accordance with the Magistrates' Courts Act 1952, s. 28, which is applied by sub-s. (4) of this section.

Sub-s. (1) (*a*) of this section ensures that a child charged with homicide and who is not released on bail will be committed to the care of the local authority.

COMMENCEMENT OF THIS SECTION
See s. 73 (2), *post*, and the note thereto.

SUB-S. (1)

Court
For meaning, see sub-s. (5) of this section.

Remands
As to remand of persons aged 17 to 20, see the Criminal Justice Act 1948, s. 27, substituted by Sch. 5, para. 24, *post*, as from a day to be appointed.

Young person
I.e., a person who has attained the age of 14 and is under 17; see s. 70 (1), *post*.
Note, however, that the Secretary of State may provide by order that any reference to a young person in sub-s. (1) shall be construed as including a child who has attained such an age as may be specified, not being over ten; see s. 34 (1) (*c*), (4), *post*; he may further provide that sub-ss. (2) or (3) shall have effect as if references to a "young person" excluded a young person who has not attained such age as may be specified; see s. 31 (4) (*e*), *post*.

Commits . . . for trial
See the note to s. 6, *ante.*

Remand centre
See the note to s. 22, *ante.*

Prison
As to prisons generally, see the Prison Act 1952 (32 Halsbury's Statutes (2nd Edn.) 623 *et seq.*).

Magistrates' court
See sub-s. (5) of this section, and also the note to s. 5, *ante.*

Jurisdiction
See the note to s. 3, *ante.*

DEFINITIONS
For "young person", "local authority", "child" and "resides", see s. 70 (1), *post*.

TRANSITIONAL PROVISION
See the second para. of the note "Young person" above.

MAGISTRATES' COURTS ACT 1952, ss. 28, 105 (5)
See 32 Halsbury's Statutes (2nd Edn.) 447, 448, 505.

24. Powers and duties of local authorities etc. with respect to persons committed to their care

(1) It shall be the duty of a local authority to whose care a person is committed by a care order or by a warrant under subsection (1) of the preceding section to receive him into their care and, notwithstanding any claim by his parent or guardian, to keep him in their care while the order or warrant is in force.

(2) A local authority shall, subject to the following provisions of this section, have the same powers and duties with respect to a person in their care by virtue of a care order or such a warrant as his parent or guardian would have apart from the order or warrant and may (without prejudice to the preceding provisions of this subsection but subject to regulations made in pursuance of section 43 of this Act) restrict his liberty to such extent as the authority consider appropriate.

(3) A local authority shall not cause a person in their care by virtue of a care order to be brought up in any religious creed other than that in which he would have been brought up apart from the order.

(4) It shall be the duty of a local authority to comply with any provision included in an interim order in pursuance of section 22 (2) of this Act and, in the case of a person in their care by virtue of the preceding section, to permit him to be removed from their care in due course of law.

(5) If a person who is subject to a care order and has attained the age of five is accommodated in a community home or other establishment which he has not been allowed to leave during the preceding three months for the purpose of ordinary attendance at an educational institution or at work and it appears to the local authority to whose care he is committed by the order that—

(*a*) communication between him and his parent or guardian has been so infrequent that it is appropriate to appoint a visitor for him; or

(*b*) he has not lived with or visited or been visited by either of his parents or his guardian during the preceding twelve months,

it shall be the duty of the authority to appoint an independent person to be his visitor for the purposes of this subsection; and a person so appointed shall—

(i) have the duty of visiting, advising and befriending the person to whom the care order relates; and

(ii) be entitled to exercise on behalf of that person his powers under section 21 (2) of this Act; and

(iii) be entitled to recover from the authority who appointed him any expenses reasonably incurred by him for the purposes of his functions under this subsection.

In this section "independent person" means a person satisfying such conditions as may be prescribed by regulations made by the Secretary of State with a view to securing that he is independent of the local authority in question and unconnected with any community home.

(6) A person's appointment as a visitor in pursuance of the preceding subsection shall be determined if the care order in question ceases to be in force or he gives notice in writing to the authority who appointed him that he resigns the appointment or the authority give him notice in writing that they terminate it; but the determination of such an appointment shall not prejudice any duty under the preceding subsection to make a further appointment.

(7) The functions conferred on a local authority by the preceding provisions of this section in respect of any person are in addition to the functions which, by virtue of section 27 of this Act, are conferred on the authority in respect of him by Part II of the Children Act 1948.

(8) While a care order other than an interim order is in force in respect of a person who has not attained the age of eighteen, it shall be the duty of his parent to keep the local authority to whose care he is committed by the order informed of the parent's address; and if the parent knows of the order and fails to perform his duty under this subsection, the parent shall be liable on summary conviction to a fine not exceeding ten pounds unless he shows that at the

material time he was residing at the address of the other parent and had
reasonable cause to believe that the other parent had kept the authority
informed of their address.

COMMENCEMENT OF THIS SECTION
See s. 73 (2), *post*, and the note thereto.

SUB-S. (1)

Parent or guardian
See the note to s. 1, *ante*.

Keep him in their care
This does not mean that the child or young person must be deprived of liberty while
he is in care; see sub-s. (2) (power to restrict liberty to the extent the authority
considers appropriate). See also (by virtue of sub-s. (7) of this section), the Children
Act 1948, s. 13 (2), as substituted by s. 49, *post*. But note that by s. 27 (3), *post*, the
Secretary of State is empowered to give directions to a local authority as to the exercise
of their powers in relation to a particular child in their care, and it is the duty of the
authority to comply with such directions. Cf. also the duty of a local authority to keep
and "detain" a person committed to their care in pursuance of arrangements made under
s. 29 (3), *post*. Cf. also the Secretary of State's power under s. 42 (2) (*c*), *post*, to make
regulations requiring his approval for the provision and use of accommodation for the
purpose of restricting the liberty of children in community homes.
      As to the removal to a borstal institution of a young person in care who has attained
the age of 15 (or such greater age as may be specified by order under s. 34 (1) (*f*), *post*),
see s. 31, *post*.

SUB-S. (3)

Cause
      In *McLeod* (or *Houston*) v. *Buchanan*, [1940] 2 All E.R. 179, H.L., at p. 187, Lord
Wright said: "To cause the user involves some express or positive mandate from the
person 'causing' to the other person, or some authority from the former to the latter,
arising in the circumstances of the case." It follows, therefore, that, in the words of
Donovan, J. (as he then was) in *Shave* v. *Rosner*, [1954] 2 All E.R. 208; [1954] 2 Q.B.
113, at p. 282 and p. 117 respectively, approved in *Shulton (Great Britain) Ltd.* v. *Slough
Borough Council*, [1967] 2 All E.R. 137, "'cause', in this context, involves . . . some
degree of dominance or of control, or some express or positive mandate, that is, in or by
the person alleged to have caused the prohibited act"; see also *Ellis* v. *Smith*, [1962]
3 All E.R. 954; and see, in particular, *Tophams, Ltd.* v. *Earl Sefton*, [1966] 1 All E.R.
1039; [1967] 1 A.C. 50.

Religious creed
      Prima facie the parents have the legal right to control the religion of a child that is
too young to have any wishes of its own; cf. the Custody of Children Act 1891, s. 4
(17 Halsbury's Statutes (3rd Edn.) 421); the Guardianship of Infants Act 1925, s. 1
(17 Halsbury's Statutes (3rd Edn.) 424); *Re Carroll (J. M.)*, [1931] 1 K.B. 317, C.A.;
and *Re Collins*, [1950] 1 All E.R. 1057; [1950] Ch 498, C.A.; and also see the
Legitimacy Act 1959, s. 3 (119 Statutes Supp.); *Re W., W.* v. *M.*, [1907] 2 Ch. 557, C.A.;
Ward v. *Laverty*, [1925] A.C. 101; [1924] All E.R. Rep. 319; and *Re Adoption Application No. 41/61*, [1962] 3 All E.R. 553; [1963] Ch. 315, C.A.

SUB-S. (4): IN DUE COURSE OF LAW
      E.g., pursuant to an application under s. 21, *ante*.

SUB-S. (5)
Certain safeguards with respect to persons committed to the care of local authorities,
are already provided for by regulations under the Children Act 1948, s. 42, and by s. 63,
post, which requires local authorities to make returns of information to the Secretary
of State with respect to children in their care, and requires the Secretary of State to lay
before Parliament annual abstracts of information received by them and reports as to the
exercise by local authorities of their functions under the Children Act 1948, s. 39 (1)
(which is to contain a reference to their functions under this Act by virtue of s. 72 (3),
Sch. 5, para. 18, *post*).
      These subsections now provide for additional safeguards against the danger of
children in care being "forgotten", by providing that where a person over 5 is kept in

care in a community home and has not been allowed to leave during the previous 3 months to attend school or go to work and either communication between him and his parents or guardian is very infrequent or he has not lived with or visited or been visited by either of his parents or his guardian during the preceding 12 months, the local authority must appoint an independent person to be his visitor. The visitor will have the duty to "advise, assist and befriend" the person in care, and be entitled to apply to the court for the discharge of the care order.

Attained the age
See the note to s. 1, *ante*.

Allowed to leave
It is submitted that a person would not be taken to have been "allowed to leave" the establishment in which he was kept in care simply because he was allowed to go to church or participate in casual outings. It should be noted that children under five have been excluded because at that age they spend most of their lives in the establishments where they live and it is not usual for children under five to be "allowed to leave" within the meaning of the subsection. The additional safeguards do not apply to children who are living with foster parents or to children who go out daily to school or to work.

Note that the authority will have some discretion to judge whether the contact between the child and parents is so infrequent that a visitor should be appointed.

Parent or guardian
See the notes to s. 1, *ante*.

Independent person
In reply to a question, the Government said that such a person should not be a member or an officer of the local authority, or anyone in the local authority's employment, direct or indirect. The kinds of person contemplated were those who would be readily available to the authority—magistrates, teachers, retired clergy, citizens of good repute—and not only of good repute but of good intent and willing to take on this work.

Commenting upon this, the Government spokesman in the House of Lords said:

> "This independent visitor will have not only the right to take the case to court at any time if he thinks that desirable, but also the duty to visit, advise and befriend the child. This means that he will be doing some of the things which the child's absent or ineffective parents might otherwise have done—visiting him, discussing his case with the staff of the establishment and of the local authority, and generally giving what help he can. I believe that this is a valuable feature of this scheme. It will ensure that cases go to court when they should; and it will also provide a source of outside help and guidance to the child, whether or not an application is made to the court. It may then mean—in fact I think it will mean—that many children who have no parents, or who have ineffective parents, may gain a friend for life."

Community home
For meaning, see s. 36 (1), *post*; and see generally ss. 34–45, *post*.

Or other establishment
E.g., a home such as is referred to in s. 64, *post*, or a voluntary home other than a community home; see the Children Act 1948, s. 13, as substituted by s. 49, *post*.

SUB-S. (6): WRITING
See the note to s. 5, *ante*.

SUB-S. (8)
This replaces s. 14 of the Children and Young Persons Act 1963 which placed a duty upon parents who had a child in an approved school to keep the local authority notified of changes in address. The new provision extends this to the parents of any child under the age of 18 subjected to a care order.

Summary conviction
Cf. the note "Summary proceedings" to s. 3, *ante*.

DEFINITIONS
For "local authority" and "reside" see s. 70 (1), *post*; for "care order", "interim order", see s. 20 (1), *ante*.

CHILDREN ACT 1948, PART II (SS. 11–22)
> See 17 Halsbury's Statutes (3rd Edn.) 549–557. Ss. 11, 13, 19 of that Act are substituted, s. 20 (1) thereof is amended and ss. 15, 16 thereof are repealed by ss. 27, 49, 50, 72 (3), (4), Sch. 5, para. 15, Sch. 6, *post*, respectively as from a day to be appointed. For a modification of s. 12 (1) of that Act, see s. 27 (2), *post*.

REGULATIONS
> See generally as to regulations under this Act, s. 69, *post*.
> No regulations had been made under sub-s. (5) of this section up to 1st May 1970.

Transfer

25. Transfers between England or Wales and Northern Ireland

(1) If it appears to the Secretary of State, on the application of the welfare authority or the managers of the training school to whose care a person is committed by a fit person order or by virtue of a training school order, that his parent or guardian resides or will reside in the area of a local authority in England or Wales, the Secretary of State may make an order committing him to the care of that local authority; and while an order under this subsection is in force it shall have effect as if it were a care order and as if sections 20 (2) and (3) and 21 (1) and (5) of this Act were omitted and in section 31 (3) (a) of this Act for the reference to section 20 (3) there were substituted a reference to subsection (3) of this section.

(2) If it appears to the Minister of Home Affairs for Northern Ireland, on the application of the local authority to whose care a person is committed by a care order other than an interim order, that his parent or guardian resides or will reside in Northern Ireland, the said Minister may make an order committing him to the care of the managers of a training school or to the care of the welfare authority in whose area his parent or guardian resides or will reside; and the provisions of the Children and Young Persons Act (Northern Ireland) 1968 (except sections 83 (3) (a), 88 (3), 90 and 91 (3)) shall apply to an order under this subsection as if it were a training school order made on the date of the care order or, as the case may be, a fit person order.

If an order under this subsection commits a person to the care of the managers of a training school, the contributions to be made in respect of him under section 161 of the said Act of 1968 shall be made by such council as may be named in that order, being the council within whose district his parent proposes to reside or is residing at the time of the order.

(3) When a person is received into the care of a local authority or welfare authority or the managers of a training school in pursuance of an order under this section, the training school order, fit person order or care order in consequence of which the order under this section was made shall cease to have effect; and the order under this section shall, unless it is discharged earlier, cease to have effect—

> (a) in the case of an order under subsection (1), on the earlier of the following dates, that is to say, the date when the person to whom the order relates attain the age of nineteen or the date when, by the effluxion of time, the fit person order aforesaid would have ceased to

have effect or, as the case may be, the period of his detention under the training school order aforesaid would have expired;

(*b*) in the case of an order under subsection (2), on the date when the care order aforesaid would have ceased to have effect by the effluxion of time or—

     (i) if the person to whom the order relates is committed by it to the care of a welfare authority and will attain the age of eighteen before that date, when he attains that age;

     (ii) if the order has effect by virtue of subsection (2) as a training school order and the period of supervision following the detention of the person in question in pursuance of the order expires before that date, when that period expires.

(4) An order under this section shall be sufficient authority for the detention in Northern Ireland, by any constable or by a person duly authorised by a local authority or welfare authority or the managers of a training school, of the person to whom the order relates until he is received into the care of the authority or managers to whose care he is committed by the order.

(5) In this section "training school", "training school order" and "welfare authority" have the same meaning as in the said Act of 1968, and "fit person order" means an order under that Act committing a person to the care of a fit person.

GENERAL NOTE

This provides for the transfer to Northern Ireland of persons who are subject to English care orders and for the transfer to England or Wales of persons who are subject to Northern Ireland training school orders or fit person orders. These transfer provisions operate, in a way similar to those affecting Scotland, only where the parents or guardians of the children live or intend to live in the other country. The situation contemplated by the provisions is that wherein, after an order has been made in relation to a child, the parents move to the other country and it is desirable that the child should go as well. A more exceptional case could involve a child resident in one country being brought before the court of another.

Cf. also General Note to following section.

COMMENCEMENT OF THIS SECTION

See s. 73 (2), *post*, and the note thereto.

SUB-S. (1)

Fit person order; training school; training school order; welfare authority
For meanings, see sub-s. (5) of this section.

Parent or guardian
See the notes to s. 1, *ante*.

May make an order
Orders under this section are not required to be made by statutory instrument; see s. 69 (1), *post*.

SUB-S. (3): ATTAINS THE AGE
Cf. the note "Attained the age" to s. 1, *ante*.

SUB-S. (4): CONSTABLE
See the note to s. 1, *ante*.

DEFINITIONS
   For "local authority" and "reside", see s. 70 (1), *post*; for "care order" and "interim
order", see s. 20 (1), *ante*.

CHILDREN AND YOUNG PERSONS ACT (NORTHERN IRELAND) 1968
   1968 c. 34 (N.I.); not printed in this work.

26. Transfers between England or Wales and the Channel Islands or Isle of Man

(1) The Secretary of State may by order designate for the purposes of this section an order of any description which—

  (*a*) a court in the Isle of Man or any of the Channel Islands is authorised to make by the law for the time being in force in that country; and

  (*b*) provides for the committal to the care of a public authority of a person who has not attained the age of eighteen; and

  (*c*) appears to the Secretary of State to be of the same nature as a care order other than an interim order;

and in this section "relevant order" means an order of a description for the time being so designated and "the relevant authority", in relation to a relevant order, means the authority in the Isle of Man or any of the Channel Islands to whose care the person to whom the order relates is, under the law of that country, committed by the order.

(2) The Secretary of State may authorise a local authority to receive into their care any person named in the authorisation who is the subject of a relevant order; and while such an authorisation is in force in respect of any person he shall, subject to the following subsection, be deemed to be the subject of a care order committing him to the care of the local authority.

(3) This Act shall have effect, in relation to a person in respect of whom an authorisation under this section is in force, as if sections 20 (2) and (3), 21 and 31 and in section 27 (4) the words from "and if" onwards were omitted; and it shall be the duty of a local authority who propose, in exercise of their powers under section 13 (2) of the Children Act 1948, to allow such a person to be under the charge and control of a person residing outside England and Wales to consult the relevant authority before exercising those powers.

(4) An authorisation given to a local authority under this section shall cease to have effect when—

  (*a*) the local authority is informed by the Secretary of State that he has revoked it; or

  (*b*) the relevant order to which the authorisation relates ceases to have effect by the effluxion of time under the law of the place where the order was made or the local authority is informed by the relevant authority that the order has been discharged under that law; or

  (*c*) the person to whom the relevant order relates is again received into the care of the relevant authority;

and if a local authority having by virtue of this section the care of a person to whom a relevant order relates is requested by the relevant authority to make arrangements for him to be received again into the care of the relevant authority, it shall be the duty of the local authority to comply with the request.

GENERAL NOTE

This section provides for the accommodation in the United Kingdom of children and young persons but who are subject to court orders made in the Channel Islands and the Isle of Man. The existing law, which was contained in s. 83 of the Children and Young Persons Act 1933 (repealed) provides that if the insular law enables children or young persons under 17 years of age to be sent to approved schools in England, a child or young person with respect to whom such an order is made may be received in such approved school as the Secretary of State may direct. The child is then treated as if it were subject to an approved school order made under mainland law. With the abolition of the approved school order in England and Wales this will no longer be possible and other arrangements are necessary. A similar problem arises with respect to fit person orders, which are also due for abolition. There can be no doubt that the islands will make their own adaptations to their law as regards these orders or may introduce new ones. The section is, however, designed to obviate any difficulties, and enables the Secretary of State to designate an insular order to be the same as a care order—provided, of course, that it partakes of substantially the same nature. A child or young person may then be received into the care of any local authority in England or Wales which is able or willing to take him.

Cf. also General Note to preceding section.

COMMENCEMENT OF THIS SECTION

See s. 73 (2), *post*, and the note thereto.

SUB-S. (I)

Isle of Man

The Isle of Man is not part of the United Kingdom but is included in the British Islands. Legislation passed by the Tynwald Court must be assented to by the Queen in Council, but legislation by the United Kingdom Parliament is confined to matters of special importance and non-local character. See 5 Halsbury's Laws (3rd Edn.) 650.

Channel Islands

I.e., Guernsey, Jersey, Alderney and Sark and their respective dependencies, cf. the Customs and Excise Act 1952, s. 37 (9 Halsbury's Statutes (3rd Edn.) 88). The functions of legislating for purely domestic matters is in practice left to the local legislative bodies, but the right of Parliament to legislate is paramount. Acts of Parliament affecting the Islands are sent to the Royal Courts of Jersey and Guernsey for registration. See 5 Halsbury's Laws (3rd Edn.) 648.

Attained the age

See the note to s. I, *ante*.

DEFINITIONS

For "care order" and "interim order", see s. 20 (I), *ante*; for "local authority" and "reside", see s. 70 (I), *post*.

CHILDREN ACT 1948, S. 13 (2)

For that section as substituted, see s. 49, *post*.

ORDER UNDER THIS SECTION

No order had been made under this section up to 1st May 1970.

Consequential modifications of ss. 11 and 12 of Children Act 1948

27. Consequential modifications of 1948 c. 43 ss. 11 and 12

(1) For section 11 of the Children Act 1948 (which specifies the children in respect of whom functions are conferred on local authorities by Part II of that Act) there shall be substituted the following section:—

11. Children to whom Part II applies

Except where the contrary intention appears, any reference in this Part of this Act to a child who is or was in the care of a local authority is a reference to a child who is or was in the care of the authority under section 1 of this Act or by virtue of a care order within the meaning of the Children and Young Persons Act 1969 or a warrant under section 23 (1) of that Act (which relates to remands in the care of local authorities).;

but nothing in the said section 11 as replaced by this subsection prejudices the application of any provision of the said Part II to any person by virtue of an enactment passed after that Act and before this Act.

(2) If it appears to a local authority that it is necessary, for the purpose of protecting members of the public, to exercise their powers in relation to a particular child in their care in a manner which may not be consistent with their general duty under section 12 (1) of the said Act of 1948 to further his best interests and afford him opportunity for proper development, the authority may, notwithstanding that duty, act in that manner.

(3) If the Secretary of State considers it necessary, for the purpose of protecting members of the public, to give directions to a local authority with respect to the exercise of their powers in relation to a particular child in their care, he may give such directions to the authority; and it shall be the duty of the authority, notwithstanding their general duty aforesaid, to comply with any such directions.

(4) Without prejudice to their general duty aforesaid, it shall be the duty of a local authority who have at any time had a child in their care throughout the preceding six months and have not during that period held a review of his case in pursuance of this subsection to review his case as soon as is practicable after the expiration of that period and, if a care order is in force with respect to him, to consider in the course of the review whether to make an application for the discharge of the order.

COMMENCEMENT OF THIS SECTION
    See s. 73 (2), *post*, and the note thereto.

SUB-S. (1)

Enactment
    For meanings, see s. 70 (4), *post*.

Passed after that Act, etc.
    The Children Act 1948 was passed (i.e. received the Royal Assent) on 30th June 1948; this Act was passed on 22nd October 1969.

SUB-S. (2)
    The necessity for local authorities to take measures for the protection of the public arises under the existing law, with the fit person order, but it may arise more frequently when local authorities are responsible under care orders, for the care and control of young persons who would at present be sent to approved school or borstal. This subsection therefore clearly lays down that authorities have the power to take such

measures should a case arise in which an authority is in doubt whether the protection of the public could be justified if the interests of the child were the sole consideration.

Members of the public
See the note to s. 19, *ante.*

Child
In this section, the expression "child" means a person under the age of 18, and a person who has attained the age of 18 and is subject to a care order; see s. 20 (1), *post.*

SUB-S. (4)
Months
See the note to s. 15, *ante.*

Practicable
See the note to s. 19, *ante.*

Application
As to applications by local authorities for the discharge of a care order, see s. 21 (1), *ante.*

DEFINITIONS
For "care order" and "local authority", see s. 70 (1), *post.*

CHILDREN ACT 1948, SS. 11, 12 (1)
See 17 Halsbury's Statutes (3rd Edn.) 549, 550.

Detention

28. Detention of child or young person in place of safety

(1) If, upon an application to a justice by any person for authority to detain a child or young person and take him to a place of safety, the justice is satisfied that the applicant has reasonable cause to believe that—

    (*a*) any of the conditions set out in section 1 (2) (*a*) to (*e*) of this Act is satisfied in respect of the child or young person; or

    (*b*) an appropriate court would find the condition set out in section 1 (2) (*b*) of this Act satisfied in respect of him; or

    (*c*) the child or young person is about to leave the United Kingdom in contravention of section 25 of the Act of 1933 (which regulates the sending abroad of juvenile entertainers),

the justice may grant the application; and the child or young person in respect of whom an authorisation is issued under this subsection may be detained in a place of safety by virtue of the authorisation for twenty-eight days beginning with the date of authorisation, or for such shorter period beginning with that date as may be specified in the authorisation.

(2) Any constable may detain a child or young person as respects whom the constable has reasonable cause to believe that any of the conditions set out in section 1 (2) (*a*) to (*d*) of this Act is satisfied or that an appropriate court would find the condition set out in section 1 (2) (*b*) of this Act satisfied or that an offence is being committed under section 10 (1) of the Act of 1933 (which penalises a vagrant who takes a juvenile from place to place).

(3) A person who detains any person in pursuance of the preceding provisions of this section shall, as soon as practicable after doing so, inform him of the reason for his detention and take such steps as are practicable for informing his parent or guardian of his detention and of the reason for it.

(4) A constable who detains any person in pursuance of subsection (2) of this section or who arrests a child without a warrant otherwise than for homicide shall as soon as practicable after doing so secure that the case is enquired into by a police officer not below the rank of inspector or by the police officer in charge of a police station, and that officer shall on completing the enquiry either—

(*a*) release the person in question; or

(*b*) if the officer considers that he ought to be further detained in his own interests or, in the case of an arrested child, because of the nature of the alleged offence, make arrangements for his detention in a place of safety and inform him, and take such steps as are practicable for informing his parent or guardian, of his right to apply to a justice under subsection (5) of this section for his release;

and subject to the said subsection (5) it shall be lawful to detain the person in question in accordance with any such arrangements.

(5) It shall not be lawful for a child arrested without a warrant otherwise than for homicide to be detained in consequence of the arrest or such arrangements as aforesaid, or for any person to be detained by virtue of subsection (2) of this section or any such arrangements, after the expiration of the period of eight days beginning with the day on which he was arrested or, as the case may be, on which his detention in pursuance of the said subsection (2) began; and if during that period the person in question applies to a justice for his release, the justice shall direct that he be released forthwith unless the justice considers that he ought to be further detained in his own interests or, in the case of an arrested child, because of the nature of the alleged offence.

(6) If while a person is detained in pursuance of this section an application for an interim order in respect of him is made to a magistrates' court or a justice, the court or justice shall either make or refuse to make the order and, in the case of a refusal, may direct that he be released forthwith.

COMMENCEMENT OF THIS SECTION
See the note to s. 73 (2), *post*, and the order thereto.

SUB-S. (1)

Place of safety
By virtue of s. 70 (1), *post* (see the third definition therein), for meaning, see the Children and Young Persons Act 1933, s. 107 (1) (17 Halsbury's Statutes (3rd Edn.) 515). That definition is amended by s. 72 (3), Sch. 5, para. 12 (2), *post*, as from a day to be appointed. A prison does not appear to be within the definition; see 101 J.P.N. 797.

Reasonable cause, etc.
It is submitted that the Act not only requires that the applicant has reasonable cause to believe but also that he does actually believe so; see *R.* v. *Banks*, [1916] 2 K.B. 621; [1916–17] All E.R. Rep. 356, and *R.* v. *Harrison*, [1938] 3 All E.R. 134; and see also *Nakkuda Ali* v. *Jayaratue (M. F. de S.)*, [1951] A.C. 66, P.C.

United Kingdom
I.e., Great Britain and Northern Ireland; see the Royal and Parliamentary Titles Act 1927, s. 2 (2) (6 Halsbury's Statutes (3rd Edn.) 520). "Great Britain" means England, Wales and Scotland by virtue of the Union with Scotland Act 1706, preamble Art. I (6 Halsbury's Statutes (3rd Edn.) 501), and the Wales and Berwick Act 1746, s. 3 (24 Halsbury's Statutes (2nd Edn.) 183).

The Channel Islands and the Isle of Man are not generally included in the expression "the United Kingdom".

Beginning with, etc.
See the note to s. 12, *ante*.

SUB-S. (2): CONSTABLE
See the note to s. 1, *ante*.

SUB-S. (3)

Any person
I.e., any child or young person.

Parent or guardian
See the notes to s. 1, *ante*.

SUB-S. (4)

Arrest
A child may not, under the terms of s. 4, *ante*, be *charged* with any offence except homicide. But he may nevertheless be *arrested* if he is suspected of committing an offence, in which case the provisions of sub-ss. (4)–(6) of this section come into play.

For power to arrest a child or young person who has absconded from the premises at which he is required to live, or from the home, remand home, special reception centre or training school at which he is required to be, see s. 32, *post*.

An arrest without warrant is not rendered unlawful *ab initio* by the fact that the person arrested has been set free without further action being taken; see *Wiltshire v. Barrett*, [1965] 2 All E.R. 271; [1966] 1 Q.B. 312, C.A.

Child
I.e., a person under the age of 14; see s. 70 (1), *post*.

Note, however, that by s. 34 (1) (*a*), (4), *post*, the Secretary of State is empowered by order to provide that the reference to a child in sub-s. (4) shall be construed as excluding a child who has attained such age as may be specified, not being under ten.

Rank of inspector
See the note to s. 8, *ante*.

Reason to believe
Cf. the note "Reasonable cause, etc." to s. 28, *ante*.

Homicide
See the note to s. 4, *ante*.

Applies . . . for his release
The parent or guardian of the child or young person may also apply for his release; see s. 70 (2), *post*.

SUB-S. (5)
Whereas children arrested for homicide or young persons arrested for any offence must, under s. 29 (5), *post*, be brought before a court within 72 hours, children arrested without a warrant otherwise than for homicide may be detained for 8 days under this subsection, subject, however, to a right to apply to a justice for release. (Sub-s. (4) (*b*) of this section provides that the parents or guardian of the young person are to be notified of this right.)

The 8-day period was justified on the following grounds: If, for example, a 13-year-old boy was found by the police loitering around a doubtful and notorious district in

Liverpool on Friday evening and it was discovered that his home was in Northampton—some 120 miles away, it might take longer than 72 hours to get in touch with his parents and sort out the situation. That would result in the boy having to make an additional and upsetting appearance in court. The new provisions therefore avoid creating the situation in which children, in respect of whom there is no question of their being sent home again, having to appear before a court more frequently than is reasonable.

TRANSITIONAL PROVISIONS
See the second paragraph of the note "Child" above.

DEFINITIONS
For "child", "young person", "place of safety", "police officer", see s. 70 (1), *post*; for "interim order", see s. 20 (1), *ante*.

ACT OF 1933
I.e., the Children and Young Persons Act 1933 (17 Halsbury's Statutes (3rd Edn.) 435 *et seq.*); see s. 70 (1), *post*
A new sub-s. (1A) is inserted after sub-s. (1) of s. 10 of that Act by s. 72 (3), Sch. 5, para. 2, *post*, as from a day to be appointed.

29. Release or further detention of arrested child or young person

(1) Where a person is arrested with or without a warrant and cannot be brought immediately before a magistrates' court, then if either—

(*a*) he appears to be a child and his arrest is for homicide; or
(*b*) he appears to be a young person and his arrest is for any offence,

the police officer in charge of the police station to which he is brought or another police officer not below the rank of inspector shall forthwith enquire into the case and, subject to subsection (2) of this section, shall release him unless—

(i) the officer considers that he ought in his own interests to be further detained; or
(ii) the officer has reason to believe that he has committed homicide or another grave crime or that his release would defeat the ends of justice or that if he were released (in a case where he was arrested without a warrant) he would fail to appear to answer to any charge which might be made.

(2) A person arrested in pursuance of a warrant shall not be released in pursuance of subsection (1) of this section unless he or his parent or guardian (with or without sureties) enters into a recognisance for such amount as the officer aforesaid considers will secure his attendance at the hearing of the charge; and a recognisance entered into in pursuance of this subsection may, if the said officer thinks fit, be conditioned for the attendance of the parent or guardian at the hearing in addition to the person arrested.

(3) An officer who enquires into a case in pursuance of subsection (1) of this section and does not release the person to whom the enquiry relates shall, unless the officer certifies that it is impracticable to do so or that he is of so unruly a character as to make it inappropriate to do so, make arrangements for him to be taken into the care of a local authority and detained by the authority, and it shall be lawful to detain him in pursuance of the arrangements; and a certificate made under this subsection in respect of any person shall be produced to the court before which that person is first brought thereafter.

(4) Where an officer decides in pursuance of subsection (1) of this section not to release a person arrested without a warrant and it appears to the officer that a decision falls to be taken in pursuance of section 5 of this Act whether to lay an information in respect of an offence alleged to have been committed by that person, it shall be the duty of the officer to inform him that such a decision falls to be taken and to specify the offence.

(5) A person detained by virtue of subsection (3) of this section shall be brought before a magistrates' court within seventy-two hours from the time of his arrest unless within that period a police officer not below the rank of inspector certifies to a magistrates' court that by reason of illness or accident he cannot be brought before a magistrates' court within that period.

(6) Where in pursuance of the preceding subsection a person is brought before a court or a certificate in respect of any person is produced to a court and the court does not proceed forthwith to inquire into the case, then—

(a) except in a case falling within paragraph (b) of this subsection, the court shall order his release; and

(b) in a case where he was arrested in pursuance of a warrant or the court considers that he ought in his own interests to be further detained or the court has reason to believe as mentioned in subsection (1) (ii) of this section, the court shall remand him;

and where a court remands a person in pursuance of this subsection otherwise than on bail it shall, if he is not represented by counsel or a solicitor, inform him that he may apply to a judge of the High Court to be admitted to bail and shall, if he is not so represented or his counsel or solicitor so requests, give him a written notice stating the reason for so remanding him.

GENERAL NOTE
This section is largely an amplification of ss. 32 and 67 of the Children and Young Persons Act 1933.

COMMENCEMENT OF THIS SECTION
See s. 73 (2), *post*, and the note thereto.

SUB-S. (1)

Young person
I.e., a person who has attained the age of 14 and is under the age of 17, see s. 70 (1), *post*.
But note that by s. 34 (1) (c), (4), *post*, the Secretary of State is empowered by order to provide that the reference to a young person in sub-s. (1) of this section shall be construed as including a child who has attained such age as may be specified, not being under ten.

Shall release him
The provisions of this section replace those of the Children and Young Persons Act 1933, s. 32 (release on bail of persons under 17). That section is consequentially repealed by s. 72, Sch. 6, *post*, as from a day to be appointed.

Magistrates' court
See the note to s. 5, *ante*.

Rank of inspector
See the note to s. 8, *ante*.

Reason to believe
Cf. the note "reasonable cause, etc." to s. 28, *ante*.

Homicide
    See the note to s. 4, *ante*.

Ends of justice
    For a case in which this phrase is discussed, see *R .v. Barnett*, [1919] 1 K.B. 640, *per* Shearman, J., at pp. 644, 645.

SUB-S. (2)

Parent or guardian
    See the notes to s. 1, *ante*.

Enters into a recognisance
    See the note to s. 1, *ante*.

Taken into . . . care . . . and detained
    The words "and detained" clearly preclude the authority from allowing the child or young person to be released to the charge and control of a parent, guardian, relative or friend.

SUB-S. (4): PERSON ARRESTED
    I.e., a young person; since they are the subjects of s. 5, *ante*. (But note the Secretary of State's power to order that the provisions of s. 5 shall apply to children; see s. 34 (1) (*b*), (*c*), (4), *post*.)

SUB-S. (5): ACCIDENT
    See the note to s. 22, *ante*.

SUB-S. (6)

Forthwith
    See the note to s. 18, *ante*.

Shall remand him
    I.e., in accordance with the provisions of s. 23, *ante*, which applies to a child or a young person who has not attained the age of 17. (Cf. the provisions of the Criminal Justice Act 1948, s. 27, as substituted (as from a day to be appointed) by Sch. 5, para. 24, *post*, which relate to a person aged 17 to 20.)

TRANSITIONAL PROVISION
    See the second para. of the note "Young person" above.

DEFINITIONS
    For "child", "police officer" and "local authority", see s. 70 (1), *post*.

30. Detention of young offenders in community homes

(1) The power to give directions under section 53 of the Act of 1933 (under which young offenders convicted on indictment of certain grave crimes may be detained in accordance with directions given by the Secretary of State) shall include power to direct detention by a local authority specified in the directions in a home so specified which is a community home provided by the authority or a controlled community home for the management, equipment and maintenance of which the authority are responsible; but a person shall not be liable to be detained in the manner provided by this section after he attains the age of nineteen.

(2) It shall be the duty of a local authority specified in directions given in pursuance of this section to detain the person to whom the directions relate in

the home specified in the directions subject to and in accordance with such instructions relating to him as the Secretary of State may give to the authority from time to time; and the authority shall be entitled to recover from the Secretary of State any expenses reasonably incurred by them in discharging that duty.

GENERAL NOTE
There are very few cases of the kind contemplated by this section. According to the Home Office, the number of offenders falling under s. 53 of the Children and Young Persons Act 1933, which is extended by this section, is about 6 a year. At present some of the youngsters go to approved schools and the purpose of the present section is to enable this to continue when approved schools become community homes. This assurance had to be given by the Government because there was considerable alarm expressed by many members of staff in residential establishments who feared an influx of persons as a result of this section and doubted their own capacity to work with delinquent children, who, in any case they did not feel ought to be put alongside other children who might only be in care from quite innocent causes.

COMMENCEMENT OF THIS SECTION
See s. 73 (2), *post*, and the note thereto.

SUB-S. (1)
Community home
For meaning, see s. 36 (1), *post*; and see generally, ss. 34-45, *post*.

Controlled community home
I.e., a voluntary home, as defined by s. 70 (1), *post*, designated a community home in accordance with s. 36 (3), *post*, managed in accordance with s. 39 (3) (*a*), (4), *post*, and is the responsibility of a local authority in accordance with s. 41, *post*.
Where the Secretary of State decides that a person is to be detained in a place provided and controlled by him—that is a prison or a borstal—he simply directs detention in that place. The power in s. 53 is, however, wide enough to enable him to arrange detention elsewhere so far as legal custody is concerned, but only with the agreement of the person providing the establishment which it is desired to use. Section 58 of the 1933 Act enables the Secretary of State to direct detention in an approved school which will ultimately be merged into the new community home system.
Assisted community homes, it will be noted, are not mentioned in this section because the local authority cannot have a duty to detain in a home which is not maintained by them. It was not thought reasonable or necessary to impose a statutory duty of this nature on a voluntary organisation.
For further details as to community homes, see s. 36 (1), *post*; and generally, ss. 35-45, *post*. Controlled community homes are voluntary homes, as defined by s. 70 (1), *post*, which are designated thus in accordance with s. 36 (3), *post*, and managed in accordance with s. 39 (3) (*a*), (4), *post*, and are the responsibility of a local authority in accordance with s. 41, *post*.

Management, equipment etc.
As to the management of controlled community homes, see s. 41, *post*.

Attains the age
Cf. the note "attained the age" to s. 1, *ante*.

DEFINITIONS
For "local authority", see s. 70 (1), *post*.

ACT OF 1933
I.e., the Children and Young Persons Act 1933 (17 Halsbury's Statutes (3rd Edn.) 435 *et seq*); see s. 70 (1), *post*.

31. Removal to borstal institutions of persons committed to care of local authorities

(1) Where a person who has attained the age of fifteen is for the time being committed to the care of a local authority by a care order (other than an interim order) and accommodated in a community home and the authority consider that he ought to be removed to a borstal institution under this section, they may with the consent of the Secretary of State bring him before a juvenile court.

(2) If the court before which a person is brought in pursuance of this section is satisfied that his behaviour is such that it will be detrimental to the persons accommodated in any community home for him to be accommodated there, the court may order him to be removed to a borstal institution.

(3) Where an order is made under subsection (2) of this section with respect to any person, the care order aforesaid shall cease to have effect and he shall be treated as if he had been sentenced to borstal training on the date of the other order, except that—

> (a) where the day on which the care order would have ceased to have effect by virtue of section 20 (3) of this Act (disregarding section 21 (1)), is earlier than the end of the period of two years beginning with the date aforesaid he shall, subject to paragraph (b) of this subsection, not be liable to be detained by virtue of this subsection after that day: and

> (b) section 45 (4) of the Prison Act 1952 shall apply to him as if for the reference to two years from the date of his sentence there were substituted a reference to that day.

(4) If the court before which a person is brought in pursuance of this section is not in a position to decide whether to make an order under subsection (2) of this section in respect of him, it may make an order for his detention in a remand centre for a period not exceeding twenty-one days.

(5) An order under the preceding subsection may from time to time be varied or extended by the court which made the order or by any other magistrates' court acting for the same area as that court, but a court shall not exercise its powers under this subsection—

> (a) if the person to whom the order relates is not before the court, unless the court is satisfied that by reason of illness or accident he cannot be present;

> (b) so as to authorise the detention of that person after the expiration of the period of eight weeks beginning with the date when the order was originally made.

(6) The provisions of the Magistrates' Courts Act 1952 and of any other enactment relating to summary proceedings (other than provisions relating to remand or legal aid) shall apply to proceedings for the removal of a person under this section as they apply to proceedings against a person charged with a summary offence.

(7) Where immediately before an order under paragraph (*f*) of section 34 (1) of this Act comes into force an order under this section is in force with respect to any person, the order under that paragraph shall not affect the other order or the application of this section to that person while the other order remains in force.

GENERAL NOTE

This section replaces three provisions in the existing law under which a person in an approved school may be removed to borstal. They are: (1) serious misconduct by a person in an approved school; (2) absconding; and (3) cases in which a person's continued detention in an approved school would be ineffective for the purposes of his own reformation or would be detrimental to the training or welfare of other persons in the school and it would be in his interests to receive borstal training. These three conditions are now replaced by a single test which covers cases where a person over the age of 15 is accommodated in a community home under a care order and his behaviour is such that it would be detrimental to other persons accommodated there, for him to remain.

Note the necessity for the consent of the Secretary of State. One important reason for this requirement is that the Home Secretary is directly responsible for the approved school system as a whole and for admissions to individual schools. Sometimes when the managers of a school apply for consent, the answer is not court proceedings with a view to removal to borstal but removal to another approved school. In other words it will very often appear to the managers that there is no alternative but borstal, but the Home Secretary, who has general control of the whole system, looking at it on a very much broader basis and enabled to have a much fuller and comprehensive picture will realise that there are other and more appropriate alternatives. He has that wider knowledge which is not available to the individual authorities as to what accommodation is available throughout the country for different young people. So the main purpose is to ensure that all the possibilities of dealing with the young offender in a home have been fully considered before the case goes to court. The Home Secretary also has the control of a small number of homes for mentally disturbed persons under s. 64 of this Act and has to approve all secure accommodation and make all the regulations that are appropriate—see s. 43 (2) (*c*), *post*. He will also be able to help in securing a place in a home not normally available to an authority—for which regulations made under s. 43 (2) (*d*), *post*, could be invoked.

COMMENCEMENT OF THIS SECTION

See s. 73 (2), *post*, and the note thereto.

SUB-S. (1)

Attained the age of fifteen

The Secretary of State may by order provide that sub-s. (1) shall have effect as if for the reference to fifteen in that subsection there were substituted such greater age as may be specified; see s. 34 (1) (*f*), *post*. Note also sub-s. (7) of this section.

See also the note "attained the age" to s. 1, *ante*.

Community home

See the note to s. 21, *ante*.

Committed to . . . care . . . by a court order

E.g., in accordance with ss. 1 (3) (*c*), 7 (7) (*a*) or 15 (1), *ante*.

Borstal institution: borstal training

See the Criminal Justice Act 1948, s. 20 (8 Halsbury's Statutes (3rd Edn.) 355), and the Criminal Justice Act 1961, ss. 1, 11 (127 Statutes Supp.). S. 20 (1) of the 1948 Act is amended, and s. 11 (1) of the 1961 Act is repealed by s. 7 (1), *ante*, s. 72 (4), Sch. 6, *post*, respectively as from a day to be appointed.

Juvenile court

See the note to s. 1, *ante*. Such a court cannot normally send a person to borstal, but must commit the case to quarter sessions. However, under the situations contemplated by this section, urgency frequently prevails and so this special power is accorded.

SUB-S. (3): BEGINNING WITH, ETC.
See the note to s. 12, *ante*.

SUB-S. (4): REMAND CENTRE
See the note to s. 22, *ante*.

SUB-S. (5)

Not before the court
Cf. the note "Is present" to s. 16, *ante*.

Accident
See the note to s. 22, *ante*.

SUB-S. (6): THE PROVISIONS OF THE MAGISTRATES' COURTS ACT 1952 AND OF ANY OTHER ENACTMENT
Provisions relating to summary jurisdiction and procedure in England and Wales are now mainly governed by the Magistrates' Courts Act 1952 (32 Halsbury's Statutes (2nd Edn.) 416), and the Magistrates' Courts Act 1957 (104 Statutes Supp.), though various amendments are made by provisions in the Criminal Justice Act 1967 (163 Statutes Supp.). Some of these provisions, such as right of appeal and the provision of legal aid are safeguards and some of them are simply procedural. The proceedings under this section are *sui generis*. They are not proceedings for an offence nor are they care proceedings. It is accordingly necessary to include in the section a provision which attracts all the requisite safeguards as well as the procedural provisions. This subsection, in its reference to the 1952 enactment consequently attracts, as well as the appropriate procedural requirements, also the right of appeal to quarter sessions.
By the Criminal Justice Act 1967, s. 73(3A), (3B), inserted by s. 33(1), Sch. 1, para. 1, *post*, where a person is or is to be brought before a juvenile court under this section, the court may order that he be given legal aid for the purpose of proceedings before the court, and where a person desires to appeal to quarter sessions in pursuance of this subsection, that court or the court from whose decision the appeal lies may order that he be given legal aid.

TRANSITIONAL PROVISION
See the note "Attained the age of fifteen" above.

DEFINITIONS
For "local authority", see s. 70 (1), *post*; for "care order" and "interim order", see s. 20 (1), *ante*.

PRISON ACT 1952, S. 45 (4)
See 32 Halsbury's Statutes (2nd Edn.) 651.

MAGISTRATES' COURTS ACT 1952
See 32 Halsbury's Statutes (2nd Edn.) 416 *et seq.*

32. Detention of absentees

(1) If any of the following persons, that is to say—

   (a) a person committed to the care of a local authority by a care order or by a warrant under section 23 of this Act; or

   (b) a person who, in pursuance of section 2 (5), 16 (3) or 28 of this Act, has been taken to a place of safety which is a community home provided by a local authority or a controlled community home; or

   (c) a person in the care of a local authority in pursuance of arrangements under section 29 (3) of this Act; or

   (d) a person sent to a remand home, special reception centre or training school or committed to the care of a fit person under the Children and Young Persons Act (Northern Ireland) 1968,

is absent from premises at which he is required by the local authority or the relevant Northern Ireland authority to live, or as the case may be is absent from the home, remand home, special reception centre or training school, at a time when he is not permitted by the local authority or the managers of the home or the relevant Northern Ireland authority to be absent from it, he may be arrested by a constable anywhere in the United Kingdom or the Channel Islands without a warrant and shall if so arrested be conducted, at the expense of the authority or managers, to the premises or other place aforesaid or such other premises as the authority or managers may direct.

(2) If a magistrates' court is satisfied by information on oath that there are reasonable grounds for believing that a person specified in the information can produce a person who is absent as mentioned in subsection (1) of this section, the court may issue a summons directed to the person so specified and requiring him to attend and produce the absent person before the court; and a person who without reasonable excuse fails to comply with any such requirement shall, without prejudice to any liability apart from this subsection, be guilty of an offence and liable on summary conviction to a fine of an amount not exceeding twenty pounds.

In the application of this subsection to Northern Ireland, "magistrates' court" means a magistrates' court within the meaning of the Magistrates' Courts Act (Northern Ireland) 1964.

(3) A person who knowingly compels, persuades, incites or assists another person to become or continue to be absent as mentioned in subsection (1) of this section shall be guilty of an offence and liable on summary conviction to imprisonment for a term not exceeding six months or a fine of an amount not exceeding one hundred pounds or both.

(4) The reference to a constable in subsection (1) of this section includes a reference to a person who is a constable under the law of any part of the United Kingdom, to a member of the police in Jersey and to an officer of police within the meaning of section 43 of the Larceny (Guernsey) Law 1958 or any corresponding law for the time being in force, and in that subsection "the relevant Northern Ireland authority" means in the case of a person committed to the care of a fit person, the fit person, and in the case of a person sent to a remand home, special reception centre or training school, the person in charge of that home or centre or the managers of that school.

(5) Nothing in this section authorises the arrest in Northern Ireland of, or the taking there of any proceedings in respect of, such a person as is mentioned in paragraph (*d*) of subsection (1) of this section.

GENERAL NOTE
This section replaces the Children and Young Persons Act 1933, ss. 72, 78 and 85.

COMMENCEMENT OF THIS SECTION
See s. 73 (2), *post*, and the note thereto.

SUB-S. (1)

Committed to . . . care . . . by a care order
See the note to s. 31, *ante*.

Place of safety
See the note to s. 28, *ante*.

Community home: controlled community home
See the notes to s. 30, *ante*.

Arrested, etc.
Cf. the note "Arrests" to s. 28, *ante*.

Constable
See sub-s. (4) of this section. See also the note to s. 1, *ante*.

United Kingdom
See the note to s. 26, *ante*.

Channel Islands
I.e., Guernsey, Jersey, Alderney and Sark and their respective dependencies; see 5 Halsbury's Laws (3rd Edn.) 647 *et seq.*

SUB-S. (2)

Magistrates' court
See the note to s. 5, *ante*.

Oath
In the case of persons allowed by law to affirm or declare instead of swearing, this includes affirmation and declaration; see the Interpretation Act 1889, s. 3 (24 Halsbury's Statutes (2nd Edn.) 207).

Reasonable excuse
What is a reasonable excuse is largely a question of fact; cf. *Leck* v. *Epsom Rural District Council*, [1922] 1 K.B. 383; [1922] All E.R. Rep. 784. Yet there is authority for saying that ignorance of the statutory provisions provides no reasonable excuse; cf. *Aldridge* v. *Warwickshire Coal Co., Ltd.* (1925), 133 L.T. 439, C.A.

Summary conviction
Cf. the note "The provisions of the Magistrates' Courts Act, etc." to s. 31, *ante*.

Fine
See the note to s. 6, *ante*.

SUB-S. (3)

Knowingly
There is authority for saying that, where a person deliberately refrains from making inquiries the results of which he might not care to have, this constitutes in law actual knowledge of the facts in question; see *Knox* v. *Boyd*, 1941 S.C. (J) 82, at p. 86, and *Taylor's Central Garages (Exeter), Ltd.* v. *Roper* (1951), 115 J.P. 445, at pp. 449, 450, *per* Devlin, J.; and see also, in particular, *Mallon* v. *Allon*, [1963] 3 All E.R. 843; [1964] 1 Q.B. 385, at p. 847 and p. 394, respectively. However, mere neglect to ascertain what would have been found out by making reasonable enquiries is not tantamount to knowledge; see *Taylor's Central Garages (Exeter), Ltd.* v. *Roper, ubi supra, per* Devlin, J.; and cf. *London Computator, Ltd.* v. *Seymour*, [1944] 2 All E.R. 11; but see also *Mallon* v. *Allon, ubi supra* and *Wallworth* v. *Balmer*, [1965] 3 All E.R. 721.

Incites
As to incitement to commit a crime generally, see 10 Halsbury's Laws (3rd Edn.) 309–310; see also *R.* v. *Macro and Others* (Times, 11th February, 1969); *R.* v. *Assistant Recorder of Kingston-upon-Hull*, [1969] 1 All E.R. 416.

Not exceeding six months
Cf. the note "Three months" to s. 6, *ante*.

SUB-S. (4): JERSEY

See the note "Channel Islands", *supra*.

DEFINITIONS
For "local authority" and "place of safety", see s. 66 (1), *post*; for "care order", see s. 20 (1), *ante*; for "controlled community home" and "Managers", see s. 36, *post*.

LARCENY (GUERNSEY) LAW 1958, S. 43
Not printed in this work.

Legal aid

33. Legal aid. 1967 c. 80

(1) Part IV of the Criminal Justice Act 1967 (which relates to legal aid in criminal proceedings) shall have effect subject to the provisions of Schedule 1 to this Act (being provisions for applying the said Part IV to certain proceedings under this Part of this Act and for modifying the said Part IV in certain minor respects in relation to juveniles).

(2) Legal aid in pursuance of the Legal Aid and Advice Act 1949 shall not be given in respect of any proceedings in respect of which legal aid may be given by virtue of the preceding subsection.

GENERAL NOTE

This section must be read in conjunction with Schedule 1, *post*. When a child is brought to court on the grounds that he has committed an offence, first of all, the offence must be proved by the criminal burden of proof. When it has been proved, the court will turn itself into a civil court and decide whether or not the child is in need of care and protection, and this raises certain problems in the granting of legal aid to children in criminal courts, because these will be civil proceedings and the court will not be able to grant legal aid as it can at the moment. Accordingly, the Government came to the conclusion that legal aid should apply in care proceedings. The Under-Secretary of State for the Home Department made the following statement:

"Section 78 of the 1967 Act (dealing with legal aid in criminal proceedings) empowers the Secretary of State to make regulations providing that in the case of infants, the resources and commitments of other persons may be taken into account. In the Legal Aid in Criminal Proceedings (Assessment of Resources) Regulations 1968, [S.I. 1968 No. 1265], the Secretary of State has made such regulations.

The persons whose resources and commitments may be taken into account are persons liable to maintain the infant, or who would be so liable if he were under the age of 16, and other persons having charge or control of him except local authorities and persons having charge or control for a temporary purpose, or by reason of any contract. The 1967 Act, however, makes no provision for the court to require such a person to complete a statement of his means before legal aid can be given to the applicant and no provision for requiring him to make a contribution or enforcing it against him.

The Government are of the opinion that in the case of children under the age of 16, it should be possible to enforce a contribution against the parents, if their means permit, in both criminal and care proceedings, and the amendments now provide for this. The reason why the age of 16 has been chosen, and not 17, which is the upper age for juvenile proceedings, or 18, which will be the new age of majority, is that it seems reasonable to be able to enforce a contribution against the parents only where they are legally liable to maintain the child. Under Section 22 of the Ministry of Social Security Act 1966, that liability comes to an end at the age of 16. The effect will be that between 16 and the new age of majority, the parents' resources and commitments may be taken into account as under the existing law, but there will be no power to enforce a contribution against a parent.

The provisions applying the criminal legal aid system to care proceedings apply also where there is an appeal to quarter sessions in those proceedings; where the child or young person is the subject of an application under [s. 15], under which the supervisor may bring a supervised person before the court; where the child or young person is the subject of an application under [s. 21 (1)], which enables the local authority to apply for a care order to be extended from 18 to 19 years of age, or under [s. 21 (2)], which deals with applications for the discharge of a care order: and also where there is an application under [s. 31], under which an order may be made removing a young person in care to borstal. Subsection (2) of the new [section] takes legal aid in care proceedings out of the civil legal aid system." (784 H. of C. Official Report 1014.)

COMMENCEMENT OF THIS SECTION

See s. 73 (2), *post*, and the note thereto.

CRIMINAL JUSTICE ACT 1967, PART IV (SS. 73–84)
   See 163 Statutes Supp. See also Schedule I, *post.*

LEGAL AID AND ADVICE ACT 1949
   See 64 Statutes Supp.

Transitional modifications of Part I for persons of specified ages

34. Transitional Modifications of Part I for persons of specified ages

(1) The Secretary of State may by order provide—

  (*a*) that any reference to a child in section 4, 13 (2) or 28 (4) or (5) of this Act shall be construed as excluding a child who has attained such age as may be specified in the order;

  (*b*) that any reference to a young person in section 5 of this Act (except subsection (8)) shall be construed as including a child, or excluding a young person, who has attained such age as may be so specified;

  (*c*) that any reference to a young person in section 5 (8), 7 (7), 7 (8), 9 (1), 23 (1) or 29 (1) of this Act shall be construed as including a child who has attained such ages as may be so specified;

  (*d*) that section 7 (1) of this Act shall have effect as if for references to seventeen years there were substituted references to sixteen years;

  (*e*) that section 23 (2) or (3) of this Act shall have effect as if the references to a young person excluded a young person who has not attained such age as may be so specified;

  (*f*) that section 22 (5) of this Act shall have effect as if for the reference to the age of fourteen, or section 31 (1) of this Act shall have effect as if for the reference to the age of fifteen, there were substituted a reference to such greater age as may be so specified.

(2) In the case of a person who has not attained the age of seventeen but has attained such lower age as the Secretary of State may by order specify, no proceedings under section 1 of this Act or for an offence shall be begun in any court unless the person proposing to begin the proceedings has, in addition to any notice falling to be given by him to a local authority in pursuance of section 2 (3) or 5 (8) of this Act, given notice of the proceedings to a probation officer for the area for which the court acts; and accordingly in the case of such a person the reference in section 1 (1) of this Act to the said section 2 (3) shall be construed as including a reference to this subsection.

(3) In the case of a person who has attained such age as the Secretary of State may by order specify, an authority shall, without prejudice to subsection (2) of section 9 of this Act, not be required by virtue of subsection (1) of that section to make investigations or provide information which it does not already possess with respect to his home surroundings if, by direction of the justices or probation and after-care committee acting for any relevant area, arrangements are in force for information with respect to his home surroundings to be furnished to the court in question by a probation officer.

(4) Except in relation to section 13 (2) of this Act references to a child in subsection (1) of this section do not include references to person under the age of ten.

(5) In relation to a child tried summarily in pursuance of section 6 of this Act, for the words "fifty pounds" in subsection (3) of that section there shall be substituted the words "ten pounds".

(6) Without prejudice to the generality of section 69 (4) of this Act, an order under this section may specify different ages for the purposes of different provisions of this Act specified in the order.

(7) A draft of any order proposed to be made under this section shall be laid before Parliament and, in the case of an order of which the effect is that the reference to a child in section 4 of this Act, includes a child who has attained an age of more than twelve, shall not be made unless the draft has been approved by a resolution of each House of Parliament.

GENERAL NOTE

This section arises from the Government's decision to raise the age of full criminal liability to 14. "But they will not move up to that age unless they have the necessary resources, nor will they do so if having moved the age level up to 12, experience is such as clearly to show that it would not be proper to move towards 14" (*per* Under-Secretary of State: Home Office, H. of C. Official Report, S.C.G., 15th April 1969, col. 219). Sub-ss. (1) to (3) of this section therefore refer back to those provisions in the Act which depend upon the availability of resources for their implementation: they provide for a series of appointed days to bring these provisions into effect gradually. The Government was at pains to point out that the difference between the normal "appointed day sections" and these provisions was that usually the law was already enacted and the "appointed day" procedure simply brought it into operation: in the case of this enactment, the alteration of an age could mean the wholesale shifting of provisions to persons not otherwise affected—as, for example, those in sub-s. (1) (*c*) under which certain proceedings affecting young persons can be made applicable to children over a specified age. Furthermore, the subsections make transitional modifications to the substance of the Act—for example, sub-s. (2) requires probation officers still to be notified of proceedings. It is recognised that under these circumstances the ordinary appointed day orders, which are not normally subject to Parliamentary proceedings would be inappropriate, and so sub-s. (7) provides that orders under this section are to be laid before Parliament in draft.

COMMENCEMENT OF THIS SECTION

See s. 73 (2), *post*, and the note thereto.

SUB-S. (1)

"Child" in this subsection means a person not under 10, except in relation to s. 13 (2), *ante*; see sub-s. (4) of this section.

As to borstal training, see s. 7 (1), *ante*.

As to unruly characters, see s. 22 (5), *ante*.

Attained such age

Cf. the note "attained the age" to s. 1, *ante*.

SUB-S. (2)

In order to maintain continuity in the work of the probation service, this subsection requires the probation officers to be notified before care proceedings are brought in respect of amended age groups.

Probation officer

See the note to s. 11, *ante*.

SUB-S. (3)

Note that while relieved by this subsection of any duty under s. 9 (1), *ante*, a local authority is still required, under sub-s. (2) of that section to provide information as requested by the court.

Probation and after-care committee

See the note to s. 13, *ante*.

SUB-S. (4)
> *Under the age of ten*
>> Cf. the note "attained the age" to s. 1, *ante*.

> *Tried summarily*
>> See the note to s. 6, *ante*.

SUB-S. (7)
> It was generally agreed that section 4 was right in relation to children aged 10 and 11, and an assurance was given by the Government that in the first instance the section would be brought into operation only up to the twelfth birthday. Concern was, however, expressed that the application of that section to the ages beyond 12 was a matter of the highest importance and was something both Houses should debate fully. The Government accepted this, and any amendment to the age of criminal responsibility beyond that of 12 may be undertaken only after a positive decision in each House of Parliament.
> For the laying of documents before Parliament generally, see Laying of Documents before Parliament (Interpretation) Act 1948 (56 Statutes Supp. 293).

DEFINITIONS
> For "young person" and "local authority", see s. 70 (1), *post*.

ORDER UNDER THIS SECTION
> For orders under this Act, see generally s. 69, *post*, and, in particular, sub-s. (2) thereof. Note also sub-s. (7) of this section.
> No orders had been made under this section up to 1st May 1970.

PART II

ACCOMMODATION ETC. FOR CHILDREN IN CARE, AND FOSTER CHILDREN

Community homes

35. Regional planning of accommodation for children in care

(1) With a view to the preparation, in pursuance of the provisions of this Part of this Act, of regional plans for the provision of accommodation for children in the care of local authorities and for the equipment and maintenance of the accommodation, the Secretary of State may by order provide that any area specified in the order shall be a separate area (in this Act referred to as a "planning area") for the purposes of those provisions.

(2) Before making an order under subsection (1) of this section, the Secretary of State shall consult each local authority whose area or any part of whose area is included in the planning area which he proposes should be specified in the order and such local authorities, if any, as he thinks fit.

(3) It shall be the duty of the local authorities whose areas are wholly or partly included in a planning area (in this Act referred to, in relation to such an area, as "the relevant authorities") to establish for the area, within such period as may be provided by the order specifying the planning area or such longer period as the Secretary of State may allow, a body to be called the children's regional planning committee.

(4) The provisions of Schedule 2 to this Act shall have effect in relation to children's regional planning committees.

(5) In the case of an order under subsection (1) of this section which (by virtue of section 69 (3) of this Act) varies or revokes a previous order under that subsection—

(a) the reference in subsection (2) of this section to the planning area which the Secretary of State proposes should be specified in the order shall be construed as a reference to the planning area as it would be if the variation were made or, as the case may be, to the planning area as it is before the revocation; and

(b) the order may contain such transitional provisions (including provisions as to the expenses and membership of any existing or former children's regional planning committee for a planning area) as the Secretary of State thinks fit.

GENERAL NOTE
This section follows a pattern which has steadily become familiar with the development of a regional system of administration. It compares very closely with s. 9 of the Transport Act 1968. It empowers the Minister to designate, by order, any area, including Greater London, as a "planning area" for the provision of community homes for the young people within its boundaries.

CHILDREN'S REGIONAL PLANNING COMMITTEE
As to the composition, etc. of which, see Sch. 2, *post*.

COMMENCEMENT OF THIS SECTION
See s. 73 (2), *post*, and the note thereto.

THIS PART OF THIS ACT
I.e., ss. 35–59.

CHILDREN
I.e., persons under the age of 18, or persons over the age of 18 subject to a care order; see s. 70 (1), *post*.

CONSULT
See the note "Consultation" to s. 19(2), *ante*.

ORDERS UNDER THIS SECTION
See, generally, as to orders under this Act, s. 69, *post*. The Children and Young Persons (Planning Areas) Order 1970, S.I. 1970 No. 335 (reproduced at p. 298, *post*), was made under this section.

36. Regional plans for community homes

(1) The children's regional planning committee for a planning area (in this and the following section referred to as "the committee") shall prepare and submit to the Secretary of State, in accordance with the following provisions of this section, a plan (in this Act referred to as a "regional plan") for the provision and maintenance of homes, to be known as community homes, for the accommodation and maintenance of children in the care of the relevant authorities.

(2) The community homes for which provision may be made by a regional plan shall be—

(a) community homes provided by the relevant authorities; and

(b) voluntary homes provided by voluntary organisations but in the management of each of which the plan proposes that a relevant authority should participate in accordance with an instrument of management.

(3) Where a regional plan makes provision for any such voluntary home as is referred to in paragraph (*b*) of subsection (2) of this section, the plan shall designate the home as either a controlled community home or an assisted community home, according as it is proposed in the plan that the management, equipment and maintenance of the home should be the responsibility of one of the relevant authorities or of the voluntary organisation by which the home is provided.

(4) Every regional plan shall contain proposals—

(*a*) with regard to the nature and purpose of each of the community homes for which the plan makes provision; and

(*b*) for the provision of facilities for the observation of the physical and mental condition of children in the care of the relevant authorities and for the assessment of the most suitable accommodation and treatment for those children.

(5) Before including provision in a regional plan that a community home should be provided by any of the relevant authorities or that a voluntary home provided by a voluntary organisation should be designated as a controlled or assisted community home, the committee shall obtain the consent of the authority or voluntary organisation by which the home is or is to be provided and, in the case of a home which is to be designated as a controlled or assisted community home, the consent of the local authority which it is proposed should be specified in the instrument of management for the home.

(6) A regional plan shall be prepared in such form and shall contain such information as the Secretary of State may direct, either generally or in relation to a particular planning area or particular kinds of plans; and the Secretary of State may direct that the regional plan for a particular planning area shall be submitted to him within such period as may be specified in the direction or such longer period as he may allow.

GENERAL NOTE

This important section provides the means whereby the abstract principles implied in Part I, *ante*, may be expressed in terms of "bricks and mortar". Having been constituted, the regional planning committees will have to set to work and prepare their initial plans. These plans should ensure that every relevant authority, however small, has access to a suitable range of facilities and that all voluntary organisations wishing to participate in the provision of community homes are fitted into the needs of the planning area as a whole. It is anticipated that this work will take at least a year before it is ready for submission to the Secretary of State. The Government has assured the local authorities that once the initial comprehensive plan has been approved, authorities and voluntary organisations should be free to carry on with a minimum of reference to the planning committee or the Home Office.

The community homes will serve a wide range of purposes, and in particular, those which are at present served by children's homes and hostels provided under the 1948 enactment. The homes provided by voluntary associations and utilised by local authorities (the present approved schools and the remand homes and hostels for persons under 17) will ultimately take the place of borstals in so far as they accommodate persons under the age of 17. The Government have indicated that "the categories of possibility within the framework of this Act will not be closed". (H. of C. Official Report, S.C.G, 6th May 1969, col. 509.)

The essential feature of this new system is that once the predominantly penal overlay which has existed in certain conditions is removed, then one makes it possible for the basis to be the need of a particular child rather than any feeling that punishment automatically follows transgression.

COMMENCEMENT OF THIS SECTION
　　See s. 73 (2), *post*, and the note thereto.

SUB-S. (1)
　　This emphasises the need for the fullest possible consultation and unified approach among the constituent members of the committee. It should be noted that the Act confers no executive powers on the regional planning committees, who cannot, then, involve the individual authorities in any financial liabilities. Therefore the ultimate implementation of any plan rests with the local authorities and the voluntary associations.

Shall prepare and submit ... a plan
　　Note that it is only plans which are to be submitted to the Secretary of State. While it is inherent in the whole relationship between central and local government that the Secretary of State has a duty to consider any representations which any such authority may wish to make to him at any time about any question of child care, it could possibly be unhelpful that, in laying a duty on the Secretary of State to consider representations on specified questions (as was suggested during the passing of the Act—for example, that he might exclude certain categories of establishment from a plan) it might imply that he had not at the moment any such duty in relation to other child care questions.

Community homes
　　The term is intended to identify, for the purposes of this Act, a residential establishment whose purpose is wholly or mainly to accommodate children in the care of the local authority and whose management is carried out wholly or partly by the local authority. Thus the expression "community home" applies to all such establishments, including those that are predominantly schools.
　　However, the term is simply a legal designation and the actual title of any community home may be anything the responsible local authority or voluntary organisation prefers. If they wish to include the word "school" in the title of the establishment there is nothing to stop them.
　　There are no restrictions in the Act as to the kind of premises which may be used as community homes provided by local authorities. Thus premises which were formerly in use as approved schools, remand homes, or approved probation hostels or homes, may be so used; see, *e.g.*, Sch. 3, para. 6 (1), *post*, which provides for the situation where an approved institution (other than one provided by a local authority) is designated as a community home to be provided by a local authority.
　　But note the Secretary of State's power by virtue of s. 43 (2) (*a*), (*c*), (*f*) and (*g*), *post*, to impose requirements as to the accommodation and equipment to be provided in community homes; to require that he should approve the provision and use of accommodation for restricting the activity of children in community homes; to prescribe the standards to which premises used for community homes are to conform; and to require that he should approve the use of buildings for the purposes of community homes and to the doing of anything which materially affects the buildings or grounds, etc. available for children in community homes.
　　As to the discontinuance of approved institutions on the establishment of community homes, see s. 46 and Sch. 3, *post*.
　　For a full explanation of the Public System of Community Homes for Children and Young Persons, see Appendix IV, *post*.

Accommodation and maintenance
　　These words are variously defined and it is submitted that their meanings are according to their current sense and have no special legal limitations.
　　There was some surprise that references to education were omitted, and indeed, in the House of Lords one speaker went so far as to say "reading this Act one would barely know that children have to go to school at all . . . one would have no idea that there is a vast educational system in this country, the primary object of which is to bring them up in the way they should go." It was, however, pointed out that this measure does not alter the position in respect of the education of children in care. Part II of the 1948 Act, s. 12 in particular, places a duty on local authorities to provide for the child's proper development, which includes education.

SUB-S. (2): INSTRUMENT OF MANAGEMENT
　　See further, s. 37, *post*.

SUB-S. (3)

Shall designate the home as a controlled . . . or assisted community home
There are no restrictions in the Act as to the kinds of voluntary homes which may be designated as controlled or assisted community homes. Homes which were formerly in use as approved schools, or approved probation hostels or homes may, for example, be so designated; see *e.g.*, Sch. 3, para. 5 (1), *post*, which provides for the situation where premises formerly in use as an approved institution are designated as a controlled or assisted community home. Cf. also s. 48 (5), *post*.

Responsibility of one of the relevant authorities or of the voluntary organisations
Note that by s. 39 (3), (4), *post*, where a voluntary home is designated as a controlled community home, two-thirds of the managers are to be appointed by the local authority, and one-third are to be "foundation managers", but where a voluntary home is designated as an "assisted community home", the position is reversed.

DEFINITIONS
For "child", see s. 70 (1), *post*; for "children's regional planning committee" and "the relevant authorities", see s. 35 (3), *ante*; for "planning area", see s. 35 (1), *ante*; for "voluntary home", see, by virtue of s. 70 (1), *post*, the Children and Young Persons Act 1933, s. 92 (17 Halsbury's Statutes (3rd Edn.) 506); for "voluntary organisation", see by virtue of s. 70 (1), *post*, the Children Act 1948, s. 59 (1) (17 Halsbury's Statutes (3rd Edn.) 578).

FURTHER PROVISIONS
As to supplementary plans to be submitted under this section where part only of the original plan is granted, see s. 36 (3), (5), *post*; as to variation or replacement of a regional plan, see s. 36 (4), (5), *post*.

37. Approval and variation of regional plans

(1) After considering any regional plan submitted to him under section 36 of this Act and after making in the plan such modifications (if any) as he may agree with the committee by which the plan was submitted and as he may consider appropriate for securing that the plan makes proper provision for the accommodation and maintenance of children in the care of the relevant authorities, the Secretary of State may approve the plan.

(2) Where the Secretary of State considers that, either with or without such modifications as are referred to in subsection (1) of this section, part but not the whole of a plan submitted to him under section 36 of this Act makes proper provision for the accommodation and maintenance of the children to whom that part of the plan relates, the Secretary of State may approve that part of the plan.

(3) Where the Secretary of State has approved part only of a regional plan, the committee for the planning area concerned shall prepare and submit to him under section 36 of this Act a further regional plan containing proposals to supplement that part of the previous plan which was approved by the Secretary of State.

(4) If, at any time after the approval of the whole or part of a regional plan by the Secretary of State, the committee for the planning area concerned consider that the plan, or such part of it as was approved, should be varied or replaced, they shall prepare and submit to the Secretary of State under section 36 of this Act a further regional plan for that purpose; and any such further regional plan may—

    (*a*) take the form of a replacement for the regional plan or part thereof which was previously approved by the Secretary of State; or (*b*) contain proposals for the amendment of that regional plan or part thereof.

(5) In relation to a further regional plan which contains proposals for supplementing or amending a regional plan or part of a regional plan which has been previously approved by the Secretary of State (in this subsection referred to as "the approved plan")—

(*a*) section 36 (4) of this Act shall have effect as if references to a regional plan were references to the approved plan as it would have effect if supplemented or amended in accordance with the proposals contained in the further regional plan; and

(*b*) subsection (1) of this section shall have effect as if the reference therein to children in the care of the relevant authorities were a reference to the children to whom the proposals in the plan relate; and

(*c*) in so far as the further regional plan contains proposals under which a home would cease to be a community home, or would become a community home of a different description, or would be used for a purpose different from that provided for in the approved plan, the committee preparing the further plan shall, before submitting it to the Secretary of State, obtain the consent of the local authority or voluntary organisation by which the home is provided and, if the proposal is for a home to become or to cease to be a controlled or assisted community home, the consent of the local authority which it is proposed should be, or which is, specified in the instrument of management for the home.

(6) Where the Secretary of State approves a regional plan, in whole or in part, he shall give notice in writing of his approval to the committee for the planning area concerned specifying the date on which the plan is to come into operation, and the committee shall send a copy of the notice to each of the relevant authorities and to any voluntary organisation whose consent was required to any provision of the plan.

GENERAL NOTE
The duty imposed upon local authorities to prepare plans for certain purposes is becoming a regular feature of regional administration and the requirement that such plans be submitted for approval is now standard. It is a reasonable condition since it ensures uniformity of standards and enables the central Government to get a "bird's-eye view" of the national structure.

For the return of statistics, etc., see s. 63, *post.*

COMMENCEMENT OF THIS SECTION
See s. 73 (2), *post,* and the note thereto.

COMMITTEE BY WHICH THE PLAN WAS SUBMITTED
I.e., the children's regional planning committee; see s. 36 (1), *ante.*

INSTRUMENT OF MANAGEMENT
See further, ss. 39, 40, *post.*

WRITING
See the note to s. 5, *ante.*

7—A.L.S. 189

DEFINITIONS
For "regional plan", see s. 36 (1), *ante*; for "the relevant authorities", see s. 35 (3), *ante;* for "planning area", see s. 35 (1), *ante*; for "child" and "local authority", see s. 70 (1), *post*; for "voluntary organisation", see, by virtue of s. 70 (1), *post*, the Children Act 1948, s. 59 (1) (17 Halsbury's Statutes (3rd Edn.) 578); for "controlled community home" and "assisted community home", see s. 36 (3), *ante*.

38. Provision of community homes by local authorities

Where a regional plan for a planning area includes provision for a community home to be provided by one of the relevant authorities, it shall be the duty of the local authority concerned to provide, manage, equip and maintain that home.

GENERAL NOTE
This section replaces s. 15 (1) of the Children Act 1948.
There is nothing in the section militating against local authorities coming to various agreements among themselves as to the sharing of facilities and for allocating expenditure proportionately with regard to the costs incidental to farming out and providing for the children and young persons in their care.
During the committee proceedings, much was made of the possible unwillingness or downright refusal of some local authorities to participate in the regional plans. It was suggested that those areas, popularly described as "superior", "sought-after" "select", etc. would simply refuse to accede to proposals for setting up community homes in their areas. Although dealing with disputes, s. 45 would not cover this problem and *semble* "there is no power given to the Secretary of State to compel local authorities to co-operate, but the principle underlying this particular measure is of fairly general application. Local authorities, being creatures of statute, are charged with carrying out a public duty, and it is felt that they can be trusted to co-operate in these circumstances. Whether mandamus would lie against them if there was an absolute refusal on the part of a local authority to participate is another matter"—*per* the Under-Secretary of State for the Home Department.

COMMENCEMENT OF THIS SECTION
See s. 73 (2), *post*, and the note thereto.

COMMUNITY HOME . . . PROVIDED BY ONE OF THE RELEVANT AUTHORITIES
See the note to s. 36, *ante*.

THE LOCAL AUTHORITY CONCERNED
I.e., the local authority which has agreed, under the schemes referred to in s. 36, *ante*, to undertake the running of the particular community home. No financial burden is automatically imposed upon the authority in whose area the establishment is situated simply by being there—but, of course, if the "host" wishes to take advantage of the amenities provided, on behalf of its own people, there is nothing to prevent it from coming to some arrangement with the authority "providing" the home. This is the case even where a community home has been placed in area "A" by the authority for area "B" and its facilities are shared with the authority for areas "C" and "D".

DEFINITIONS
For "regional plan", see s. 36 (1), *ante*; for "planning area", see s. 35 (1), *ante*; for "the relevant authorities", see s. 35 (3), *ante*; for "local authority", see s. 70 (1), *post*.

39. Instruments of management for assisted and controlled community homes

(1) The Secretary of State may by order make an instrument of management providing for the constitution of a body of managers for any voluntary home which, in accordance with a regional plan approved by him, is designated as a controlled or assisted community home.

(2) Where in accordance with a regional plan approved by the Secretary of State, two or more voluntary homes are designated as controlled community homes or as assisted community homes, then if—

    (*a*) those homes are, or are to be, provided by the same voluntary organisation; and

    (*b*) the same local authority is to be represented on the body of managers for those homes,

a single instrument of management may be made by the Secretary of State under this section constituting one body of managers for those homes or for any two or more of them.

(3) The number of persons who, in accordance with an instrument of management under this section, constitute the body of managers for a voluntary home shall be such number, being a multiple of three, as may be specified in the instrument of management, but the instrument shall provide that a proportion of the managers shall be appointed by such local authority as may be so specified and—

    (*a*) in the case of a voluntary home which is designated in a regional plan as a controlled community home, the proportion shall be two-thirds; and

    (*b*) in the case of a voluntary home which is so designated as an assisted community home, the proportion shall be one-third.

(4) An instrument of management shall provide that the "foundation managers", that is to say, those of the managers of the voluntary home to which the instrument relates who are not appointed by a local authority in accordance with subsection (3) of this section, shall be appointed, in such manner and by such persons as may be specified in the instrument,—

    (*a*) so as to represent the interests of the voluntary organisation by which the home is, or is to be, provided; and

    (*b*) for the purpose of securing that, as far as practicable, the character of the home as a voluntary home will be preserved and that, subject to section 40 (3) of this Act, the terms of any trust deed relating to the home are observed.

(5) An instrument of management under this section shall come into force on such date as may be specified in the instrument, and if such an instrument is in force in relation to a voluntary home the home shall be and be known as a controlled community home or an assisted community home, according to its designation in the regional plan.

GENERAL NOTE
    This section replaces, *inter alia*, Sch. 4 to the Children and Young Persons Act 1933.

COMMENCEMENT OF THIS SECTION
    See s. 73 (2), *post*, and the note thereto.

INSTRUMENT OF MANAGEMENT
    As to the contents of such instruments see sub-ss. (3) and (4) of this section and s. 40 (1), (2), *post*; as to the variation or revocation of such instrument, see s. 40 (4), *post*.

A BODY OF MANAGERS

The Government stressed that the valuable services rendered in the past by co-opted voluntary managers of these homes would not be jettisoned. There was no need to fear any diminution in the powers of lay managers and an increase in the power of the "professional". The Government were only too well aware that the fresh outlook and independent reasoning which the voluntary worker could bring to the administration of the children's service acted as a salutary discipline upon the professional worker.

For the rights of Staff, etc., see Sch. 3, *post*.

DESIGNATED AS A CONTROLLED OR ASSISTED COMMUNITY HOME

The Under-Secretary of State for the Home Department made the following statement:

"The question whether the home or school becomes a controlled or an assisted establishment is one which can be settled only by negotiation. One must remember all the time that no establishment has a right to go to the regional planning committee and say, 'We want to be included in your scheme.' Conversely, no regional planning authority can go to any establishment and say, 'You must be included in our scheme.' It is all a matter of bilateral agreement and it is largely a matter of choice in the first instance whether they wish to apply to be included as a controlled or an assisted establishment. The controlled status will mean involving the surrender of majority control—which will be two-thirds—belonging to the local authority. On the other hand, the responsibility for maintenance, etc. will be removed from them.

It may be that they would opt for greater freedom but less assistance and prefer to remain an unassisted establishment. All that is a matter of choice in the first instance as to which form of application they wish to make and then it is a matter of negotiation and agreement, for the whole of this must depend upon agreement in each case." (H. of C. Official Report, S.C.G., 6th May 1969, col. 525.)

DEFINITIONS

For "voluntary home", "voluntary organisation" and "local authority", see s. 70 (1), *post*; for "regional plan", see s. 36 (1), *ante*.

ORDERS UNDER THIS SECTION

By s. 69 (1), *post*, orders under this section are not required to be made by statutory instrument. Such orders will not be noted in this work.

40. Supplementary provisions as to instruments of management and trust deeds

(1) An instrument of management for a controlled or assisted community home shall contain such provisions as the Secretary of State considers appropriate for giving effect to the provisions of the regional plan by which the home is designated as a controlled or assisted community home, but nothing in the instrument of management for such a home shall affect the purposes for which the premises comprising the home are held.

(2) Without prejudice to the generality of subsection (1) of this section, an instrument of management may contain—

(a) provisions specifying the nature and purpose of the home or each of the homes to which it relates;

(b) provisions requiring a specified number or proportion of the places in that home or those homes to be made available to local authorities and to any other body specified in the instrument; and

(c) provisions relating to the management of that home or those homes and the charging of fees in respect of children placed therein or places made available to any local authority or other body.

(3) Subject to subsection (1) of this section, in the event of any inconsistency between the provisions of any trust deed and the instrument of management

relating to a controlled or assisted community home, the instrument of management shall prevail over the provisions of the trust deed in so far as they relate to that home.

(4) After consultation with the voluntary organisation by which a controlled or assisted community home is provided and with the local authority specified in the instrument of management for the time being in force for that home, the Secretary of State may vary or revoke any provisions of that instrument of management by a further instrument of management.

(5) In this Act the expression "trust deed", in relation to a voluntary home, means any instrument (other than an instrument of management) regulating the maintenance, management or conduct of the home or the constitution of a body of managers or trustees of the home.

GENERAL NOTE

The aim of this section is to facilitate the participation of voluntary homes in the regional scheme. In particular, power is given to the Secretary of State to modify the terms of the original trust deeds of voluntary bodies.

COMMENCEMENT OF THIS SECTION

See s. 73 (2), *post*, and the note thereto.

SUB-S. (1): DESIGNATED AS A CONTROLLED OR ASSISTED COMMUNITY HOME

I.e., in accordance with s. 36 (3), *ante*. See the note to s. 36, *ante*.

SUB-S. (2)

An instrument . . . may contain

Whereas an instrument of management must provide that the body of managers of the home be in the proportion specified in s. 39 (3), *ante*, and that the "foundation managers" be appointed in accordance with s. 39 (4), *ante*, and must contain such provisions as the Secretary of State considers appropriate for giving effect to the regional plan, it may or may not contain the provisions specified in sub-s. (2) of this section.

A specified number or proportion of the places

See paras. 9 and 11 of Appendix IV, *post*.

SUB-S. (4): CONSULTATION

See the note to s. 19 (2), *ante*.

DEFINITIONS

For "child", "instrument of management", "local authority" and "voluntary home", see s. 70 (1), *post*; for "regional plan", see s. 36 (1), *ante*.

41. Management of controlled community homes

(1) The management, equipment and maintenance of a controlled community home shall be the responsibility of the local authority specified in the instrument of management for that home, and in the following provisions of this section "the responsible authority", in relation to such a home, means the local authority responsible for its management, equipment and maintenance.

(2) Subject to the following provisions of this section, the responsible authority shall exercise their functions in relation to a controlled community home through the body of managers constituted by the instrument of management for the home, and any thing done, liability incurred or property acquired

by the managers shall be done, incurred or acquired by the managers as agents of the responsible authority.

(3) In so far as any matter is reserved for the decision of the responsible authority, either by subsection (4) of this section or by the instrument of management for the controlled community home in question or by the service by the responsible authority on the managers or any of them of a notice reserving any matter, that matter shall be dealt with by the responsible authority themselves and not by the managers, but in dealing with any matter so reserved, the responsible authority shall have regard to any representations made to them by the managers.

(4) The employment of persons at a controlled community home shall be a matter reserved for the decision of the responsible authority, but where the instrument of management so provides the responsible authority may enter into arrangements with the voluntary organisation by which the home is provided whereby, in accordance with such terms as may be agreed between the responsible authority and the voluntary organisation, persons who are not in the employment of the responsible authority shall undertake duties at the home.

(5) The accounting year of the managers of a controlled community home shall be such as may be specified by the responsible authority and, before such date in each accounting year as may be so specified, the managers of a controlled community home shall submit to the responsible authority estimates, in such form as the authority may require, of expenditure and receipts in respect of the next accounting year; and any expenses incurred by the manager of a controlled community home with the approval of the responsible authority shall be defrayed by that authority.

(6) The managers of a controlled community home shall keep proper accounts in respect of that home and proper records in relation to the accounts, but where an instrument of management relates to more than one controlled community home, one set of accounts and records may be kept in respect of all the homes to which the instrument relates.

GENERAL NOTE

The principal difference between this section and the one that follows (dealing with assisted community homes) relates to staffing; see sub-s. (4) of this section.

Denominational bodies will naturally wish to recruit staff, particularly teachers, from their own followers, and, in certain cases, will wish them to be ordained. In the case of a home becoming "controlled", a valuable feature would be lost if this right to draw exclusively from a certain source were not preserved. Thus, although the employment of staff at a controlled community home is, in general, "reserved for the decision of the responsible authority", special arrangements are permitted whereby persons not employed by the authority may staff the home.

COMMENCEMENT OF THIS SECTION

See s. 73 (2), *post*, and the note thereto.

CONTROLLED COMMUNITY HOME

I.e., a voluntary home, as defined by s. 70 (1), *post*, so designated in accordance with s. 36 (3), *ante*, and managed in accordance with s. 39 (3) (a), (4), *ante*.

DEFINITIONS

For "instrument of management" and "voluntary organisation", see s. 70 (1), *post*.

42. Management of assisted community homes

(1) The management, equipment and maintenance of an assisted community home shall be the responsibility of the voluntary organisation by which the home is provided, and in the following provisions of this section "the responsible organisation", in relation to such a home, means the voluntary organisation responsible for its management, equipment and maintenance.

(2) Subject to the following provisions of this section, the responsible organisation shall exercise its functions in relation to the home through the body of managers constituted by the instrument of management for the home, and any thing done, liability incurred or property acquired by the managers shall be done, incurred or acquired by the managers as agents of the responsible organisation.

(3) In so far as any matter is reserved for the decision of the responsible organisation, either by subsection (4) of this section or by the instrument of management for the assisted community home in question or by the service by the responsible organisation on the managers or any of them a notice reserving any matter, that matter shall be dealt with by the responsible organisation itself and not by the managers, but in dealing with any matter so reserved the responsible organisation shall have regard to any representations made to the organisation by the managers.

(4) The employment of persons at an assisted community home shall be a matter reserved for the decision of the responsible organisation but, subject to subsection (5) of this section,—

(*a*) where the responsible organisation proposes to engage any person to work at the home or to terminate without notice the employment of any person at the home, the responsible organisation shall consult the local authority specified in the instrument of management and, if the local authority so directs, the responsible organisation shall not carry out its proposal without the consent of the local authority; and

(*b*) the local authority may, after consultation with the responsible organisation, require the organisation to terminate the employment of any person at the home.

(5) Paragraphs (*a*) and (*b*) of subsection (4) of this section shall not apply—

(*a*) in such cases or circumstances as may be specified by notice in writing given by the local authority to the responsible organisation; and

(*b*) in relation to the employment of any persons or class of persons specified in the instrument of management.

(6) The accounting year of the managers of an assisted community home shall be such as may be specified by the responsible organisation and, before such date in each accounting year as may be so specified, the managers of an assisted community home shall submit to the responsible organisation estimates, in such form as the organisation may require, of expenditure and receipts in respect of the next financial year; and all expenses incurred by the managers of an assisted community home with the approval of the responsible organisation shall be defrayed by the organisation.

(7) The managers of an assisted community home shall keep proper accounts in respect of that home and proper records in relation to those accounts, but where an instrument of management relates to more than one assisted community home, one set of accounts and records may be kept in respect of all the homes to which the instrument relates.

GENERAL NOTE
 The principal difference between this and the previous section relates to staffing; see sub-s. (4) of this section.
 The staffing of an assisted community home is in general "reserved for the decision of the responsible organisation", but, subject to sub-s. (5), the voluntary organisation must consult the local authority before engaging any one to work at the home, and before dismissing any one without notice—there is no necessity for consultation where a contract is terminated with due notice. Furthermore, the local authority may, after consultation with the responsible organisation, require the organisation to dismiss a member of the staff.
 However, by virtue of sub-s. (5), the authority's powers in relation to staff do not apply at all to the employment of any persons or class of persons specified in the instrument of management, and they may also be excluded in such circumstances as may be specified by the authority in a written notice to the voluntary organisation.

COMMENCEMENT OF THIS SECTION
 See s. 73 (2), *post*, and the note thereto.

ASSISTED COMMUNITY HOME
 I.e., a voluntary home, as defined by s. 70 (1), *ante*, so designated in accordance with s. 36 (3), *ante*, and managed in accordance with s. 39 (3) (*b*), (4), *ante*.

CONSULT; CONSULTATION
 See the note to s. 19 (2), *ante*.

SUB-S. (7)
 An assisted home is the responsibility of a voluntary organisation and their accounts consequently come under the provisions of the Charities Act 1960, s. 8.

DEFINITIONS
 For "instrument of management", "local authority" and "voluntary organisation", see s. 70 (1), *post*.

FURTHER PROVISION
 For the Secretary of State's power to make grants to voluntary organisations towards expenditure incurred by them in establishing, maintaining or improving assisted community homes, see s. 65 (1), *post*.

43. Control of premises used for, and conduct of, community homes

(1) The Secretary of State may make regulations with respect to the conduct of community homes and for securing the welfare of the children in community homes.

(2) Without prejudice to the generality of subsection (1) of this section, regulations under this section may—

 (*a*) impose requirements as to the accommodation and equipment to be provided in community homes and as to the medical arrangements to be made for protecting the health of the children in the homes;

 (*b*) impose requirements as to the facilities which are to be provided for giving religious instruction to children in community homes;

(c) require the approval of the Secretary of State for the provision and use of accommodation for the purpose of restricting the liberty of children in community homes and impose other requirements as to the placing of a child in accommodation provided for that purpose, including a requirement to obtain the permission of the local authority or voluntary organisation in whose care the child is;

(d) authorise the Secretary of State to give and revoke directions requiring the local authority by whom a community home is provided or who are specified in the instrument of management for a controlled community home or the voluntary organisation by which an assisted community home is provided to accommodate in the home a child in the care of a local authority for whom no places are made available in that home or to take such action in relation to a child accommodated in the home as may be specified in the directions;

(e) require reviews of any permission given in pursuance of paragraph (c) above and provide for such a review to be conducted in a manner approved by the Secretary of State by a committee of persons representing the local authority or voluntary organisation in question but including at least one person satisfying such conditions as may be prescribed by the regulations with a view to securing that he is independent of the authority or organisation and unconnected with any community home containing such accommodation as is mentioned in the said paragraph (c);

(f) prescribe standards to which premises used for community homes are to conform;

(g) require the approval of the Secretary of State to the use of buildings for the purpose of community homes and to the doing of anything (whether by way of addition, diminution or alteration) which materially affects the buildings or grounds or other facilities or amenities available for children in community homes;

(h) provide that, to such extent as may be provided for in the regulations, the Secretary of State may direct that any provision of regulations under this section which is specified in the direction and makes any such provision as is referred to in paragraph (a), (f), or (g) above shall not apply in relation to a particular community home or the premises used for it, and may provide for the variation or revocation of any such direction by the Secretary of State.

(3) Without prejudice to the power to make regulations under this section conferring functions on the local authority or voluntary organisation by which a community home is provided or on the managers of a controlled or assisted community home, regulations under this section may confer functions in relation to a controlled or assisted community home on the local authority named in the instrument of management for the home.

(4) Where it appears to the Secretary of State that any premises used for the purposes of a community home are unsuitable for those purposes, or that the conduct of a community home is not in accordance with regulations made by him under this section or is otherwise unsatisfactory, he may by notice in

writing served on the responsible body, direct that as from such date as may be specified in the notice the premises shall not be used for the purposes of a community home.

(5) Where the Secretary of State has given a direction in relation to a controlled or assisted community home under subsection (4) of this section and the direction has not been revoked, the Secretary of State may at any time by order revoke the instrument of management for that home.

(6) For the purposes of subsection (4) of this section the responsible body—

(a) in relation to a community home provided by a local authority, is that local authority;

(b) in relation to a controlled community home, is the local authority specified in the instrument of management for that home; and

(c) in relation to an assisted community home, is the voluntary organisation by which the home is provided.

GENERAL NOTE

This section enables the Home Secretary to make regulations for the running of community homes.

COMMENCEMENT OF THIS SECTION

See s. 73 (2), *post*, and the note thereto.

COMMUNITY HOME

I.e., (1) a community home provided by a local authority in accordance with s. 38, *ante*; (2) a controlled community home, being a voluntary home, as defined in s. 70 (1), *post*, which is so designated in accordance with s. 36 (3), *ante*, is managed in accordance with s. 39 (3) (a), (4), *ante*, and is the responsibility of the local authority in accordance with s. 41, *ante*; or (3) an assisted community home, being a voluntary home, as defined in s. 20 (1), *post*, which is so designated in accordance with s. 36 (3), *ante*, is managed in accordance with s. 39 (3) (b), (4), *ante*, and is the responsibility of a voluntary organisation in accordance with s. 42, *ante*.

SUB-S. (2), PARAS. (c) AND (e): PERMISSIONS TO PLACE A CHILD IN SECURE ACCOMMODATION

Regulations made under paras (c) and (e) will provide safeguards in connection with the removal of a child from an open home into one where his liberty is restricted. The Home Secretary made the following statement in relation to these safeguards:

"The safeguards provided by [ss. 21 (2) and 27 (4)] are substantial. [Section 27 (4) places] a statutory duty on local authorities to review each child's case at least once every six months, but the children accommodated in secure conditions are special cases and the local authority must be fully answerable for the welfare of such children. I have no doubt that the local authorities will take great pains but having considered what was said in Committee, it is right that the law should provide that there should be no risk, however slight, of a child being kept in secure accommodation for perhaps a protracted period without some independent person having a say in what is being done." (784 H. of C. Official Report 1169.)

Section 21 (2), *ante*, entitles a person in care, or his parent or guardian, to apply for his discharge.

See also the note to s. 20 (3), *ante*.

AMENITIES

In considering the meaning of this expression as used in the Housing, Town Planning, etc., Act 1909, s. 59 (repealed), Scrutton, L.J., in *Re Ellis* v. *Ruislip–Northwood Urban Council*, [1920] 1 K.B. 343, at p. 370, considered that it appeared to mean "pleasant circumstances, or features, advantages".

WRITING

See the note to s. 5, *ante*.

DEFINITIONS
For "child", "instrument of management", "local authority" and "voluntary organisation", see s. 70 (1), *post*.

REGULATIONS UNDER THIS SECTION
    See generally, as to regulations under this Act, s. 69, *post*.
    No regulations had been made under this section up to 1st May 1970.

ORDERS UNDER SUB-S. (5)
    By s. 69 (1), *post*, orders under sub-s. (5) are not required to be made by statutory instrument. Such orders will not be noted in this work.

44. Controlled and assisted community homes exempted from certain provisions as to voluntary homes

While a voluntary home is a controlled or assisted community home, the following enactments shall not apply in relation to it, that is to say,—

(a) sections 29 and 30 of the Children Act 1948 (compulsory registration of voluntary homes);

(b) section 31 of that Act (regulations as to conduct of voluntary homes); and

(c) section 93 of the Act of 1933 and section 32 of the Children Act 1948 (notification to Secretary of State of certain particulars relating to voluntary homes).

GENERAL NOTE
    This section is purely administrative: there would be no point in requiring the separate registration of and the separate return of particulars to the Secretary of State by voluntary bodies participating in a community home scheme—which has already been approved by him. The establishments are, in any case, subject to other controls in this Act; see s. 43, *ante*.

COMMENCEMENT OF THIS SECTION
    See s. 73 (2), *post*, and the note thereto.

CONTROLLED . . . COMMUNITY HOME
    I.e., a voluntary home, as defined by s. 70 (1), *post*, so designated in accordance with s. 36 (3), *ante*, and managed in accordance with s. 39 (3) (a), (4), *ante*, and is the responsibility of the local authority in accordance with s. 41, *ante*.

ASSISTED COMMUNITY HOME
    I.e., a voluntary home, as defined by s. 70 (1), *post*, so designated in accordance with s. 36 (3), *ante*, managed in accordance with s. 39 (3) (b), (4), *ante*, and is the responsibility of a voluntary organisation in accordance with s. 41, *ante*.

CHILDREN ACT 1948, SS. 29-32
    See 17 Halsbury's Statutes (3rd Edn.) 561–564.

ACT OF 1933
    I.e., the Children and Young Persons Act 1933; see s. 70 (1), *post*. For s. 93 of that Act, see 12 Halsbury's Statutes (2nd Edn.) 1043.

45. Determination of disputes relating to controlled and assisted community homes

(1) Subject to subsection (5) of this section, where any dispute relating to a controlled community home arises between the local authority specified in the instrument of management and either the voluntary organisation by which the

home is provided or any other local authority who have placed, or desire or are required to place, a child in their care in the home, the dispute may be referred by either party to the Secretary of State for his determination.

(2) Subject to subsection (5) of this section, where any dispute relating to an assisted community home arises between the voluntary organisation by which the home is provided and any local authority who have placed, or desire to place, a child in their care in the home, the dispute may be referred by either party to the Secretary of State for his determination.

(3) Where a dispute is referred to the Secretary of State under this section he may, in order to give effect to his determination of the dispute, give such directions as he thinks fit to the local authority or voluntary organisation concerned.

(4) The provisions of this section shall apply notwithstanding that the matter in dispute may be one which, under or by virtue of the preceding provisions of this Part of this Act, is reserved for the decision, or is the responsibility, of the local authority specified in the instrument of management or, as the case may be, the voluntary organisation by which the home is provided.

(5) Where any trust deed relating to a controlled or assisted community home contains provision whereby a bishop or any other ecclesiastical or denominational authority has power to decide questions relating to religious instruction given in the home, no dispute which is capable of being dealt with in accordance with that provision shall be referred to the Secretary of State under this section.

COMMENCEMENT OF THIS SECTION
    See s. 73 (2), *post*, and the note thereto.

CONTROLLED COMMUNITY HOME; ASSISTED COMMUNITY HOME
    See the notes to s. 44, *ante*.

LOCAL AUTHORITY SPECIFIED IN THE INSTRUMENT OF MANAGEMENT
    I.e., in accordance with s. 39 (3), *ante*.

DEFINITIONS
    For "child", "instrument of management", "local authority" and "voluntary organisation", see s. 70 (1), *post*; for "trust deed", see s. 40 (5), *ante*.

46. Discontinuance of approved schools etc. on establishment of community homes

(1) If in the case of any approved school, remand home, approved probation hostel or approved probation home within the meaning of the Criminal Justice Act 1948 (hereafter in this section referred to as an "approved institution") it appears to the Secretary of State that in consequence of the establishment of community homes for a planning area the institution as such is no longer required, he may by order provide that it shall cease to be an approved institution on a date specified in the order.

(2) The provisions of Schedule 3 to this Act shall have effect in relation to institutions which are, or by virtue of this section have ceased to be, approved institutions.

GENERAL NOTE

    It should be noted that the section does not imply that after being discontinued such establishment as were formerly "approved" will have no further part to play in the regional scheme: the expression "the institution *as such* is no longer required" plainly indicates that it may undertake other forms of care and treatment.

COMMENCEMENT OF THIS SECTION

    See s. 73 (2), *post*, and the note thereto.

DEFINITIONS

    For "approved school", "remand home", "approved probation hostel" and "approved probation home", see the Criminal Justice Act 1948, s. 80 (1), 28 Halsbury's Statutes (2nd Edn.) 393.

ORDERS UNDER THIS SECTION

    See, generally, as to orders under this Act, s. 69, *post*. Order under this section, being local in nature, will not be noted in this work.

47. Discontinuance by voluntary organisation of controlled or assisted community home

(1) The voluntary organisation by which a controlled or assisted community home is provided shall not cease to provide the home except after giving to the Secretary of State and the local authority specified in the instrument of management not less than two years' notice in writing of their intention to do so.

(2) A notice under subsection (1) of this section shall specify the date from which the voluntary organisation intends to cease to provide the home as a community home; and where such a notice is given and is not withdrawn before the date specified in it, then, subject to subsection (4) of this section the instrument of management for the home shall cease to have effect on that date and accordingly the home shall then cease to be a controlled or assisted community home.

(3) Where a notice is given under subsection (1) of this section, the local authority to whom the notice is given shall inform the children's regional planning committee responsible for the regional plan under which the voluntary home in question was designated as a controlled or assisted community home of the receipt and content of the notice.

(4) Where a notice is given under subsection (1) of this section and the body of managers for the home to which the notice relates give notice in writing to the Secretary of State that they are unable or unwilling to continue as managers of the home until the date specified in the first-mentioned notice, the Secretary of State may by order—

    (*a*) revoke the instrument of management; and

    (*b*) require the local authority who were specified in that instrument to conduct the home, until the date specified in the notice under subsection (1) of this section or much earlier date (if any) as may be specified for the purposes of this paragraph in the order, as if it were a community home provided by the local authority.

(5) Where the Secretary of State makes such a requirement as is specified in subsection (4) (*b*) of this section,—

    (*a*) nothing in the trust deed for the home in question shall affect the conduct of the home by the local authority; and (*b*) the Secretary of State may by order direct that for the purposes of any provision specified in the direction and made by or under any enactment relating to community homes (other than this section) the home shall, until the date or earlier date specified as mentioned in subsection (4) (*b*) of this section, be treated as an assisted community home or as a controlled community home, but except in so far as the Secretary of State so directs, the home shall until that date be treated for the purposes of any such enactment as a community home provided by the local authority; and

(*c*) on the date or earlier date specified as mentioned in subsection (4) (*b*) of this section the home shall cease to be a community home.

COMMENCEMENT OF THIS SECTION
    See s. 73 (2), *post*, and the note thereto.

SUB-S. (I)
    Controlled . . . community home; assisted community home
        See the notes to s. 44, *ante*.

    Local authority specified in the instrument of management
        I.e., in accordance with s. 39 (3), *ante*.

    Writing
        See the note to s. 5 (5), *ante*.

SUB-SS. (4) (*b*) AND (5) (*c*): SUCH EARLIER DATE
    The references to an earlier date are designed to prevent an authority from suddenly finding themselves saddled with a home which might have been forced to discontinue for reasons which would bear equally as hard upon the local authority—*e.g.* grave staff shortages. Under such circumstances it would be only reasonable for there to be a much shorter period than the two years specified in sub-s. (I).

SUB-S. (5) (*b*)
    The purpose of this subsection is to make it clear that a voluntary community home which is being temporarily managed by the local authority may still be regarded as a voluntary home where the Secretary of State so directs. For example, if the voluntary body had undertaken, say, building works under the promise of a grant awarded under s. 65 (I), *post*, the work might have to cease because the local authority would not be eligible—unless they were prepared to lose money. By treating the local authority in this way as if it were a voluntary body, the situation is remedied.

DEFINITIONS
    For "children's regional planning committee", see s. 35 (3), *ante*; for "regional plan", see s. 36 (I), *ante*; for "instrument of management", "local authority" and "voluntary organisation", see s. 70 (I), *post*; for "trust deed", see s. 40 (5), *ante*.

ORDERS UNDER THIS SECTION
    See, generally, as to orders under this Act, s. 69, *post*. Orders under this section, being local in nature, will not be noted in this work.

48. Financial provisions applicable on cessation of controlled or assisted community home

(I) Where the instrument of management for a controlled or assisted community home ceases to have effect by virtue either of an order under section 43 (5) of this Act or of subsection (2) or subsection (4) (*a*) of section 47 of this Act, the voluntary organisation by which the home was provided or, if the premises used for the purposes of the home are not vested in that organisation, the persons in whom those premises are vested (in this section referred to as "the trustees of the home"), shall become liable, in accordance with the following provisions of this section, to make repayment in respect of any increase in the value of the premises and other property belonging to the voluntary organisation or the trustees of the home which is attributable to the expenditure of public money thereon.

(2) Where an instrument of management has ceased to have effect as mentioned in subsection (1) of this section and the instrument related—

(*a*) to a controlled community home; or

(*b*) to an assisted community home which, at any time before that instrument of management came into force, was a controlled community home,

then, on the home ceasing to be a community home, the voluntary organisation by which the home was provided or, as the case may be, the trustees of the home, shall pay to the local authority specified in that instrument of management a sum equal to that part of the value of any relevant premises which is attributable to expenditure by the local authority who at the time the expenditure was incurred had responsibility for the management, equipment and maintenance of the home by virtue of section 41 (1) of this Act.

(3) For the purposes of subsection (2) of this section, "relevant premises", in relation to a controlled or assisted community home, means premises used for the purposes of the home and belonging to the voluntary organisation or the trustees of the home but erected, extended or improved, at any time while the home was a controlled community home, by the local authority having, at that time, such responsibility in relation to the home as is mentioned in subsection (2) of this section.

(4) Where an instrument of management has ceased to have effect as mentioned in subsection (1) of this section and the instrument related—

(*a*) to an assisted community home; or

(*b*) to a controlled community home which, at any time before that instrument of management came into force, was an assisted community home,

then, on the home ceasing to be a community home, the voluntary organisation by which the home was provided or, as the case may be, the trustees of the home, shall pay to the Secretary of State a sum equal to that part of the value of the premises and any other property used for the purposes of the home which is attributable to the expenditure of money provided by way of grant under section 65 of this Act.

(5) Where an instrument of management has ceased to have effect as mentioned in subsection (1) of this section and the controlled or assisted community home to which it related was conducted in premises which formerly were used as an approved school or were an approved probation hostel or home but which were designated as a community home in a regional plan approved by the Secretary of State, then, on the home ceasing to be a community home, the voluntary organisation by which the home was provided or, as the case may be, the trustees of the home, shall pay to the Secretary of State a sum equal to that part of the value of the premises concerned and of any other property used for the

purposes of the home and belonging to the voluntary organisation or the trustees of the home which is attributable to the expenditure—

> (*a*) of sums paid towards the expenses of the managers of an approved school under section 104 of the Act of 1933; or
>
> (*b*) of sums paid under section 77 (3) (*b*) of the Criminal Justice Act 1948 in relation to expenditure on approved probation hostels or homes.

(6) The amount of any sum payable under this section by the voluntary organisation by which a controlled or assisted community home was provided or by the trustees of the home shall be determined in accordance with such arrangements—

> (*a*) as may be agreed between the voluntary organisation by which the home was provided and the local authority concerned or, as the case may be, the Secretary of State; or
>
> (*b*) in default of agreement, as may be determined by the Secretary of State;

and with the agreement of the local authority concerned or the Secretary of State, as the case may be, the liability to pay any sum under this section may be discharged, in whole or in part, by the transfer of any premises or other property used for the purposes of the home in question.

(7) The provisions of this section shall have effect notwithstanding anything in any trust deed for a controlled or assisted community home and notwithstanding the provisions of any enactment or instrument governing the disposition of the property of a voluntary organisation.

(8) Any sums received by the Secretary of State under this section shall be paid into the Consolidated Fund.

GENERAL NOTE

The purpose of this section is to provide the means whereby, if grants have been made out of public money to a voluntary body, and that body ceases to participate in the scheme, the money should be paid back. Three points should be noticed: (1) The principle of repayment applies only to capital sums: this accounts for the wording in sub-s. (1)—"in respect of any increase in the value of the premises and any other property belonging to the voluntary body". Consequently, if a capital grant has been paid out which has not brought about any enhancement of the premises, no repayment is necessary; if there has been any enhancement the organisation has enjoyed a commensurate benefit and the money must be repaid. (2) The section applies to sums paid to voluntary organisations before the commencement of this Act; see sub-s. (5) of this section. (3) Housing grants are not affected by this section in any way.

It should be noted that a local authority has no discretion to waive payments to it under sub-s. (2) on the discontinuance of a former controlled community home, but it may accept property in lieu of cash.

COMMENCEMENT OF THIS SECTION

See s. 73 (2), *post*, and the note thereto.

CONTROLLED . . . COMMUNITY HOME; ASSISTED COMMUNITY HOME

See the notes to s. 44, *ante*.

APPROVED SCHOOL; APPROVED PROBATION HOSTEL; APPROVED PROBATION HOME

For meanings, see The Criminal Justice Act 1948, s. 80 (1), 8 Halsbury's Statutes (3rd Edn.) 370.

The Consolidated Fund of the United Kingdom was established under the Consolidated Fund Act 1816, s. 1, 21 Halsbury's Statutes (2nd Edn.) 31. By the Finance Act 1954, s. 34 (3) (86 Statutes Supp.), any charge on the Fund extends to the growing produce of the Fund. See also, as to payment out of the Fund, the Exchequer and Audit Departments Act 1866, s. 13, 21 Halsbury's Statutes (2nd Edn.) 210, as amended, in conjunction with the Finance Act 1936, s. 34, 21 Halsbury's Statutes (2nd Edn.) 1171, and with the Exchequer and Audit Departments Act 1957, 37 Halsbury's Statutes (2nd Edn.) 925.

DEFINITIONS
For "instrument of management", "local authority" and "voluntary organisation", see s. 70 (1), *post*; for "the relevant premises", see sub-s. (3) of this section; for "trustees of the home", see sub-s. (1) of this section; for "trust deed", see s. 40 (5), *ante*.

Consequential modifications of ss. 13 *and* 19 *of Children Act* 1948

49. Provision of accommodation and maintenance for children in care

For section 13 of the Children Act 1948 there shall be substituted the following section:—

13. Provision of accommodation and maintenance for children in care.

(1) A local authority shall discharge their duty to provide accommodation and maintenance for a child in their care in such one of the following ways as they think fit, namely,—

(*a*) by boarding him out on such terms as to payment by the authority and otherwise as the authority may, subject to the provisions of this Act and regulations thereunder, determine; or

(*b*) by maintaining him in a community home or in any such home as is referred to in section 64 of the Children and Young Persons Act 1969; or

(*c*) by maintaining him in a voluntary home (other than a community home) the managers of which are willing to receive him;

or by making such other arrangements as seem appropriate to the local authority.

(2) Without prejudice to the generality of subsection (1) of this section, a local authority may allow a child in their care, either for a fixed period or until the local authority otherwise determine, to be under the charge and control of a parent, guardian, relative or friend.

(3) The terms, as to payment and other matters, on which a child may be accommodated and maintained in any such home as is referred to in section 64 of that Act shall be such as the Secretary of State may from time to time determine.

GENERAL NOTE
Section 13, as formerly enacted, broadly arranged for a child in the care of a local authority to be boarded out where possible, and expressed this matter in such terms as to imply that residential accommodation was necessarily a second best alternative— for which it was often criticised. The new s. 13 differs from the former section in the following respects: The new sub-s. (1) is completely neutral as between boarding out and receiving into a home. The old sub-ss. (2) and (3) referred to the poor law which now

no longer is in use. Sub-s. (4) formerly authorised the accommodation of a child in a hostel under certain conditions: the distinction between homes and hostels having been eliminated, this requirement is no longer necessary. Sub-ss. (5)–(7) of the former section have been omitted as being inapplicable to the new community home system.

COMMENCEMENT OF THIS SECTION
    See s. 73 (2), *post*, and the note thereto.

CHILD
    I.e., a person under the age of eighteen years and any person who has attained that age and is the subject of a care order within the meaning of the Children and Young Persons Act 1969; see the Children Act 1948, s. 59, 17 Halsbury's Statutes (3rd Edn.) 578, as amended by Sch. 5, para. 22, *post*.

COMMUNITY HOME
    For meaning, see s. 36 (1), *ante*, and see generally ss. 35–45, *ante*.

ANY SUCH HOME AS IS REFERRED TO IN SECTION 64
    I.e., a home for the accommodation of children who are in the care of local authorities and are in need of particular facilities and services which are provided in those homes and are, in the opinion of the Secretary of State, unlikely to be readily available in community homes.

DEFINITIONS
    For "guardian", "parent" and "voluntary home", see the Children Act 1948, s. 59 (1), 17 Halsbury's Statutes (3rd Edn.) 578. For "local authority", see *ibid.*, s. 38, *ibid.*, p. 1132, as amended. For "relative", see the Adoption of Children Act 1949, s. 13 (1), (61 Statutes Supp.), by virtue of *ibid.*, s. 13 (2), *ibid.*, p. 776.

CHILDREN ACT 1948, S. 13
    See 17 Halsbury's Statutes (3rd Edn.) 550.

REGULATIONS
    See, generally, as to regulations under the Children Act 1948, s. 58 of that Act, 17 Halsbury's Statutes (3rd Edn.), 577.
    As to boarding out regulations, see *ibid.*, s. 14, *ibid.*, p. 1116.

50. Accommodation of persons over school age in convenient community home

For section 19 of the Children Act 1948 there shall be substituted the following section:—

19. Accommodation of persons over school age in convenient community home

A local authority may provide accommodation in a community home for any person who is over compulsory school age but has not attained the age of twenty-one if the community home is provided for children who are over compulsory school age and is near the place where that person is employed or seeking employment or receiving education or training.

GENERAL NOTE
    This section obtained an enthusiastic welcome from many parties. Under the present system, at the age of 16 children are forced to leave the haven of a community home, and frequently have difficulty in finding good, cheap lodgings. Too often the lack of a stabilising influence such as the community home and the pseudo-parental discipline provided has in the past brought disaster. This section now provides them with a home and some sort of continuity of care.

COMMENCEMENT OF THIS SECTION
    See s. 73 (2), *post*, and the note thereto.

COMMUNITY HOME
As to the establishment, see generally ss. 35–45, *ante.*

It is a cardinal principle of the new scheme that a single statutory class of residential establishments should supersede the various classes of establishment which at present have separate statutory existence, and accordingly "hostels" for persons over school age are given no special name, but are simply another variety of community homes. Their special nature and purpose will have been specified in the regional plan submitted to the Secretary of State for his approval under s. 36, *ante.*

COMPULSORY SCHOOL AGE
A person is over compulsory school age as soon as he has attained the age of fifteen years; see the Education Act 1944, s. 35 (11 Halsbury's Statutes (3rd Edn.) 194), the proviso to which enables the upper limit of compulsory school age to be raised to sixteen by Order in Council, but this is subject to qualification in the case of registered pupils at special schools who are not deemed to be over compulsory school age until they have attained sixteen years, *ibid.*, s. 38, *ibid.*, p. 197.

ATTAINED THE AGE OF
See the note to s. 1, *ante.*

DEFINITION
For "local authority", see the Children Act 1948, s. 38, 17 Halsbury's Statutes (3rd Edn.) 566.

CHILDREN ACT 1948, S. 19
See 17 Halsbury's Statutes (3rd Edn.) 555.

Foster children

51. Modification of general duty of local authorities with respect to foster children

For section 1 of the Children Act 1958 (which imposes a duty on every local authority to secure that foster children are visited by officers of the authority) there shall be substituted the following section:—

1. Duty of local authorities to ensure well-being of foster children

It shall be the duty of every local authority to satisfy themselves as to the well-being of children within their area who are foster children within the meaning of this Part of this Act and, for that purpose, to secure that, so far as appears to the authority to be appropriate, the children are visited from time to time by officers of the authority and that such advice is given as to the care and maintenance of the children as appears to be needed.

GENERAL NOTE
The amendment in this section is designed to make the duty of local authorities more flexible so as to enable them to concentrate greater effort on those cases in which supervision is more desirable—and often really necessary. The demand for foster homes has increased very rapidly since the passing of the Act of 1958 and is expected steadily to continue to do so. This increase is due very largely to the number of immigrants—particularly Commonwealth and African students, who seek foster homes for their children, and, because of the heavy pressure on accommodation, find it difficult to be discriminating in their choice.

As originally enacted, s. 1 of the 1958 Act imposed an absolute requirement to visit all foster children from time to time, irrespective of whether supervision is necessary. Under the new section local authorities need only visit foster homes as it appears to them to be appropriate.

COMMENCEMENT OF THIS SECTION
See s. 73 (2), *post*, and the note thereto.

DEFINITIONS
    For "foster children", see the Children Act 1958, s. 2, as reproduced in Sch. 7, *post*.
    For "local authority", see *ibid.*, s. 17 (112 Statutes Supp.).

CHILDREN ACT 1958, S. 1
    See 112 Statutes Supp.

52. Amendments of definitions of "foster child" and "protected child"

(1) In subsection (1) of section 2 of the Children Act 1958 (which, subject to the following provisions of that section, defines a foster child for the purposes of Part I of that Act as a child below the upper limit of the compulsory school age whose care and maintenance are undertaken for reward for a period exceeding one month by a person who is not a relative or guardian of his) the words from "for reward" to "one month" shall be omitted.

(2) At the end of paragraph (c) of subsection (3) of the said section 2 (which provides that a child is not a foster child while he is in the care of any person in a school) there shall be added the words "in which he is receiving full time education".

(3) After subsection (3) of the said section 2 there shall be inserted the following subsection:—

(3A) A child is not a foster child within the meaning of this Part of this Act at any time while his care and maintenance are undertaken by a person, other than a relative or guardian of his, if at that time—

(a) that person does not intend to, and does not in fact, undertake his care and maintenance for a continuous period of more than six days; or

(b) that person is not a regular foster parent and does not intend to, and does not in fact, undertake his care and maintenance for a continuous period of more than twenty-seven days;

and for the purposes of this subsection a person is a regular foster parent if, during the period of twelve months immediately preceding the date on which he begins to undertake the care and maintenance of the child in question, he had, otherwise than as a relative or guardian, the care and maintenance of one or more children either for a period of, or periods amounting in the aggregate to, not less than three months or for at least three continuous periods each of which was of more than six days.

(4) Section 37 of the Adoption Act 1958 (which defines "protected child" for the purposes of Part IV of that Act) shall have effect subject to the following modifications:—

(a) in paragraph (a) of subsection (1) which refers to arrangements for placing a child in the care of a person who is not a parent, guardian or relative of his) after the words "relative of his" there shall be inserted the words "but who proposes to adopt him";

(b) in subsection (1) (which among other matters excludes a foster child from the definition of "a protected child") the words "but is not a foster child within the meaning of Part I of the Children Act 1958" shall be omitted; and

(c) in subsection (2) (which excludes certain children from the definition of protected child, including children only temporarily in the care and possession of a person under such arrangements as are referred to in subsection (1) (*a*) of that section) the words from "by reason" to "that subsection, nor" shall be omitted.

(5) In consequence of the modifications of the definition of "protected child" specified in subsection (4) of this section, after subsection (4) of section 2 of the Children Act 1958 there shall be inserted the following subsection:—

"(4A) A child is not a foster child for the purposes of this Part of this Act while he is placed in the care and possession of a person who proposes to adopt him under arrangements made by such a local authority or registered adoption society as is referred to in Part II of the Adoption Act 1958 or while he is a protected child within the meaning of Part IV of that Act."

GENERAL NOTE
This section (1) amends the definition of a foster child in s. 2 of the Children Act 1958 so as to include cases in which the foster parents obtain no remuneration; (2) closes the gap between the Nurseries and Child Minders Act 1948, which covers periods up to six days, and the 1958 Act, which operated in cases where a child was being fostered beyond a month; and (3) increases the protection accorded to children who are living on school premises but not being educated there.

COMMENCEMENT OF THIS SECTION
See s. 73 (2), *post*, and the note thereto.

NOT A FOSTER CHILD
As to the categories of children who are not "foster children" within the meaning of Part I of the Children Act 1958, see s. 2 (2)–(4) of that Act, as reproduced in Sch. 7, *post*.

MONTHS
See the note to s. 15 (1), *ante*.

SUB-SS. (4), (5)
The force of the amendments referred to in these subsections are (*a*) to bring foster children within the meaning of "protected child"; and (*b*) to provide that neither a child whom it is proposed to adopt nor a protected child within Part IV of the Act of 1958 is a "foster child" within the meaning of s. 2 of that Act.

DEFINITIONS
For "child", "local authority" and "relative", see the Children Act 1958, s. 17, 112 Statutes Supp.

CHILDREN ACT 1958, S. 2, PART I
See 112 Statutes Supp.

ADOPTION ACT 1958, S. 37, PARTS II AND IV
See 115 Statutes Supp.

53. Modification of duty of persons maintaining foster children to notify local authority

(1) Section 3 of the Children Act 1958 (which requires any person maintaining foster children to notify the local authority on each occasion on which he receives a foster child) shall have effect subject to the following provisions of this section.

(2) In subsection (1) of the section (which requires at least two weeks advance notice of, or, in an emergency, notice within one week after, the reception of a foster child) at the beginning there shall be inserted the words "Subject to the following provisions of this section", after the words "two weeks" there shall be inserted the words "and not more than four weeks" and for the words "one week" there shall be substituted the words "forty-eight hours".

(3) In subsection (2) of the section (which relates to the content of the notice) after the word "specify" there shall be inserted the words "the date on which it is intended that the child should be received or, as the case may be, on which the child was in fact received or became a foster child and".

(4) After subsection (2) of the section there shall be inserted the following subsection:—

(2A) A person shall not be required to give notice under subsection (1) of this section in relation to a child if—

> (a) he has on a previous occasion given notice under that subsection in respect of that or any other child, specifying the premises at which he proposes to keep the child in question; and
> (b) he has not, at any time since that notice was given, ceased to maintain at least one foster child at those premises and been required by virtue of the following provisions of this section to give notice under subsection (5A) of this section in respect of those premises.

(5) In subsection (3) of the section (which relates to notification of changes of address of foster parents and requires similar periods of notice as under subsection (1))—

> (a) for the words "a foster child" there shall be substituted the words "one or more foster children";
> (b) for the words "the child is kept" there shall be substituted the words "the child is, or the children are, kept";
> (c) after the words "two weeks" there shall be inserted the words "and not more than four weeks"; and
> (d) for the words "one week" there shall be substituted the words "forty-eight hours".

(6) So much of subsection (4) of the section as requires notification that a foster child has been removed or has removed himself from the care of the person maintaining him shall cease to have effect and, accordingly, in that subsection for the words "that person" there shall be substituted the words "the person who was maintaining him" and in subsection (5) of the section (which dispenses with the need for such a notice where a child ceases to be a foster child on his removal from a foster parent but empowers the local authority concerned to require certain particulars in such a case)—

> (a) for the words "ceases to be a foster child on his removal" there shall be substituted the words "is removed or removes himself";
> (b) the words "need not give notice under subsection (4) of this section but" shall be omitted; and

    (*c*) for the words from "the same" onwards there shall be substituted the words "the name and address, if known, of the person (if any) into whose care the child has been removed".

(7) After subsection (5) of the section there shall be inserted the following subsections:—

    (5A) Subject to the provisions of the following subsection, where a person who has been maintaining one or more foster children at any premises ceases to maintain foster children at those premises and the circumstances are such that no notice is required to be given under subsection (3) or subsection (4) of this section, that person shall, within forty-eight hours after he ceases to maintain any foster child at those premises, give notice in writing thereof to the local authority.

    (5B) A person need not give the notice required by the preceding subsection in consequence of his ceasing to maintain foster children at any premises if, at the time he so ceases, he intends within twenty-seven days again to maintain any of them as a foster child at those premises; but if he subsequently abandons that intention or the said period expires without his having given effect to it he shall give the said notice within forty-eight hours of that event.

GENERAL NOTE
    This section amends the Children Act 1958, s. 3, so as to relax the obligation to notify the local authority of the arrival or departure of a foster child in certain cases, and thus to eliminate unnecessary work by foster parents and local authorities.
    But note that the interests of children may still be safeguarded by recourse to the provision in s. 4 (2) (*h*) of the 1958 Act—for which see s. 55 (2), *post*.

COMMENCEMENT OF THIS SECTION
    See s. 73 (2), *post*, and the note thereto.

WRITING
    See the note to s. 5, *ante*.

DEFINITIONS
    For "child" and "local authority", see the Children Act 1958, s. 17 (112 Statutes Supp.).
    For "foster child" see *ibid*., s. 2, as reproduced in Sch. 7, *post*.

CHILDREN ACT 1958, S. 3
    See 112 Statutes Supp.

54. Inspection of premises in which foster children are kept

(1) In section 4 (1) of the Children Act 1958 (which empowers an officer of a local authority to inspect premises in the local authority's area in which foster children are being kept) after the word "in" in the second place where it occurs there shall be inserted the words "the whole or any part of".

(2) After the said section 4 (1) there shall be inserted the following subsection:—

    (1A) If it is shown to the satisfaction of a justice of the peace on sworn information in writing—

        (*a*) that there is reasonable cause to believe that a foster child is being kept in any premises, or in any part thereof, and (*b*) that admission to those premises or that part thereof has been refused to a duly authorised officer of the local authority or that such a refusal is apprehended or that the occupier is temporarily absent,

the justice may by warrant under his hand authorise an officer of the local authority to enter the premises, if need be by force, at any reasonable time within forty-eight hours of the issue of the warrant, for the purpose of inspecting the premises.

(3) At the end of paragraph (*b*) of section 14 (1) of the Children Act 1958 (which makes it an offence under that section to refuse to allow an inspection of any premises under section 4 (1) of that Act) there shall be added the words "or wilfully obstructs a person entitled to enter any premises by virtue of a warrant under subsection (1A) of that section".

GENERAL NOTE

This section substantially expands the text of s. 4 of the Children Act 1958 to give the local authority greater powers to inspect premises which are wholly or partly used for the reception of foster children.

COMMENCEMENT

See s. 73 (2), *post*, and the note thereto.

SUB-S. (2)

Note the reference to "force" in the new sub-s. (1A).

WRITING

See the note to s. 5, *ante*.

WILFULLY

This expression "means that the act is done deliberately and intentionally, not by accident or inadvertence, but so that the mind of the person who does the act goes with it"; see *R.* v. *Senior*, [1899] 1 Q.B. 283, at pp. 290, 291, *per* Lord Russell of Killowen, C.J. See also, in particular, *R.* v. *Walker* (1934), 24 Cr. App. Rep. 117; *Eaton* v. *Cobb*, [1950] 1 All E.R. 1016; *Arrowsmith* v. *Jenkins*, [1963] 2 Q.B. 561; [1963] 2 All E.R. 210; and *Rice* v. *Connolly*, [1966] 2 Q.B. 414; [1966] 2 All E.R. 649.

DEFINITIONS

For "foster child", see the Children Act 1958, s. 2, as reproduced in Sch. 7, *post*. For "local authority", see *ibid.*, s. 17 (112 Statutes Supp.).

CHILDREN ACT 1958, SS. (4) (1), 14 (1)

See 112 Statutes Supp.

55. Imposition of requirements and prohibitions relating to the keeping of foster children

(1) In section 4 (2) of the Children Act 1958 (which empowers a local authority to impose certain requirements on a person who keeps or proposes to keep foster children in premises used wholly or mainly for that purpose) for the word "mainly" there shall be substituted the word "partly".

(2) After paragraph (*f*) of the said section 4 (2) there shall be inserted the following paragraphs:—

(*g*) the fire precautions to be taken in the premises;

(*h*) the giving of particulars of any foster child received in the premises and of any change in the number or identity of the foster children kept therein.

(3) In the words following the several paragraphs of the said section 4 (2), after the word "but" there shall be inserted the words "any such requirement may be limited to a particular class of foster children kept in the premises and" and for the words "(*b*) to (*f*)" there shall be substituted the words "(*b*) to (*h*)".

(4) For subsection (3) of section 4 to the Children Act 1958 (which empowers a local authority to prohibit a person from keeping a particular foster child or any foster children at particular premises) there shall be substituted the following subsections:—

(3) Where a person proposes to keep a foster child in any premises and the local authority are of the opinion that—

(*a*) the premises are not suitable premises in which to keep foster children; or

(*b*) that person is not a suitable person to have the care and maintenance of foster children; or

(*c*) it would be detrimental to that child to be kept by that person in those premises;

the local authority may impose a prohibition on that person under subsection (3A) of this section.

(3A) A prohibition imposed on any person under this subsection may—

(*a*) prohibit him from keeping any foster child in premises specified in the prohibition; or

(*b*) prohibit him from keeping any foster child in any premises in the area of the local authority; or

(*c*) prohibit him from keeping a particular child specified in the prohibition in premises so specified.

(3B) Where a local authority have imposed a prohibition on any person under subsection (3A) of this section, the local authority may, if they think fit, cancel the prohibition, either of their own motion or on an application made by that person on the ground of a change in the circumstances in which a foster child would be kept by him.

(5) In section 5 (1) of the Children Act 1958 (which confers a right of appeal to a juvenile court within fourteen days of the imposition of a requirement or prohibition under section 4 of that Act) after the word "prohibition", in the second place where it occurs, there shall be inserted the words "or, in the case of a prohibition imposed under subsection (3A) of that section, within fourteen days from the refusal by the local authority to accede to an application by him for the cancellation of the prohibition".

GENERAL NOTE

This section greatly extends the powers of local authorities to impose requirements in respect of premises in which foster children are kept and it clarifies and extends their powers to prohibit the reception of a foster child by an unsuitable person or in unsuitable premises. Note that s. 4 (3) of the Children Act 1958 as substituted by sub-s. (4) of this section does not apply to existing foster homes, but applies only where a person "proposes" to keep a foster child.

See also the Children Act 1958, s. 7 (removal of children from unsuitable surroundings).

See s. 73 (2), *post*, and the note thereto.

WITHIN FOURTEEN DAYS FROM
In calculating this period the *dies a quo* is not to be reckoned; see, in particular, *Gold-smiths' Co.* v. *West Metropolitan Rail. Co.*, [1904] 1 K.B. 1, [1900–3] All E.R. Rep. 667, C.A.; and *Stewart* v. *Chapman*, [1951] 2 K.B. 792; [1951] 2 All E.R. 613 (and contrast *Hare* v. *Gocher*, [1962] 2 Q.B. 641; [1962] 2 All E.R. 763, and *Trow* v. *Ind. Coope (West Midlands), Ltd.*, [1967] 2 Q.B. 899; [1967] 2 All E.R. 900, C.A.).

DEFINITIONS
For "foster child", see the Children Act 1958, s. 2, as reproduced in Sch. 7, *post*. For "local authority", see *ibid.*, s. 17 (112 Statutes Supp.).

CHILDREN ACT 1958, SS. 4 (2), (3), 5 (1)
See 112 Statutes Supp.

56. Extension of disqualification for keeping foster children

(1) In section 6 of the Children Act 1958 (which provides that a person shall not, without the consent of the local authority, maintain a foster child if one or more of a variety of orders has been made against him) there shall be made the following amendments, that is to say—

    (a) in paragraph (b), after the word "1933", there shall be inserted the words "the Children and Young Persons Act 1969" and for the words from "in respect of" to "of which the" there shall be substituted the words "and by virtue of the order or requirement a";

    (b) at the end of paragraph (c) there shall be inserted the words "or has been placed on probation or discharged absolutely or conditionally for any such offence";

    (c) in paragraph (e), after the word "subsection" there shall be inserted the words "(3) or" and for the words from "refusing" onwards there shall be substituted the words "refusing, or an order under section five of that Act cancelling, the registration of any premises occupied by him or his registration"; and

    (d) after paragraph (e) there shall be inserted the following paragraph:—

        (f) an order has been made under section 43 of the Adoption Act 1958 for the removal of a protected child who was being kept or was about to be received by him.

(2) At the end of the said section 6 there shall be added the following sub-section:—

    (2) Where this section applies to any person, otherwise than by virtue of this subsection, it shall apply also to any other person who lives in the same premises as he does or who lives in premises at which he is employed;

and accordingly the said section 6 as amended by the preceding subsection shall be subsection (1) of that section.

GENERAL NOTE
The amendments made in this section are designed to extend the classes of people who may not keep a foster child without the local authority's consent. It should be noted that being refused registration under s. 1 (4) of the Nurseries and Child Minders Act 1948 is not a complete bar to keeping foster children, but the consent of the local authority must be obtained where persons have been refused registration or there has been a cancellation of the registration of their premises under that enactment.

See s. 73 (2), *post*, and the note thereto.

PROTECTED CHILD
For meaning in Part IV of the Adoption Act 1958, see s. 37 of that Act (115 Statutes Supp.), and note the amendments to that section contained in s. 52 (4), *ante*.

CHILDREN ACT 1958, S. 6
See 112 Statutes Supp.

ADOPTION ACT 1958, S. 43
See 115 Statutes Supp.

57. Modifications of provisions as to offences

(1) After subsection (1) of section 14 of the Children Act 1958 (which, among other matters, makes it an offence to maintain a foster child in contravention of section 6 of that Act) there shall be inserted the following subsection:—

(1A) Where section 6 of this Act applies to any person by virtue only of subsection (2) of that section, he shall not be guilty of an offence under paragraph (*d*) of subsection (1) of this section if he proves that he did not know, and had no reasonable ground for believing, that a person living or employed in the premises in which he lives was a person to whom that section applies.

(2) After subsection (2) of the said section 14 (which provides that offences under that section are punishable summarily) there shall be added the following subsection:—

(2A) If any person who is required, under any provision of this Part of this Act, to give a notice fails to give the notice within the time specified in that provision, then, notwithstanding anything in section 104 of the Magistrates' Courts Act 1952 (time limit for proceedings) proceedings for the offence may be brought at any time within six months from the date when evidence of the offence came to the knowledge of the local authority.

GENERAL NOTE
This section makes two amendments to the Children Act 1958, designed (1) to protect persons who inadvertently fail to comply with s. 6 of that Act, and (2) in the case of an offence involving a failure to give notice under any provisions of that Act, to enable proceedings to be brought within six months of the *discovery* of the offence instead of within six months of the commission of the offence, as at present provided (see the Magistrates' Courts Act 1952, s. 104).

COMMENCEMENT
See s. 73 (2), *post*, and the note thereto.

THIS PART OF THIS ACT
I.e., the Children Act 1958, ss. 1–17 (112 Statutes Supp.).

NOTICE
As to the service of notices by post, see the Children Act 1958, s. 15 (112 Statutes Supp.), and the note thereto.

WITHIN SIX MONTHS FROM
See the note "Within fourteen days from" to s. 55, *ante*.
"Months" means calendar months; see the Interpretation Act 1889, s. 3 (24 Halsbury's Statutes (2nd Edn.) 207.

DEFINITION
For "local authority", see the Children Act 1958, s. 17 (112 Statutes Supp.).

CHILDREN ACT 1958, ss. 6, 14 (1), (2)
See Sch. 7, *post.*

MAGISTRATES' COURTS ACT 1952, S. 104
See 125 Statutes Supp.

Inspection

58. Inspection of children's homes etc. by persons authorised by Secretary of State

(1) Subject to subsection (2) of this section, the Secretary of State may cause to be inspected from time to time—

  (a) any community home provided by a local authority under section 38 of this Act;

  (b) any voluntary home (whether a community home or not);

  (c) any other premises at which one or more children in the care of a loca authority are being accommodated and maintained;

  (d) any other premises at which one or more children are being boarded out by a voluntary organisation; and

  (e) any other premises where a foster child within the meaning of Part I of the Children Act 1958 or a child to whom any of the provisions of that Part are extended by section 12 or section 13 of that Act, or a protected child within the meaning of Part IV of the Adoption Act 1958 is being accommodated or maintained.

(2) Subsection (1) of this section does not apply to any home or other premises which is, as a whole, subject to inspection by or under the authority of a governmental department.

(3) An inspection under this section shall be conducted by a person authorised in that behalf by the Secretary of State, but an officer of a local authority shall not be so authorised except with the consent of that authority.

(4) Any person inspecting a home or other premises under this section may inspect the children therein and make such examination into the state and management of the home of other premises and the treatment of children therein as he thinks fit.

GENERAL NOTE
This section replaces s. 94 of the Children and Young Persons Act 1933.

COMMENCEMENT
See s. 73 (2), *post,* and the note thereto.

SUB-S. (1)
Note that voluntary organisations are required to transmit particulars in respect of accommodation and maintenance of children in their care under s. 63 (2), *post.*

Children
  I.e., persons under the age of eighteen or persons over the age of eighteen subject to a care order; see s. 70 (1), *post.*

Boarded out
    See s. 13 (1) (*a*) of the Children Act 1948, as substituted by s. 49, *ante*. For regulations as to boarding out, see s. 14 of the 1948 Act.

Foster child
    For meaning in Part I of the Children Act 1958, see s. 2 of that Act, as reproduced in Sch. 7, *post*.

Protected child
    For meaning in Part IV of the Adoption Act 1958, see s. 37 of that Act (115 Statutes Supp.) and note the amendments to that section contained in s. 52, *ante*.

SUB-S. (2): INSPECTION . . . BY A PERSON AUTHORISED
    For powers of entry, see s. 59, *post*.

DEFINITIONS
    For "local authority", "voluntary home" and "voluntary organisation", see s. 70 (1), *post*.

CHILDREN ACT 1958, SS. 12, 13, PART I
    See 112 Statutes Supp.

59. Powers of entry supplemental to s. 58

(1) A person authorised to inspect any home or other premises under section 58 of this Act shall have a right to enter the home or other premises for that purpose and for any other purpose specified in subsection (4) of that section, but shall if so required produce some duly authenticated document showing his authority to exercise the power of entry conferred by this subsection.

(2) A person who obstructs the exercise by a person authorised as mentioned in subsection (1) of this section of a power of entry conferred thereby shall be liable on summary conviction to a fine not exceeding five pounds or, in the case of a second or subsequent conviction, to a fine not exceeding twenty pounds.

(3) A refusal to allow any such person as is mentioned in subsection (1) of this section to enter any such home or other premises as are mentioned in section 58 (1) of this Act shall be deemed, for the purposes of section 40 of the Act of 1933 (which relates to search warrants), to be a reasonable cause to suspect that a child or young person in the home or other premises is being neglected in a manner likely to cause him unnecessary suffering or injury to health.

GENERAL NOTE
    This section replaces the Children and Young Persons Act 1933, s. 94.

COMMENCEMENT OF THIS SECTION
    See s. 73 (2), *post*, and the note thereto.

OBSTRUCTS
    Obstruction need not involve physical violence; see, in particular, *Borrow* v. *Howland* (1896), 74 L. T. 787, and *Hinchliffe* v. *Sheldon*, [1955] 3 All E.R. 406. In fact there is authority for saying that anything which makes it more difficult for a person to carry out his duty amounts to obstruction: see *Hinchliffe* v. *Sheldon, supra.* Yet, standing by and doing nothing is not obstruction unless there is a legal duty to act; see *Swallow* v. *London County Council*, [1916] 1 K.B. 224; [1914–15] All E.R. Rep. 403; and contrast *Baker* v. *Ellison*, [1914] 2 K.B. 762; but see *Rice* v. *Connolly*, [1966] 2 Q.B. 414; [1966] 2 All E.R. 649.

SUMMARY CONVICTION
    See the note "Summary proceedings" to s. 3, *ante*.

DEFINITIONS
    For "child" and "young person", see s. 70 (1), *post*.

ACT OF 1933
    I.e., the Children and Young Persons Act 1933; see s. 70 (1), *post*. For s. 40 of that Act, see 17 Halsbury's Statutes (3rd Edn.) 465.

PART III
MISCELLANEOUS AND GENERAL
Miscellaneous

60. Extradition offences

(1) There shall be included—

(*a*) in the list of extradition crimes contained in Schedule I to the Extradition Act 1870; and

(*b*) among the descriptions of offences set out in Schedule I to the Fugitive Offenders Act 1967,

any offences of the kind described in section 1 of the Act of 1933 (which relates to cruelty to persons under sixteen) and any offence of the kind described in section 1 of the Indecency with Children Act 1960.

(2) Nothing in this Act shall be construed as derogating from the provisions of section 17 of the said Act of 1870 or section 16 (2) or 17 of the said Act of 1967 in their application to any provisions of those Acts respectively as amended by the preceding subsection.

COMMENCEMENT OF THIS SECTION
    See s. 73 (2), *post*, and the note thereto.

EXTRADITION ACT 1870, S. 17, SCH. 1
    See 13 Halsbury's Statutes (3rd Edn.) 261, 266.

FUGITIVE OFFENDERS ACT 1967, SS. 16 (2), 17, SCH. 1
    See 164 Statutes Supp.

ACT OF 1933
    I.e., the Children and Young Persons Act 1933; see s. 70 (1), *post*. For s. 1 of that Act, see 17 Halsbury's Statutes (3rd Edn.) 438.

INDECENCY WITH CHILDREN ACT 1960, S. 1
    123 Statutes Supp.

61. Rules relating to juvenile court panels and composition of juvenile courts

(1) Without prejudice to the generality of the power to make rules under section 15 of the Justices of the Peace Act 1949 relating to the procedure and practice to be followed by magistrates' courts, provision may be made by such rules with respect to any of the following matters, namely,—

(*a*) the formation and revision of juvenile court panels, that is to say, panels of justices specially qualified to deal with juvenile cases and the eligibility of justices to be members of such panels;

(*b*) the appointment of persons as chairmen of juvenile courts; and

(*c*) the composition of juvenile courts.

(2) Rules making any such provisions as are referred to in subsection (1) of this section may confer powers on the Lord Chancellor with respect to any of the matters specified in the rules and may, in particular, provide for the appointment of juvenile court panels by him and for the removal from a juvenile court panel of any justice who, in his opinion, is unsuitable to serve on a juvenile court.

(3) Rules made by virtue of this section may make different provision in relation to different areas for which juvenile court panels are formed; and in the application of this section to the county palatine of Lancaster, for any reference in the preceding subsection to the Lord Chancellor there shall be substituted a reference to the Chancellor of the Duchy.

(4) Nothing in this section or in any rules made under section 15 of the said Act of 1949 shall affect—

(a) the areas for which juvenile court panels are formed and juvenile courts are constituted;

(b) the provisions of Part I of Schedule 2 to the Act of 1963 (and, as it has effect by virtue of section 17 (1) of that Act, Part I of Schedule 2 to the Act of 1933) with respect to the making of recommendations and orders relating to the formation of combined juvenile court panels; or

(c) the provisions of paragraph 14 of that Schedule relating to the divisions of the metropolitan area for which juvenile courts sit;

but rules under the said section 15 may repeal, either generally or with respect to any part of the metropolitan area, any provision contained in paragraphs 15 to 18 of that Schedule (which contain provisions applicable in the metropolitan area with respect to certain of the matters referred to in subsection (1) of this section) and in subsections (2) and (3) of section 12 of the Administration of Justice Act 1964 (which amend those paragraphs).

(5) In this section "the metropolitan area" means the inner London area and the City of London.

GENERAL NOTE

This section extends the rule-making power of the Lord Chancellor with respect to juvenile court panels and the composition of juvenile courts. Sub-s. (2) of the section extends to the whole of England and Wales the system, at present confined to Inner London, whereby the juvenile court panels are appointed by the Lord Chancellor. Under the present system, the justices for each petty sessions area (outside Inner London) in every third year appoint from among themselves justices specially qualified for dealing with juvenile cases; see the Juvenile Courts (Constitution) Rules 1954, S.I. 1954 No. 1711, rule 1 (11 Halsbury's Statutory Instruments, title Infants, Part 4). By sub-s. (3) of this section, different provision may be made for different parts of the country.

It was explained in Parliament that in making appointments to juvenile court panels, the Lord Chancellor will act on the advice of a local committee, composed largely of juvenile court magistrates whose duty it will be to get to know the merits of all the justices in that area and the needs of local benches.

COMMENCEMENT OF THIS SECTION

See s. 73 (2), *post*, and the note thereto.

JUVENILE COURTS

See the note to s. 1, *ante*.

THE METROPOLITAN AREA

See sub-s. (5) of this section.

62. Contributions in respect of children and young persons in care

(1) The provisions of sections 86 to 88 of the Act of 1933 (which, as originally enacted, provided for contributions in respect of children and young persons committed to the care of a fit person or sent to an approved school) shall apply in relation to children and young persons committed to the care of a local authority by a care order which is not an interim order.

(2) Whether or not a contribution order has been made in respect of any child or young person in the care of a local authority, no contribution shall be payable in respect of him for any period during which he is allowed by the local authority to be under the charge and control of a parent, guardian, relative or friend, although remaining in the care of the local authority.

(3) Where a person (in this section referred to as a "contributory") is liable under section 86 of the Act of 1933 to make a contribution in respect of a child or young person in the care of a local authority, then, subject to the following provisions of this section, the amount of his contribution shall be such as may be proposed by the local authority and agreed by the contributory or, in default of agreement, as may be determined by a court in proceedings for, or for the variation of, a contribution order.

(4) The maximum contribution which may be proposed by a local authority in respect of a child or young person in their care shall be a weekly amount equal to the weekly amount which, in the opinion of the local authority, they would normally be prepared to pay if a child or young person of the same age were boarded out by them (whether or not the child or young person in respect of whom the contribution is proposed is in fact so boarded out and, if he is, whether or not the local authority are in fact paying that amount).

(5) No contribution order shall be made on a contributory in respect of a child or young person unless—

   (a) the local authority in whose care he is have, by notice in writing given to the contributory, proposed an amount as the amount of his contribution; and

   (b) either the contributory and the local authority have not, within the period of one month beginning with the day on which the notice was given to the contributory, agreed on the amount of his contribution or the contributory has defaulted in making one or more contributions of an amount which has been agreed.

(6) In proceedings for a contribution order, the court shall not order a contributory to pay a contribution greater than that proposed in the notice given to him under subsection (5) (*a*) of this section.

(7) In proceedings for the variation of a contribution order, the local authority concerned shall specify the weekly amount which, having regard to subsection (4) of this section, they propose should be the amount of the contribution and the court shall not vary the contribution order so as to require the contributory to pay a contribution greater than that proposed by the local authority.

(8) In this section—

"contribution" means a contribution under section 86 of the Act of 1933; and

"contribution order" means an order under section 87 of that Act.

GENERAL NOTE

This section provides that the maximum amount of a parental contribution which may be ordered in respect of a child or young person in care should be a weekly amount corresponding to that which the authority normally pay to foster parents in respect of a child or young person of the same age (sub-s. (4)). Under the present system the practice of local authorities varies. Some do not attempt to recover more than the cost of maintaining the child, so that the parent may be asked for a greater contribution if a child is in a children's home than if he is boarded out with foster parents. Other authorities take the view that this is inequitable, because the parent has no control over the decision where the child in care is to live. Some have maximum charges for all children, whether boarded out or in children's homes. These maxima vary from about £3·50 to £5·00 a week. In the case of children committed to approved schools, where the only responsibility of the local authority is a financial one, the maximum charges are often higher.

The present practice whereby the local authority ask the parent for a contribution after obtaining from him a statement of means and, if the contribution is not forthcoming, then make an application to the court is preserved (sub-s. (3)).

COMMENCEMENT OF THIS SECTION

See s. 73 (3), *post*, and the note thereto.

CHILDREN

I.e., persons under the age of fourteen.

SUB-S. (2)

This subsection replaces s. 87 (3) of the Act of 1933 and is designed to prevent the parent or guardian from paying "twice over" for the maintenance of the child.

Contribution order; contribution

See sub-s. (8) of this section.

SUB-S. (4)

The principle behind this provision is that the parents should be required—if their means so permit—to pay for their child's board and lodging, so that they are in no way better off as a result of the child's being in care; but that they should not be required to pay for any additional treatment which their child requires, for, in such a case, they rarely have any discretion or choice. The reference to the "foster children" arises from the fact that it would be unfair for local authorities to take from parents more than they would be prepared to pay to their own foster parents.

Parent

See the note to s. 1, *ante*.

Writing

See the note to s. 5, *ante*.

8—A.L.S. 189

63. Returns of information and presentation of reports etc. to Parliament

(1) Every local authority shall, at such times and in such form as the Secretary of State may direct, transmit to the Secretary of State such particulars as he may require—

> (*a*) with respect to the performance by the local authority of all or any of the functions specified in section 39 (1) of the Children Act 1948 (which relates to the establishment of children's committees); and
>
> (*b*) with respect to the children in relation to whom the authority have exercised those functions.

(2) Every voluntary organisation shall, at such times and in such form as the Secretary of State may direct, transmit to him such particulars as he may require with respect to the children who are accommodated and maintained in voluntary homes provided by the organisation or who have been boarded out by the organisation.

(3) The clerk of each juvenile court shall, at such times and in such form as the Secretary of State may direct, transmit to him such particulars as he may require with respect to the proceedings of the court.

(4) The Secretary of State shall in each year lay before Parliament a consolidated and classified abstract of the information transmitted to him under the preceding provisions of this section.

(5) The Secretary of State shall lay before Parliament in 1973 and in every third subsequent year a report with respect to the exercise by local authorities of the functions specified in section 39 (1) of the Children Act 1948, the provision by voluntary organisations of facilities for children and such other matters relating to children as he thinks fit.

GENERAL NOTE

> This section (1) requires local authorities to give to the Secretary of State particulars of the exercise of their child-care functions; (2) requires voluntary organisations to give to the Secretary of State particulars of children in their care or boarded out by them; (3) requires the clerks of juvenile courts to give to the Secretary of State particulars of juvenile court proceedings; and (4) provides that the Secretary of State is (a) to lay before Parliament a consolidated and classified abstract of the information so received, and (b) in every third year to lay before Parliament a report as to the exercise of local authority child-care functions, the provision of facilities for children by voluntary organisations and such other matters relating to children as he thinks fit.

COMMENCEMENT OF THIS SECTION

> See s. 73 (2), *post*, and the note thereto.

CHILDREN

> *I.e.*, persons under the age of eighteen or persons over the age of eighteen subject to a care order; see s. 70 (1), *post*.

SUB-S. (3)

> The purpose of this subsection is to enable statistics of care proceedings to be compiled and published. At present statistics of care, protection or control proceedings are included in the criminal statistics. As with criminal proceedings, the information is obtained from returns made by the police. The Adams Committee on Civil Judicial Statistics, which reported in July 1968, recommended that the publication of statistics of non-criminal proceedings in magistrates' courts in the "Criminal Statistics" be discontinued and that the courts, rather than the police, should be responsible for supplying the information on which the statistics are based.

Clerks of juvenile courts are already required to maintain a separate Juvenile Court Register and the information which will be required under this subsection will already be kept.

It is intended that the police will continue to supply figures as to the number of alleged offenders cautioned.

JUVENILE COURT
See the note to s. 1, *ante*.

LAY BEFORE PARLIAMENT
For provisions as to laying of documents before Parliament, see the Laying of Documents before Parliament (Interpretation) Act 1948, s. 1 (1) (24 Halsbury's Statutes (2nd Edn.) 448).

DEFINITIONS
For "local authority", "voluntary home" and "voluntary organisation", see s. 70 (1), *post*.

CHILDREN ACT 1948, s. 39 (1)
See 17 Halsbury's Statutes (3rd Edn.) 567.

Financial provisions

64. Expenses of Secretary of State in providing homes offering specialised facilities

There shall be defrayed out of moneys provided by Parliament any expenses incurred by the Secretary of State in providing, equipping and maintaining homes for the accommodation of children who are in the care of local authorities and are in need of particular facilities and services which are provided in those homes and are, in the opinion of the Secretary of State, unlikely to be readily available in community homes.

GENERAL NOTE
The homes envisaged under this section will specialise in meeting the needs of severely disturbed boys and girls and are intended to combine the training and treatment facilities of a school, a children's home and a hospital. There will also be a certain amount of secure accommodation and substantial provision for psychiatric observation and therapy. Special emphasis is to be given to the needs of severely disturbed girls.

COMMENCEMENT OF THIS SECTION
See s. 73 (2), *post*, and the note thereto.

CHILDREN
I.e., persons under the age of eighteen or over eighteen and the subject of a care order; see s. 70 (1), *post*.

COMMUNITY HOMES
As to the establishment of these homes, see, generally, ss. 35-45, *ante*.

65. Grants to voluntary organisations etc.

(1) The Secretary of State may make out of moneys provided by Parliament grants to voluntary organisations of such amounts and subject to such conditions as he may with the consent of the Treasury determine towards expenditure incurred by them in connection with the establishment, maintenance or improvement of voluntary homes which at the time the expenditure was incurred were assisted community homes or were designated as such in a regional plan

which was then in operation, including expenses incurred by them in respect of the borrowing of money to defray any such expenditure.

(2) The power of the Secretary of State to make grants to voluntary organisations under section 46 of the Children Act 1948 (which relates to grants in respect of certain expenses incurred in connection with voluntary homes) shall not apply to expenditure incurred in connection with a voluntary home which, at the time the expenditure was incurred, was a controlled or assisted community home or was designated as such in a regional plan which was then in operation.

(3) Where an order has been made under section 46 of this Act in relation to an approved institution within the meaning of that section and no such provision as is referred to in paragraph 9 (1) of Schedule 3 to this Act is made by a regional plan in relation to any part of the premises of the institution, the Secretary of State may with the consent of the Treasury make out of moneys provided by Parliament grants towards the discharge by any person of any liability, other than an obligation to which paragraph 11 of that Schedule applies, which was incurred by that person in connection with the establishment, maintenance or improvement of the institution.

(4) No grant shall be made under subsection (3) of this section in respect of a liability relating to an institution unless it appears to the Secretary of State that, on or within a reasonable time after the date specified in the order referred to in that subsection, the premises of the institution are to be used for a purpose which is of benefit to children; and any grant made under that subsection shall be subject to such conditions as the Secretary of State may with the approval of the Treasury determine, including conditions with respect to the repayment in whole or in part of the grant, either by the person to whom the grant was made or by some other person who, before the grant was made, consented to accept the liability.

(5) Any sums received by the Secretary of State by virtue of any such condition as is referred to in subsection (4) of this section shall be paid into the Consolidated Fund.

GENERAL NOTE
    This section enables the Secretary of State, with the consent of the Treasury, to make grants to voluntary organisations for expenditure incurred on assisted community homes.
    Note as to the repayment of sums received under this section on the discontinuance of an assisted community home, s. 48 (4), *ante.*
    Note also in relation to trust deeds, s. 40, *ante.*

COMMENCEMENT OF THIS SECTION
    See s. 73 (2), *post,* and the note thereto.

TREASURY
    This expression means the Lord High Treasurer for the time being or the Commissioners for the time being of Her Majesty's Treasury; see the Interpretation Act 1889, s. 12 (2) (24 Halsbury's Statutes (2nd Edn.) 211).

ASSISTED COMMUNITY HOMES
    See the note to s. 44, *ante.*

CONTROLLED COMMUNITY HOME
    See the note to s. 44, *ante.*

CONSOLIDATED FUND
See the note to s. 48, *ante*.

DEFINITIONS
For "regional plan", "voluntary home" and "voluntary organisation", see s. 70 (1), *post*.

CHILDREN ACT 1948, S. 46
See 17 Halsbury's Statutes (3rd Edn.) 572.

66. Increase of rate support grants

(1) The power to make an order under section 3 (1) of the Local Government Act 1966 increasing the amounts fixed by a rate support grant order for a particular year shall be exercisable, in accordance with subsection (2) of this section, in relation to any rate support grant order made before the date of the coming into operation of any provision of this Act (in this section referred to as "the relevant provision") for a grant period ending after that date.

(2) Without prejudice to subsection (4) of the said section 3 (which empowers an order under subsection (1) of that section to vary the matters prescribed by a rate support grant order), an order under subsection (1) of that section made by virtue of this section may be made for such year or years comprised in the grant period concerned as may be specified in the order and in respect of the year or each of the years so specified shall increase the amounts fixed by the relevant rate support grant order as the aggregate amounts of the rate support grants and any elements of the grants for that year to such extent and in such a manner as may appear to the Minister of Housing and Local Government to be appropriate, having regard to any additional expenditure incurred or likely to be incurred by local authorities in consequence of the coming into operation of the relevant provision.

(3) In this section "grant period" means the period for which a rate support grant order is made.

(4) There shall be defrayed out of moneys provided by Parliament any increase in rate support grants attributable to this Act.

GENERAL NOTE
Under the Local Government Act 1966, a new system of financial aid to local authorities was introduced which can be expressed, very generally, by this formula:

Total expenditure incurred by local authorities	£x
Less sums paid by Exchequer in respect of specific purposes	£y
	£z

The remainder (£z) is the sum available for rate support grants. Each authority is allocated a proportion of £z in accordance with a specified formula, particularly with regard to its expenses: the costs arising out of the application of this Act are to be included as expenses going towards calculating how much (if any) of the rate support grant it may be entitled to.

For a full account, see the text and annotations in 155 Statutes Supp. 100, dealing with the Local Government Act 1966.

COMMENCEMENT OF THIS SECTION
See s. 73 (2), *post*, and the note thereto.

COMING INTO OPERATION OF ANY PROVISION OF THIS ACT
See s. 73 (2), *post*, and the note thereto.

GRANT PERIOD
For meaning, see sub-s. (3) of this section.

RELEVANT PROVISION
For meaning, see sub-s. (1) of this section.

DEFINITION
For "local authority", see s. 70 (1), *post.*

LOCAL GOVERNMENT ACT 1966, S. 3 (1)
See 155 Statutes Supp.

ORDERS
No orders had been made under the Local Government Act 1966, s. 3 (1), by virtue of this section up to 1st May 1970.

67. Administrative expenses

Any administrative expenses of the Secretary of State under this Act shall be defrayed out of moneys provided by Parliament.

COMMENCEMENT OF THIS SECTION
See s. 73 (2), *post*, and the note thereto.

Supplemental

68. Compulsory acquisition of land

(1) A local authority other than a county council may be authorised by the Secretary of State to purchase compulsorily any land, whether situated inside or outside their area, for the purposes of their functions under this Act or section 1 of the Act of 1963.

(2) The Acquisition of Land (Authorisation Procedure) Act 1946 shall apply in relation to the compulsory purchase of land in pursuance of subsection (1) of this section as if that subsection were contained in an Act in force immediately before the commencement of that Act.

(3) In the application to the functions of a county council under this Act or section 1 of the Act of 1963 of section 159 (1) of the Local Government Act 1933 (under which a county council may be authorised to purchase land compulsorily) the power to authorise a compulsory purchase shall be vested in the Secretary of State.

GENERAL NOTE
The purpose of this section is to enable the Secretary of State to authorise a county borough council or one of the London boroughs or the Common Council of the City of London to effect the compulsory purchase of any land, inside or outside their area, for the purpose of any functions under this Act or s. 1 of that of 1963 (which places a duty upon local authorities to make available such advice, guidance and assistance as may promote the welfare of certain children).
County councils are excluded from the provisions of this section because they already have, under s. 159 (1) of the Local Government Act 1933, a general power to purchase land compulsorily when authorised by the appropriate Minister, provided they are doing so in order to carry out any of their functions as permitted under any public general Act. In respect of county borough councils or of London borough councils powers under s. 56 of the Local Government Act 1948 (extended by the London Government Act 1963) have been conferred upon them to enable them to carry out functions under that enactment. The powers suffer, however, from being more confined than the general power exercised by county councils under the 1933 Act.
For compulsory acquisition see 10 Halsbury's Laws (3rd Edn.) 3 *et seq.*

COMMENCEMENT OF THIS SECTION
See s. 73 (2), *post*, and the note thereto.

COUNTY COUNCIL
I.e., the chairman, county aldermen and county councillors of an administrative county; see the Local Government Act 1933, s. 2 (1), 2nd Edn., Vol. 14, p. 362.

IN FORCE IMMEDIATELY BEFORE THE COMMENCEMENT OF THAT ACT
The Acquisition of Land (Authorisation Procedure) Act 1946 came into force on receiving the Royal Assent on 18th April 1946. Many of the enactments extending that Act provide that that Act shall apply to compulsory acquisition under the enactment concerned as if it had been in force immediately before the commencement of that Act.

DEFINITION
For "local authority", see s. 70 (1), *post*.

ACT OF 1963
I.e., the Children and Young Persons Act 1963; see s. 70 (1), *post*. For s. 1 of that Act, see 139 Statutes Supp.

ACQUISITION OF LAND (AUTHORISATION PROCEDURE) ACT 1946
See 39 Statutes Supp.

LOCAL GOVERNMENT ACT 1933, S. 159 (1)
See 14 Halsbury's Statutes (2nd Edn.) 437.

69. Orders and regulations etc.

(1) Any power conferred on the Secretary of State by this Act to make an order or regulations, except an order under section 25, 39 or 43 (5) or paragraph 23 or 24 of Schedule 4, shall be exercisable by statutory instrument; and any statutory instrument made in pursuance of this subsection, except an instrument containing only regulations under paragraph 8 (2) of Schedule 3 or an order under section 1 (6), 26, 46, 47, 72 (2) or 73 (2), or paragraph 11 (2) of Schedule 3, shall be subject to annulment in pursuance of a resolution of either House of Parliament.

(2) A statutory instrument containing regulations under subsection (4) of section 5 or an order under section 34 of this Act shall not be subject to annulment as aforesaid, but no such regulations or order shall be included in a statutory instrument containing provisions which do not require approval in pursuance of the said subsection (4) or, as the case may be, to which subsection (7) of the said section 34 does not apply.

(3) An order made or directions given by the Secretary of State under any provision of this Act, except an order under section 7 (5), may be revoked or varied by a subsequent order or subsequent directions under that provision.

(4) Any order or regulations made by the Secretary of State under this Act may—

(a) make different provisions for different circumstances;

(b) provide for exemptions from any provisions of the order or regulations; and

(c) contain such incidental and supplemental provisions as the Secretary of State considers expedient for the purposes of the order or regulations.

SUB-S. (1)
Most of the instruments which may be made under this Act are subject to annulment procedure, but those which define an authorised person (s. 1 (6)); which discontinue

approved schools and voluntary homes (ss. 46 and 47); and which bring the Act generally and certain transitional provisions into force (ss. 72 (2) and 73 (2)) are exempt from this procedure.

SUB-S. (2)
By s. 5 (4), *ante,* no regulations may be made thereunder unless a draft of the regulations has first been approved by a resolution of each House of Parliament.

By s. 34 (7), *ante,* drafts of all orders proposed to be made under s. 34 are to be laid before Parliament and no order is to be made providing for raising beyond the age of 12 the age at which a child is subject to criminal proceedings unless a draft thereof has been approved by each House of Parliament.

The present subsection exempts regulations under s. 5 (4) and orders under s. 34 from the annulment procedure, and provides that such regulations and orders are not to be included in an instrument containing regulations and orders not requiring to be approved in draft or laid before Parliament, as the case may be.

SUB-S. (4) (C): EXPEDIENT
This expression is not defined, but it is used in s. 57 of the Trustee Act 1925, and was discussed in *Re Craven's Estate, Lloyds Bank, Ltd.* v. *Cockburn (No.* 2), [1937] Ch. 431. The tenor of that judgment was that "expedient" means what is good for the objects of the Act as a whole.

COMMENCEMENT OF THIS SECTION
See s. 73 (2), *post,* and the note thereto.

STATUTORY INSTRUMENT; SUBJECT TO ANNULMENT
Provisions as to statutory instruments generally are contained in the Statutory Instruments Act 1946 (24 Halsbury's Statutes (2nd Edn.) 440). As to statutory instruments which are subject to annulment, see ss. 5 (1) and 7 (1) of that Act *(ibid.).*

REVOKED OR VARIED
An express power of revocation or variation is required since the general power in that behalf in the Interpretation Act 1889, s. 32 (3) (24 Halsbury's Statutes (2nd Edn.) 226), does not extend to orders or directions.

70. Interpretation and ancillary provisions

(1) In this Act, unless the contrary intention appears, the following expressions have the following meanings:—

"the Act of 1933" means the Children and Young Persons Act 1933;

"the Act of 1963" means the Children and Young Persons Act 1963;

"approved school order", "guardian" and "place of safety" have the same meanings as in the Act of 1933;

"care order" has the meaning assigned to it by section 20 of this Act;

"child", except in Part II (including Schedule 3) and sections 27, 63, 64 and 65 of this Act, means a person under the age of fourteen, and in that Part (including that Schedule) and those sections means a person under the age of eighteen and a person who has attained the age of eighteen and is the subject of a care order;

"instrument of management" means an instrument of management made under section 39 of this Act;

"interim order" has the meaning assigned to it by section 20 of this Act;

"local authority" means the council of a county, county borough or London borough or the Common Council of the City of London;

"petty sessions area" has the same meaning as in the Magistrates' Courts Act 1952 except that, in relation to a juvenile court constituted for the metropolitan area within the meaning of Part II of Schedule 2 to the Act of 1963, it means such a division of that area as is mentioned in paragraph 14 of that Schedule;

"planning area" has the meaning assigned to it by section 35 (1) of this Act;

"police officer" means a member of a police force;

"regional plan" has the meaning assigned to it by section 36 (1) of this Act;

"the relevant authorities", in relation to a planning area, has the meaning assigned to it by section 35 (3) of this Act;

"reside" means habitually reside, and cognate expressions shall be construed accordingly except in section 12 (4) and (5) of this Act;

"supervision order", "supervised person" and "supervisor" have the meanings assigned to them by section 11 of this Act;

"trust deed", in relation to a voluntary home, has the meaning assigned to it by section 40 (5) of this Act;

"voluntary home" has the same meaning as in Part V of the Act of 1933;

"voluntary organisation" has the same meaning as in the Children Act 1948; and

"young person" means a person who has attained the age of fourteen and is under the age of seventeen;

and it is hereby declared that, in the expression "care or control", "care" includes protection and guidance and "control" includes discipline.

(2) Without prejudice to any power apart from this subsection to bring proceedings on behalf of another person, any power to make an application which is exercisable by a child or young person by virtue of section 15 (1), 21 (2), 22 (4) or (6) or 28 (5) of this Act shall also be exercisable on his behalf by his parent or guardian; and in this subsection "guardian" includes any person who was a guardian of the child or young person in question at the time when any supervision order, care order or warrant to which the application relates was originally made.

(3) In section 99 (1) of the Act of 1933 (under which the age which a court presumes or declares to be the age of a person brought before it is deemed to be his true age for the purposes of that Act) the references to that Act shall be construed as including references to this Act.

(4) Subject to the following subsection, any reference in this Act to any enactment is a reference to it as amended, and includes a reference to it as applied, by or under any other enactment including this Act.

(5) Any reference in this Act to an enactment of the Parliament of Northern Ireland shall be construed as a reference to that enactment as amended by any Act of that Parliament, whether passed before or after this Act, and to any enactment of that Parliament for the time being in force which re-enacts the said enactment with or without modifications.

COMMENCEMENT OF THIS SECTION
See s. 73 (2), *post*, and the note thereto.

SUB-S. (1)
Attained the age of
See the note to s. 1, *ante*.

County
This expression clearly refers to an administrative county, for only such a county has a council. The existing administrative counties in England and Wales are those

specified in the Local Government Act 1933, Sch. 1, Part I (14 Halsbury's Statutes (2nd Edn.) 515) (see s. 1 (1), (2), (a) of that Act), as amended by Orders made by the Minister of Housing and Local Government under the Local Government Act 1958, Part II (114 Statutes Supp.) now repealed, with savings, by the Local Government (Termination of Reviews) Act 1967, s. 1 (3) and Schedule (47 Halsbury's Statutes (2nd Edn.) 973, 975).

County Borough
   The existing county boroughs in England and Wales are the boroughs specified in the Local Government Act 1933, Sch. 1, Part II (14 Halsbury's Statutes (2nd Edn.) 513), as amended by the London Government Act 1963, ss. 3 (1), 93 (1) and Sch. 18, Part II (138A Statutes Supp.) (abolishing the county boroughs of Croydon, East Ham and West Ham), and as affected by Orders made by the Minister of Housing and Local Government, under the Local Government Act 1958, Part II (114 Statutes Supp.), now repealed with savings, by the Local Government (Termination of Reviews) Act 1967, s. 1 (1) and Schedule (47 Halsbury's Statutes (2nd Edn.) 973, 975).

London Borough
   I.e., a borough constituted by the London Government Act 1963, s. 1 (1), Sch. 1, Part I (138A Statutes Supp.).

Common Council of the City of London
   I.e., the mayor, aldermen and commons of the City of London in common council assembled; see the City of London (Various Powers) Act 1958, s. 5 (38 Halsbury's Statutes (2nd Edn.) 774).

SUB-S. (2)
   This subsection enables the parents or guardian of a child or young person to exercise on his behalf the right to apply under s. 15 (1), *ante*, for the variation or discharge of a supervision order; to apply under s. 21 (2), *ante*, for the discharge of a care order; to apply under s. 22 (4), *ante*, for the discharge of an interim order; to apply under s. 22 (6) *ante*, for the discharge of a warrant of committal to a remand centre; and to apply under s. 28(5), *ante*, for release from arrest or detention.

SUB-S. (5): PASSED BEFORE OR AFTER THIS ACT
   This Act was passed, *i.e.*, received the Royal Assent, on 22nd October 1969.

CHILDREN AND YOUNG PERSONS ACT 1933
   See 17 Halsbury's Statutes (3rd Edn.) 435 *et seq.*

CHILDREN AND YOUNG PERSONS ACT 1963
   See 139 Statutes Supp.

MAGISTRATES' COURTS ACT 1952
   See 125 Statutes Supp.

CHILDREN ACT 1948
   See 17 Halsbury's Statutes (3rd Edn.) 538.

71. Application to Isles of Scilly

This Act shall have effect, in its application to the Isles of Scilly, with such modifications as the Secretary of State may by order specify.

COMMENCEMENT OF THIS SECTION
   See s. 73 (2), *post*, and the note thereto.

ORDERS UNDER THIS SECTION
   See, generally, as to orders under this Act, s. 69, *ante*. No orders had been made under this section up to 1st May 1970.

72. Transitional provisions, minor amendments and repeals etc.

(1) The transitional provisions and savings set out in Part I of Schedule 4 to this Act shall have effect.

(2) The transitional provisions set out in Part II of Schedule 4 to this Act shall have effect until such day as the Secretary of State may by order specify for the purposes of this subsection (being the day on and after which those provisions will in his opinion be unnecessary in consequence of the coming into force of provisions of the Social Work (Scotland) Act 1968) and shall be deemed to have been repealed on that day by an Act of Parliament passed after this Act.

(3) The enactments mentioned in Schedule 5 to this Act shall have effect subject to the amendments specified in that Schedule (which are minor amendments and amendments consequential on the provisions of this Act).

(4) Subject to subsection (1) of this section, the enactments mentioned in the first and second columns of Schedule 6 to this Act are hereby repealed to the extent specified in the third column of that Schedule.

(5) In accordance with Part II of this Act and the said Schedules 5 and 6, sections 1 to 6 and 14 of the Children Act 1958 are to have effect, after the coming into force of so much of that Part and those Schedules as relates to those sections, as set out in Schedule 7 to this Act, but without prejudice to any other enactment affecting the operation of those sections.

GENERAL NOTE

Subsection (2) is especially complicated and arises from the fact that an entirely new system of child care is developing for Scotland since the passing of the Social Work (Scotland) Act 1968 and, in many respects does not correspond with that of England and Wales. In addition certain provisions of the English Act will be in operation before those of the Scottish one, and so it is necessary to provide during a brief transitional period for movement between the new English and the old Scottish system—which is what Part II of Sch. 4 does. The subsection provides that the provisions of that Part of the Schedule shall have effect until such day as the Secretary of State may specify, which will be when they become unnecessary because of the coming into force of provisions of the Scottish Act, and shall then be deemed to have been repealed.

For a brief summary of the relevant provisions of the Scottish Act, see note to Sch. 4, Part II, *post.*

COMMENCEMENT OF THIS SECTION

See s. 73 (2), *post*, and the note thereto.

PASSED AFTER THIS ACT

This Act was passed, *i.e.*, received the Royal Assent, on 22nd October 1969.

CHILDREN ACT 1958, SS. 1–6, 14

See Sch. 7, *post.*

ORDERS UNDER THIS SECTION

See, generally, as to orders under this Act, s. 69, *ante*. No orders had been made under this section up to 1st May 1970.

73. Citation, commencement and extent

(1) This Act may be cited as the Children and Young Persons Act 1969, and this Act and the Children and Young Persons Acts 1933 to 1963 may be cited together as the Children and Young Persons Acts 1933 to 1969.

(2) This Act shall come into force on such day as the Secretary of State may by order appoint, and different days may be appointed under this subsection for different provisions of this Act or for different provisions of this Act so far as they apply to such cases only as may be specified in the order.

(3) Without prejudice to the generality of section 69 (4) of this Act, an order under the preceding subsection may make such transitional provision as the Secretary of State considers appropriate in connection with the provisions brought into force by the order, including such adaptations of those provisions and of any other provisions of this Act then in force as appear to him appropriate for the purposes or in consequence of the operation of any provision of this Act before the coming into force of any other provision of this Act or of a provision of the Social Work (Scotland) Act 1968.

(4) This section and the following provisions only of this Act extend to Scotland, that is to say—

(a) sections 10 (1) and (2), 32 (1), (3) and (4), 56 and 57 (1);

(b) section 72 (2) and Part II of Schedule 4;

(c) paragraphs 25, 26, 33, 35, 38, 42, 43, 53, 54 and 57 to 83 of Schedule 5 and section 72 (3) so far as it relates to those paragraphs;

(d) section 72 (4) and Schedule 6 so far as they relate to the Merchant Shipping Act 1894, the Superannuation (Miscellaneous Provisions) Act 1948, sections 10, 53, 55 and 59 of the Act of 1963, the Family Allowances Act 1965 and the Social Work (Scotland) Act 1968.

(5) This section and the following provisions only of this Act extend to Northern Ireland, that is to say—

(a) sections 25 and 32;

(b) section 72 (3) and Schedule 5 so far as they relate to section 29 of the Criminal Justice Act 1961 and provisions of the Social Work (Scotland) Act 1968 which extend to Northern Ireland; and

(c) section 72 (4) and Schedule 6 so far as they relate to section 83 of the Act of 1933, paragraph 13 of Schedule 2 to the Children and Young Persons (Scotland) Act 1937, section 29 of the Criminal Justice Act 1961, sections 10 (1) and (2), 53 (1) and 65 (5) of, and paragraphs 27, 34 and 50 of Schedule 3 to, the Act of 1963 and sections 73 (2), 76 (1) and (2) and 77 (1) (b) of the Social Work (Scotland) Act 1968;

and section 32 (2) and (3) of this Act shall be treated for the purposes of section 6 of the Government of Ireland Act 1920 as if it had been passed before the day appointed for the said section 6 to come into operation.

(6) Section 26 of this Act and this section, and section 72 (4) of this Act and Schedule 6 to this Act so far as they relate to paragraph 13 of Schedule 2 to the Children and Young Persons (Scotland) Act 1937 and section 53 (1) of, and paragraph 34 of Schedule 3 to, the Act of 1963, extend to the Channel Islands and the Isle of Man, and section 32 (1) and (4) of this Act and this section extend to the Channel Islands.

(7) It is hereby declared that the provisions of sections 69 and 70 of this Act extend to each of the countries aforesaid so far as is appropriate for the purposes of any other provisions of this Act extending to the country in question.

SCOTLAND, NORTHERN IRELAND, CHANNEL ISLANDS, ISLE OF MAN
There are certain provisions in this Act, which must, by their nature, extend to Scotland, Northern Ireland, the Channel Islands or the Isle of Man. These provisions fall generally into four categories. First, the prohibitions against press reports of court proceedings—the same newspapers circulate both in Scotland and England; secondly, the arrangements for absconders who do not necessarily remain within their original jurisdiction; thirdly the amendments to provisions of common enactments (*e.g.*, the Children Act 1958, s. 6) and, finally, the arrangements for the transfer of persons between different parts of the British Isles. The subsections furnish the necessary modifications to various enactments (including the Government of Ireland Act 1920 ("reserved matters")) to secure a common code.
For the constitutional status of the Channel Islands—which include Jersey, Guernsey, Alderney, Brechon, Great Sark, Little Sark, Herm, Jelhou and Lihou—see 5 Halsbury's Laws (3rd Edn.) 647; for the Isle of Man, *ibid.*, 650.

CHILDREN AND YOUNG PERSONS ACTS 1933 TO 1969
The Acts under this heading are those of 1933 (12 Halsbury's Statutes (2nd Edn.) 974); 1952 (an Amendment Act) (77 Statutes Supp. 95) and 1963 (139 Statutes Supp.). The Acts of 1938 and 1956, formerly included under this citation have been repealed.

SOCIAL WORK (SCOTLAND) ACT 1968
17 Halsbury's Statutes (3rd Edn.) 757.

MERCHANT SHIPPING ACT 1894
23 Halsbury's Statutes (2nd Edn.) 395.

SUPERANNUATION (MISCELLANEOUS PROVISIONS) ACT 1948
53 Statutes Supp.

ACT OF 1963
I.e., the Children and Young Persons Act 1963 (139 Statutes Supp.); see s. 70 (1), *ante*.

FAMILY ALLOWANCES ACT 1965
See 45 Halsbury's Statutes (2nd Edn.) 1191.

ACT OF 1933
I.e., the Children and Young Persons Act 1933; see s. 70 (1), *ante*. For s. 83 of that Act, see 17 Halsbury's Statutes (3rd Edn.) 494.

CHILDREN AND YOUNG PERSONS (SCOTLAND) ACT 1937
1 Edw. 8 & Geo. 6 c. 37; not printed in this work.

CRIMINAL JUSTICE ACT 1961, S. 29
See 127 Statutes Supp.

GOVERNMENT OF IRELAND ACT 1920, S. 6
See 17 Halsbury's Statutes (2nd Edn.) 56.
The day appointed for that section to come into operation was 3rd May 1921.

ORDERS UNDER THIS SECTION
See, generally, as to orders under this Act, s. 69, *ante*.
By the Children and Young Persons Act 1969 (Commencement Nos. 1 and 2) Orders 1969, S.I. 1969 Nos. 1552, 1565, the following provisions of this Act were brought into force on the dates specified below:

S. 33 (1) (so far as it relates to Sch. 1, para. 6)	1st December 1969
Ss. 35–45	1st December 1969
S. 46 (except sub-s. (2) so far as it relates to Sch. 3, paras. 3, 4, 8)	1st December 1969
Ss. 47–50	1st December 1969
Ss. 51–55	1st January 1970
S. 56 (except sub-s. (1) (*a*))	1st January 1970
S. 57	1st January 1970
Ss. 58–60	1st December 1969
S. 62 (2)	1st December 1969
Ss. 63–68	1st December 1969

Ss. 69–70 .. .. 16th November 1969
S. 71 .. .. 1st December 1969
S. 72 (1) (so far as it relates to Sch. 4, paras. 13, 14) .. 1st December 1969

S. 72 (3) so far as it relates to—

(a) Sch. 5, paras. 63, 64 (1), 69, 73, 75, 76 .. .. 16th November 1969
(b) the provisions of Sch. 5 specified in Appendix A to
Sch. 1 to the No. 2 Order (subject to transitional modifications contained in Sch. 3 to the No. 2 Order) .. 1st December 1969
(c) the provisions of Sch. 5 specified in Appendix A to
Sch. 2 to the No. 2 Order .. .. 1st January 1970

S. 72 (4) so far as it relates to—

(a) the repeal set out in the Appendix to the Schedule to
the No. 1 Order .. .. 16th November 1969
(b) the repeals set out in Appendix B to Sch. 1 to the No. 2
Order .. .. 1st December 1969
(c) the repeals set out in Appendix B to Sch. 2 to the No. 2
Order .. .. 1st January 1970

S. 72 (5) (except so far as it relates to the Children Act 1958,
ss. 2 (4), 6 (1) (b)) .. .. 1st January 1970
S. 73 .. .. 16th November 1969
Sch. 1, para. 6 .. .. 1st December 1969
Sch. 2 .. .. 1st December 1969
Sch. 3 (except paras. 3, 4, 8).. .. .. 1st December 1969
Sch. 4, paras. 13, 14 .. .. 1st December 1969
Sch. 5, paras. 63, 64 (1), 69, 73, 75, 76 .. .. .. 16th November 1969
provisions specified in Appendix A to Sch. 1 to the No. 2
Order .. .. 1st December 1969
provisions specified in Appendix A to Sch. 2 to the No. 2
Order .. .. 1st January 1970

Sch. 6 so far as it relates to—

(a) the repeal set out in the Appendix to the Schedule to
the No. 1 Order .. .. 16th November 1969
(b) the repeals set out in Appendix B to Sch. 1 to the
No. 2 Order .. .. 1st December 1969
(c) the repeals set out in Appendix B to Sch. 2 to the
No. 2 Order .. .. 1st January 1970

Sch. 7 (except so far as it relates to the Children Act 1958,
ss. 2 (4), 6 (1) (b)) .. .. 1st January 1970

Provisions not mentioned in the two commencement orders are ss. 1–32, 33 (except sub-s. (1) thereof in so far as it relates to Sch. 1, para. 6), 34, 46 (2) (so far as it relates to Sch. 3, paras. 3, 4, 8), 56 (1) (a), 61, 62 (1), (3)–(5), 72 (1) (except in so far as it relates to Sch. 4, paras. 13, 14), (2), (3) (except as noted above), (4) (except as noted above), (5) (so far as it relates to the Children Act 1958, ss. 2 (4), 6 (1) (b)), Sch. 1, paras. 1–5, 7–8, Sch. 3, paras. 3, 4 and 8, Sch. 4, paras. 1–12, 15–18, Sch. 5 (except as noted above), Sch. 6 (except as noted above), Sch. 7 (so far as it relates to the Children Act 1958, ss. 2 (4), 6 (1) (b)). It is intended to bring most of those provisions into force on 1st October 1970 (see 790 H. of C. Official Report 188).

SCHEDULES

SCHEDULE 1   Section 33 (1)

MODIFICATIONS OF PART IV OF CRIMINAL JUSTICE ACT 1967

GENERAL NOTE

This Schedule is consequential to s. 33, *ante*, which provides that legal aid is to be available in care proceedings.

1.—(1) In section 73 (1), after the word "proceedings" there shall be inserted the words "and the proceedings mentioned in subsections (3A) and (3B) of this section".

(2) At the end of section 73 (2) there shall be inserted the words "and any other magistrates' court to which the case is remitted in pursuance of section 56 (1) of the Children and Young Persons Act 1933".

(3) In section 73, after subsection (3) there shall be inserted the following subsections:—

(3A) Where a person—

   (a) is or is to be brought before a juvenile court under section 1 of the Children and Young Persons Act 1969; or

   (b) is the subject of an application to a magistrates' court under section 15 or section 21 of that Act; or

   (c) is or is to be brought before a juvenile court under section 31 of that Act,

the court may order that he shall be given legal aid for the purpose of proceedings before the court and, in a case falling within paragraph (a) of this subsection, before any juvenile court to which the case is remitted.

(3B) Where a person desires to appeal to a court of quarter sessions in pursuance of section 2 (12), 3 (8), 16 (8), 21 (4) or 31 (6) of the said Act of 1969, that court or the court from whose decision the appeal lies may order that he be given legal aid for the purpose of the appeal.

2.—(1) At the end of section 74 (2) there shall be inserted the words "and except in the case of proceedings under section 1 of the Children and Young Persons Act 1969 where it is alleged that the condition set out in subsection (2) (f) of that section is satisfied in consequence of an indictable offence and where the court is of the opinion aforesaid".

(2) In section 74 (3), after "(3)" there shall be inserted the word "(3B)" and for the word "either" there shall be substituted the word "any".

(3) In section 74 (5), after the word "(2)" there shall be inserted the words "or (3A)".

(4) In section 74 (6), after the word "section", there shall be inserted the words "or to any person by a legal aid order under subsection (3B) of that section" and after the word "sentence" there shall be inserted the words "or, as the case may be, dismissing the appeal mentioned in the said subsection (3B) or otherwise altering the order to which the appeal relates".

3. In section 75, after subsection (4) there shall be inserted the following subsection:—

(4A) Subsections (3) and (4) of this section shall have effect, in their application to a person who has not attained the age of sixteen, as if the words "he", "him" and "his" referred to that person and a person who is an appropriate contributor in relation to him or such of them as the court selects, and as if for the word "shall" in subsection (4) there were substituted the word "may"; and the court may require that a statement furnished by an appropriate contributor in pursuance of subsection (4) shall specify both his means and those of the other person aforesaid.

4.—(1) In section 76, after subsection (1) there shall be inserted the following subsection:—

(1A) In a case where a legally assisted person has not attained the age of sixteen, the power conferred by the last foregoing subsection to order him to pay contributions in respect of the relevant costs shall include power to order any person who is an appropriate contributor in relation to him to pay such contributions; and for the purposes of any order proposed to be made by virtue of this subsection in connection with a legal aid order, an appropriate contributor who has failed to furnish a statement which he was required to furnish in pursuance of section 75 (4) of this Act in connection with the legal aid order shall be deemed to have resources and commitments which are such that he may reasonably be ordered to pay the whole amount of the costs in question.

(2) In section 76 (4) (a), after the words "that magistrates' court" there shall be inserted the words ", or any other magistrates' court to which the case is remitted in pursuance of section 56 (1) of the Children and Young Persons Act 1933."

(3) At the end of section 76 there shall be inserted the following subsection:—

(5) Nothing in subsection (4) of this subsection applies in a case where the legal aid order in question was made by virtue of section 73 (3A) or (3B) of this Act, and in such a case an order under this section may be made—

(a) where the legal aid was ordered to be given for the purpose of proceedings before a magistrates' court, by that court, or any other magistrates' court to which the case is remitted in pursuance of section 2 (11) of the Children and Young Persons Act 1969, after disposing of the case; and

(b) where the legal aid was ordered to be given for the purposes of an appeal to a court of quarter sessions, by that court after disposing of the appeal.

5. In section 77 (1), after the words "assisted person", there shall be inserted the words ", or a person who is an appropriate contributor in relation to him,", for the words "into his means" there shall be substituted the words "into the means of that person and any such contributor or of either or any of them" and the words "on his means" shall be omitted.

6. In section 78 (1), after the words "that he" there shall be inserted the words "or any other person".

7.—(1) In section 79 (2), after the word "by" there shall be inserted the words "or in respect of", and for the words "to him" there shall be substituted the words—

"(a) where the contribution was made by one person only, to him; and

(b) where the contribution was made by two or more persons, to them in proportion to the amounts contributed by them".

(2) In section 79 (3) and section 79 (6) after the words "assisted person" there shall be inserted the words "or an appropriate contributor".

8.—(1) In section 84, in the definition of "appropriate authority", after paragraph (a) there shall be inserted the following paragraph:—

(aa) in relation to legal aid ordered by virtue of section 73 (3A) or (3B) of this Act, the clerk of the magistrates' court before which the proceedings were heard or from which the appeal was brought or the clerk of the magistrates' court nominated for the purposes of this paragraph by the first-mentioned court.

(2) In section 84, after the definition aforesaid there shall be inserted the following:—

"appropriate contributor", in relation to a person who has not attained the age of sixteen, means his father, any person who has been adjudged to be his putative father and (whether or not he is legitimate) his mother.

(3) At the end of section 84 there shall be inserted the following subsections:—

(2) Any power to make an application in pursuance of this Part of this Act which is exercisable by a person who has not attained the age of seventeen shall also be exercisable by his parent or guardian on his behalf, without prejudice to any powers of the parent or guardian apart from this subsection; and in this subsection "guardian" has the same meaning as in section 70 (2) of the Children and Young Persons Act 1969.

(3) A person who attains the age of sixteen after a legal aid order is made in respect of him or, in a case where such an order is made in pursuance of an application, after the application is made, shall be treated for the purposes of this Part of this Act, in relation to the order, as not having attained that age.

and accordingly the said section 84 as amended by sub-paragraphs (1) and (2) of this paragraph shall be subsection (1) of that section.

COMMENCEMENT OF THIS SCHEDULE
See s. 73 (2), *ante*, and the note thereto.

ATTAINED THE AGE OF
See the note to s. 1, *ante*.

APPROPRIATE CONTRIBUTOR
See para. 8 (2) of this Schedule.

CRIMINAL JUSTICE ACT 1967, SS. 73 (1), (2), (3), 74 (2), (3), (5), (6), 75 (4), 76 (1), (4) (*a*), 77 (1), 78 (1), 79 (2), (3), (6), 84
See 163 Statutes Supp.

SCHEDULE 2 Section 35 (4)

CHILDREN'S REGIONAL PLANNING COMMITTEES

1.—(1) Subject to the following provisions of this Schedule, the children's regional planning committee for a planning area (in this Schedule referred to as "the committee") shall consist of such number of persons selected and appointed in such manner and holding office on such terms as the relevant authorities may from time to time approve.

(2) No person who is disqualified by virtue of section 59 of the Local Government Act 1933 from being a member of any local authority which is one of the relevant authorities for a planning area may be a member of the committee for that area.

2.—(1) Subject to sub-paragraph (2) of this paragraph, the relevant authorities for a planning area shall so exercise their powers under paragraph 1 (1) of this Schedule as to secure that each authority nominates as a member of the committee for the area at least one person who is not so nominated by any other of the relevant authorities.

(2) If the Secretary of State considers that owing to special circumstances the requirement imposed by sub-paragraph (1) of this paragraph should be dispensed with in the case of a particular authority he may direct accordingly.

(3) The members of the committee for a planning area who are nominated by the relevant authorities are in the following provisions of this Schedule referred to as "the nominated members".

3.—(1) Without prejudice to any power of co-option conferred on the committee for a planning area under paragraph 1 (1) of this Schedule, but subject to paragraph 4 of this Schedule, the nominated members of the committee may co-opt other persons to serve as members of the committee, either generally or in relation only to such matters as may be specified by the nominated members.

(2) Where any persons are co-opted to serve as members of the committee for a planning area in relation only to such matters as are specified by the nominated members then, subject to any directions given by the relevant authorities, the extent to which those persons shall be entitled to attend, speak and vote at meetings of the committee shall be such as may be determined by the nominated members.

4. The relevant authorities for a planning area shall so exercise their powers under paragraph 1 (1) of this Schedule, and the nominated members of the committee for a planning area shall so limit any exercise of their power under paragraph 3 of this Schedule, as to secure that at all times a majority of the members of the committee for the planning area are members of the relevant authorities.

5. Subject to any directions given by the relevant authorities, the procedure and quorum of the committee for a planning area shall be such as may be determined by the nominated members.

6. Section 93 (1) of the Local Government Act 1933 (which relates to the expenses of joint committees of local authorities) shall apply to the committee for a planning area as it applies to such a joint committee as is mentioned in that section, but as if—

(a) for references to the local authorities by whom the committee is appointed there were substituted references to the relevant authorities; and
(b) for paragraphs (a) and (b) of subsection (1) of that section there were substituted the words "by the Secretary of State";

and Part X of that Act (which relates to accounts and audit) shall apply to the accounts of the committee for a planning area as it applies to the accounts of such a joint committee as is mentioned in section 219 (c) of that Act.

GENERAL NOTE
This Schedule, which must be read in conjunction with s. 35 (4), *ante*, provides for the composition of the children's regional planning committee.

The committee is essentially a body which acts on behalf of the relevant authorities, as defined in s. 35 (3), *ante*. Its purpose is not only to arrange for the provision of community homes in its region, but also to decide schemes of the various types of facilities which it is hoped will ultimately be available as intermediate treatment for persons under supervision. Because it is desirable that they act together in planning such accommodation and such facilities, ss. 19 and 35, *ante*, require the "relevant authorities" to act in these matters through a regional planning committee and not undertake anything independently. The Schedule, with this object in view, places the composition of the committee entirely in the hands of the authorities for which the committee is to act.

COMMENCEMENT OF THIS SCHEDULE
 See s. 73 (2), *ante*, and the note thereto.

PARA. I: NO PERSON WHO IS DISQUALIFIED
 The current legislation is contained in several enactments, and with regard to teachers and other persons employed in schools maintained by a local education authority, the operative section is s. 94 of the Local Government Act 1933, as amended by s. 10 of the Education Act 1946 and by s. 13 of the Education (Miscellaneous Provisions) Act 1953. The effect is that "being a teacher or otherwise employed in (a school, college or other educational establishment) maintained or assisted by a local education authority" does not disqualify that person from being co-opted by the authority to membership of the education committee, any committee dealing with mental deficiency, any committee dealing with libraries or the children's committee. Thus a local authority is not debarred from co-opting to the children's committee a member of the staff of a school administered by them as education authority. They are, however, debarred from co-opting any other employee, including a member of the staff of a local authority approved school, since they do not administer such a school as an education authority but rather as an authority for the purpose set out in s. 39 of the Children Act 1948.
 The conditions thus indicated gave rise to expressions of regret that the experience and valuable advice from headmasters and matrons accustomed to the work which the new committees were to arrange, would be sacrificed. To this the Government pointed out that there was no need to make such officers members of any committee in order to secure that the skill and knowledge would be at the disposal of the committee: it could just as easily be secured by inviting any person specially qualified to participate fully in its discussions and to be one of a working group, etc.

PARA. 2
 Sub-para. (1) of this para. ensures that all those local authorities responsible for providing community homes under the regional committee are, in fact, represented, or that they will at least be consulted before plans are submitted.

Secretary of State . . . may direct
 See, generally, as to directions, s. 69 (3), *ante*.

PARA. 3
 It is envisaged that the number of persons outside the local authority child care field who have something of value to contribute to the activities of planning committees will be many times the number of persons who will be nominated members. The total number of co-opted members, therefore, may be several times the number of nominated members. It may be that it would be appropriate that different co-opted members should attend different meetings for different subjects, and also that different co-opted members should attend the same meeting for different items on the agenda. To preserve the controlling position of the nominated members at all times there must be some machinery for telling co-opted members to what extent they may attend particular meetings. This is not something which can be done in advance: it depends upon the committee's programme of work and the agenda for particular meetings. Accordingly, sub-para. (2) of this paragraph provides that the machinery will remain in the hands of the nominated members, that they will retain the power to run the meeting, the agenda, the business, the arrangements at all times as the exigencies arise. It is thought that the rights of co-opted members will be decided upon as a matter of general policy and enshrined in standing orders.

PARA. 4: A MAJORITY OF THE MEMBERS
 This provision is to provide the means whereby, for example, the interests of those furnishing facilities under the Education Acts, the national health services, voluntary associations, etc. may be represented on the regional planning committees, although they are not "relevant authorities". The requirement that the latter should always remain in the majority is simply that such authorities are ultimately responsible for the schemes and the financial arrangements involved.

DEFINITIONS
 By virtue of s. 70 (1), *ante*, for "planning area", see s. 35 (1), *ante*, and for "relevant authorities", see s. 35 (3), *ante*. For "nominated members", see para. 2 (3) of this Schedule.

LOCAL GOVERNMENT ACT 1933, SS. 59, 93 (1), PART X
 See 19 Halsbury's Statutes (3rd Edn.) 429, 449, 523–537.

SCHEDULE 3

APPROVED SCHOOLS AND OTHER INSTITUTIONS

Provisions as to staff

1.—(1) This paragraph applies where it appears to the Secretary of State that on the date specified in an order under section 46 of this Act (in the following provisions of this Schedule referred to as a "section 46 order") all or any of the premises used for the purposes of the institution to which the order relates are to be used for the purposes—

    (*a*) of a community home, or

    (*b*) of a school of any of the following descriptions, namely, a county school, a voluntary school which is a controlled or aided school, or a special school;

and in this Schedule "the specified date", in relation to an institution to which a section 46 order relates, means the date specified in that order.

(2) Where this paragraph applies the Secretary of State may, by the section 46 order, make such provision as he considers appropriate with respect to—

    (*a*) the transfer of existing staff to the employment of the authority, voluntary organisation or other body of persons responsible for the employment of persons at the community home or school, as the case may be; and

    (*b*) the transfer to a local authority or voluntary organisation specified in the order of any liabilities (including contingent and future liabilities) with respect to the payment of superannuation and other benefits to or in respect of existing staff and retired staff.

(3) If any such superannuation or other benefits as are referred to in sub-paragraph (2) (*b*) of this paragraph are not benefits to which the Pensions (Increase) Acts 1920 to 1969 or any of those Acts apply, the section 46 order may contain such provisions as the Secretary of State considers appropriate—

    (*a*) for securing the continued payment of additional amounts (calculated by reference to increases under those Acts) which were paid before the specified date in respect of any such benefits; and

    (*b*) for securing the payment of additional amounts (calculated by reference to increases under those Acts) in respect of any such benefits to which any person became entitled before the specified date but in respect of which no similar additional amounts were paid before that date.

(4) Where this paragraph applies the section 46 order—

    (*a*) shall contain provisions for the protection of the interests of any existing staff whose employment is transferred as mentioned in sub-paragraph (2) (*a*) of this paragraph;

    (*b*) may contain provisions for the protection of the interests of existing staff whose employment is not so transferred; and

    (*c*) may contain provisions applying, amending or repealing any provision made by or under any enactment and relating to the conditions of service of existing staff or the payment of superannuation and other benefits to or in respect of existing or retired staff;

and in a case falling within sub-paragraph (1) (*b*) of this paragraph any provisions made under paragraph (*a*) of this sub-paragraph shall have effect notwithstanding any provision made by or under any enactment and relating to the remuneration of teachers.

(5) In this paragraph "existing staff" in relation to a section 46 order means persons who, immediately before the specified date, were employed for the purposes of the institution to which the order relates, and "retired staff" in relation to such an order means persons who, at some time before the specified date, were employed for those purposes but ceased to be so employed before the specified date.

2.—(1) Regulations under section 60 of the Local Government Act 1958 may make provision in relation to persons who suffer loss of employment or loss or diminution of emoluments as a result of a section 46 order and, if in such a case the Minister by whom the regulations are made thinks fit, the regulations may provide for the payment of compensation by the Secretary of State instead of by an authority prescribed by or determined under the regulations.

(2) In accordance with sub-paragraph (1) of this paragraph, subsection (2) of the said section 60 shall be amended as follows:

(a) after the words "under the regulations" there shall be inserted the words "or, in a case to which paragraph 2 of Schedule 3 to the Children and Young Persons Act 1969 applies, by the Secretary of State"; and

(b) after the words "order under Part I of the Police Act 1964" there shall be inserted the words "or of an order under section 46 of the Children and Young Persons Act 1969".

(3) Where a section 46 order is made in relation to an approved institution but paragraph 1 of this Schedule does not apply in relation to that institution, the section 46 order may make such provision as the Secretary of State considers appropriate with respect to the transfer to him of any such liabilities as are referred to in sub-paragraph (2) (b) of that paragraph and the payment by him of any such additional amount as is referred to in sub-paragraph (3) of that paragraph.

COMMENCEMENT
    See s. 73 (2), *ante*, and the note thereto.

PARA. 1
    Paragraph 1 deals with the contents of an order which may close an approved school, probation home or hostel. Note that while sub-para. (4) (a) provides that the order *must* contain provisions for the protection of the interests of existing staff who may be transferred, sub-para. (4) (b) provides only that it *may* make such provision in the case of staff who are not transferred.
    If the latter provision had been mandatory and not permissive (as was suggested) an intolerable situation could arise since in many cases it would bind private employers to obligations for which there was no moral or legal justification. The protection afforded by the Act to such persons is to be found in paragraph 2 which provides for the making of regulations for the compensation of persons who lose their employment or suffer loss of emolument.

PARA. 2
    During the passing of the Act, objections were taken to this paragraph on the grounds that teachers in approved schools were inadequately protected. The Burnham Regulations are rather more favourable than those under s. 60 of the Local Government Act 1958, which, according to para. 2, would apply following a re-organisation in the development of community homes. The Burnham Report provides that teachers in primary or secondary schools are not to suffer a diminution of salary as a result of closure or reorganisation (Section T). In practice ordinary teachers are unaffected, and only those who are in receipt of special responsibility allowances are subject to the consideration. The Government announced that it is intended to adopt this rule in the case of approved school teachers, all of whom receive a special allowance in any case, and so the salaries of such staff would be unaffected.

Community home
    As to the establishment of such homes, see ss. 35–45, *ante*.

DEFINITIONS

For "local authority" and "voluntary organisation", see s. 70 (1), *ante*. For "approved institution" see para. 12 of this Schedule.

PENSIONS (INCREASE) ACTS 1920 TO 1969

For the Acts which may be cited by this collective title, see the Pensions (Increase) Act 1969, s. 5 (2), p. 16 (69 Halsbury's Statutes (2nd Edn.) 16).

LOCAL GOVERNMENT ACT 1958, S. 60

See 114 Statutes Supp.

ORDERS UNDER S. 46

For the orders made under s. 46, *ante*, see the notes to that section.

REGULATIONS

No regulations under the Local Government Act 1958, s. 60, as amended by para. 2 of this Schedule had been made up to 1st May 1970.

Use of premises as homes for children in care

3.—(1) If on the day specified for the purposes of section 7 (5) of this Act premises are used for the purposes of an approved school, then during the period (in this Schedule referred to, in relation to an approved school, as "the interim period") beginning immediately after that day and ending on the day on which the school ceases to be an approved school (whether by virtue of a section 46 order or otherwise) those premises may be used for the accommodation and maintenance of children in the care of local authorities.

(2) If during the interim period the premises of an approved school are used for the accommodation and maintenance of children in the care of a local authority then, during that period,

(a) any reference in section 21 (1) or section 31 of this Act to a community home includes a reference to those premises; and

(b) for the reference in section 18 (1) (c) of the Criminal Justice Act 1961 (directions of Secretary of State as to management of approved schools) to persons under the care of the managers there shall be substituted a reference to the children in the care of local authorities who are accommodated and maintained in those premises.

(3) At the request of the managers of an approved school the Secretary of State may, at any time during the interim period, give a direction—

(a) that so much as may be specified in the direction of any rules made under paragraph 1 (1) of Schedule 4 to the Act of 1933 (approved school rules) and of any rules made by the managers and approved by him under paragraph 1 (2) of that Schedule shall no longer apply in relation to that school; and

(b) that, in place of those rules, so much as may be specified in the direction of any regulations made under section 43 of this Act shall apply, subject to such adaptations and modifications as may be so specified, in relation to the approved school as if it were a community home.

(4) If the effect of the application, by a direction under sub-paragraph (3) above, of any provision of regulations made under section 43 of this Act in relation to an approved school would be to impose any duty or confer any power on a local authority in relation to that school, the Secretary of State shall not give a direction applying that provision except with the consent of the local authority concerned.

4.—(1) If on the day specified for the purposes of section 7 (5) of this Act a remand home was designated under section 11 of the Act of 1963 as a classifying centre then, during the period beginning immediately after that day and ending on the date specified in a section 46 order relating to that home, the home may be used for the accommodation and maintenance of children in the care of local authorities.

(2) In this Schedule "classifying centre" means a remand home designated as mentioned in sub-paragraph (1) of this paragraph and, in relation to a classifying centre, the period specified in that sub-paragraph is referred to as "the interim period".

(3) During the interim period—

(a) the expenses of a local authority in providing and maintaining a classifying centre in relation to the whole or part of the expenses of which a direction has been given by the Secretary of State under section 11 (3) of the Act of 1963 shall be treated for the purposes of section 104 of the Act of 1933 as if they were expenses incurred by the authority as managers of an approved school;

(b) subsections (4) and (5) of section 106 of the Act of 1933 shall apply in relation to a classifying centre as they apply in relation to an approved school the managers of which are a local authority; and

(c) any reference in section 21 (1) or section 31 of this Act to a community home includes a reference to a classifying centre.

5.—(1) Where a section 46 order is made in relation to an approved school or approved probation hostel or home and, in a regional plan approved by the Secretary of State, the whole or any part of the premises of the institution is designated as a controlled or assisted community home, the premises so designated may, after the specified date, be used for the purpose specified in the regional plan.

(2) Without prejudice to any power to vary the provisions of a trust deed relating to a community home consisting of premises designated as mentioned in sub-paragraph (1) of this paragraph, the purpose referred to in that sub-paragraph shall be deemed to be included among the purposes for which the premises are held in accordance with a trust deed relating to that home.

6.—(1) Where a section 46 order is made in relation to an approved institution (other than an institution provided by a local authority) and, in a regional plan approved by the Secretary of State, the whole or any part of the premises of the institution is designated as a community home to be provided by a local authority, then if the Secretary of State is satisfied that the premises so designated were to a substantial extent provided with the assistance of grants under section 104 of the Act of 1933 or section 77 of the Criminal Justice Act 1948, he may, by an authorisation in writing under this paragraph, authorise the transfer of the premises so designated to that local authority.

(2) The transfer of any premises in pursuance of an authorisation under this paragraph—

(a) shall be on such terms, as to payment and other matters, as may be agreed between the local authority concerned and the trustees or other persons in whom the premises are vested and, if the authorisation so provides, as may be approved by the Secretary of State;

(b) shall not take effect before the specified date; and

(c) shall operate to vest the premises transferred in the local authority free from any charitable trust and from any other obligation requiring the use of the premises for the purposes of an approved institution.

(3) Before giving an authorisation under this paragraph authorising the transfer of any premises belonging to a charity or otherwise held on charitable trusts, the Secretary of State shall consult the Charity Commissioners.

7. The provisions of paragraphs 3 to 6 of this Schedule shall have effect notwithstanding anything in the law relating to charities or in any deed or other instrument regulating the purposes for which any premises may be used.

COMMENCEMENT
See s. 73 (2), *ante*, and the note thereto.

DAY SPECIFIED FOR THE PURPOSES OF S. 7 (5)
See the note "Orders under this section" to s. 7, *ante*.

SECRETARY OF STATE MAY . . . GIVE A DIRECTION
See, generally, s. 69 (3), *ante*.

CONTROLLED OR ASSISTED COMMUNITY HOME
See s. 36 (3) *ante*.

WRITING
See the note to s. 5, *ante*.

CHARITY COMMISSIONERS
I.e., the Charity Commissioners for England and Wales. As to the contribution, etc., of the Charity Commissioners, see the Charities Act 1960, s. 1, Sch. 1 (132 Statutes Supp.).

DEFINITIONS
For "children", "local authority" and "regional plan", see s. 70 (1), *ante*. For "interim period", see para. 3 (1) of this Schedule, and for "classifying centre", see para. 4 (2) of this Schedule. For "section 46 orders", see para. 12 of this Schedule.

CRIMINAL JUSTICE ACT 1961, S. 18 (1) (c)
See 127 Statutes Supp.

ACT OF 1933
I.e., the Children and Young Persons Act 1933; see s. 70 (1), *ante*. For that Act, see 17 Halsbury's Statutes (3rd Edn.) 435.

ACT OF 1963
I.e., the Children and Young Persons Act 1963; see s. 70 (1), *ante*. For that Act see 139 Statutes Supp.

CRIMINAL JUSTICE ACT 1948, S. 77
See 8 Halsbury's Statutes (3rd Edn.) 368.

Financial provisions

8.—(1) During the period which is the interim period in relation to an approved school or to a classifying centre falling within paragraph 4 (3) (*a*) of this Schedule contributions shall be payable by local authorities to the managers of that school or, as the case may be, the local authority providing the classifying centre in respect of children in the care of the authorities who are accommodated and maintained in the school premises or the classifying centre in accordance with paragraph 3 (1) or paragraph 4 (1) of this Schedule.

(2) The contributions payable by a local authority under sub-paragraph (1) above in respect of a child in their care shall be payable throughout the time during which the child is accommodated and maintained in the approved school or classifying centre concerned and shall be such as may be prescribed by regulations made by the Secretary of State.

9.—(1) Where a section 46 order is made in relation to an approved institution, other than an institution provided by a local authority, and in a regional plan approved by the Secretary of State the whole or any part of the premises of the approved institution is designated as a community home, then,—

(a) on the coming into force of an instrument of management for a voluntary home which consists of or includes the premises so designated; or

(b) on the transfer of the premises so designated to a local authority in pursuance of an authorisation under paragraph 6 of this Schedule,

any such obligation relating to that institution as is referred to in sub-paragraph (2) of this paragraph shall cease.

(2) Sub-paragraph (1) of this paragraph applies to any obligation arising by virtue of a condition imposed under either of the following enactments, namely,—

(a) section 104 of the Act of 1933 (expenses of managers of an approved school); or

(b) section 77 of the Criminal Justice Act 1948 (expenditure in connection with approved probation hostels or homes).

(3) In a case falling within sub-paragraph (1) of this paragraph, the section 46 order may contain provisions requiring the responsible authority or organisation or, as the case may be, the local authority to whom the premises are transferred, to pay to the Secretary of State such sum as he may determine in accordance with sub-paragraph (4) of this paragraph by way of repayment of a proportion of any grants made in relation to the former approved institution under either of the enactments referred to in sub-paragraph (2) of this paragraph, but where the community home concerned is an assisted community home, the section 46 order may provide that, with the consent of the Treasury, the Secretary of State may reduce the sum to be paid to him in accordance with the preceding provisions of this sub-paragraph to such sum as he thinks fit.

(4) For the purpose of determining any such sum as is mentioned in sub-paragraph (3) of this paragraph, the Secretary of State shall assess—

(a) the amount which in his opinion represents the proportion of the total amount of the grants paid in respect of expenditure in connection with the former approved institution which was attributable to expenditure of a capital nature; and

(b) the amount which in his opinion represents the proportion of the contributions paid by local authorities under section 90 of the Act of 1933 or, as the case may be, the proportion of the sums paid by probation committees under rules made under Schedule 5 to the Criminal Justice Act 1948 which (in either case) should be treated as having been paid on account of expenditure of a capital nature in connection with the former approved institution;

and the sum determined by the Secretary of State for the purpose of sub-paragraph (3) of this paragraph shall be equal to the amount by which the amount assessed under paragraph (a) above exceeds twice the amount assessed under paragraph (b) above.

(5) If the instrument of management for an assisted community home ceases to have effect as mentioned in subsection (1) of section 48 of this Act there shall be deducted from any sum which is payable to the Secretary of State under subsection (5) of that section any sums paid to him by the responsible organisation in respect of the assisted community home in pursuance of any such provisions of a section 46 order relating to the former approved institution as are referred to in sub-paragraph (3) of this paragraph.

(6) In this paragraph "the former approved institution", in relation to a community home, means the approved institution the whole or part of the premises of which are comprised in that home.

10.—(1) The provisions of this paragraph apply where in a regional plan approved by the Secretary of State, the whole or any part of the premises of an approved institution to which a section 46 order relates is designated as a controlled or assisted community home and an instrument of management for a community home which consists of or includes the premises so designated has come into force; and in this paragraph "the former approved institution", in relation to such a community home, means the approved institution the whole or part of the premises of which are comprised in that home.

(2) Where this paragraph applies and the community home concerned is a controlled community home, then—

    (*a*) the Secretary of State may, by the section 46 order, make such provision as he considers appropriate for the transfer to the responsible authority of any rights, liabilities and obligations which, immediately before the specified date, were rights, liabilities and obligations of the managers of, or the society or person carrying on, the former approved institution; and

    (*b*) except in so far as the section 46 order otherwise provides, any legal proceedings pending immediately before the specified date by or against those managers or that society or person shall be continued on and after that date, with the substitution of the responsible authority for those managers or that society or person as a party to the proceedings.

(3) Where this paragraph applies and the community home concerned is an assisted community home but the responsible organisation does not consist of the persons who were the managers of or, as the case may be, is not the society or person who carried on, the former approved institution, paragraphs (*a*) and (*b*) of sub-paragraph (2) of this paragraph shall apply with the substitution for any reference to the responsible authority of a reference to the responsible organisation.

(4) If any liabilities of a voluntary organisation which is the responsible organisation in relation to an assisted community home falling within sub-paragraph (1) of this paragraph were incurred by the organisation before the specified date or were transferred to the organisation by the section 46 order (by virtue of sub-paragraph (3) of this paragraph) and, in either case, had the former approved institution continued to be an approved institution, any expenditure incurred in meeting those liabilities would have been eligible for a grant out of moneys provided by Parliament—

    (*a*) under section 104 (1) (*a*) of the Act of 1933 as the expenses of the managers of an approved school, or

    (*b*) under section 77 (3) (*b*) of the Criminal Justice Act 1948, as expenditure falling within that section and relating to an approved probation hostel or home, then any expenditure incurred after the specified date by the responsible organisation in meeting those liabilities shall be deemed for the purposes of section 65 (1) of this Act to be expenditure incurred by the responsible organisation in connection with the assisted community home in question.

11.—(1) Where a section 46 order is made in relation to an approved institution and no such provision as is referred to in sub-paragraph (1) of paragraph 9 of this Schedule is made by a regional plan in relation to any part of the premises of the institution, the person or persons on whom falls any such obligation (in this paragraph referred to as a "repayment obligation") relating to the institution as is referred to in sub-paragraph (2) of that paragraph may apply to the Secretary of State for an order under this paragraph.

(2) If, on an application under sub-paragraph (1) of this paragraph, it appears to the Secretary of State that on or within a reasonable time after the specified date the premises of the institution concerned or the proceeds of sale of the whole or any part of those premises are to be used for a purpose which is of benefit to children, he may with the consent of the Treasury make an order—

    (a) substituting for the conditions under which the repayment obligation arose such different conditions as he considers appropriate with respect to the repayment of any sum to which the repayment obligation relates; and

    (b) if the person or persons on whom the repayment obligation falls so request, imposing any liability to repay a sum in pursuance of the substituted conditions referred to in paragraph (a) above on such other person or persons as consent to accept the liability and as, in the opinion of the Secretary of State, will be able to discharge that liability.

COMMENCEMENT
    See s. 73 (2), *ante*, and the note thereto.

TREASURY
    See the note to s. 65, *ante*.

ASSISTED COMMUNITY HOME; CONTROLLED COMMUNITY HOME
    See the notes to s. 44 *ante*.

DEFINITIONS
    For "instrument of management", "local authority" and "regional plan", see s. 70 (1), *ante*. For "interim period", see para. 3 (1) of this Schedule and for classifying centre", see para. 4 (2) of this Schedule. For "section 46 order", see para. 12 of this Schedule.

ACT OF 1933
    I.e., the Children and Young Persons Act 1933; see s. 70 (1), *ante*. For that Act, see 17 Halsbury's Statutes (3rd Edn.) 435.

CRIMINAL JUSTICE ACT 1948, SS. 77, 77 (3) (*b*), SCH. 5
    See 8 Halsbury's Statutes (3rd Edn.) 368, 375.

REGULATIONS
    See generally as to regulations under this Act, s. 69, *ante*; and see in particular, sub-s. (1) thereof. No regulations had been made under para. 8 (2) of this Schedule up to 1st May 1970.

ORDER
    See generally as to orders under this Act, s. 69, *ante*, and see in particular sub-s. (1) thereof. Orders under para. 11 (2) of this Schedule, being local in nature, will not be noted in this work.

Interpretation

12. In this Schedule—

"approved institution" has the same meaning as in section 46 of this Act;
"the responsible authority", in relation to a controlled community home, has the same meaning as in section 41 of this Act;
"the responsible organisation", in relation to an assisted community home, has the same meaning as in section 42 of this Act; and
"section 46 order" and, in relation to an institution to which such an order relates, "specified date" have the meanings assigned to them by paragraph 1 (1) of this Schedule.

COMMENCEMENT
    See s. 73 (2), *ante*, and the note thereto.

Section 72 (1), (2)   SCHEDULE 4

TRANSITIONAL PROVISIONS AND SAVINGS

PART I

GENERAL

1. For the purposes of subsection (4) of section 1 and subsection (7) of section 7 of this Act, any order under the Act of 1933 committing a child or young person to the care of a fit person other than a local authority, any supervision order under that Act and any order to enter into recognisances in pursuance of section 62 (1) (c) of that Act shall be deemed to be such an earlier order as is mentioned in those subsections.

COMMENCEMENT
    See s. 73 (2), *ante*, and the note thereto.

FIT PERSON
    See the Children and Young Persons Act 1933, s. 84 (17 Halsbury's Statutes (3rd Edn.) 495). S. 84 of that Act is repealed by s. 72 (4), Sch. 6, *post*, as from a day to be appointed, but orders made before the coming into force of these provisions of this Act are saved by para. 18 of this Schedule.

SUPERVISION ORDER
    See the Children and Young Persons Act 1933, s. 62 (17 Halsbury's Statutes (3rd Edn.) 477). S. 62 of that Act is repealed by s. 72 (4), Sch. 6, *post*, as from a day to be appointed. Orders made before the coming into force of these provisions of this Act are saved by para. 18 of this Schedule. For meaning of "supervision order" in this Act, see s. 11, *ante*.

ACT OF 1933
    I.e., the Children and Young Persons Act 1933; see s. 70 (1), *ante*. For that Act, see 17 Halsbury's Statutes (3rd Edn.) 435.

2.—(1) Nothing in section 4 of this Act affects any proceedings against a person for an offence with which by virtue of that section he has ceased to be chargeable since the proceedings were begun; but where a person is found guilty of an offence and by reason of that section could not have been charged with it on the date of finding, then, subject to sections 1 (5) and 2 (13) of this Act, the court may make an order under section 1 of this Act in respect of the offender or an order discharging him absolutely but shall not have power to make any other order in consequence of the finding.

(2) Nothing in section 4 of this Act shall be construed as preventing any act or omission which occurred outside the United Kingdom from being a civil offence for the purposes of the Army Act 1955, the Air Force Act 1955, or the Naval Discipline Act 1957, or from being dealt with under any of those Acts.

COMMENCEMENT
See s. 73 (2), *ante*, and the note thereto.

PARA. 2
The references in sub-para. (2) to the Army Acts, etc., arise from the fact that certain provisions of the service discipline codes apply to civilians, including children, who accompany servicemen on overseas postings. Under these provisions a member of a serviceman's family can be dealt with by the appropriate British service authorities. Whether or not this is the most desirable way of dealing with a British child who gets into trouble overseas, it is usually the only alternative to his being hauled up before a foreign court. In certain circumstances the jurisdiction of the service authorities over such children is to be preferred to that of a foreign system, and this provision is inserted to protect their interests.

UNITED KINGDOM
See the note to s. 28, *ante*.

ARMY ACT 1955
See 35 Halsbury's Statutes (2nd Edn.) 443.

AIR FORCE ACT 1955
See 35 Halsbury's Statutes (2nd Edn.) 608.

NAVAL DISCIPLINE ACT 1957
See 37 Halsbury's Statutes (2nd Edn.) 948.

3. Nothing in section 5 of this Act affects any information laid in respect of a person before the date on which apart from this paragraph the information would have been required by virtue of that section to contain a statement of his age.

4. Where a person is committed for trial by a jury before subsection (1) of section 6 of this Act comes into force, or claims to be tried by a jury before subsection (2) of that section comes into force, proceedings in respect of the offence in question shall not be affected by the coming into force of that subsection.

5.—(1) The coming into force of section 7 (1) or of an order under section 34 (1) (*d*) of this Act shall not affect any sentence of borstal training passed before the date when the said section 7 (1) or the order came into force or any committal for sentence before that date under section 28 (1) of the Magistrates' Courts Act 1952; but a sentence of borstal training shall not be passed on any person (including a person to whom such a committal relates) if on the date of the relevant conviction he had not attained the minimum age which is for the time being specified in section 20 (1) of the Criminal Justice Act 1948.

(2) Nothing in section 7 (2) of this Act affects a probation order made before the coming into force of the said section 7 (2).

6. No order shall be made under section 19 (1) of the Criminal Justice Act 1948, at any time after the coming into force of this paragraph and before the coming into force of paragraph 23 of Schedule 5 to this Act, in respect of a person under the age of seventeen in consequence of a default within the meaning of the Criminal Justice Act 1961.

COMMENCEMENT
See s. 73 (2), *ante*, and the note thereto.

AGE
See the note "attained the age" to s. 1, *ante*.

COMING INTO FORCE OF SS. 6 (1), (2), 7 (1), (2), SCH. 5, PARA. 23
See s. 73 (2), *ante*, and the note thereto.

PARA. 5 (1) AND (2)
This transitional provision preserves sentences of borstal training passed, or probation orders made, before the coming into force of s. 7, *ante*. It also preserves a committal for sentence under s. 28 of the Magistrates' Courts Act 1952 under which a magistrates' court may commit to quarter sessions with a view to a sentence of borstal. This might have been interpreted as giving quarter sessions power to pass a sentence of borstal training even though borstal for young persons of the appropriate age had been abolished. The terms of para. 5 make it clear that, while the committal to quarter sessions is not affected by the coming into force of s. 7, that body may not pass a sentence of borstal training on a young person who, at the time of the conviction, had not attained the new minimum age for borstal. Quarter sessions will be able to deal with him by making a care order or any of the other orders available in the case of juveniles.

DEFAULT
By virtue of this para., for meaning, see the Criminal Justice Act 1961, s. 39 (1) (127 Statutes Supp.).

MAGISTRATES' COURTS ACT 1952, S. 28 (1)
See 32 Halsbury's Statutes (2nd Edn.) 447.

CRIMINAL JUSTICE ACT 1948, SS. 20 (1)
See 8 Halsbury's Statutes (3rd Edn.) 355. For s. 19 (1), see 14 Halsbury's Statutes (2nd Edn.) 1003.

7.—(1) Every approved school order in force on the specified day shall cease to have effect at the end of that day; and after that day—

(*a*) no person shall be detained by virtue of section 73 or section 82 of the Act of 1933 or an order under paragraph 2 of Schedule 2 to the said Act of 1961 or be subject to supervision in pursuance of that Schedule; and

(*b*) no person who has attained the age of nineteen shall be detained by virtue of a warrant under section 15 of the said Act of 1961.

(2) A person who has not attained the age of nineteen on the specified day and who, but for sub-paragraph (1) of this paragraph, would after that day have been the subject of an approved school order or liable to be detained or subject to supervision as mentioned in that sub-paragraph shall be deemed from the end of that day—

(*a*) to be the subject of a care order made by the court which made the approved school order in question on the same day as that order and committing him to the care of the local authority named in the approved school order in pursuance of section 70 (2) of the Act of 1933 or, if no authority is so named, of a local authority nominated in relation to him by the Secretary of State; and

(*b*) in the case where he would have been subject to supervision as aforesaid, to have been allowed by the said local authority to be under the charge and control of the person last nominated in relation to him in pursuance of paragraph 1 (1) of Schedule 2 to the said Act of 1961;

but nothing in this paragraph shall be construed as affecting the validity of a warrant under the said section 15 in relation to a person who has not attained the age of nineteen.

In relation to a person in respect of whom two or more approved school orders would have been in force after the specified day but for sub-paragraph (1) of this paragraph, references to such an order in paragraph (*a*) of this sub-paragraph are to the later or latest of the orders.

(3) The Secretary of State may from time to time nominate another local authority in the place of a local authority nominated by him in pursuance of the preceding sub-paragraph or this sub-paragraph.

(4) A person who is the subject of a care order by virtue of sub-paragraph (2) of this paragraph and who was unlawfully absent on the specified day from an approved school in which he was then required to be shall, until the local authority to whose care he is committed by the order direct otherwise, be deemed for the purposes of section 32 of this Act to be duly required by the authority to live after that day in the premises which on that day constituted the school.

(5) A person who on the specified day is the subject of an approved school order or subject to supervision in pursuance of the said Schedule 2 or eligible for assistance under paragraph 7 of that Schedule and is not the subject of a care order from the end of that day by virtue of sub-paragraph (2) of this paragraph shall be deemed for the purposes of section 20 of the Children Act 1948 and section 58 of the Act of 1963 (which authorise local authorities to provide assistance for persons formerly in care) to have been in the care of a local authority under the Children Act 1948 on that day, notwithstanding that he may then have attained the age of eighteen; and in relation to such a person the reference in the said section 58 to the local authority shall be construed as a reference to any local authority.

(6) If an order under section 88 of the Act of 1933 is in force at the end of the specified day in respect of payments under an affiliation order made for the mainten-ance of a person who is deemed by virtue of this paragraph to be subject to a care order after that day, the order under that section shall after that day be deemed to have been made, by virtue of the care order, under that section as modified by this Act.

(7) A direction restricting discharge which was given under section 74 of the Mental Health Act 1959 in respect of a person detained by virtue of an approved school order and which is in force at the end of the specified day shall cease to have effect at the end of that day.

(8) References to an approved school order in this paragraph, except in sub-paragraph (2) (*a*), include references to an order of the competent authority under subsection (1) of section 83 of the Act of 1933 and such an order as is mentioned in subsection (3) of that section; and in relation to those orders this paragraph shall have effect as if for sub-paragraph (2) (*a*) there were substituted the following—

> "(*a*) to be the subject of a care order made by a court in England on the date when the order for his detention in a school was made under the relevant law mentioned in section 83 of the Act of 1933 and committing him to the care of a local authority nominated in relation to him by the Secretary of State; and"

(9) In this paragraph "the specified day" means the day specified for the pur-poses of section 7 (5) of this Act.

8.—(1) An order under the Act of 1933 committing a child or young person to the care of a local authority as a fit person and in force on the date when section 7 (6) of this Act comes into force shall be deemed on and after that date to be a care order committing him to the care of that authority.

(2) Sub-paragraph (6) of the preceding paragraph shall have effect for the purposes of this paragraph as if for references to that paragraph and the specified day there were substituted respectively references to this paragraph and the day preceding the date mentioned in the preceding sub-paragraph.

9. Except as provided by paragraph 1 of this Schedule and this paragraph, nothing in this Act affects—

(a) an order under the Act of 1933 committing a child or young person to the care of a fit person other than a local authority and in force on the date when section 7 (6) of this Act comes into force; or

(b) the operation of any enactment in relation to such an order;

but where an application for the variation or revocation of the order is considered on or after that date by a juvenile court in pursuance of section 84 (6) of the Act of 1933, the court shall have power (to the exclusion of its powers under the said section 84 (6)) to refuse the application or to revoke the order and, where it revokes the order, to make a care order in respect of the child or young person in question.

10. Without prejudice to the preceding paragraph, a person who is subject to such an order as is mentioned in sub-paragraph (a) of that paragraph is not a foster-child within the meaning of Part I of the Children Act 1958.

11. Notwithstanding anything in section 20 (3) or 21 (1) of this Act, an order which is a care order by virtue of paragraph 8 of this Schedule and a care order made by virtue of paragraph 9 of this Schedule shall, unless previously revoked, cease to have effect when the child or young person in question attains the age of eighteen.

COMMENCEMENT
See s. 73 (2), *ante,* and the note thereto.

PARAS. 7 AND 8
Paragraph 7 (2) of this Schedule provides that, on the appointed day, persons under 19 subject to approved school orders are to be deemed to be subject to a care order made by the court which made the approved school order on the same day as that order. Para. 8 makes similar provision for those persons subject to orders made under s. 83 of the Children and Young Persons Act 1933. That section enables persons detained in a school in Scotland or Northern Ireland to be transferred to an approved school in England and persons subject to approved school orders made in the Channel Islands or the Isle of Man to be received into an approved school in England. All such persons are treated in like manner as persons subject to an approved school order made in England by a juvenile court, that is to say, they are deemed to be subject to an English care order. This ensures that a child will get the same kind of treatment as he would have got if he had been able to stay in the area where the sentence was passed.

Approved school order
See the note to s. 7 (5), *ante.*

Specified day
For meaning, see sub-para. (9) of this para.

Attained the age of
See the note to s. 1, *ante.*

S. 7 (6) of this Act comes into force
See s. 73 (2), *ante,* and the note thereto.

Foster child
For meaning in Part I of the Children Act 1958, see s. 2 of that Act as reproduced in Sch. 7, *post.*

DEFINITIONS
For "approved school order", "care order", "local authority", see s. 70 (1), *ante.*

ACT OF 1933
I.e., the Children and Young Persons Act 1933; see s. 70 (1), *ante.* For ss. 70 (2), 73, 82, 83, 84 (6), 88 of that Act, see 17 Halsbury's Statutes (3rd Edn.) 435.

ACT OF 1961
I.e., the Criminal Justice Act 1961; see s. 70 (1), *ante.* For s. 15 of, and Sch. 2, para. 1 (1), 2 to, that Act, see 127 Statutes Supp.

CHILDREN ACT 1948, S. 20
See 17 Halsbury's Statutes (3rd Edn.) 556.

ACT OF 1963
I.e., the Children and Young Persons Act 1963; see s. 70 (1), *ante.* For s. 58 of that Act, see 139 Statutes Supp.

MENTAL HEALTH ACT 1959, S. 74
See 39 Halsbury's Statutes (2nd Edn.) 1029.

12.—(1) Where a supervision order under the Children and Young Persons Acts 1933 to 1963 is in force on the date when this paragraph comes into force or where an order under section 52 of the Act of 1963 (whether made before, on or after that date) falls to be treated by virtue of subsection (3) of that section as a supervision order under the Act of 1933, the order and, in relation to the order, any enactment amended or repealed by this Act shall, subject to the following provisions of this paragraph, have effect as if this Act had not been passed; and the order may be altered or revoked accordingly.

(2) A juvenile court before which the person to whom such a supervision order relates is brought after the date aforesaid in pursuance of subsection (1) of section 66 of the Act of 1933 shall not have power to make such an order as is mentioned in that subsection in respect of him but shall instead have power to revoke the supervision order and make a care order in respect of him on being satisfied that he is unlikely to receive the care or control he needs unless the court makes a care order; and section 6 (1) of the Act of 1963 shall not apply in a case where the court exercises its power under this sub-paragraph.

(3) Where such a supervision order contains a provision requiring residence in an institution which has become a community home, the provision shall be construed as requiring residence in the home; and in such a case any reference to an institution of the kind in question in rules under the Criminal Justice Act 1948 providing for the making of payments to the body or person by whom the institution is managed shall be construed as a reference to the home.

(4) References to a supervision order in sub-paragraphs (2) and (3) of this paragraph include references to an order under the said section 52.

13.—(1) During the period beginning with the coming into force of section 35 of this Act and ending with the coming into operation of a regional plan for a particular planning area—

   (a) sections 15 and 16 of the Children Act 1948 shall continue to apply in relation to each of the relevant authorities; and

   (b) each of the relevant authorities may continue to exercise the power conferred by subsection (2) of section 19 of that Act, as it had effect immediately before the passing of this Act, to accommodate persons in hostels provided under that section; and

(c) section 77 (1) of the Act of 1933 shall continue to apply in relation to each of the relevant authorities as if for the words "the duty of" there were substituted the words "lawful for".

(2) Where different parts of the area of a local authority are comprised in different planning areas then, in relation to that local authority, the period specified in sub-paragraph (1) of this paragraph shall not expire until a regional plan has come into operation for each of those planning areas.

(3) If on the submission of a regional plan for a planning area to the Secretary of State part only of the plan is approved by him, any reference in the preceding provisions of this paragraph to the coming into operation of a regional plan for that area shall be construed as a reference to the coming into operation of a further regional plan containing all necessary supplementary proposals for that area.

COMMENCEMENT
　　See s. 73 (2), *ante*, and the note thereto.

PARA. 12
　　This paragraph makes transitional provision for supervision orders made under the Children and Young Persons Acts 1933 to 1963 which are in force when the new code of supervision in ss. 11 to 19, *ante*, comes into force.

PERIOD BEGINNING WITH
　　See the note to s. 12(3), *ante*.

PASSING OF THIS ACT
　　This Act was passed, *i.e.*, received the Royal Assent, on 22nd October 1969.

DEFINITIONS
　　For "planning area", "regional plan" and "residence", see s. 70 (1), *ante*.

CHILDREN AND YOUNG PERSONS ACTS 1933 TO 1963
　　For the Acts which may be cited by this collective title, see the Children and Young Persons Act 1963, s. 65 (2) (139 Statutes Supp.).

ACT OF 1963
　　I.e., the Children and Young Persons Act 1963, see s. 70 (1), *ante*. For ss. 6 (1), 52 of that Act, see 139 Statutes Supp.

ACT OF 1933
　　I.e., the Children and Young Persons Act 1933; see s. 70 (1), *ante*. For that Act, see 17 Halsbury's Statutes (3rd Edn.) 435.

CHILDREN ACT 1948, SS. 15, 16, 19 (2)
　　See 17 Halsbury's Statutes (3rd Edn.) 538.

14. If immediately before the coming into force of section 49 of this Act any person has, under section 3 (3) of the Children Act 1948, the care and control of a child (within the meaning of that Act) with respect to whom a resolution under section 2 of that Act is in force, then after the coming into force of that section the child shall again be in the care of the local authority by whom the resolution was passed but shall be deemed to have been allowed by that authority, under section 13 (2) of that Act (as substituted by the said section 49), to be under the charge and control of that person, on the same terms as were applicable under the said section 3 (3).

15. It shall be lawful for a person detained in any place in pursuance of section 27 of the Criminal Justice Act 1948 at the time when paragraph 24 of Schedule 5 to this Act comes into force to be detained there thereafter, until he is next delivered thence in due course of law, as if that paragraph had not come into force.

16. Nothing in paragraph 29 of Schedule 5 to this Act affects the operation of section 2 (4) of the Children Act 1958 in relation to a supervision order made under the Children and Young Persons (Scotland) Act 1937.

17. Nothing in Schedule 6 to this Act affects the operation of section 15 (3) of the Adoption Act 1958 in relation to a fit person order made under the Children and Young Persons (Scotland) Act 1937.

18. Nothing in any provision of Schedule 6 to this Act affects any order which, immediately before the coming into force of that provision, is in force by virtue of any enactment repealed by that provision.

COMMENCEMENT
    See s. 73 (2), *ante,* and the note thereto.

COMING INTO FORCE OF S. 49, SCH. 6
    See s. 73 (2), *ante,* and the note thereto.

PARAS. 16 AND 17
    These paragraphs make transitional provisions in relation to Scotland before the relevant provisions of the Social Work (Scotland) Act 1968 come into force.

CHILDREN ACT 1948, SS. 2, 3 (3), 13 (2)
    See 17 Halsbury's Statutes (3rd Edn.) 538.

CRIMINAL JUSTICE ACT 1948, S. 27
    See 14 Halsbury's Statutes (2nd Edn.) 1009.

CHILDREN AND YOUNG PERSONS (SCOTLAND) ACT 1937
    1 Edw. 8 & Geo. 6 c. 37; not printed in this work.

ADOPTION ACT 1958, S. 15 (3)
    See 115 Statutes Supp.

PART II

INTERIM PROVISIONS PENDING COMMENCEMENT OF PROVISIONS OF SOCIAL WORK (SCOTLAND) ACT 1968

19. Where a court in England or Wales by which a child or young person is found guilty of an offence is satisfied that he resides or will reside in Scotland, the court shall have power, without prejudice to its other powers and notwithstanding anything in section 7 (2) of this Act, to make a probation order in respect of him in accordance with sections 3 and 9 of the Criminal Justice Act 1948.

20. In section 51 (1) of the Act of 1963, for the words "principal Act" there shall be substituted the words "Children and Young Persons Act 1969 in proceedings under section 1 of that Act".

21. In section 51 (2) of the Act of 1963, for the words from "proposes" to "this Act" there shall be substituted ", or a supervision order under the Children and Young Persons Act 1969 has been made in proceedings under section 1 of that Act, proposes to reside or is residing in Scotland" and for the words "specified in the supervision order" there shall be substituted the words "for which the supervision order would have continued in force if it had been allowed to continue in force until it ceased to have effect by the effluxion of time."

22. Where a juvenile court in England or Wales is satisfied that a person who has not attained the age of eighteen and in respect of whom a supervision order made by virtue of section 7 (7) (*b*) of this Act or section 7A (4) of the Criminal Justice

(Scotland) Act 1949 is in force resides or will reside in Scotland, the court may discharge the order and exercise the like powers to make a probation order in accordance with sections 3 and 9 of the Criminal Justice Act 1948 in respect of him as if in the proceedings it had duly found him guilty of the offence in consequence of which the supervision order was made and section 7 (2) of this Act had not been passed; but a probation order made by virtue of this paragraph shall not continue in force after the date on which the discharged supervision order would have ceased to have effect by the effluxion of time.

23.—(1) Where it appears to the local authority to whose care a person is committed by a care order that his parent or guardian resides or will reside in Scotland and that it is appropriate to transfer him to the care of the managers of an approved school in Scotland, the authority shall make a report on the case to the Secretary of State; and thereupon the Secretary of State may, if he thinks fit, make an order transferring the person in question to the care of the managers of such a school.

(2) The provisions of the Children and Young Persons (Scotland) Acts 1937 to 1963 shall apply to an order made under this paragraph as if it were an approved school order made by a juvenile court in Scotland on the date on which the care order in question was originally made; but notwithstanding anything in section 75 of the said Act of 1937 such an order shall cease to have effect on the date when the care order in question would have ceased to have effect by the effluxion of time and the contributions to be made under section 94 of the said Act of 1937 in respect of the person to whom the order under this paragraph relates shall be made by the authority nominated for the purpose in the order under this paragraph, being the education authority within whose area it appears to the Secretary of State at the time that order is made that his parent or guardian resides or will reside.

(3) When a person is received into the care of the managers of an approved school in pursuance of an order under this paragraph, the care order in question shall cease to have effect.

24. If it appears to the Secretary of State that the parent or guardian of a person who has not attained the age of nineteen and is the subject of an approved school order in force under the Children and Young Persons (Scotland) Act 1937, or such other order as is mentioned in subsection (1) or subsection (3) of section 87 of that Act, resides or will reside in the area of a local authority in England or Wales, the Secretary of State may make an order committing that person to the care of that authority; and an order under this paragraph shall have effect as if it were a care order made on the date on which the approved school or other order was made, but as if sections 20 (2) and 21 (5) of this Act were omitted.

GENERAL NOTE
The Social Work (Scotland) Act 1968 introduced an entirely new system in Scotland but the relevant provisions are not yet in force and they are not expected to be brought into operation before the end of 1970. The Act abolishes the prosecution of children under 16 except on the authority of the Lord Advocate and provides for children who commit offences, or who are broadly in situations equivalent to those referred to in paragraphs (a) to (d) of s. 1 (2), ante, to appear before children's hearings. The hearings have power to make supervision requirements which may require children to reside in residential establishments and which are effective up to the age of 18.

COMMENCEMENT
See s. 73 (2), ante, and the note thereto.

ATTAINED THE AGE OF
See the note to s. 1, ante.

DEFINITIONS
    For "approved school orders", "care order", "child", "guardian", "local authority", "reside", "supervision order" and "young person", see s. 70 (1), *ante.*

CRIMINAL JUSTICE ACT 1948, SS. 3, 9
    See 8 Halsbury's Statutes (3rd Edn.) 339, 349.

ACT OF 1963
    I.e., the Children and Young Persons Act 1933; see s. 70 (1), *ante.* For that Act, see 17 Halsbury's Statutes (3rd Edn.) 435.

CRIMINAL JUSTICE (SCOTLAND) ACT 1949
    13 & 14 Geo. 6 c. 94; not printed in this work.

CHILDREN AND YOUNG PERSONS (SCOTLAND) ACTS 1937 TO 1963
    1 Edw. 8 & Geo. 6 c. 37; not printed in this work.

Section 72 (3)   SCHEDULE 5

MINOR AND CONSEQUENTIAL AMENDMENTS OF ENACTMENTS

GENERAL NOTE
    This makes the necessary minor and consequential amendments to a range of enactments relevant to children and young persons, dating from 1897 to 1961. Many of them are designed to co-ordinate the law of England and Scotland.

The Police (Property) Act 1897

1. The Police (Property) Act 1897 (which makes provision for the disposal of property in the possession of the police) shall apply to property which has come into the possession of the police in connection with an allegation, in proceedings under section 1 of this Act, that the condition set out in subsection 2 (*f*) of that section is satisfied as it applies to property which has come into the possession of the police in the circumstances mentioned in that Act.

COMMENCEMENT
    See s. 73 (2), *ante,* and the note thereto.

POLICE (PROPERTY) ACT 1897
    See 18 Halsbury's Statutes (2nd Edn.) 111.

The Act of 1933

2. In section 10 of the Act of 1933, after subsection (1) there shall be inserted the following subsection:—

    (1A) Proceedings for an offence under this section shall not be instituted except by a local education authority; and before instituting such proceedings the authority shall consider whether it would be appropriate, instead of or as well as instituting the proceedings, to bring the child or young person in question before a juvenile court under section 1 of the Children and Young Persons Act 1969.

3. In section 34 (2) of the Act of 1933, after the words "be taken" there shall be inserted the words "by the person who arrested him".

4. In section 46 of the Act of 1933, after subsection (1) there shall be inserted the following subsection:—

> (1A) If a notification that the accused desires to plead guilty without appearing before the court is received by the clerk of a court in pursuance of section 1 of the Magistrates' Courts Act 1957 and the court has no reason to believe that the accused is a child or young person, then, if he is a child or young person he shall be deemed to have attained the age of seventeen for the purposes of subsection (1) of this section in its application to the proceedings in question.

5. In section 55 (1) of the Act of 1933, for the words "charged with" there shall be substituted the words "found guilty of" and after the word "care" there shall be inserted the words "or control".

6. In section 56 (1) of the Act of 1933, for the word "resides" there shall be substituted the words "habitually resides".

7. Section 63 of the Act of 1933 shall cease to have effect.

8. In section 86 (1) of the Act of 1933 for the words from "an order" to "approved school" there shall be substituted the words "a care order which is not an interim order has been made in respect of a child or young person".

9.—(1) In subsection (1) of section 87 of the Act of 1933, for the words from "an order has" to "same time, and" there shall be substituted the words "a care order which is not an interim order has been made in respect of a child or young person then, subject to section 62 of the Children and Young Persons Act 1969".

(2) For subsection (2) of that section, there shall be substituted the following subsection:—

> (2) A contribution order in respect of a child or young person may be made on the application of the local authority entitled to receive contributions in respect of him.

(3) In subsection (3) of that section for the words from "in the case", in the first place where they occur, onwards there shall be substituted the words "as long as the child or young person to whom it relates is in the care of the local authority concerned".

10.—(1) In subsection (1) of section 88 of the Act of 1933 for the words from "ordered" to "approved school" there shall be substituted the words "the subject of a care order (other than an interim order)"; for the words "that court" there shall be substituted the words "the court which makes the order"; for the words "the person who is" there shall be substituted the words "the local authority who are", and for the words "the persons by whom, and in the circumstances in which" there shall be substituted the words "the local authorities by whom".

(2) In subsection 2 (*c*) of that section, for the words "person who was" there shall be substituted the words "local authority who were".

(3) In subsection (4) of that section, for paragraphs (*a*) and (*b*) there shall be substituted the words "after the child or young person to whom that order relates has ceased to be the subject of the care order by virtue of which the order under this section was made or, where this section applies by virtue of section 23 of the Children Act 1948, after he has ceased to be in the care of a local authority under section 1 of that Act or, in either case, if he is allowed by the local authority to be under the

charge and control of a parent, guardian, relative or friend, although remaining in the care of the local authority".

11. In section 106 (2) (*a*) of the Act of 1933, for the words from "fifty-seven" to "Schedule to" there shall be substituted the words "eighty-seven and eighty-eight of".

12.—(1) In section 107 (1) of the Act of 1933, after the words "that is to say" there shall be inserted the following words:—

> "care order" and "interim order" have the same meanings as in the Children and Young Persons Act 1969.

(2) In the said section 107 (1), in the definition of "place of safety", for the words "any home provided by a local authority under Part II of the Children Act 1948 any remand home or" there shall be substituted the words "a community home provided by a local authority or a controlled community home, any".

(3) Section 107 (2) of the Act of 1933 shall cease to have effect.

COMMENCEMENT
See s. 73 (2), *ante*, and the note thereto.

JUVENILE COURT
See the note to s. 1, *ante*.

ATTAINED THE AGE OF
See the note to s. 1, *ante*.

CARE ORDER; INTERIM ORDER
For meanings, by virtue of para. 12 (1) of this Schedule, see s. 70 (1), *ante*.

ACT OF 1933
I.e., the Children and Young Persons Act 1933; see s. 70 (1), *ante*. For ss. 10 (1), 34 (2), 46 (1), 55 (1), 56 (1), 63, 86 (1), 87 (1), (2), (3), 88 (1), (2) (*c*), (4), 106 (2) (*a*), 107 (1), (2) of that Act, see 17 Halsbury's Statutes (3rd Edn.) 435.

The Education Act 1944

13. For subsections (2) to (5) of section 40 of the Education Act 1944 there shall be substituted the following subsections:—

> (2) Proceedings for such offences as aforesaid shall not be instituted except by a local education authority; and before instituting such proceedings the authority shall consider whether it would be appropriate, instead of or as well as instituting the proceedings, to bring the child in question before a juvenile court under section 1 of the Children and Young Persons Act 1969.

> (3) The court by which a person is convicted of an offence against section 37 of this Act or before which a person is charged with an offence against section 39 of this Act may if it thinks fit direct the authority who instituted the proceedings to bring the child to whom the proceedings relate before a juvenile court under the said section 1; and it shall be the duty of the authority to comply with the direction.

> (4) Where a child in respect of whom a school attendance order is in force is brought before a juvenile court by a local education authority under the said section 1 and the court finds that the condition set out in subsection (2) (*e*) of that section is not satisfied with respect to him, the court may direct that the order shall cease to be in force.

COMMENCEMENT
    See s. 73 (2), *ante*, and the note thereto.

JUVENILE COURT
    See the note to s. 1, *ante*.

EDUCATION ACT 1944, SS. 37, 39, 40 (2)–(5)
    See 11 Halsbury's Statutes (3rd Edn.) 196, 198, 200.

The Children Act 1948

14. In section 4 (3) of the Children Act 1948, the proviso shall cease to have effect.

15. In section 20 (1) of the said Act of 1948, for the words "any such person as is mentioned in subsection (1) of the last foregoing section" there shall be substituted the words "any person over compulsory school age but under the age of twenty one who is, or has at any time after ceasing to be of compulsory school age been, in the care of a local authority".

16. In section 23 (1) of the said Act of 1948 for the words from "committed" in the second place where it occurs to the end of the subsection there shall be substituted the words "in the care of a local authority by virtue of such an order as is mentioned in subsection (1) of the said section 86".

17.—(1) In section 26 (1) of the said Act of 1948 for paragraph (*b*) there shall be substituted the following paragraph:—

    (*b*) an illegitimate child is in the care of a local authority by virtue of such an order as is mentioned in section 86 (1) of the Children and Young Persons Act 1933, or.

(2) In subsections (3) and (4) (*b*) of the said section 26, for the words "person who is" there shall be substituted the words "local authority who are", and in subsection (4) of that section for the words "(*b*) or (*c*)" there shall be substituted the words "or (*b*)".

18. In section 39 (1) of the said Act of 1948 after paragraph (*h*) there shall be inserted the following paragraph:—

    (*i*) the Children and Young Persons Act 1969.

19. In section 43 (1) of the said Act of 1948 for the words from "Parts IV and V" onwards there shall be substituted the words "the Children and Young Persons Acts 1933 to 1969, the Adoption Act 1958 and the Adoption Act 1968".

20.—(1) In subsection (1) of section 51 of the said Act of 1948, for the words from "homes" to "this Act" there shall be substituted the words "community homes provided by them or in controlled community homes" and at the end of that subsection there shall be added the words "or sections 2 (5), 16 (3) or 28 of the Children and Young Persons Act 1969 and of children detained by them in pursuance of arrangements under section 29 (3) of that Act".

(2) In subsection (3) of the said section 51, for the words from "home" to "this Act" there shall be substituted the words "community home provided by a local authority or a controlled community home".

21.—(1) In subsection (3) of section 54 of the said Act of 1948, after the word "area" in the first place where it occurs there shall be inserted the words "other than community homes" and after the word "any" in the last place where it occurs, there shall be inserted the word "such".

(2) In subsection (4) of that section, for the words from "as a fit person" to the end of the subsection there shall be substituted the words "by a care order within the meaning of the Children and Young Persons Act 1969 or by a warrant under section 23 (1) of that Act."

(3) In subsection (5) of that section, for the words from "ninety-four" to "1933" there shall be substituted the words "section 58 of the Children and Young Persons Act 1969".

22. In section 59 (1) of the said Act of 1948, at the end of the definition of "child" there shall be added the words "and any person who has attained that age and is the subject of a care order within the meaning of the Children and Young Persons Act 1969".

COMMENCEMENT
See s. 73 (2), *ante,* and the note thereto.

COMPULSORY SCHOOL AGE
See the note to s. 50, *ante.*

AGE
See the note "attained the age" to s. 1, *ante.*

COMMUNITY HOME; CONTROLLED COMMUNITY HOME
See the notes to s. 30, *ante.*

CARE ORDER
For meaning, see s. 70 (1), *ante.*

CHILDREN ACT 1948, SS. 4 (3), 20 (1), 23 (1), 26 (1), (3), (4) (*b*), 39 (1), 43 (1), 51 (1), (3), 54 (3), (4), (5), 59 (1)
See 17 Halsbury's Statutes (3rd Edn.) 538.

The Criminal Justice Act 1948

23. In section 19 (1) of the Criminal Justice Act 1948, after the words "who is" there shall be inserted the words "not less than seventeen but".

24. For section 27 of the said Act of 1948 there shall be substituted the following section:—

27. Remand of persons aged 17 to 20

(1) Where a court remands a person charged with or convicted of an offence or commits him for trial or sentence and he is not less than seventeen but under twenty-one years old and is not released on bail, then, if the court has been notified by the Secretary of State that a remand centre is available for the reception from the court of persons of his class or description, it shall commit him to a remand centre and, if it has not been so notified, it shall commit him to a prison.

(2) Where a person is committed to a remand centre in pursuance of this section, the centre shall be specified in the warrant and he shall be detained there for the period for which he is remanded or until he is delivered thence in due course of law.

(3) In this section "court" includes a justice; and nothing in this section affects the provisions of section 105 (5) of the Magistrates' Courts Act 1952 (which provides for remands to the custody of a constable).

COMMENCEMENT
See s. 73 (2), *ante*, and the note thereto.

NOT LESS THAN SEVENTEEN
As to the time when a person attains a particular age, see the note "attained the age" to s. 1, *ante*.

CRIMINAL JUSTICE ACT 1948, SS. 19 (1), 27
See 14 Halsbury's Statutes (2nd Edn.) 1003, 1009–1110.

MAGISTRATES' COURTS ACT 1952, S. 105 (5)
See 32 Halsbury's Statutes (2nd Edn.) 505.

The Criminal Justice (Scotland) Act 1949

25. In section 7 of the Criminal Justice (Scotland) Act 1949, after the words "that the offender" in subsection (1) and "that the probationer" in subsection (2) there shall be inserted the words "has attained the age of seventeen and".

26. After section 7 of the said Act of 1949 there shall be inserted the following section:—

7A. Further provisions as to probation orders relating to persons residing or formerly residing in England

(1) Where the court by which a probation order is made under section 2 of this Act or subsection (6) of this section is satisfied that the person to whom the order relates is under the age of seventeen and resides or will reside in England, subsection (2) of the said section 2 shall not apply to the order but the order shall name the petty sessions area in which that person resides or will reside and the court shall send notification of the order to the clerk to the justices for that area.

(2) Where a probation order has been made under section 2 of this Act or subsection (6) of this section and the court which made the order or the appropriate court is satisfied that the person to whom the order relates is under the age of seventeen and proposes to reside or is residing in England, the power of that court to amend the order under Schedule 2 to this Act shall include power, without summoning him and without his consent, to insert in the order the name of the petty sessions area aforesaid; and where the court exercises the power conferred on it by virtue of this subsection it shall send notification of the order to the clerk aforesaid.

(3) A court which sends a notification to a clerk in pursuance of the foregoing provisions of this section shall send to him with it three copies of the probation order in question and such other documents and information relating to the case as it considers likely to be of assistance to the juvenile court mentioned in the following subsection.

(4) It shall be the duty of the clerk to whom a notification is sent in pursuance of the foregoing provisions of this section to refer the notification to a juvenile court acting for the petty sessions area named in the order, and on such a reference the court—

(a) may make a supervision order under the Children and Young Persons Act 1969 in respect of a person to whom the notification relates; and

(b) if it does not make such an order, shall dismiss the case.

(5) A supervision order made by virtue of the foregoing subsection shall not include a requirement authorised by section 12 of the said Act of 1969 unless the supervised person is before the court when the supervision order is made, and in relation to a supervision order made by virtue of that subsection—

(*a*) section 15 of that Act shall have effect as if in subsection (4), paragraph (*b*) and the words following it were omitted; and

(*b*) section 17 (*a*) of that Act shall have effect as if the second reference to the supervision order were a reference to the probation order in consequence of which the supervision order is made;

and when a juvenile court disposes of a case referred to it in pursuance of the foregoing subsection, the probation order in consequence of which the reference was made shall cease to have effect.

(6) The court which, in pursuance of subsection (1) of section 73 of the Social Work (Scotland) Act 1968, considers a case referred to it in consequence of a notification under paragraph (i) of that subsection (which relates to a case in which a person subject to a supervision order made by virtue of this section moves to Scotland)—

(*a*) may, if it is of opinion that the person to whom the notification relates should continue to be under supervision, make a probation order in respect of him for a period specified in the order; and

(*b*) if it does not make such an order, shall dismiss the case;

and when the court disposes of a case in pursuance of this subsection the supervision order aforesaid shall cease to have effect.

(7) Notwithstanding any provision to the contrary in section 2 of this Act, a probation order made by virtue of the foregoing subsection which includes only requirements having the like effect as any requirement or provision of the supervision order to which the notification relates may be made without summoning the person to whom the notification relates and without his consent, and shall specify a period of supervision which shall expire not later than the date on which that supervision order would have ceased to have effect by the effluxion of time; and, except as aforesaid, Part I of this Act shall apply to that probation order.

(8) In this section "petty sessions area" has the same meaning as in the said Act of 1969.

The Sexual Offences Act 1956

27. In section 37 (7) of the Sexual Offences Act 1956, for the words "section twenty or twenty-one of the Magistrates' Courts Act 1952 (which relate" in paragraph (*a*) there shall be substituted the words "section 6 of the Children and Young Persons Act 1969 (which relates" and for the words "that Act" in paragraph (*b*) there shall be substituted the words "the Magistrates' Courts Act 1952".

COMMENCEMENT
See s. 73 (2), *ante*, and the note thereto.

SEXUAL OFFENCES ACT 1956, S. 37 (7)
See 102 Statutes Supp.

MAGISTRATES' COURTS ACT 1952
See 125 Statutes Supp.

The Affiliation Proceedings Act 1957

28.—(1) In section 5 (2) (*a*) of the Affiliation Proceedings Act 1957, for the words from "fit person" to "school" there shall be substituted the words "local authority".

(2) In section 7 (4) of that Act, for paragraph (*a*) there shall be substituted the following paragraph:—

> (*a*) subject to the next following subsection, so as to require payments there-under to be made in respect of any period when the child is in the care of a local authority under section 1 of the Children Act 1948 or by virtue of a care order (other than an interim order) within the meaning of the Children and Young Persons Act 1969;

(3) In section 7 (6) of that Act, for the words from "a person" onwards there shall be substituted the words "by virtue of such a care order as aforesaid".

COMMENCEMENT
    See s. 73 (2), *ante*, and the note thereto.

CARE ORDER
    For meaning, see s. 70 (1), *ante*.

AFFILIATION PROCEEDINGS ACT 1957, SS. 5 (2) (A), 7 (4), (6)
    See 1 Halsbury's Statutes (3rd Edn.) 81, 83.

The Children Act 1958

29. In section 2 (4) of the Children Act 1958, for the words "supervision order or" there shall be substituted the words "supervision order within the meaning of the Children and Young Persons Act 1969 or a".

30. In section 9 of the said Act of 1958, after the words "foster child" there shall be inserted the words "for reward".

31. In section 12 (1) of the said Act of 1958, for the words "one month" there shall be substituted the words "two weeks".

32. In section 17 of the said Act of 1958, after the words "that is to say" there shall be inserted the words "approved school" has the same meaning as in the Children and Young Persons (Scotland) Act 1937;" and, in the definition of "place of safety", for the word "home" in the first place where it occurs there shall be substituted the words "community home" and for the words "under Part II of the Children Act 1948, remand" there shall be substituted the words "a controlled community".

COMMENCEMENT
    See s. 73 (2), *ante*, and the note thereto.

SUPERVISION ORDER
    For meaning, see s. 70 (1), *ante*.

COMMUNITY HOME
    As to the establishment of community homes, see generally ss. 35–45, *ante*.

CHILDREN ACT 1958, SS. 2 (4), 9, 12 (1), 17
    See 112 Statutes Supp.

CHILDREN AND YOUNG PERSONS (SCOTLAND) ACT 1937
    1 Edw. 8 & Geo. 6 c. 37; not printed in this work.

The Adoption Act 1958

33.—(1) In section 4 (3) of the Adoption Act 1958, for paragraph (*a*) there shall be substituted the following paragraph:—

    (*a*) section 24 of the Children and Young Persons Act 1969 (which relates to the powers and duties of local authorities with respect to persons committed to their care in pursuance of that Act).

34. In section 15 (3) of the said Act of 1958, for the words "the last mentioned order" there shall be substituted the words "or to the care of a local authority by a care order (other than an interim order) in force under the Children and Young Persons Act 1969, the fit person order or care order as the case may be".

35. In section 37 (2) of the said Act of 1958, for the words "(4) or (5)" there shall be substituted the words "or (4)".

36. In section 57 (1) of the said Act of 1958, in the definition of "place of safety", for the word "home" in the first place where it occurs there shall be substituted the words "community home" and for the words "under Part II of the Children Act 1948, remand" there shall be substituted the words "a controlled community".

COMMENCEMENT
    See s. 73 (2), *ante*, and the note thereto.

CARE ORDER; INTERIM ORDER
    For meaning, see s. 70 (1), *ante*.

ADOPTION ACT 1958, SS. 4 (3), 15 (3), 37 (2), 57 (1)
    See 115 Statutes Supp.

CHILDREN ACT 1948, PART II
    See 17 Halsbury's Statutes (3rd Edn.) 549.

The Mental Health Act 1959

37.—(1) In subsection (1) of section 9 of the Mental Health Act 1959 for the words from "or other accommodation" to "section fifteen of that Act" there shall be substituted the words "provided under section 38 of the Children and Young Persons Act 1969" and for the words "that Act" there shall be substituted the words "the Children Act 1948".

(2) In subsection (2) of the said section 9, for the words "or other accommodation provided under the said section fifteen" there shall be substituted the words "provided under the said section 38".

38. In section 10 (1) (*a*) of the said Act of 1959 for sub-paragraph (i) there shall be substituted the following sub-paragraph:—

    (i) section 24 of the Children and Young Persons Act 1969 (which relates to the powers and duties of local authorities with respect to persons committed to their care in pursuance of that Act).

39. In section 50 of the said Act of 1959, for paragraph (*a*) there shall be substituted the following paragraph:—

    (*a*) section 24 of the Children and Young Persons Act 1969 (which relates to the powers and duties of local authorities with respect to persons committed to their care in pursuance of that Act).

40. In section 60 (6) of the said Act of 1959, after the word "offence" there shall be inserted the words "or make any such order as is mentioned in paragraphs (*b*) or

(*c*) of section 7 (7) of the Children and Young Persons Act 1969 in respect of the offender".

41. In section 62 (4) of the said Act of 1959 for the words "section 62 of the Children and Young Persons Act 1933" there shall be substituted the words "section 1 of the Children and Young Persons Act 1969".

COMMENCEMENT
See s. 73 (2), *ante*, and the note thereto.

MENTAL HEALTH ACT 1959, SS. 9 (1), (2), 10 (1) (A), 50, 60 (6), 62 (4)
See 39 Halsbury's Statutes (2nd Edn.) 970, 1006, 1014.

CHILDREN ACT 1948
See 17 Halsbury's Statutes (3rd Edn.) 538.

The Mental Health (Scotland) Act 1960

42. In section 10 (1) (*a*) of the Mental Health (Scotland) Act 1960, for sub-paragraph (ii) there shall be substituted the following sub-paragraph:—

(ii) section 24 of the Children and Young Persons Act 1969 (which relates to the powers and duties of local authorities in England and Wales with respect to persons committed to their care).

43. In section 46 of the said Act of 1960, for paragraph (*b*) there shall be substituted the following paragraph:—

(*b*) section 24 of the Children and Young Persons Act 1969 (which relates to the powers and duties of local authorities in England and Wales with respect to persons committed to their care).

COMMENCEMENT
See s. 73 (2), *ante*, and the note thereto.

MENTAL HEALTH (SCOTLAND) ACT 1960, S. 10 (1) (A)
See 40 Halsbury's Statutes (2nd Edn.) 590.

The Criminal Justice Act 1967

44. For section 5 (1) of the Criminal Justice Act 1961 there shall be substituted the following:—

5. Defaulters already detained in detention centre

(1) Where a court has power to commit a person to prison for any term for a default and that person has attained the age of seventeen and is detained in a detention centre under a previous sentence or warrant, the court may, subject to the provisions of this section, commit him to a detention centre for a term not exceeding the term aforesaid or six months, whichever is the shorter.

and subsection (3) of section 6 of that Act shall be subsection (6) of section 5 of that Act.

45. In section 9 of the said Act of 1961, for the words from the beginning to "that Act", where they first occur, there shall be substituted the words "Where an order for conditional discharge under section seven of the Criminal Justice Act 1948".

46. In section 29 (3) (*a*) of the said Act of 1961, for the words "that Act" there shall be substituted the words "the Children and Young Persons Act 1933".

COMMENCEMENT
See s. 73 (2), *ante*, and the note thereto.

ATTAINED THE AGE OF
See the note to s. 1, *ante*.

MONTHS
See the note to s. 15, *ante*.

CRIMINAL JUSTICE ACT 1961, SS. 5 (1), 6 (3), 9
See 127 Statutes Supp. S. 29 (3) (*a*) was added by the Children and Young Persons Act 1963, s. 64 (1), Sch. 3, para. 50 (139 Statutes Supp).

The Act of 1963

47. In section 3 (1) of the Act of 1963, for the words "section 62 of the principal Act" there shall be substituted the words "section 1 of the Children and Young Persons Act 1969".

48. In section 23 of the Act of 1963, in subsection (1) (*b*), for the words "that Act" there shall be substituted the words "the principal Act" and, in subsection (5), for the words from "for his detention" onwards there shall be substituted the words "within the meaning of the Children and Young Persons Act 1969".

49. In section 29 (1) of the Act of 1963, for the words "before a juvenile court under section 62 or section 65 of the principal Act" there shall be substituted the words "under section 1 of the Children and Young Persons Act 1969 or for an offence"; and section 29 (2) of the Act of 1963 shall cease to have effect.

50.—(1) In subsection (1) of section 30 of the Act of 1963, for the words "the person who" there shall be substituted the words "the local authority who".

(2) In subsection (3) of that section, for the words "subsections (3) and (4)" there shall be substituted "subsection (3)" and at the end of that subsection there shall be added the words "section 62 of the Children and Young Persons Act 1969".

(3) In subsection (4) of that section for the words from "a magistrates' court", in the first place where they occur, to the end of the subsection there shall be substituted the words "a magistrates' court acting for the area or part of the area of the local authority which is the applicant."

(4) In subsection (5) of that section for the words "14 (1) of this Act keep the person" there shall be substituted the words "24 (8) of the Children and Young Persons Act 1969 keep the local authority".

51. In section 45 (1) of the Act of 1963, after the words "the Children Act 1958" there shall be inserted the words "the Children and Young Persons Act 1969".

52. In section 49 (1) of the Act of 1963, for the words "section 3 (3)", there shall be substituted the words "section 13 (2)" and for the words "over the care" in both places there shall be substituted the word "charge".

53. For subsection (3) of section 57 of the Act of 1963 there shall be substituted the following subsection:—

(3) The said sections 39 and 49 shall extend to Scotland and the said sections 46 and 54 shall extend to England and Wales, but—

    (*a*) references to a court in the said sections 39 and 49 shall not include a court in Scotland; and

    (*b*) references to a court in the said sections 46 and 54 shall not include a court in England or Wales.

COMMENCEMENT
 See s. 73 (2), *ante*, and the note thereto.

ACT OF 1963
 I.e., the Children and Young Persons Act 1963, see s. 70 (1), *ante*. For ss. 3 (1), 23 (1)
(*b*), (5), 29 (1), (2), 30 (1), (3), (4), (5), 45 (1), 49 (1), 57 (3) of that Act, see 139 Statutes
Supp.

The Family Allowances Act 1965

54.—(1) In subsection (1) (*b*) of section 11 of the Family Allowances Act 1965,
for the words "said Act of" there shall be substituted the words "Children and Young
Persons Act".

(2) In subsection (2) of that section for the words "said Act of 1933" there shall
be substituted the words "Children and Young Persons Act 1969 (other than an
interim order)" and for the words from "5 (1)" to "1956" there shall be substituted
the words "13 (2) of the Children Act 1948".

(3) In subsection (3) of that section, for the words "3 or 4" there shall be substituted the words "4 or 13 (2)".

COMMENCEMENT
 See s. 73 (2), *ante*, and the note thereto.

FAMILY ALLOWANCES ACT 1965, SS. 11 (1) (B), (2), (3)
 See 45 Halsbury's Statutes (2nd Edn.) 1198.

The Criminal Justice Act 1967

55. In sections 2 and 9 of the Criminal Justice Act 1967, after subsection (3)
of each section there shall be inserted the following subsection:—

 (3A) In the case of a statement which indicates in pursuance of subsection
 (3) (*a*) of this section that the person making it has not attained the age of fourteen, subsection (2) (*b*) of this section shall have effect as if for the words from
 "made" onwards there were substituted the words "understands the importance
 of telling the truth in it."

56. In section 3 (3) of the Criminal Justice Act 1967, for the words "19 or 20 of
the Magistrates' Courts Act 1952" there shall be substituted the words "or 19 of the
Magistrates' Courts Act 1952 or section 6 of the Children and Young Persons Act
1969".

COMMENCEMENT
 See s. 73 (2), *ante*, and the note thereto.

ATTAINED THE AGE OF
 See the note to s. 1, *ante*.

CRIMINAL JUSTICE ACT 1967, SS. 2, 3 (3)
 See 163 Statutes Supp.

MAGISTRATES' COURTS ACT 1952, S. 19
 See 32 Halsbury's Statutes (2nd Edn.) 438

The Social Work (Scotland) Act 1968

57. After section 44 (1) of the Social Work (Scotland) Act 1968, there shall be inserted the following subsection:—

(1A) A supervision requirement imposing a condition as to the place where a child is to reside in England or Wales shall be a like authority as in Scotland for the person in charge of the place to restrict the child's liberty to such an extent as that person may consider appropriate having regard to the terms of the supervision requirement.

58.—(1) In section 72 of the said Act of 1968, after subsection (1) there shall be inserted the following subsection:—

(1A) The juvenile court in England or Wales to which notification of a supervision requirement is sent under this section may make a supervision order in respect of the person to whom the notification relates but, notwithstanding anything in section 76 (1) of this Act, shall not include in the order a requirement authorised by section 12 of the Children and Young Persons Act 1969 unless that person is before the court when the supervision order is made; and in a relation to a supervision order made by virtue of this subsection—

(a) section 15 of that Act shall have effect as if subsection (2) were omitted; and

(b) section 17 of that Act shall have effect as if in paragraph (a) the references to three years and the date on which the order was originally made were respectively references to one year and the date on which the said notification was sent and as if in paragraph (b) the words from "the order was" to "and" were omitted.

(2) In subsection (2) of that section, after the word "court" there shall be inserted the words "in Northern Ireland".

(3) In subsection (4) of that section for the words from "includes" to "1963" there shall be substituted the words " in relation to England and Wales, has the same meaning as in the said Act of 1969".

59.—(1) In section 73 of the said Act of 1968, in subsection (1), after the word "reporter", in the second place where it occurs, there shall be inserted the following words:—

(i) in the case of a supervision order made by virtue of section 7A (4) of the Criminal Justice (Scotland) Act 1969, to notify the appropriate court and to transmit to that court all documents and certified copies of documents relating to the case which the reporter has received by virtue of section 76 of this Act;

(ii) in any other case.

and at the end of that subsection there shall be inserted the following paragraph:—

In this subsection "the appropriate court" means the sheriff having jurisdiction in the area in which the child proposes to reside or is residing or, where the original probation order was imposed by the High Court of Justiciary, that Court.

(2) After subsection (1) of that section there shall be inserted the following subsection:—

(1A) Where a court in England or Wales is satisfied that a child in respect of whom the court proposes to make a supervision order is residing or proposes to reside in Scotland, the court may make the order notwithstanding anything in subsection (1) of section 18 of the Children and Young Persons Act 1969 (which relates to residence of the supervised person in England or Wales); and where the court makes a supervision order by virtue of this subsection—

(*a*) the areas to be named in the order in pursuance of subsection (2) (*a*) of the said section 18 shall be those in which the court is sitting;

(*b*) the order may require the supervised person to comply with directions of the supervisor with respect to his departure to Scotland, and any such requirement shall, for the purposes of sections 15 and 16 of that Act (which relate to the variation and discharge of supervision orders), be deemed to be included in the order in pursuance of section 12 (2) of that Act; and

(*c*) the court shall send notification of the order as mentioned in paragraph (*b*) of the foregoing subsection and the provisions of that subsection relating to the duty of the reporter shall apply accordingly.

(3) In subsection (2) of that section for the word "subsection" there shall be substituted the words "provisions of this section".

60. In section 74 of the said Act of 1968, after subsection (5) there shall be inserted the following subsection:—

(6) An order under this section committing a child to the care of a local authority shall have effect as if it were a care order under the Children and Young Persons Act 1969, but as if sections 20 (2) and 21 (5) of that Act and in section 20 (3) of that Act paragraph (*a*) and the words 'in any other case' in paragraph (*b*) were omitted.

61.—(1) In section 75 of the said Act of 1968, in subsection (1) after the word "order" there shall be inserted the words "or an order under section 74 (3) of this Act relating to a training school".

(2) In subsection (2) of that section, for the words from "under", where it first occurs, to "1944" there shall be substituted the words "by a care order (other than an interim order) within the meaning of the Children and Young Persons Act 1969 or an order under section 74 (3) of this Act" and after the word "1947" there shall be inserted the words "or the said section 74 (3)".

(3) In subsection (3) of that section, after the words "training school order" there shall be inserted the words "or order under the said section 74 (3) relating to a training school".

(4) In subsection (4) of that section after the word "order" there shall be inserted the words "under the said section 74 (3) or".

62. In section 76 (4) of the said Act of 1968, after the word "order" there shall be inserted the words "or order under section 74 (3) of this Act relating to a training school".

63. In section 90 (1) of the said Act of 1968, the words "or to prescribe any matter," shall be omitted.

64. In section 94 (1) of the said Act of 1968—

(1) after the definition of "place of safety" there shall be inserted the words—
        "prescribed" means—
            (*a*) in section 3, prescribed by regulations,
            (*b*) in section 44, prescribed by rules, and

(c) in sections 62 (2), 66 (1) and (2), 94, paragraphs 2 (2) and (3), 4 (3) and (4) of Schedule 7, prescribed by order,

(2) in the definition of "supervision order" after the word "1963" there shall be inserted the words "and includes a supervision order within the meaning of the Children and Young Persons Act 1969".

65. In section 97 (1) of the said Act of 1968—

(1) after the words "that is to say—" there shall be inserted the words "section 44 (1) (except head (b)) and (1A)",

(2) after the words "Part V" there shall be inserted the words "section 98 (3)" and "Schedule 2, paragraphs 7 and 13".

66. In section 98 of the said Act of 1968, after subsection (2) there shall be inserted the following subsection:—

(3) An order under this section may make such transitional provisions as appear to the Secretary of State to be necessary or expedient in connection with the provisions thereby brought into force, including such adaptations of those provisions or of any provision of this Act then in force as appear to the Secretary of State necessary or expedient for the purposes or in consequence of the operation of any provision of this Act before the coming into force of any other provision of this Act or of the Children and Young Persons Act 1969.

67. In Schedule 2 to the said Act of 1968, in paragraph 10, to section 50 of the Children and Young Persons (Scotland) Act 1937 as substituted by that paragraph, there shall be added the following subsection:—

(2) The provisions of the foregoing subsection so far as they relate to section 54 of this Act shall extend to England and Wales.

68. In Schedule 2 to the said Act of 1968, in paragraph 19, after the word "'children'" there shall be inserted the words ", for the word 'offenders' there shall be substituted the word 'children', and for the word 'offender' in the three places where that word occurs there shall be substituted the word 'child'".

69. In Schedule 7 to the said Act of 1968, in paragraph 1 (1) (a), for the words "section 63" there shall be substituted the words "section 62".

70. In Schedule 8 to the said Act of 1968, in paragraph 7—

(a) for sub-paragraph (1) of that paragraph there shall be substituted the following sub-paragraph:—

(1) In section 87, for subsection (1), there shall be substituted the following subsection—

(1) Any person detained in a training school under the law in force in Northern Ireland may, with the consent of the Secretary of State, be transferred by order of the competent authority in Northern Ireland to such place in Scotland as the Secretary of State may direct for the purposes of undergoing residential training, and shall be subject to the provisions of this Act and of the Criminal Justice (Scotland) Act 1963 as if the order sending him to the school in Northern Ireland were an order for committal for residential training made under section 58A of this Act made upon the same date, and as if the order were an

authority for his detention for a period not exceeding the period for which he might be detained under the training school order made in respect of him;

(*b*) in sub-paragraph (2) of that paragraph at the end there shall be inserted the words "; and in section 87 (2) and (4) the words "England or", wherever they occur, shall be omitted";

(*c*) in sub-paragraph (3) of that paragraph the words "to such" shall be omitted;

(*d*) after sub-paragraph (3) of that paragraph there shall be inserted the following sub-paragraphs—

(4) In section 87 (5) the words "in relation to England, the Secretary of State, and," shall be omitted.

(5) In section 87 subsection (6) shall be omitted.

71. In Schedule 8 to the said Act of 1968, in paragraph 9 (2), for the word "for" there shall be substituted the word "of".

72. In Schedule 8 to the said Act of 1968, in paragraph 10, at the end there shall be inserted the following words—

"after the definition of "Street" there shall be inserted the following definition—

'Training school order' has the same meaning as in the Social Work (Scotland) Act 1968'".

73. In Schedule 8 to the said Act of 1968, in paragraph 17 (1), for the words "in Scotland" there shall be substituted the words ", within the meaning of the Social Work (Scotland) Act 1968".

74. In Schedule 8 to the said Act of 1968, in paragraph 38, for the words "In section 15 (4)" there shall be substituted the words—

"(1) In section 15 (3), for the words "the last mentioned order" there shall be substituted the words "or to the care of a local authority by a care order (other than an interim order) in force under the Children and Young Persons Act 1969, the fit person order or care order as the case may be".

(2) In subsection (4)".

75. In Schedule 8 to the said Act of 1968, in sub-paragraph (1) of paragraph 51, for the words from "include" where it secondly occurs to the end of the sub-paragraph there shall be substituted the words "include"; and paragraph (*e*) shall be omitted."

76. In Schedule 8 to the said Act of 1968, in paragraph 54, for the word "and" where that word first occurs there shall be substituted the word "or" and after the words ""by virtue of"" there shall be inserted the words "where those words secondly occur".

77. In Schedule 8 to the said Act of 1968, after paragraph 59, there shall be inserted the following paragraph:—

Criminal Justice Act 1961

59A. In section 32 (2), after paragraph (*g*), there shall be inserted the following paragraph—

(*h*) section 58A of the Children and Young Persons (Scotland) Act 1937.

78. In Schedule 8 to the said Act of 1968, for paragraph 74 (1), there shall be substituted the following sub-paragraph—

74.—(1) For section 11 (1) (*a*) there shall be substituted the following paragraph—

(*a*) during which his or her residence in a residential establishment is required by a supervision requirement made under section 44 of the Social Work (Scotland) Act 1968, and the child is not absent from the residential establishment under supervision;

in paragraph (*b*), for the words "the said Act of 1937", there shall be substituted the words "the Children and Young Persons (Scotland) Act 1937", after paragraph (*b*) there shall be inserted the following paragraph:—

(*bb*) during which the child is liable to undergo residential training under committal by virtue of section 58A of the said Act of 1937, and is not released under that section;

and for paragraph (*c*) there shall be substituted the following paragraph:—

(*c*) during which the child is accommodated by virtue of rules made by the Secretary of State under section 45 of the Social Work (Scotland) Act 1968".

79. In Part I of Schedule 9 to the said Act of 1968, in the entry relating to the Children and Young Persons (Scotland) Act 1937, in the third column, after the words "Sections 68 to 86" there shall be inserted the following words:—

"In section 87 (2) and (4) the words "England or" wherever they occur, in subsection (5) the words "in relation to England, the Secretary of State, and" and subsection (6)."

80. In Part I of Schedule 9 to the said Act of 1968, in the entry relating to the Children Act 1958, in the third column, for the words "Section 2 (6) and (7)" there shall be substituted the words—

In section 2, in subsection (4) the words from "or by virtue of" to "of an approved school", and subsections (6) and (7).

81. In Part I of Schedule 9 to the said Act of 1968, in the entry relating to section 15 (3) of the Adoption Act 1958, in the third column, for the words "'or the Children' to '1937'" there shall be substituted the following words "'fit person by' to 'care of a' and the words 'fit person order or' and 'as the case may be'".

82. In Part II of Schedule 9 to the said Act of 1968, in the entry relating to the Children Act 1958, in the third column, the entry relating to section 17 shall be omitted.

83. In Part II of Schedule 9 to the said Act of 1968, in the entry relating to the Family Allowances Act 1965, in the third column, for the words from "11," to "(2)," there shall be substituted the word "11 (2),".

COMMENCEMENT
See s. 73 (2), *ante*, and the note thereto.

SOCIAL WORK (SCOTLAND) ACT 1968, SS. 72 (1), (2), (4), 73 (1), (2), 74 (5), 75 (1), (2), (3), (4), 76 (4), 94 (1), 97 (1), 98 (2), SCH. 8, SCH. 9, PART II
See 17 Halsbury's Statutes (3rd Edn.) 757.

CRIMINAL JUSTICE (SCOTLAND) ACT 1949
13 & 14 Geo. 6 c. 94; not printed in this work.

CRIMINAL JUSTICE ACT 1961, S. 32 (2)
See 127 Statutes Supp.

CHILDREN AND YOUNG PERSONS (SCOTLAND) ACT 1937
1 Edw. 8 & Geo. 6 c. 37; not printed in this work.

CHILDREN ACT 1958, SS. 2 (6), (7), 17.
See 112 Statutes Supp.

ADOPTION ACT 1958, S. 15 (3)
See 115 Statutes Supp.

FAMILY ALLOWANCES ACT 1965
See 45 Halsbury's Statutes (2nd Edn.) 1191.

SCHEDULE 6

Section 72 (4)

REPEALS

Chapter	Short title	Extent of repeal
1894 c. 60	The Merchant Shipping Act 1894	In section 183 (3), the proviso.
1918 c. 57	The War Pensions (Administrative Provisions) Act 1918	Section 9 (4).
1920 c. 23	The War Pensions Act 1920	Section 9.
1933 c. 12	The Children and Young Persons Act 1933	In section 10 (2) the words from "and may" onwards. Sections 26 (6), 29 (3) and 32. In section 34 (2) the words "or taken to a place of safety". Section 35. In section 44, in subsection (1) the words from "being" to "as", and subsection (2). In section 48 (2) the words "a probationer or" and "any failure to comply with the requirements of the probation order or" and the words from "or to amend" onwards. Section 54. In section 55 the words "child or" wherever they occur, in subsection (1) the words "in any case and shall if the offender is a child," subsection (2), and in subsection (4) the words "or on forfeiture of any such security as aforesaid". In section 56 (1) the words "child or". Sections 57 and 58.

Chapter	Short title	Extent of repeal
1933 c. 12—*cont.*	The Children and Young Persons Act 1933—*cont.*	In section 59 (1) the words "children and" and "child or". Sections 62 to 85. In section 86, subsection (2), in subsection (3) the words "or ordered to be sent to an approved school" and the words from "and", in the first place where it occurs, to the end of the subsection, and subsection (4). Sections 89 (1), 90, 91 and 94. In section 102, paragraphs (*a*) and (*b*) of subsection (1), and in subsection (2) the words from "the rights" to "Act or". Sections 103 and 104. In section 106, subsections (3) to (5). In section 107 (1) the definitions of "approved school", "approved school order", "managers" and "special reception centre". Section 107 (2). Section 108 (2) and (3). Schedule 4.
1937 c. 37	The Children and Young Persons (Scotland) Act 1937	Sections 82, 86, 87 and 89. In Schedule 2, paragraph 13.
1938 c. 40	The Children and Young Persons Act 1938	The whole Act.
1944 c. 31	The Education Act 1944	Section 40A.
1948 c. 33	The Superannuation (Miscellaneous Provisions) Act 1948	Section 14.
1948 c. 40	The Education (Miscellaneous Provisions) Act 1948	In Schedule 1, the entries relating to section 40 of the Education Act 1944.
1948 c. 43	The Children Act 1948	Section 3 (3) to (5). In section 4 (3), the proviso. Sections 5, 6 (3) and (4), 7, 15 and 16. In section 23, in subsection (1), the words from "(which" to "aliment)" and subsection (3). Section 25. In section 26 (1), paragraph (*c*), and in paragraph (ii) the words "or (*c*)" and the words from "or", in the second place where it occurs, onwards.

Chapter	Short title	Extent of repeal
1948 c. 43—*cont.*	The Children Act 1948—*cont.*	Section 39 (1) (*e*). In section 49 (1), the words from "other than" onwards. Section 51 (2). Section 54 (1) and (2). In section 59, in subsection (1) the definition of "approved school order", and subsection (2). In Schedule 3, the entries relating to sections 70, 82, 84, 90 and 107 of the Act of 1933.
1948 c. 58	The Criminal Justice Act 1948	In section 3 (5), the words from "if the" to "age". In section 11 (1) the words from the beginning to "behaviour" in the first place where it occurs. In sections 46 (1) and 47 (1) the words "or a supervision order". Sections 48 (4), 49, 71, 72 and 75. In section 77, in subsection (1) the words "or in remand homes or approved schools", in subsection (4) (*c*) the words "in remand homes or" and "or in approved schools", and subsection (6). In section 80 (1), the definitions of "approved school", "remand home" and "supervision order" and in the definition of "sentence" the words from "an", in the second place where it occurs, to "school". In Schedule 9, the entries relating to sections 54, 58, 70, 77, 78, 82 and 90 of the Act of 1933, in the entry relating to section 48 (2) of the Act of 1933 the words "a probationer or" and "any failure to comply with the requirements of the probation order or" and the words from "or to amend" to the end of the entry, and the entry relating to the Children and Young Persons Act 1938.
1949 c. 101	The Justices of the Peace Act 1949	Section 14.

Chapter	Short title	Extent of repeal
1950 c. 37	The Maintenance Orders Act 1950	In Schedule 1, in the entry relating to section 86 of the Act of 1933, the words from "or as" onwards.
1952 c. 50	The Children and Young Persons (Amendment) Act 1952	Sections 2 to 5. In the Schedule, paragraphs 2, 3, 5, 8, 9 and 11 to 16.
1952 c. 52	The Prison Act 1952	In section 49 (2) the words "remand home or", where they first occur, and the words "remand home" wherever else they occur. In section 50, the words from "and subsection" onwards. In section 53 (1) the definition of "remand home".
1952 c. 55	The Magistrates' Courts Act 1952	Sections 20, 21 and 26 (2). Section 32. In section 38 (1), the words from "The provisions of this" onwards.
1953 c. 33	The Education (Miscellaneous Provisions) Act 1953	Section 11.
1956 c. 24	The Children and Young Persons Act 1956	The whole Act.
1956 c. 50	The Family Allowances and National Insurance Act 1956	Section 5.
1957 c. 55	The Affiliation Proceedings Act 1957	In section 5 (2) (*d*) the words from "or" onwards. In section 7 (5), the words "Sub-paragraph (ii) of".
1958 c. 55	The Local Government Act 1958	In Schedule 8, in paragraph 2, sub-paragraph (3), in sub-paragraph (4) the words "paragraph (*b*) of", and sub-paragraph (5).
1958 c. 65	The Children Act 1958	In section 2, in subsection (1) the words from "for reward" to "one month", in subsection (2) the words from "by" in the first place where it occurs to "or" where that word first subsequently occurs, in subsection (4) the words "the Children and Young Persons Act 1933 or of", and subsections (6) and (7). In section 3, in subsection (4), the words from "or is removed" to "maintaining him" and the words from "or removal" onwards, in subsection (5) the words "need not

Chapter	Short title	Extent of repeal
1958 c. 65—*cont.*	The Children Act 1958—*cont.*	give a notice under subsection (4) of this section but", and subsection (6). In section 17, in the definition of "fit person order" the words "the Children and Young Persons Act 1933 or". In Schedule 2 the entry relating to section 54 of the Children Act 1948.
1958 c. 5 (7 & 8 Eliz. 2)	The Adoption Act 1958	In section 15 (3) the words from "fit person by" to "care of a" and the words "fit person order or" and "as the case may be". In section 37, in subsection (1) the words "but is not a foster child within the meaning of Part I of the Children Act 1958", in subsection (2) the words from "by reason" to "subsection nor", and in subsection (3) the words "in an approved school or".
1959 c. 72	The Mental Health Act 1959	In section 60 (6) the words from "including" onwards. Section 61. Section 70 (2). In section 72 (6) (*a*) the words from "or made" to "Act 1933" and from "or an order" onwards. In section 75 (1), the words "(other than a person detained in a remand home)" and in paragraph (*b*) the words from "or as" to "have been remitted", and in section 75 (2) the words from "including" to "1963". Section 79. In section 80 (1), the definitions of "approved school" and "remand home".
1961 c. 39	The Criminal Justice Act 1961	In section 1, subsection (1) and the proviso to subsection (2). In section 4, in subsection (1) the words "but not less than fourteen", and in subsection (2) (*a*) the words from "the offender" to "and". In section 5 (2), paragraph (*a*) and the words following paragraph (*b*), and section 5 (3).

Chapter	Short title	Extent of repeal
1961 c. 39—*cont.*	The Criminal Justice Act 1961 —*cont.*	In section 6, subsections (1) and (2), and in subsection (3) the words from "or ordering" to "home" in paragraph (*a*), the words from "or" to "home" in paragraph (*b*), and the words "or remand home" and "a prison is so named and". In section 7, subsection (2), and in subsection (3) the words from "and where" onwards. Section 8 (1) and (2). In section 9, paragraph (*a*). In section 10 (2) (*a*), the words from "except" to "excessive". Sections 14 to 19, 22 (4) and 25. In section 29 (1), the words "remand home" and "special reception centre or other" and in section 29 (3) the words from "special" to "1933 and". Schedule 2. In Schedule 4 the entries relating to sections 54, 72, 78, 82, 83 and 88 of the Act of 1933 and to Schedule 4 to that Act and the entries relating to the Children and Young Persons Act 1938, section 72 and the change in the definition of "sentence" in section 80 (1) of the Criminal Justice Act 1948, sections 20 and 32 of the Magistrates' Courts Act 1952, and section 79 of the Mental Health Act 1959.
1963 c. 33	The London Government Act 1963	In section 47, in subsection (1) the words "and in the definition of 'remand home' in any enactment", and in subsection (3) the reference in paragraph (*c*) to section 49 of the Criminal Justice Act 1948. In Schedule 17, paragraph 18 (*c*).
1963 c. 37	The Children and Young Persons Act 1963	Sections 1 (4), 2 and 4 to 15. Section 22. In section 23, in subsection (1), paragraph (*a*) and the word "authority", subsection (2), in subsection (3) the words "or subsection (2)" in both places and the words "takes

Chapter	Short title	Extent of repeal
1963 c. 37—*cont.*	The Children and Young Persons Act 1963—*cont.*	refuge there or", and subsections (6) to (8). Section 24. In section 25 (1) the words "or taken to a place of safety", and section 25 (2). In section 29, in subsection (1) the words "continue to" and subsection (2). Section 33. Section 53 (1) and (2). In section 55 the words from "section 84 (5)" to "principal Act", the word "or" immediately preceding the words "section 17" and the words from "(which relate" onwards. Sections 59 and 61. In section 65 (5), the words "subsections (1) and (2) of section 10 and", "and 53 (1)" and "27" and "34". Schedule 1. In Schedule 3, paragraphs 10, 15 to 23, 25 to 27, 33, 34, 35, 36, 44, 46, 48 and 49, and in paragraph 50 the words "special reception centre or other", and "'special reception centre' has the same meaning as in the Children and Young Persons Act 1933 and".
1963 c. 39	The Criminal Justice (Scotland) Act 1963	In Schedule 5, the entry relating to the Children Act 1948.
1965 c. 53	The Family Allowances Act 1965	In section 11 (1), sub-paragraph (i) of paragraph (*a*) and in paragraph (*c*) the words from "made" to "order".
1967 c. 80	The Criminal Justice Act 1967	In section 55, the words "or any provision of the Children and Young Persons Act 1933" and the words from "and accordingly" onwards. In section 77 (1), the words "on his means". In Part I of Schedule 3, the entries relating to sections 72 (5) and 82 (5) of the Act of 1933 and section 14 of the Act of 1963.

Chapter	Short title	Extent of repeal
1968 c. 49	The Social Work (Scotland) Act 1968	In section 72 (2), the words "of the Children and Young Persons Acts 1933 to 1963 or, as the case may be", the word "respectively" and the words "to a supervision order within the meaning of section 5 of the Children and Young Persons Act 1963 or". In section 73 (2), the word "juvenile". In section 74, in subsection (3) the words "in England or Wales or" and "if he thinks fit" and the words from "an approved" to "be" where it first occurs, in subsection (4) the words from "the Children" to "be of", the words "an approved school or" in the first, second and third places where they occur, the word "of" and "in" following those words in the first and third of those places respectively and the words "section 71 of the said Act of 1933 or" and "section 90 of the said Act of 1933 or under", and in subsection (5) the words "of the Acts of 1933 to 1963 or, as the case may be", the words "of a local authority or, as the case may be" and the words "those Acts or". In section 75, in subsection (1) the words "the Secretary of State or" and "approved school or", and in subsection (3) the words "approved school or". In section 76, in subsections (1) and (2) the word "juvenile" wherever it occurs, and in subsection (4) the words "approved school or" and "of the approved school or". Section 77 (1) (*b*). In section 90 (1) the words "or to prescribe any matter". In Schedule 2, in paragraph 10 the words from "and" to "1933". In Schedule 8, paragraphs 2 to 5, 18, 21 and 35.

GENERAL NOTE
By virtue of Sch. 4, para. 18, *ante*, nothing in any provision of this Schedule affects any order which, immediately before the coming into force of this Schedule, is in force by virtue of any enactment repealed by that provision.

COMMENCEMENT
See s. 73 (2), *ante*, and the note thereto.

SCHEDULE 7

Section 72 (5)

SECTIONS 1 TO 6 AND 14 OF THE CHILDREN ACT 1958 AS AMENDED

1. Duty of local authorities to ensure well-being of foster children

It shall be the duty of every local authority to satisfy themselves as to the well-being of children within their area who are foster children within the meaning of this Part of this Act and, for that purpose, to secure that, so far as appears to the authority to be appropriate, the children are visited from time to time by officers of the authority and that such advice is given as to the care and maintenance of the children as appears to be needed.

2. Meaning of "foster child"

(1) In this Part of this Act "foster child" means, subject to the following provisions of this section, a child below the upper limit of the compulsory school age whose care and maintenance are undertaken by a person who is not a relative or guardian of his.

(2) A child is not a foster child within the meaning of this Part of this Act while he is in the care of a local authority or a voluntary organisation or is boarded out by a local health authority or a local education authority (or, in Scotland, an education authority).

(3) A child is not a foster child within the meaning of this Part of this Act while he is in the care of any person—

    (*a*) in premises in which any parent, adult relative or guardian of his is for the time being residing;

    (*b*) in any voluntary home within the meaning of Part V of the Children and Young Persons Act 1933, or in any residential establishment within the meaning of the Social Work (Scotland) Act 1968;

    (*c*) in any school within the meaning of the Education Acts 1944 to 1953, or the Education (Scotland) Acts 1939 to 1956 in which he is receiving full-time education;

    (*d*) in any hospital or in any nursing home registered or exempted from registration under Part VI of the Public Health Act 1936, Part XI of the Public Health (London) Act 1936, or the Nursing Homes Registration (Scotland) Act 1938; or

    (*e*) in any home or institution not specified in this section but maintained by a public or local authority.

(3A) A child is not a foster child within the meaning of this Part of this Act at any time while his care and maintenance are undertaken by a person, other than a relative or guardian of his, if at that time—

(*a*) that person does not intend to, and does not in fact, undertake his care and maintenance for a continuous period of more than six days; or

(*b*) that person is not a regular foster parent and does not intend to, and does not in fact, undertake his care and maintenance for a continuous period of more than twenty-seven days;

and for the purposes of this subsection a person is a regular foster parent if, during the period of twelve months immediately preceding the date on which he begins to undertake the care and maintenance of the child in question, he had, otherwise than as a relative or guardian, the care and maintenance of one or more children either for a period of, or periods amounting in the aggregate to, not less than three months or for at least three continuous periods each of which was of more than six days.

(4) A child is not a foster child within the meaning of this Part of this Act while he is in the care of any person in compliance with a supervision order within the meaning of the Children and Young Persons Act 1969 or a probation order or supervision requirement or by virtue of a fit person order or while he is in an approved school or is deemed for the purposes of the Children and Young Persons (Scotland) Act 1937, to be under the care of the managers of an approved school or while he is liable to be detained or subject to guardianship under the Mental Health Act 1959, or the Mental Health (Scotland) Act 1960, or is resident in a residential home for mentally disordered persons within the meaning of Part III of the Mental Health Act 1959, or in a residential home for persons suffering from mental disorder within the meaning of Part III of the Mental Health (Scotland) Act 1960.

(4A) A child is not a foster child for the purposes of this Part of this Act while he is placed in the care and possession of a person who proposes to adopt him under arrangements made by such a local authority or registered adoption society as is referred to in Part II of the Adoption Act 1958 or while he is a protected child within the meaning of Part IV of that Act.

3. Duty of persons maintaining foster children to notify local authority

(1) Subject to the following provisions of this section, a person who proposes to maintain as a foster child a child not already in his care shall give written notice thereof to the local authority not less than two weeks and not more than four weeks before he receives the child, unless he receives him in an emergency; and a person who maintains a foster child whom he received in an emergency or who became a foster child while in his care shall give written notice thereof to the local authority not later than forty-eight hours after he receives the child or, as the case may be, after the child becomes a foster child.

(2) Every such notice shall specify the date on which it is intended that the child should be received or, as the case may be, on which the child was in fact received or became a foster child and the premises in which the child is to be or is being kept and shall be given to the local authority for the area in which those premises are situated.

(2A) A person shall not be required to give notice under subsection (1) of this section in relation to a child if—

(*a*) he has on a previous occasion given notice under that subsection in respect of that or any other child, specifying the premises at which he proposes to keep the child in question; and (*b*) he has not, at any time since that notice was given, ceased to maintain at least one foster child at those premises and been required by virtue of the following provisions of this section to give notice under subsection (5A) of this section in respect of those premises.

(3) Where a person who is maintaining one or more foster children changes his permanent address or the premises in which the child is, or the children are, kept he shall, not less than two weeks and not more than four weeks before the change or, if the change is made in an emergency, not later than forty-eight hours after the change, give written notice to the said local authority, specifying the new address or premises, and if the new premises are in the area of another local authority, the authority to whom the notice is given shall inform that other local authority and give them such of the particulars mentioned in subsection (7) of this section as are known to them.

(4) If a foster child dies the person who was maintaining him shall, within forty-eight hours thereof, give to the local authority and to the person from whom the child was received notice in writing of the death.

(5) Where a foster child is removed or removes himself from the care of the person maintaining him, that person shall at the request of the local authority give them the name and address, if known, of the person (if any) into whose care the child has been removed.

(5A) Subject to the provisions of the following subsection, where a person who has been maintaining one or more foster children at any premises ceases to maintain foster children at those premises and the circumstances are such that no notice is required to be given under subsection (3) or subsection (4) of this section, that person shall, within forty-eight hours after he ceases to maintain any foster child at those premises, give notice in writing thereof to the local authority.

(5B) A person need not give the notice required by the preceding subsection in consequence of his ceasing to maintain foster children at any premises if, at the time he so ceases, he intends within twenty-seven days again to maintain any of them as a foster child at those premises; but if he subsequently abandons that intention or the said period expires without his having given effect to it he shall give the said notice within forty-eight hours of that event.

(7) A person maintaining or proposing to maintain a foster child shall at the request of the local authority give them the following particulars, so far as known to him, that is to say, the name, sex, and date and place of birth of the child, and the name and address of every person who is a parent or guardian or acts as a guardian of the child or from whom the child has been or is to be received.

4. Power to inspect premises, impose conditions, or prohibit the keeping of foster children

(1) Any officer of a local authority authorised to visit foster children may, after producing, if asked to do so, some duly authenticated document showing that he is so authorised, inspect any premises in the area of the authority in the whole or any part of which foster children are to be or are being kept.

(1A) If it is shown to the satisfaction of a justice of the peace on sworn information in writing—

(*a*) that there is reasonable cause to believe that a foster child is being kept in any premises, or in any part thereof; and (*b*) that admission to those premises or that part thereof has been refused to a duly authorised officer of the local authority or that such a refusal is apprehended or that the occupier is temporarily absent,

the justice may by warrant under his hand authorise an officer of the local authority to enter the premises if need be by force, at any reasonable time within forty-eight hours of the issue of the warrant, for the purpose of inspecting the premises.

(2) Where a person is keeping or proposes to keep foster children in premises used (while foster children are kept therein) wholly or partly for that purpose, the local authority may impose on him requirements, to be complied with, after such time as the authority may specify, whenever a foster child is kept in the premises, as to—

(*a*) the number, age and sex of the foster children who may be kept at any one time in the premises or any part thereof;
(*b*) the accommodation and equipment to be provided for the children;
(*c*) the medical arrangements to be made for protecting the health of the children;
(*d*) the giving of particulars of the person for the time being in charge of the children;
(*e*) the number, qualifications or experience of the persons employed in looking after the children;
(*f*) the keeping of records;
(*g*) the fire precautions to be taken in the premises;
(*h*) the giving of particulars of any foster child received in the premises and of any change in the number or identity of the foster children kept therein;

but any such requirement may be limited to a particular class of foster children kept in the premises and any requirement imposed under paragraphs (*b*) to (*h*) of this subsection may be limited by the authority so as to apply only when the number of foster children kept in the premises exceeds a specified number.

(3) Where a person proposes to keep a foster child in any premises and the local authority are of the opinion that—

(*a*) the premises are not suitable premises in which to keep foster children; or
(*b*) that person is not a suitable person to have the care and maintenance of foster children; or
(*c*) it would be detrimental to that child to be kept by that person in those premises;

the local authority may impose a prohibition on that person under subsection (3A) of this section.

(3A) A prohibition imposed on any person under this subsection may—

(*a*) prohibit him from keeping any foster child in premises specified in the prohibition; or
(*b*) prohibit him from keeping any foster child in any premises in the area of the local authority; or
(*c*) prohibit him from keeping a particular child specified in the prohibition in premises so specified.

(3B) Where a local authority have imposed a prohibition on any person under subsection (3A) of this section, the local authority may, if they think fit, cancel the prohibition, either of their own motion or on an application made by that person on the ground of a change in the circumstances in which a foster child would be kept by him.

(4) Where a local authority impose a requirement on any person under subsection (2) of this section as respects any premises, they may prohibit him from keeping foster children in the premises after the time specified for compliance with the requirement unless the requirement is complied with.

(5) Any requirement or prohibition imposed under this section shall be imposed by notice in writing addressed to the person on whom it is imposed.

5. Appeal to juvenile court against requirement or prohibition imposed under section four

(1) Any person aggrieved by any requirement or prohibition imposed under section four of this Act may, within fourteen days from the date on which he is notified of the requirement or prohibition, or, in the case of a prohibition imposed under subsection (3A) of that section, within fourteen days from the refusal by the local authority to accede to an application by him for the cancellation of the prohibition, appeal to a juvenile court, and where the appeal is against such a requirement the requirement shall not have effect while the appeal is pending.

(2) Where the court allows such an appeal it may, instead of cancelling the requirement or prohibition, vary the requirement or allow more time for compliance with it or, where an absolute prohibition has been imposed, substitute for it a prohibition to use the premises after such time as the court may specify unless such specified requirements as the local authority had power to impose under section four of this Act are complied with.

(3) Any notice by which a requirement or prohibition is imposed on any person under section four of this Act shall contain a statement informing him of his right to appeal against the requirement or prohibition and of the time within which he may do so.

(4) Any requirement or prohibition specified or substituted under this section by the court shall be deemed for the purposes of this Part of this Act other than this section to have been imposed by the local authority under section four of this Act.

(5) In the application of this section to Scotland, for references to a juvenile court there shall be substituted references to the sheriff.

6. Disqualification for keeping foster children

(1) A person shall not maintain a foster child if—

    (a) an order has been made against him under this Part of this Act removing a child from his care;

    (b) an order has been made under the Children and Young Persons Act 1933, the Children and Young Persons Act 1969, or the Children and Young Persons (Scotland) Act 1937, or a supervision requirement has been made under the Social Work (Scotland) Act 1968 and by virtue of the order or requirement a child was removed from his care;

    (c) he has been convicted of any offence specified in the First Schedule to the said Act of 1933 or the First Schedule to the said Act of 1937 or has been placed on probation or discharged absolutely or conditionally for any such offence;

    (d) his rights and powers with respect to a child have been vested in a local authority under section two of the Children Act 1948 or under section 16 of the Social Work (Scotland) Act 1968;

    (e) a local health authority or in Scotland a local authority have made an order under subsection (3) or (4) of section one of the Nurseries and Child-

Minders Regulation Act 1948 refusing, or an order under section five of that Act cancelling, the registration of any premises occupied by him or his registration;

(*f*) an order has been made under section 43 of the Adoption Act 1958 for the removal of a protected child who was being kept or was about to be received by him,

unless he has disclosed that fact to the local authority and obtained their consent.

(2) Where this section applies to any person, otherwise than by virtue of this subsection, it shall apply also to any other person who lives in the same premises as he does or who lives in premises at which he is employed.

14. Offences

(1) A person shall be guilty of an offence if—

(*a*) being required, under any provision of this Part of this Act, to give any notice or information, he fails to give the notice within the time specified in that provision or fails to give the information within a reasonable time, or knowingly makes or causes or procures another person to make any false or misleading statement in the notice or information;

(*b*) he refuses to allow the visiting of any foster child by a duly authorised officer of a local authority or the inspection, under the power conferred by subsection (1) of section four of this Act, of any premises or wilfully obstructs a person entitled to enter any premises by virtue of a warrant under subsection (1A) of that section;

(*c*) he fails to comply with any requirement imposed by a local authority under this Part of this Act or keeps any foster child in any premises in contravention of a prohibition so imposed;

(*d*) he maintains a foster child in contravention of section six of this Act; or

(*e*) he refuses to comply with an order under this Part of this Act for the removal of any child or obstructs any person in the execution of such an order.

(1A) Where section 6 of this Act applies to any person by virtue only of subsection (2) of that section, he shall not be guilty of an offence under paragraph (*d*) of subsection (1) of this section if he proves that he did not know, and had no reasonable ground for believing, that a person living or employed in the premises in which he lives was a person to whom that section applies.

(2) A person guilty of an offence under this section shall be liable on summary conviction to imprisonment for a term not exceeding six months or a fine not exceeding one hundred pounds or both.

(2A) If any person who is required, under any provision of this Part of this Act, to give a notice fails to give the notice within the time specified in that provision, then, notwithstanding anything in section 104 of the Magistrates' Courts Act 1952 (time limit for proceedings) proceedings for the offence may be brought at any time within six months from the date when evidence of the offence came to the knowledge of the local authority.

(3) In England and Wales, a local authority may institute proceedings for an offence under this section.

COMMENCEMENT
See s. 73 (2), *ante*, and the note thereto.

THE TATTOOING OF MINORS ACT 1969

(1969 c. 24)

PRELIMINARY NOTE

This Act came into force on 16th June 1969, and extends to England, Wales and Scotland, but not to Northern Ireland (see s. 4, *post*).

An Act to prohibit the tattooing of persons under the age of eighteen years

[16th May 1969]

1. Prohibition of tattooing of minors

It shall be an offence to tattoo a person under the age of eighteen except when the tattoo is performed for medical reasons by a duly qualified medical practitioner or by a person working under his direction, but it shall be a defence for a person charged to show that at the time the tattoo was performed he had reasonable cause to believe that the person tattooed was of or over the age of eighteen and did in fact so believe.

IT SHALL BE AN OFFENCE
 This categorically puts the act of tattooing a minor within the scope of the criminal law. As the law originally stood, some restriction was certainly possible in that a tattooist might have been convicted of assault were he to tattoo a young person, even after having obtained his consent. It had, however, to be shown that the subject was unable to appreciate the nature of the act to which he had consented. The difficulties attendant upon this application of the law were clearly brought out by *Burrell* v. *Harmer* (1966), unreported; but see 1967 Crim. L.R. 169, and *New Law Journal*, 15th December 1966. As to the penalties for the commission of this offence, see s. 2, *post*.

TO TATTOO
 This is defined in s. 3, *post*. Note that it is the act of tattooing which is the essence of the offence and not the presence of the tattoo itself—see the note "At the time the tattoo was performed", *post*.

A PERSON
 This includes both male and female; see the Interpretation Act 1889, s. 1.

AGE OF EIGHTEEN
 For the legal significance of this expression, see the Family Law Reform Act 1969, s. 1 (1), *ante*. During the passage of the present Act, its sponsor stated that he had purposely chosen the age of 18 because of the Latey Report's recommendation to adopt 18

as the age of majority. To suggestions that it should be made an offence on the part of a young person to represent himself as being over 18, it was pointed out that it was not in line with current social and penal thinking to enact new criminal offences for youngsters to commit. If tattooists had reasonable cause to suppose that a client was over 18, the provisions of this Act left them clear. It was recommended by the legislature that if a tattooist was in any doubt whatsoever about a person's age he would be well-advised not to operate.

EXCEPT WHEN THE TATTOO IS PERFORMED FOR MEDICAL REASONS
During the Parliamentary debates it was explained that a surgeon might wish to indicate by a small tattoo mark that, for example, although an operation leaving a scar has been performed, the patient's appendix, for example, has not been removed.
It is submitted that putting a small tattoo on a child to hide a birth-mark would fall within the exception. Otherwise it is not certain whether the same would go for putting an identification mark upon a little child, should there be fears of his being separated from his parents during hostilities or following a catastrophe.
For consent to medical treatment, see the Family Law Reform Act 1969, s. 8, *ante.*

DULY QUALIFIED MEDICAL PRACTITIONER
For the meaning of this expression, see the Medical Act 1956, s. 52 (1) (36 Halsbury's Statutes (2nd Edn.) 567). During the committee stage it was pointed out that without the word "duly", a doctor who had been struck off the register might perform or direct the performance of tattoos: this could lead to surreptitious dealings from which undesirable consequences would most certainly flow.

OR BY A PERSON WORKING UNDER HIS DIRECTION
Very few medical practitioners would regard themselves as competent to affix a tattoo, however desirable they thought its application might be for the well-being of a patient. It is anticipated that regular tattooists—possibly only those affiliated to the British Guild of Tattooing—will be invited to undertake much of the work as being better qualified in this respect than the average doctor.

TO SHOW
The burden of proof on the accused is, in such cases as this, considerably less than that lying upon the prosecution: the standard of proof which should be accepted is not necessarily that which puts the matter "beyond any reasonable doubt" but that which, "upon a balance of probabilities" raises sufficient doubt of which the party ought to be given the benefit; see *R. v. Carr-Briant*, [1943] 2 All E.R. 156 and *R. v. Dunbar*, [1957] 2 All E.R. 737.

AT THE TIME THE TATTOO WAS PERFORMED
This expression would have significance, when, for example, a practising tattooist is at first induced to begin work on a young person who has succeeded in making him believe that he is over eighteen, and then, discovering the real age of his client, has refused to continue the process. *Cf. R. v. Packer* (1886), 16 Cox C.C. 57.

HAD REASONABLE CAUSE TO BELIEVE
Whether or not the accused did actually believe what he says he believed is for the court to decide. Matters adduced in evidence, *e.g.*, reasonable precautions; absence of grounds for suspicion; nature of information asked for and given regarding age so as to prevail upon the accused to perform the tattoo; proof that the accused did in fact direct his mind to the point (see *R. v. Harrison*, [1938] 3 All E.R. 134) are matters of fact and a court must clearly indicate to what extent such facts have influenced its decision: see *Coppen v. Moore*, [1895–99] All E.R. Rep. 926 (presentation of facts on case stated).

THAT THE PERSON TATTOOED
It is submitted that the word "tattooed" must be taken to refer to the act and not the result of the process. Otherwise some attempts may be made to evade the prohibition by deliberately postponing, until the client was of full age, the inclusion of some insignificant detail of a tattooed design. It might then be sought to show that since the adornment was not complete, the person was not, in a professional sense at least "tattooed".
See also the note to the words "At the time the tattoo was performed," above.

WAS OF OR OVER THE AGE OF EIGHTEEN
>The time at which a person attains a particular age expressed in years is the commencement of the relevant anniversary of the date of his birth; see Family Law Reform Act 1969, s. 9 (1), *ante.*
>
>Since this offence may be taken to involve "bodily injury to a child or young person", the special provisions as to age, contained in the Children and Young Persons Act 1933, s. 99 (2) are applicable (12 Halsbury's Statutes (2nd Edn.) 1046).

AND DID IN FACT SO BELIEVE
>This is the statutory acknowledgement of what had long been an established interpretation of the words "having reasonable cause to believe . . ." so frequently appearing in previous enactments: see *R.* v. *Banks*, [1916–17] All E.R. Rep. 356, and *R.* v. *Harrison*, [1938] 3 All E.R. 134.

2. Penalties

Any person committing such an offence shall be liable on summary conviction to a fine not exceeding fifty pounds, or, in the case of a second or subsequent conviction, to a fine not exceeding one hundred pounds.

SUMMARY CONVICTION
>Summary jurisdiction and procedure in England and Wales are now mainly governed by the Magistrates' Courts Act 1952 (125 Statutes Supp.) and the Magistrates' Courts Act 1957 (104 Statutes Supp.), and provisions in the Criminal Justice Act 1967 (163 Statutes Supp.).

SECOND OR SUBSEQUENT CONVICTION
>A second or subsequent conviction is a conviction of an offence committed after the first conviction; see *R.* v. *South Shields Licensing Justices*, [1911] 2 K.B. 1.

FINE NOT EXCEEDING £50; £100
>During its passage through Parliament it was objected that the Act compared poorly with the penalties under corresponding child legislation and the Act ought to prescribe for more severe sanctions. Young people, it was suggested, out of sheer bravado, might seek out an unscrupulous tattooist and be operated upon surreptitiously—the tattooist being prepared to meet the occasional fine of up to £100, which, it was alleged, he could easily recoup from inflated fees. To this, however, it was pointed out that where the authorities managed to track down such a tattooist, it would not, as a rule, be on account of one transaction: it would invariably be found that he had worked upon one person who could be questioned as to who it was who had first introduced him to the artist and this would probably ensue in a chain of tattooees being brought in. So it was quite possible that an offender would face a multiplicity of charges, and if he were to be fined for each, the aggregate might prove to be a considerable sum.
>
>As to time for payment and payment by instalments, see Magistrates' Courts Act 1952, s. 63 (32 Halsbury's Statutes (2nd Edn.) 470.)

3. Definition

For the purposes of this Act "tattoo" shall mean the insertion into the skin of any colouring material designed to leave a permanent mark.

DEFINITION OF "TATTOO"
>This definition, the adequacy of which remains to be tested, corresponds more or less with those appearing in standard dictionaries: "an indelible mark or figure fixed upon the surface of the body by the insertion of pigments under the skin" (Webster); "to mark permanently (as the skin) with figures by pricking-in colouring-matter" (Chambers); "to make permanent marks or designs upon the skin by puncturing it and inserting a pigment or pigments" (Oxford). While the statutory definition obviously contemplates the process followed by a regular tattooist, it is sufficiently wide to catch

the crude methods employed by youngsters who succeed in marking themselves, first with a pointed instrument (often a mapping-pen nib or a needle), and afterwards rubbing into the wound some colouring-matter, such as indian ink or, sometimes, gun-powder.

4. Short title, commencement and extent

(1) This Act may be cited as the Tattooing of Minors Act 1969.

(2) This Act shall come into force at the expiration of one month beginning with the date it is passed.

(3) This Act shall not extend to Northern Ireland.

ONE MONTH BEGINNING WITH, ETC.

In calculating the period of one month, the day on which the Act was passed is to be included; see *Trow* v. *Ind Coope (West Midlands), Ltd.*, [1967] 2 All E.R. 900; [1967] 2 Q.B. 899, at p. 909, C.A., applying *Hare* v. *Gocher*, [1962] 2 All E.R. 763, and distinguishing *Goldsmiths' Co.* v. *West Metropolitan Rail. Co.*, [1904] 1 K.B. 1; [1900–3] All E.R. Rep. 667, C.A. "Month" means a calendar month; see the Interpretation Act 1889, s. 3 (24 Halsbury's Statutes (2nd Edn.) 207). The Act was passed (*i.e.*, received the Royal Assent) on 16th May 1969, and accordingly came into force on 16th June 1969.

MINORS

The use of this expression, in preference to "infants" follows upon the recommendation contained in the Report of the Committee on the Age of Majority (Cmnd. 3342: 1967; para. 133). Cf. also the provisions of the Family Law Reform Act 1969, s. 12.

SUB-S. (3)

It was explained that although the social problems which had inspired this enactment were not as acute in Scotland as in England, the Scottish Office recognised the value of its provisions and did not object to its application in that country. In the case of Northern Ireland, however, the matter lies exclusively within the legislative powers of the Northern Ireland Parliament.

THE CHILDREN AND YOUNG PERSONS (PLANNING AREAS) ORDER 1970

S.I. 1970 No. 335

Made	*2nd March* 1970
Laid before Parliament	*11th March* 1970
Came into operation	*1st April* 1970

Citation and operation

1. This Order may be cited as the Children and Young Persons (Planning Areas) Order 1970 and shall come into operation on 1st April 1970.

Interpretation

2.—(1) In this Order the expression "the Act" means the Children and Young Persons Act 1969.

(2) The Interpretation Act 1889 shall apply to the interpretation of this Order as it applies to the interpretation of an Act of Parliament.

Planning areas

3. For the purposes of Part II of the Act there shall be the twelve planning areas designated in column 1 of the Schedule to this Order comprising, respectively, the local authority areas specified opposite thereto in column 2 of that Schedule.

Period for the establishment of children's regional planning committees

4. The period first mentioned in section 35 (3) of the Act (which provides that it shall be the duty of the local authorities whose areas are included in a planning area to establish a children's regional planning committee for that area within such period as may be provided by the order specifying the planning area or such longer period as the Secretary of State may allow) shall be the period ending on 30th June 1970.

Article 3   SCHEDULE

                          PLANNING AREAS

Planning Area	Areas comprised in planning area
Area No. 1	The counties of Cumberland, Durham, Northumberland and Westmorland and the county boroughs of Carlisle, Darlington, Gateshead, Hartlepool, Newcastle upon Tyne, South Shields, Sunderland, Teesside and Tynemouth.
Area No. 2	The counties of the East Riding, the North Riding and the West Riding of Yorkshire and the county boroughs of Barnsley, Bradford, Dewsbury, Doncaster, Halifax, Huddersfield, Kingston upon Hull, Leeds, Rotherham, Sheffield, Wakefield and York.
Area No. 3	The counties of Chester and Lancaster and the county boroughs of Barrow-in-Furness, Birkenhead, Blackburn, Blackpool, Bolton, Bootle, Burnley, Bury, Chester, Liverpool, Manchester, Oldham, Preston, Rochdale, St. Helens, Salford, Southport, Stockport, Wallasey, Warrington and Wigan.
Area No. 4	The counties of Herefordshire, Salop, Staffordshire, Warwickshire and Worcestershire and the county boroughs of Birmingham, Burton upon Trent, Coventry, Dudley, Solihull, Stoke-on-Trent, Walsall, Warley, West Bromwich, Wolverhampton and Worcester.
Area No. 5	The counties of Derbyshire, Leicester, Lincoln—Parts of Holland, Lincoln—Parts of Kesteven, Lincoln—Parts of Lindsey, Northamptonshire, Nottinghamshire and Rutland and the county boroughs of Derby, Grimsby, Leicester, Lincoln, Northampton and Nottingham.
Area No. 6	The counties of Cambridgeshire and Isle of Ely, Essex, Huntingdon and Peterborough, Norfolk, East Suffolk and West Suffolk and the county boroughs of Great Yarmouth, Ipswich, Norwich and Southend-on-Sea.
Area No. 7	The counties of Bedford, Berkshire, Buckingham, Hertfordshire and Oxford and the county boroughs of Luton, Oxford and Reading.
Area No. 8	The City of London and all the London boroughs.
Area No. 9	The counties of Kent, Surrey, East Sussex and West Sussex and the county boroughs of Brighton, Canterbury, Eastbourne and Hastings.
Area No. 10	The counties of Dorset, Hampshire, Isle of Wight and Wiltshire and the county boroughs of Bournemouth, Portsmouth and Southampton.
Area No. 11	The counties of Cornwall, Devon, Gloucestershire and Somerset and the county boroughs of Bath, Bristol, Exeter, Gloucester, Plymouth and Torbay.
Area No. 12	All the counties and county boroughs in Wales, the county of Monmouthshire and the county borough of Newport.

EXPLANATORY NOTE

(This Note is not part of the Order.)

This Order constitutes twelve planning areas for the purpose of Part II of the *Children and Young Persons Act* 1969 and specifies the period ending on 30th June 1970 as that within which children's regional planning committees are to be established under section 35 (3) of the Act.

APPENDIX I

AGE OF MAJORITY: THE HISTORICAL BACKGROUND
(*Family Law Reform Act 1969, Part I*)

During the Parliamentary debates on the Family Law Reform Bill there were frequent references to the fact that the choice of 21 as the age of majority was based upon historical factors which had no relevance today. The Committee on the Age of Majority (Cmnd. 3342: 1967) went to some trouble to delve into the matter and included the following passages in its Report.

"Roman historians state that the barbarians reckoned their young were old enough to carry arms and be counted as grown up at 15. And 15 became the general age of majority in Britain and Northern Europe during the 9th, 10th and 11th centuries, though not specifically linked with fighting ability. But by the time of the Norman Conquest there was a change of emphasis. The role of the mounted knight became more and more important, the armour heavier and heavier and the horses more enormous as time went on. By the time of Magna Carta the age for those holding in knight service had been raised to 21, and there is strong authority for the view that this was directly linked with the ability to hold up a heavy suit of armour and lift a lance or sword at the same time. For example, St. Palaye (*Memories sur l'Ancienne Chevalerie*, 1759) says 'the profession of arms demanded an ability and strength not to be acquired until the age of 21. This also became the age for judicial combat and the acceptance of a duel.' It seems that originally the actual age was fixed at 20 but another year was allowed for a ward to claim his inheritance and his lord to hand it over.

A tenant in socage however (an agricultural and not knightly rank) did not trundle about in heavy armour and had no need to learn how to handle a sword or to understand chivalry. His heir was reckoned an adult as soon as he became capable of husbandry and of 'conducting his rustic employs'. 21 was therefore the age of majority for everyone 'except the common people', who came of age at 15, and it was only later that 21 filtered down and became the universal age for all classes.

An authoritative work summarises the matter as follows:

'There is more than one "full age". The young burgess is of full age when he can count money and measure cloth; the young sokeman when he is 15, the tenant by knight's service when he is 21 years old. In past times boys and girls had soon attained full age; life was rude and there was not much to learn. The prolongation of the disabilities and privileges of infancy, which must have taken place sooner or later, has been hastened by the introduction of heavy armour. But here again we have a good instance

301

of the manner in which the law for the gentry becomes English common
law. The military tenant is kept in ward until he is 21 years old; the tenant in socage is out of ward six or seven years earlier. Gradually however
the knightly majority is becoming the majority of the common law. . . .
In later days our law drew various lines at various stages in a child's life;
Coke [in 1628] tells us of the seven ages of a woman; but the only line of
general importance is drawn at the age of one and twenty; and *infant*—the
one technical word that we have as a contrast for the person of full age—
stands equally well for the new-born babe and the youth who is in his 21st
year.'

In 1660 in the reign of Charles II military tenure was abolished and what
had been military lands were turned into socage. Under socage their holders
would all have come of age at 15; so to prevent this, Charles II enacted by the
Tenures Abolition Act 1660 that a father could in all cases appoint a guardian
by deed or will until his child became 21. Later, even if the father had omitted
to provide a guardian the Courts often did, so as to stop an infant squandering
his patrimony before he was 21.

So it was that the knightly age of majority gradually came to apply to
everyone."

APPENDIX II

FORMS OF CONSENT TO SURGICAL, MEDICAL AND DENTAL TREATMENT

(*Family Law Reform Act* 1969, s. 8)

The following document, which is reproduced by courtesy of Northampton and District Hospital Management Committee, is a good illustration of the type of consent required by the Family Law Reform Act 1969, s. 8 (1), *ante*.

..............HOSPITAL MANAGEMENT COMMITTEE

..............GENERAL HOSPITAL

1. CONSENT BY PATIENT

To: The Medical Staff and Management Committee.

I, ...

of ....

consent to undergo the operation of..

the effect and nature of which have been explained to me by*........................

House Officer/Registrar/S.H.M.O./Consultant.   (Signature)

I also consent to such further or alternative measures as may be found to be necessary during the course of such operation, and to the administration of a local or other anaesthetic for the purpose of the same.

I understand that an assurance has not been given that the operation will be performed by a particular surgeon.

Dated this................... day of....................................19......

(*SIGNED*)..............................

Folder No. ....

Ward................................

* Name and designation must be filled in before signature.

303

2. CONSENT BY PARENT OR GUARDIAN

To: The Medical Staff and Management Committee.

I, ...

of ....

consent to the operation of...

being performed on...

The effect and nature of the operation have been explained to me by*....................

.... House Officer/Registrar/S.H.M.O./Consultant.
(Signature)

I also consent to such further or alternative measures as may be found to be necessary during the course of the operation and to the administration of a local or other anaesthetic for the purpose of the same.

I understand that an assurance has not been given that the operation will be performed by a particular surgeon.

I certify that my child has had nothing to eat or drink since................a.m./p.m.

Dated this...................day of....................................19......

(*SIGNED*)....................................

Relationship to patient..................

Folder No............................ Ward.................................

* Name and designation must be filled in before signature.

APPENDIX III

THE NATURE OF BLOOD GROUP EVIDENCE
(*Family Law Reform Act* 1969 *Part* III)

The Law Commission's Report on "Blood Tests and the Proof of Paternity in Civil Proceedings" (Law Com. No. 16: 1967) included the following useful summary of the nature of blood group evidence which is Crown copyright and is reproduced by permission of H.M.S.O.

1. The existence of blood groups, first demonstrated at the beginning of this century by Landsteiner,[1] explained the hitherto unintelligible disasters (such as death or severe illness) which occurred frequently when blood transfusions were given to patients. Landsteiner found that when blood serum from one individual was added to samples of red blood cells from other individuals, in some cases, but not others, the red blood cells formed dense clusters—a phenomenon known as agglutination. He deduced from this that the red blood cells of some individuals contained different chemical substances from the red blood cells of others and that agglutination occurred only when the cells contained a chemical which was "incompatible" with the particular serum being used in the experiment. He found that he could classify all blood into four specific groups, termed O, A, B and AB, and that red blood cells from one group were either compatible or incompatible with the serum from the other groups according to a predictable pattern. Since Landsteiner's original discovery several other systems of blood groups have been found, including the MN and Rhesus systems. The substances which differentiate these groups cannot, as yet, be identified in terms of their chemical constitution but their presence or absence can be shown by the technique of agglutination which we have mentioned.

2. Subsequently other types of tests such as the Hp and Gc tests have been evolved. With these the technique is entirely different, for complex proteins in the blood are separated out and identified by a process called electrophoresis. This process depends upon the fact that an electric field can cause the chemicals concerned to move through a medium such as starch gel and that they move at different rates, dependent on their molecular size and charge. Thus Hp.1 takes up a characteristic position in the gel some distance from Hp.2 and the two substances can be separated from each other.

---

[1] Karl Landsteiner (1868–1943), an Austro-American pathologist, born in Vienna. His reputation stands on the researches and discoveries he made in blood diseases, particularly hæmoglobinuria, and infantile paralysis. His discovery of blood groups paved the way for the great transfusion service which is now regarded as an essential part of any medical treatment. It was for this that he was awarded the Nobel Prize in 1930. Many awards and honours were accorded him and he was invited to undertake research at the Rockefeller Institute, which he did from 1922 to 1939.

3. The value of our knowledge of blood groups for the determination of paternity lies in the fact that the different factors present in each group are transmitted from one generation to another by the recognised principles of heredity. The mode of inheritance of blood groups has been established with a high degree of certainty by an enormous mass of research in many countries, involving many thousands of families, and the results of these experiments are completely in accord with the accepted rules of genetics. Without embarking on a detailed discussion of the mechanism of heredity a brief description can be given of how this mechanism applies to the inheritance of blood groups. In the nucleus of every normal human body cell there are 46 visually identifiable bodies known as chromosomes, arranged in 23 pairs. Apart from the chromosomes which determine sex, each chromosome of the pair is the same shape as the other. These chromosomes each carry a number of smaller bodies called genes and, put very simply, the transmission of every inherited characteristic from one generation to another depends upon the transmission of the corresponding gene or groups of genes. The human germ cells (i.e. ova and spermatozoa as opposed to normal body cells) contain only 23 chromosomes, only one of each pair of chromosomes from the normal 46-chromosome nucleus being used in the formation of the germ cell nucleus. Let us take, by way of illustration, a father who has the O factor in each of the relevant pair of chromosomes and a mother who has the A factor in one chromosome of the relevant pair and the O factor in the other chromosome of that pair. When the paired chromosomes divide in the formation of germ cells the father will produce germ cells which can only contain the O factor. The mother can, however, produce germ cells with either the A factor or the O factor, depending on which chromosome of the pair the germ cells take. The diagram below shows the possible combination of factors which the child of this mother and father can have, depending on which germ cells from the father fertilizes which germ cell from the mother.

FATHER　　　　　　　**MOTHER**

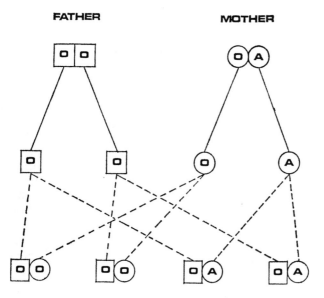

Normal body cells with paired chromosomes showing the blood factors carried by each chromosome of the pair.

Germ cells formed by division of the paired chromosomes.

Possible offspring from the fusion of either of the father's germ cells with either of the mother's.

(It should be borne in mind that when a germ cell is fertilized by another germ cell the 23 chromosomes in each germ cell pair to give an embryo with the normal 46 chromosomes.)

It can be seen that a child of these two parents cannot possess the B factor. If the mother has a child which possesses the B factor then its father must be a man whose chromosomes contain the B factor and cannot be the man in our illustration. [On p. 310 *post*], we set out tables (dealing only with the ABO and MN systems) showing possible and impossible combinations of factors in children of parents whose ABO or MN groups are known.

4. There is, theoretically, a possibility that in dividing to form germ cells the chromosomes may undergo a change in chemical composition so that, for example, a chromosome containing the O factor could change to possess the B factor instead. Clearly, if this change, termed a mutation, were to occur it would invalidate the reasoning behind the diagram in the preceding paragraph. However, mutations in nature are known to be extremely rare and so far as blood factors are concerned only one possible example has been demonstrated in all the millions of cases investigated. Even that one is not regarded by the leading authorities in this country as more than fairly convincing.[2]

5. A second fact which bears on the reliability of blood tests is that in any laboratory test there is the possibility of human observer-error. However, a vast experience of the techniques of blood grouping has been acquired in connection with the blood transfusion services in many countries. While observer-error is always a possibility, this can be virtually eliminated by repeating the tests on several samples of blood and the risk of observer-error is probably less than that involved in the identification of finger-prints.[3]

6. It is particularly important that the serologists conducting blood tests for the purposes of determining paternity are specially trained.[4] Routine training in pathology and/or haematology and clinical pathology does not necessarily qualify one to do this type of blood testing. It cannot be overstressed that only properly qualified and experienced serologists should be appointed to carry out this work. In America, for example, serious errors have been found to occur because the person carrying out the tests was not sufficiently experienced. It is also important that the standard of the materials used in testing should be carefully controlled. These considerations make it essential that testing should be carried out only at specified centres which employ expert serologists and use standard materials.[5]

7. A further source of possible error must be mentioned. Where, for example, the alleged father is of group MM (his blood reacting only for the M and not for the N factor) and the mother is MN, it is assumed that the child must be of group M or MN and cannot be N. This assumption depends, of course, upon a further assumption that there does not exist a third allelic gene, for the product of which gene no specific reagent or other means of recognition has yet been discovered. This assumption may, on occasions, be proved false. The discovery of a third allelic gene, now known as Mg, which gives rise to an antigen

---

[2] See *F. v. F.*, [1968] 2 W.L.R. 190 at 197 where Rees J. refers to the evidence given by a serologist as to the possibility of mutation. See also the Family Law Reform Act 1969, s. 25, *ante*.
[3] See *ibid.*, s. 22, *ante*.
[4] See *ibid.*, s. 22 (1) (e), *ante*.
[5] See *ibid.*, s. 25 (1) (e), *ante*.

Mg not reacting either with anti-M or anti-N serum is a case in point. Since errors of this type depend upon the existence of rare undiscovered factors, the errors themselves are bound to be rare. Furthermore they will usually tend to occur where exclusion of paternity is based on testing only the child and putative father, and not the mother.[6]

8. We have seen how blood groups can be determined and how the transmission of factors from one generation to another works in principle. Additional valuable evidence, so far as paternity findings are concerned, is provided by a statistical analysis of the distribution of factors in the population of any country. In Great Britain the distribution of the ABO groups is approximately:—

$$O — 46 \text{ per cent}$$
$$A — 42 \text{ per cent}$$
$$B — 9 \text{ per cent}$$
$$AB — 3 \text{ per cent}$$

Statistical calculations show that using these groups alone the chances of being able positively to exclude a given man average about 17 per cent although if the child is group B or AB a greater proportion of men would be excluded as so few Englishmen have B to give.

9. Since Landsteiner's original discovery and particularly since 1940, a considerable number of other blood groups have been discovered, i.e. a considerable number of other chemical substances have been shown to exist on the red cells. These substances are inherited independently of one another and so are described as different blood group systems. The relevant ones for determining parentage are set out below, together with the cumulative chances of excluding a given person by determining the group of the child and of the mother and putative father, if all the available tests are employed.

	Exclusion by each system (per cent)	*Cumulative Exclusion (per cent)*
1. ABO	17·6	17·6
2. MNS	23·9	37·2
3. Rh. (D, C, c, E)	25·2	53·0
4. Kell (K)	3·7	54·8
5. Lutheran (Lua)	3·3	56·3
6. Duffy (Fya)	4·7	58·4
7. Kidd (Jka)	2·0	59·6

These tests alone offer, on average, a 60 per cent chance of exclusion. It must be remembered that this table applies only to inhabitants of Great Britain though its application to other Western Europeans produces broadly similar results.

10. In individual cases the prospects of exclusion may be considerably higher than the figures in the table, if either the child or the putative father is found to have an uncommon blood group or a combination of uncommon groups. In extreme cases the chance of two unrelated men having the same combination of uncommon groups may be as low as 1·6 in one hundred million. In other

---

[6] Cf. *ibid.*, s. 20 (1), *ante*, and the note thereto.

cases the chance may be of the order of one in ten thousand or one in fifty thousand. In such cases proof that both child and putative father have the same rare or very rare combination is valuable positive evidence that the putative father is in fact the father.[7]

11. The blood groups mentioned in the table above are all based on chemicals found on the red cells of the blood. There are, in addition, other chemical substances which can be identified in the blood serum, i.e. the liquid component of the blood. These substances have also been shown to be transmissible from one generation to another in accordance with the rules of heredity and can therefore assist us in the determination of parentage. As we have already briefly stated, the techniques involved are quite different from those used in the identification of blood groups, but they are equally reliable in skilled hands. Two such substances are now being used in paternity cases and have been approved by the medico-legal authorities of Denmark and other Scandinavian countries. These are the haptoglobin groups[8] and Gc groups. It is possible to classify all samples of sera into three haptoglobin groups and three Gc groups described as Hp.1-1, Hp. 1-2 and Hp. 2-2 and Gc.1-1, Gc.1-2 and Gc.2-2. Approximately 15 per cent of the population of Western Europe are Hp. 1-1, 47 per cent are Hp.1-2 and 36 per cent are Hp. 2-2. The haptoglobins alone exclude 18 per cent of men erroneously alleged to be the father of the child and the Gc groups exclude 15 per cent. Since the Hp and Gc groups are inherited independently of one another and of the groups mentioned before, the combined exclusion rate if those tests are used also is raised from 59·6 per cent (see table above) to approximately 72 per cent. The haptoglobin and Gc tests have to be used carefully, for haptoglobins are not definitely developed in a child under three months old and ill health may sometimes make it difficult to identify these substances.

12. Another system of blood grouping is by identification of inherited variants of the Gamma-globulin, discovered by Grubb in 1956. He showed that the blood sera of normal persons could be divided into two groups, Gm (a+) and Gm (a−) according to whether or not their serum prevented agglutination of anti-D coated rhesus positive cells by an antibody present in the serum of a proportion of rheumatoid arthritis sufferers and occasional normal individuals, ability to inhibit agglutination being inherited as a Mendelian dominant character. Other Gm groups have since been discovered. Gm(a) and Gm(b) have been used in evidence in paternity cases in Norway since 1962 and a third factor, Gm(x) has been employed in some countries. Most of the Gamma-globulin present in the newborn child is of maternal origin and it is not until the child is some months old that its Gm groups can be determined.

13. We understand that phosphoglucomutase grouping is likely to be employed in paternity testing before very long. Here the lead is in this country. This is an inherited system of blood-tissue enzymes which is already being used in anthropological studies and forensic identification tests. Grouping is by starch gel electrophoresis (like the haptoglobin grouping) followed by a special enzyme staining technique.

14. Another group of substances present in blood serum, the lipo proteins, are at present under intensive study and it is possible that in the near future these will be valuable in the determination of parentage.

---

[7] See *ibid.*, s. 20 (*b*) and (*c*), *ante.*
[8] See *Stocker* v. *Stocker*, [1966] 1 W.L.R. 190, where evidence of haptoglobin grouping was used.

INHERITANCE OF THE OAB AND MN FACTORS

Parents' Blood Groups	*Their Children's Blood Groups*	
	Possible	*Impossible*
O–O	O	A, B, AB
O–A	O, A	B, AB
O–B	O, B	A, AB
O–AB	A, B	O, AB
A–A	A, O	B, AB
B–B	B, O	A, AB
A–B	O, A, B, AB	None
A–AB	A, B, AB	O
B–AB	B, A, AB	O
AB–AB	A, B, AB	O

INHERITANCE OF THE MN FACTORS

M–M	M	N, MN
N–N	N	M, MN
M–N	MN	M, N
M–MN	M, MN	N
N–MN	N, MN	M
MN–MN	M, N, MN	None

IMPOSSIBLE FATHER/CHILD COMBINATIONS

Man	*Child*
O	AB
AB	O
M	N
N	M

APPENDIX IV

THE PUBLIC SYSTEM OF COMMUNITY HOMES FOR CHILDREN AND YOUNG PERSONS

(Children and Young Persons Act 1969, *Part* II)

The White Paper "Children in Trouble" (Cmnd. 3601: 1969) sets out the details of the Community Home System in an Appendix which is Crown copyright and is reproduced here by permission of H.M.S.O.

1. There will be three categories of community home:—

Local authority homes.
Assisted voluntary homes.
Controlled voluntary homes.

The sole purpose of these legal descriptions will be to distinguish the various categories of homes, which will be subject to different statutory provisions. The actual title of each individual home will be for the local authority or managers to decide.

Local authority homes

2. Homes provided and maintained by local authorities, including existing local authority approved schools, will be known as local authority homes. It will be for local authorities to make arrangements for their management.

3. It will also be made possible for a voluntary approved school, or a voluntary children's home registered under section 29 of the Children Act 1948, to become a local authority home. It will then be transferred, as a going concern, to the local authority specified for the purpose in an area development plan.

Voluntary homes

4. These will be community homes provided, maintained and managed by a partnership between public and voluntary effort. Their functions and status will be those specified in an approved area development plan. In the case of what are now voluntary approved schools, it will be for the joint planning committee for the area in which the school is situated to initiate discussions with the school authorities about its future functions and status. In view of the uneven geographical distribution of approved schools, however, a school might eventually be included in the development plan of a neighbouring area. In the case of voluntary children's homes it will be open to the managers to make proposals to a joint planning committee, or for the committee to approach the managers, if they wish the home to be considered for inclusion within the public system. Neither will be under any obligation to make or

accept such proposals. The role which each existing voluntary establishment plays under a development plan will depend upon the joint planning committee's agreement to this role, and the Secretary of State's approval of the plan.

5. Every assisted or controlled voluntary home will be conducted in accordance with its trust, supplemented by rules of management to be made by the Secretary of State. He will also make an instrument of management constituting the homes' managing body, for the purposes of the public system of community homes, after consultation with the trustees or other representatives of the original foundation or voluntary body concerned and with the local authority or authorities who are to be its major users. The premises or other assets will be vested in trustees or other representatives of the original foundation, to whom control and use will revert if at any time it ceases to form part of the public system. If the property is then sold, or is used for any purpose other than one approved by the Secretary of State, the trustees will be required to pay the Exchequer a sum equivalent to any value then attaching to the property as a result of the expenditure of public funds.

6. Responsibility for arranging for the assessment of the needs of children and young persons, and for deciding allocations to particular homes, transfers to other homes or forms of treatment and discharges from residential care will rest with the local authority having the child in its care. Where the home offers a variety of treatments it will also be the responsibility of the authority having the child in its care to decide, after considering the advice of the managers, the general character of the child's care, control or treatment. Other decisions about the treatment of a child while residing in a voluntary home will be taken by the managers or directing staff, within the framework of the general statutory rules and the rules of management for each home.

Assisted status

7. The provision, enlargement and maintenance of an assisted voluntary home will be the responsibility of the managers, who will charge fees for the use of facilities they provide for children in the care of local authorities. It will be eligible for Exchequer grant at the rate of 100 per cent. of the approved cost of any building work, or other provision on capital account, needed to fit it for the purpose defined for it in the development plan. The rate at which building work or other capital expenditure can be approved will depend on the country's economic circumstances.

8. The instrument of management will provide for two-thirds of the managers to be appointed by the trustees or other representatives of the original foundation. The particular responsibility of these foundation managers will be to ensure that the home is conducted in accordance with its trust deed or similar document. The remaining one-third of the managers (the representative managers) will normally be appointed by the local authority or authorities which are its major users. In the case of homes serving national needs, representative managers may be appointed by the Secretary of State.

9. Rules of management will provide that the managers must at all times make available 50 per cent. of the places for children or young persons in the care of local authorities, and must accept any child who is recommended for that home by the observation centre or other agency locally responsible for observation and assessment. They may also be required to make available a further 25 per cent. of places, on the same conditions, after reasonable notice has been given by the local authority or authorities represented on the managing body. It will be open to them to accept

as many local authority placements as they wish. Beyond the 50 per cent. of reserved places, or the 75 per cent. if the option to increase is exercised, the managers' consent to the acceptance of any particular child will be required.

10. When considering proposals in development plans, the Secretary of State will normally be prepared to accord assisted status only to homes which have the support of an organisation larger than their own managing body (e.g., a religious community or charitable foundation).

Controlled status

11. The arrangements will be generally similar to those described in paragraphs 7 to 9, but with the following three specific differences. First, financial responsibility on both capital and current account will be wholly assumed by the local authorities defined for this purpose in the relevant area development plan. Secondly, the instrument of management will provide for two-thirds of the managers to be representative managers, and one-third foundation managers. Thirdly, the Rules of Management will require 90 per cent. of the places to be available for children in the care of local authorities, should the authorities wish to take them up.

General

12. All community homes within the public system will be subject to inspection by members of the Home Office Children's Inspectorate. Minimum standards of accommodation, and general principles for their conduct, will be prescribed by statutory rules. The Secretary of State will have power to determine any dispute between a local authority and the managers of an assisted or controlled voluntary home, including disputes about the fees charged to local authorities.

APPENDIX V

LIST OF OFFICIAL PUBLICATIONS AND PARLIAMENTARY PROCEEDINGS

I. REPRESENTATION OF THE PEOPLE ACT 1969

Official Publications

Conclusions on Review of the Law Relating to Parliamentary Elections (Cmnd. 3717: 1968).

Parliamentary Proceedings

Commons.	2nd Reading: (18th November 1968) 773 H. of C. Official Report 913.
	Committee: (26th, 27th November 1968) 774 H. of C. Official Report 309, 514; (10th, 11th December 1968) 775 H. of C. Official Report 221, 338, 349, 438.
	Concluding Stages: (18th December 1968) 775 H. of C. Official Report 1398.
Lords.	2nd Reading: (23rd January 1969) 298 H. of L. Official Report 1030, 1048.
	Committee: (6th, 11th February 1969) 299 H. of L. Official Report 213, 342.
	Report: (27th February 1969) 299 H. of L. Official Report 1221.
	Return to Commons: (6th March 1969) 300 H. of L. Official Report 278.
	Final Proceedings: (15th April 1969) 301 H. of L. Official Report 15.
Royal Assent:	17th April 1969.

2. FAMILY LAW REFORM ACT 1969

Official Publications

Report of the Committee on the Age of Majority—generally called the "Latey Report" (Cmnd. 3342: 1967).

Report of the Committee on the Law of Succession in Relation to Illegitimate Persons—generally called the "Russell Report" (Cmnd. 3051: 1966).

The Law Commission: Blood Tests and the Proof of Paternity in Civil Proceedings (Law Com. No. 16: 1967).

Parliamentary Proceedings

Lords.	2nd Reading: (26th November 1968) 297 H. of L. Official Report 1132.
	Committee: (17th December 1968) 298 H. of L. Official Report 712.
	Report: (21st January 1969) 298 H. of L. Official Report 907.
Commons.	2nd Reading: (17th February 1969) 778 H. of C. Official Report 38.
	Proceedings of Standing Committee "B": H. of C. Official Report, S.C.B., 17th, 22nd, 24th, and 29th April 1969, cols. 1–170.
	Report and Return to Lords: (9th July 1969) 786 H. of C. Official Report 1407.
	Final Proceedings in Lords: (23rd July 1969) 304 H. of L. Official Report 981.
Royal Assent:	25th July 1969.

3. CHILDREN AND YOUNG PERSONS ACT 1969

Official Publications

The Child, the Family and the Young Offender (Cmnd. 2742: 1965).

Children in Trouble (Cmnd. 3601: 1968).

Report of the Committee on Local Authority and Allied Personal Social Services —generally called the "Seebohm Report" (Cmnd. 3703: 1968).

Parliamentary Proceedings

Commons.	2nd Reading: (11th March 1969) 779 H. of C. Official Report 1176.
	Proceedings of Standing Committee "G": H. of C. Official Report, S.C.G., 20th, 25th, 27th March 1969, 1st, 15th, 17th, 22nd, 24th, 29th April 1969, 1st, 6th, 8th, 13th May 1969, cols. 1–646.
	Report and Final Stages: (9th June 1969) 784 H. of C. Official Report 975, 1095.
Lords.	2nd Reading: (19th June 1969) 302 H. of L. Official Report 1128.
	Committee: (3rd, 7th, 9th July 1969) 303 H. of L. Official Report 748, 766, 790, 1107.
	Report: (18th, 23rd July 1969) 304 H. of L. Official Report 888, 1018.
	3rd Reading: (13th October 1969) 304 H. of L. Official Report 1213, 1245.
	Final Stages: (21st October 1969) 304 H. of L. Official Report 1628.
Royal Assent:	23rd October 1969.

4. TATTOOING OF MINORS ACT 1969

There are no official publications. A debate on the subject took place in the Lords on 31st January 1967.

Parliamentary Proceedings

Commons.   2nd Reading: (24th January 1969) 776 H. of C. Official Report 896.

                       Proceedings of Standing Committee "C": H. of C. Official Report, S.C.C., 26th February 1969, cols. 1–14.

                       3rd Reading: (28th March 1969) 780 H. of C. Official Report 1944.

Lords.   2nd Reading: (28th April 1969) 301 H. of L. Official Report 642. (No other proceedings.)

Royal Assent: 16th May 1969.

INDEX

A

CHILD
    accommodation for, in care, regional planning of, 190–196
    arrest of, 176, [177]
    attendance in court, 23, 112, [115]
    care and treatment—
        services providing, 29
        through court proceedings, 22, 29
    care, in—
        accommodation and maintenance for, 28–30, 211, [212]
        contribution by—
            local authority in respect of, 251
            parent in respect of, 226, 227
    care of—
        assessment of parents' contribution, 34
        in Scotland, [237]
    care proceedings in juvenile court in respect of, 104–111
    circumstances justifying court proceedings, 22
    conditions of which court must be satisfied before making an order, 104, 105, [107], [108]
    criminal proceedings in respect of, 24, 122
    definition of. *See* WORDS AND PHRASES
    detention of—
        extension of, 178–180
        in place of safety, 175–178
    enquiries by local authority, 23, 111
    Her Majesty, of, modifications of enactments relating to, 8, 62, [62], [63]
    homicide by, [122]
    illegitimate—
        maintenance for, [53], 55
        property rights of, 9–12
        protection of trustees and personal representatives who are unaware of, 14
        references to, in dispositions of property, 69–74
        right of—
            parents to succeed on child's intestacy, 10, 11
            succession in cases of intestacy. *See* INTESTACY; ILLEGITIMATE CHILD
            to succeed on parents' intestacy, 10, 11
    legal aid, for, 187
    limitation on publication of particulars of, 135, 136
    maintenance for—
        continuation after ceasing to be minor, 6, 51–55
                to age of 21, 6, 51–55
    meaning of. *See* WORDS AND PHRASES
    mentally ill, hospital order in respect of, 104, [110]
    order for custody of, [55]
    orders in respect of, 23
    parties entitled to bring proceedings in respect of, 23
    prohibition of criminal proceedings for offences by, 24, 122
    provision in supervision order placing child under supervision of probation officer, 142, [143]
    recognisance by parent of, 130, [131]
    references to—
        in a disposition of property presumed to include illegitimate children, 11–14, 69–74
        to include an illegitimate child, 11–14, 65, 69–74
    release of, 178–180
    remand of, in cases of homicide, 165, [166]
    remedial treatment of, to be left to local authority, 30
    review of case when in care, 28
    right to make application for payments under an affiliation order, 54, [55]
    supervision of, 26, 101
    trial of, on indictment, 25, 127
    unruly character, committal to remand centre, 163, 164
    visitors for, in community home, 27
    void or voidable marriages, of, [74]
    ward of court, as, put in care of local authority, 58

CONSENT,
  parent or guardian, of, to an order requiring a recognisance, 104, [110]
  required for taking of blood tests, 18, 85–86
  surgical, medical, or dental treatment, to, 7, 59, [59], [60], [61]

CONSOLIDATED FUND, 210, [211], 230

CONSTABLE,
  meaning of, [105–106], 185
  power to detain child or young person, 175–178

CONTRIBUTION,
  local authority, by, in respect of child in its care, 251
  maximum, for child or young persons in care, 226, [227]
  parents, by, in respect of children and young persons in care, 226, 227

CONTRIBUTION ORDER, 226, 227

CONTROLLED COMMUNITY HOMES. *See* COMMUNITY HOMES

COSTS,
  blood tests, of, 81, [85]

COUNSELLOR OF STATE,
  minimum age of, 5

COUNTY COUNCIL,
  meaning of, [233]

COURT PROCEEDINGS,
  restrictions on reporting, 135, 136

COURTS,
  discretionary power of, in relation to blood tests, 80, [82]
  jurisdiction of, in wardship proceedings, [56], [57]
  meaning of, [82], 166
  power to require use of blood tests, 80–85

CRIMINAL JUSTICE ACT 1967,
  modifications to, 241–243

CRIMINAL LIABILITY,
  reduction of age of, modification of enactments, [189]

CRIMINAL PROCEEDINGS,
  children against, 24
  laying an information in respect of young persons, 123, [125]
  prohibition of, in respect of offences by children, 122
  restriction on, in respect of offences by young persons, 123–126
  tests to apply in deciding whether to prosecute young persons, 123, [125]
  young persons, against, 24
    Home Office regulations, 25
    private prosecutions, 25
    summary trial, 25
    trial on indictment, 25

CROSS-EXAMINATION,
  questioning validity of blood tests by, [85]

CUSTODY,
  court order for, [55]
  infant being held in, for care proceedings, 112, [115]

CUSTODY ORDERS,
  transitional provisions affecting, 99

D

DEEDS,
  statutory provisions incorporated in, 100

L

LATEY COMMITTEE, 6, 7

LATEY REPORT, 1, 3, [44], [47], [49], [52], [56], [58], [59], [60], [61], [63]

LAW COMMISSION,
report on proof of paternity in civil proceedings, 3, 6, 15, [81], [89]

LAYING AN INFORMATION,
duty of—
informant to notify local authority, 123, 124, [125], [126]
justices to quash, 123, 124
not invalidated by failure to contain age, 255
procedure for, [125]
qualified informant in respect of, 123, 124, [125], [126]
young persons, in respect of, 123, [125]

LAYING OF DOCUMENTS,
before Parliament, [190]

LEGAL AID,
extension to proceedings involving young persons, 28
offences committed by children and young persons, for, 187

LEGAL CAPACITY,
age of, 3

LEGITIMACY,
presumption of, 19
rebuttal of, 91, 92
by failure to take blood tests, 88, [89]

LEGITIMATED CHILD,
reference to illegitimate child deemed to include, 70, [73]
rights to take interests in property, [69]
seniority in respect of other children, 70, [73], [74]

LIMITATION OF ACTIONS, 5, 100

LOCAL AUTHORITY,
care of wards of court by, 57, 58
child or young person remanded to be committed to care of, 165
committal to care of, 27
community homes provided by, 311
contributions by, in respect of child in its care, 251
definition of. *See* WORDS AND PHRASES
duty of—
in respect of a laying of information, [125]
community homes, 30–32
foster children, 213, 288
persons in its care, 167–170
to bring care proceedings, 23
after enquiry, 111
carry out investigations before proceedings, 134, [135]
ensure well-being of foster children, 288
give Secretary of State particulars of its child-care operations, 228, [228]
make enquiries where there are grounds for bringing care proceedings, 23, 111
manage, equip and maintain community homes, 196
protect public when young person in care of, 173, 174
provide accommodation for child in its care, 211, 212
maintenance for child in its care, 211, 212
review case of child in care, 174 [175]
visit all foster children, 33
under Part II of the Children Act 1948, modification of, 28
expenditure of—
on assisted or controlled community home to be repaid, 209
supervisor to be paid by, 153, [154]

LOCAL AUTHORITY—*continued*
 financial provisions in respect of child welfare facilities provided by, 250–254
 foster children. *See* duty of, *above*
 meaning of, 58, [105], 234
 means test by, to assess contribution for child or young person in care, [227]
 notification of—
  by persons maintaining foster children, 215–217, 289, 290
   qualified informant, 124, [126]
  to, of care proceedings, 23
 orders for committal to care of, 156/8–161
 payments to, in respect of classifying centres, 250
 power of—
  in respect of persons in its care, 167–170
  to impose requirements and prohibitions relating to keeping foster children, 218–220,
   290–292
   inspect premises in which foster children kept, 217, 218, 290–292
   prohibit the keeping of foster children, 290–292
   protect foster children, 33
  power to impose requirements in respect of premises where foster children kept, 34
 removal to borstal of person in care of, 182–184
 responsibility of—
  for management of controlled community homes, 199, 200
  in respect of supervision facilities, 154, [155]

LOCAL GOVERNMENT ELECTION,
 qualifying date as elector for, 38, [39]

LORD CHANCELLOR,
 power of—
  to amend local enactments, 44, [46]
  with respect to composition of juvenile courts, 224–226

M

MAGISTRATES' COURT,
 duty to remit case to juvenile court, 130, [132], [133]
 jurisdiction in maintenance proceedings, [52], [53]
 meaning of, 166
 power to order finger-printing of suspected young persons, 133, [134]
 procedure in, [184]
 summary jurisdiction of, [184]

MAINTENANCE,
 application for—
  by ward of court, 56
  effect of blood tests in previous paternity suit, 19
 children, of, modification of enactments relating to, 6
 continuation of—
  after person ceases to be minor, 6, 51
  until 21, 6, 51
 illegitimate child, for, [53], 55
 minor, for, courts having jurisdiction to hear applications, [52], [53]
 modification of enactments relating to, 51, 52, [53], 54
 student not living at home, for, [52]
 wards of court, for, 6, 55, 56, [57]
  after ceasing to be a minor, 56
 wilful neglect, for, [55]

MAINTENANCE ORDER
 court's power to vary, 56
 effect on income of a protective trust, [73]
 enforcement of, 52, [53]
 minor aged 18 or over, in respect of, [52]
 requiring parent to pay maintenance for ward of court, 55
 under the Guardianship of Infants Acts, 6